BIBLIOGRAPHY OF
BRITISH ECONOMIC
AND SOCIAL HISTORY

ALSO AVAILABLE

Bibliography of European Economic and Social History
compiled by Derek H. Aldcroft
and Richard Rodger

BIBLIOGRAPHY OF
BRITISH ECONOMIC AND SOCIAL HISTORY

COMPILED BY

W. H. CHALONER

(William Henry)

Emeritus Professor of Modern Economic History
University of Manchester

R. C. RICHARDSON

Head of History and Archaeology
King Alfred's College, Winchester

MANCHESTER
UNIVERSITY PRESS

PUBLISHED BY
MANCHESTER UNIVERSITY PRESS
Oxford Road, Manchester, M13 9PL, U.K.
51 Washington Street, Dover, N. H. 03820, U.S.A.

BRITISH LIBRARY CATALOGUING IN PUBLICATION DATA

Chaloner, W. H.
   Bibliography of British economic and social history.
   1. Great Britain—Social conditions—Bibliography
I. Title II. Richardson, R. C.
   016.941   Z2016
ISBN 0-7190-0888-3

LIBRARY OF CONGRESS CATALOGING IN PUBLICATION DATA

Chaloner, W. H. (William Henry)
   Bibliography of British economic and social history.
   Rev. ed. of: British economic and social history. c1976.
   Includes index.
   1. Great Britain—Economic conditions—Bibliography.
   2. Great Britain—Social conditions—Bibliography.
I. Richardson, R. C. II. Title.
Z7165.G8C46 1983 [HC253] 016.306′0941 83-12045
ISBN 0-7190-0888-3

PHOTOTYPESET
BY Elliott Brothers & Yeoman Limited, Liverpool

PRINTED IN GREAT BRITAIN
BY Bell & Bain Limited, Glasgow

CONTENTS

v

CONTENTS

ENGLAND 1300-1500

ENGLAND 1500-1700

CONTENTS

CONTENTS

CONTENTS

CONTENTS

PREFACE

The literature of British economic and social history has busily proliferated in the course of the last few decades with the appearance of textbook surveys, monographs and innumerable articles in a growing range of specialised periodicals. Surprisingly, however, the growth of the subject has not been matched by the proper provision of bibliographies. It was to meet this need among students and their teachers that the first edition of this work was published in 1976. Its title was deliberately chosen. It was designed as a guide to – and not a definitively comprehensive list of – the dauntingly enormous literature of British economic and social history from 1066 to 1970. No single-volume bibliography could have included everything and to have done so would in any case have been self-defeating. (It was principally for this reason that we restricted ourselves to material written in English.) But we prefaced the 1976 edition with the hope – far too optimistic, no doubt – that little of the first importance had been left out and that nothing which could be considered useless had been put in.

Since the first edition has been out of print for some time an enlarged, up-dated second edition is now called for. The case for a select bibliographical guide of this type remains as strong as ever; indeed, in a real sense it is stronger. No competitor to the 1976 edition has appeared, and new material on British economic and social history continues to be published at an alarming rate. The latest annual list of publications in the *Economic History Review* runs to over forty pages of dense print.

Like its predecessor this enlarged bibliographical guide is chronologically divided at 1300, 1500 and 1700, and arranged by subject within the different periods. The items in each subject area are then listed under their authors in alphabetical order. All items are numbered, and it is these numbers – not page numbers – which are given in cross-references and in the index. A particular work, of course, is separately numbered only once. Any further reference to that item will be abbreviated and will direct the reader to the entry in the book where fuller bibliographical details can be found. Places of publication are given only when these were outside the British Isles. In each sub-section source material is listed before the secondary works.

This second edition contains 5,800 entries as compared with the 4,200 of the first. But as well as being substantially larger it differs from the 1976 edition in a number of important respects. The sections on Scotland and Ireland – rightly criticised for their thinness in 1976 – have been considerably expanded. The separate section on Wales now gathers together all material on that country before as well as after 1700. There are new sections and sub-sections on England, reflecting the growth of interest in family history, leisure and recreation, and the history of crime. Other parts of the bibliography have been re-positioned in more appropriate places or subdivided to make for greater ease of reference. A number of items listed in the 1976 edition have been omitted from the new one so as to help make way for new inclusions.

Though this remains very much a joint work the main responsibility for revising the bibliographical guide and for preparing the index has been Dr Richardson's. He records his gratitude to King Alfred's College for a term's study leave in 1982 which made possible the completion of the work. Special thanks are also due to the following for their comments, suggestions or active assistance: John Armstrong, Philip Bagwell, Barbara Cave, Geoffrey Channon, Keith Evans, William Forsyth, Adrian Hallett and T. S. Willan. Every effort has been made in compiling the guide to reach the highest standard of accuracy, but doubtless undetected errors still remain in a work of this length. The editors would be grateful, therefore, to receive correspondence pointing out such mistakes and would welcome suggestions for changes and additions to any subsequent reissue.

W. H. C.
R. C. R.   *September 1982*

PRINCIPAL
ABBREVIATIONS

Though this is not a complete list of abbreviations
used in the text, all others should be self-explanatory.
Ass.: Association, Ec.: Economic, J.: Journal,
Proc.: Proceedings, R.: Review, Soc.: Society, throughout.

Ag.H. *Agricultural History*
Ag.H.R. *Agricultural History Review*
A.H.R. *American Historical Review*
Arch.Cant. *Archaeologia Cantiana*
Arch.J. *Archaeological Journal*
B.I.H.R. *Bulletin of the Institute of Historical Research*
B. John Rylands Lib. *Bulletin of the John Rylands Library*
B.Bd.Celtic Studs. *Bulletin of the Board of Celtic Studies*
Brit.J.Soc. *British Journal of Sociology*
Bus.H. *Business History*
Bus.H.R. *Business History Review*
Canadian J.Ec.&Pol. Science *Canadian Journal of Economics and Political Science*
Chet.Soc. *Chetham Society*
Church H. *Church History*
Comp.Studs.Soc.&H. *Comparative Studies in Society and History*
East Yorks.Loc.H.Soc. *East Yorkshire Local History Society*
Ec.H.R. *Economic History Review*
Ec.J.Ec.H.Supp. *Economic Journal Economic History Supplement*
E.H.R. *English Historical Review*
Essex R. *Essex Review*
Expl.Entrepren.H. *Explorations in Entrepreneurial History*

Geog. *Geography*
Geog.R. *Geographical Review*
Hist. *History*
H.Today *History Today*
Hist.Ass. *Historical Association*
H.Educ. *History of Education*
H.& Theory *History and Theory*
Hist.Studs. *Historical Studies*
Hug.Soc. *Huguenot Society*
Ind.Arch.R. *Industrial Archaeology Review*
Internat.R.Soc.H. *International Review of Social History*
Irish Hist.Studs. *Irish Historical Studies*
J.Brit.Studs. *Journal of British Studies*
J.Contemp.H. *Journal of Contemporary History*
J.Ec.H. *Journal of Economic History*
J.Ec.& Bus.H. *Journal of Economic and Business History*
J.Eccles.H. *Journal of Ecclesiastical History*
J.Educ.Admin.& H. *Journal of Educational Administration and History*
J.Europ.Ec.H. *Journal of European Economic History*
J.H.Geog. *Journal of Historical Geography*
J.H.Ideas *Journal of the History of Ideas*
J.Interdis.H. *Journal of Interdisciplinary History*
J.Peasant Studs. *Journal of Peasant Studies*
J.Pol.Econ. *Journal of Political Economy*
J.Roy.Stat.Soc. *Journal of the Royal Statistical*

Society
J.Soc.H. *Journal of Social History*
J.Trans.H. *Journal of Transport History*
Lit.& H. *Literature and History*
Loc.Historian *Local Historian*
Loc.Pop.Studs. *Local Population Studies*
Nat.Lib.WalesJ. *National Library of Wales Journal*
Northern H. *Northern History*
Northern Scot. *Northern Scotland*
P.P. *Past and Present*
Pop.Studs. *Population Studies*
Proc.Brit.Acad. *Proceedings of the British Academy*
Proc.Dorset Nat.H. & Arch.Soc. *Proceedings of the Dorset Natural History and Archaeological Society*
Proc.Hug.Soc. *Proceedings of the Huguenot Society*
Renaiss. & Mod.Studs. *Renaissance and Modern Studies*
Scand.Ec.H.R. *Scandinavian Economic History Review*
Scot.H.R. *Scottish Historical Review*
Scot.J.Pol.Econ. *Scottish Journal of Political Economy*
Soc.R. *Sociological Review*

Southern H. *Southern History*
Studs.Med.& Renaiss.H. *Studies in Medieval and Renaissance History*
T.H.S.L.C. *Transactions of the Historic Society of Lancashire and Cheshire*
T.L.C.A.S. *Transactions of the Lancashire and Cheshire Antiquarian Society*
T.Cumb.& West.Antiq.& Arch. Soc. *Transactions of the Cumberland and Westmorland Antiquarian and Archaeological Society*
T.Hon.Soc.Cymmrod. *Transactions of the Honourable Society of Cymmrodorion*
T.I.B.G. *Transactions of the Institute of British Geographers*
T.Jewish H.Soc. *Transactions of the Jewish Historical Society*
T.R.H.S. *Transactions of the Royal Historical Society*
Trans.H. *Transport History*
Urban H.Yearbook *Urban History Yearbook*
V.C.H. *Victoria County History*
Vict.Studs. *Victorian Studies*
Welsh H.R. *Welsh History Review*
Worcs.H.Soc. *Worcestershire Historical Society*
Yorks.B. *Yorkshire Bulletin*

GENERAL
WORKS

HISTORIOGRAPHY AND METHODOLOGY

1 **Abrams**, P. 'History, Sociology, Historical Sociology', *P.P.*, 87, 1980, 3-16.
2 **Aitken**, H. G. J., 'On the present state of economic
history', *Canadian J. Ec. and Pol. Science*,
XXVI, 1960, 87-95.
3 **Andreano**, R., ed., *The New Economic History.
Recent Papers on Methodology*, N. Y., 1970.
4 **Ashley**, W. J., *Surveys, Historic and Economic*,
1900. Includes two chapters on the study of
economic history (1-30).
5 —— 'The place of economic history in university
studies', *Ec.H.R.*, I, 1927-8, 1-11. On Ashley see:
6 **Scott**, W. R., 'Memoir: Sir William Ashley', *Ec.
H.R.*, I, 1927-8, 319-21.
7 **Ashton**, T. S., 'The relation of economic history to
economic theory', 1946. In Harte, ed. (86), listed
below. On Ashton see:
8 **John**, A. H., 'Thomas Southcliffe Ashton,
1889-1968', *Ec.H.R.*, 2nd ser., XXI, 1968, iii-v.
9 **Sayers**, R. S., 'Thomas Southcliffe Ashton,
1889-1968', *Proc.Brit.Acad.*, LVI, 1972, 263-81.
10 **Ashworth**, W., 'The study of modern economic
history', 1958. In Harte, ed. (86), listed below.
11 **Aydelotte**, W. O., *Quantification in History*,
Reading, Mass., 1971.
12 **Ballard**, M., ed., *New Movement in the Study
and Teaching of History*, 1970.
13 **Barker**, T. C., 'The beginnings of the Economic
History Society', *Ec.H.R.*, 2nd ser., XXX, 1977,
1-19.
14 **Barzun**, J., *Clio and the Doctors: Psycho-history,
Quanto-history and History*, Chicago, 1974.

15 **Basmann**, R. L., 'The role of the economic historian in the productive testing of proffered
"economic laws" ', *Expl. Entrepren. H.*, 2nd ser.,
II, 1965, 159-86.
16 **Beresford**, M. W., 'Time and place', 1960. In
Harte, ed. (86), listed below.
17 —— *History on the Ground*, 2nd ed., 1971.
18 **Bertaux**, D., ed., *Biography and Society: the life
history approach in the social sciences*, 1982.
19 **Birkos**, A. S., *Historiography, Method, History
Teaching: A Bibliography of Books and Articles
in English, 1965-73*, Hamden, Conn., 1975.
20 **Bloch**, M., *The Historian's Craft*, 1954.
21 **Bridbury**, A. R., *Historians and the Open Society*, 1972.
22 **Buchanan**, R. A., *History and Industrial Civilisation*, 1970.
23 —— 'Technology and History', *Soc.Studs. in
ence*, V, 1975, 488-99.
24 **Burke**, P., *Sociology and History*, 1980.
25 **Butt**, J., 'Achievement and Prospect: Transport
History in the 1970s and 1980s', *J.Trans.H.*, 3rd
ser., II, 1981, 1-24.
26 **Cameron**, R., 'Economic history: pure and
applied', *J.Ec.H.*, XXXVI, 1976, 3-27.
27 **Cantor**, N. F., *Perspectives on the European
Past: Conversations with Historians*, N. Y., 2
vols., 1971. Amongst the historians included in this
collection of interviews are R. M. Hartwell on 'The
Industrial Revolution', D. S. Landes on 'Labour
and the Labour Movement', A. P. Thornton on
'Imperialism' and A. Briggs on 'Modern Britain'.

28 **Cardwell**, D. S. L., 'The history of technology: now and in the future', *Ind.Arch.R.*, II, 1978, 103-10.

29 **Carus-Wilson**, Eleanora M. See Youings, Joyce, 'Eleanora M. Carus-Wilson, 1897-1977', *Ec.H.R.*, 2nd ser., XXX, 2, 1977, iii-v.

30 **Chambers**, J. D., 'The place of economic history in historical studies', 1960. In Harte, ed. (86), listed below. On Chambers see:

31 **Mingay**, G. E., 'The contribution of a regional historian: J. D. Chambers 1898-1970', *Studs. in Burke and his Time*, XIII, 1972, 2002-2010.

32 **Chandler**, J. D. and Galambos, L., eds., *Economic History: Retrospect and Prospect. Papers Presented at the Thirtieth Annual Meeting of the Economic History Association*, 1971 (A special issue of the *J.Ec.H.*, XXXI, 1, 1971). Contains papers by W. N. Parker, A. Fishlow and R. W. Fogel, J. Swanson and J. Williamson, P. Temin and D. C. North.

33 **Church**, C. H., 'Disciplinary dynamics', *Studs.Higher Ed.*, I, 1976, 101-18.

34 **Church**, R. A., 'Business history in England', *J.Europ.Ec.H.*, V, 1976, 209-28.

35 **Clapham**, J. H., 'The study of economic history', 1929. In Harte, ed. (86), listed below. On Clapham see:

36 **Heaton**, H., 'Clapham's contribution to economic history', *Pol. Sci. Quart.*, LIII, 1938, 599-602.

37 **Postan**, M. M., 'Sir John Clapham', *Univ. Leeds.R.*, XVII, 1974, 129-36, and Court (46), below.

38 **Clark**, G. N., 'The study of economic history', 1932. In Harte, ed. (86), listed below.

39 **Coats**, A. W., 'Economic growth. The economic and social historian's dilemma', 1966. In Harte, ed. (86), listed below.

40 —— 'The historical context of the "New Economic History"', *J.Europ.Ec.H.*, IX, 1980, 185-207.

41 **Cohen**, J. S., 'The achievements of economic history: the Marxist School', *J.Ec.H.*, XXXVIII, 1978, 29-57.

42 **Cohn**, B. S., 'History and Anthropology: the state of play', *Comp.Studs. Soc. & H.*, XXII, 1980, 198-221.

43 **Cole**, W. A., *Economic History as a Social Science*, 1967.

44 **Conrad**, A. H., 'Economic theory, statistical inference and economic history', *J.Ec.H.*, XVII, 1957, 524-44.

45 —— and Meyer, J. R., *Studies in Econometric History*, 1965.

46 **Court**, W. H. B., *Scarcity and Choice in History*, 1970. A collection of essays, including a valuable study of 'Two economic historians: R. H. Tawney and Sir John Clapham', 127-50.

47 **Cruise**, H. F., 'The economic historian and the growth debate', *Austral.Ec.H.R.*, XV, 1975, 83-106.

48 **David**, P., 'Economic history through the looking glass', *Econometrica*, XXXII, 1964, 694-6.

49 **Davis**, L. E., 'Professor Fogel and the new economic history', *Ec.H.R.*, 2nd ser., XIX, 1966, 657-63.

50 —— ' "And it will never be literature": the new economic history: a critique', *Expl.Entrepren.H.*, 2nd ser., VI, 1969, 75-92.

51 —— *et al.*, 'Aspects of quantitative research in economic history', *J.Ec.H.*, XX, 1960, 539-47.

52 **Davis**, R., 'History and the social sciences', 1965. In Harte ed. (86), listed below.

53 **Degler**, C. N., *Is there a History of Women?*, 1975.

54 **Delzell**, C. F., ed., *The Future of History*, Nashville, Tenn., 1977. Includes essays on the new urban history and on history and the social sciences.

55 **Desai**, M., 'Some issues in econometric history', *Ec.H.R.*, 2nd ser., XXI, 1968, 1-16.

56 **Dobb**, M., 'Historical materialism and the role of the economic factor', *Hist.*, XXXVI, 1951, 1-11.

57 **Dollar**, C. M., and Jewsen, R. J. N., *Historian's Guide to Statistics: Quantitative Analysis and Historical Research*, N. Y., 1971.

58 **Douring**, F., *History as a Social Science*, The Hague, 1960.

59 **Drake**, M., ed., *Applied Historical Studies: An Introductory Reader*, 1973. Contains a general introductory chapter on 'Sociology and the historical perspective'.

60 **Elton**, G. R., *The Practice of History*, 1967.

61 —— 'The historian's social function', *T.R.H.S.*, 5th ser., XXVII, 1977, 197-211.

62 **Erickson**, Charlotte, 'Quantitative history', *A.H.R.*, LXXX, 1975, 351-65.

63 **Farnie**, D. A., 'Three historians of the cotton industry: Thomas Ellison, Gerhart von Schulze-Gaevernitz and Sydney Chapman', *Textile H.*, IX, 1978, 75-89.

64 **Federn**, K., *The Materialist Conception of History: A Critical Analysis*, 1939.

65 **Finberg**, H. P. R., *The Local Historian and his Theme*, 1952.

66 —— *Local History in the University*, 1964.

67 —— ed., *Approaches to History: A Symposium*, 1962. Includes essays on economic, social and local history.

68 **Fisher**, F. M., 'On the analysis of history and the interdependence of the social sciences', *Philosophy of Science*, XXVII, 1960, 147-58.

69 **Fishlow**, A., and Fogel, R. W., 'Quantitative economic history. An interim evaluation; past trends and present tendencies', *J.Ec.H.*, XXXI, 1971, 15-42.

70 **Floud**, R., *An Introduction to Quantitative Method for Historians*, 1973.

71 —— 'Quantitative history: evolution of methods and techniques', *J.Soc.Archivists*, V, 1977, 407-17.

72 **Fogel**, R. W., 'The specification problem in economic history', *J.Ec.H.*, XXVII, 1967, 283-308.

73 —— 'The new economic history: its findings and methods', *Ec.H.R.*, 2nd ser., XIX, 1966, 642-56.

74 —— 'The limits of quantitative methods in history', *A.H.R.*, LXXX, 1975, 329-50.

75 **Gallman**, R. E., ed., *Recent Developments in the Study of Business and Economic History*, Greenwich, Conn., 1977.

76 **Glynn**, S., 'Approaches to urban history: the case for caution', *Austral. Ec.H.R.*, X, 1970, 218-25.

77 **Goodrich**, C. L., 'Economic history: one field or two?', *J.Ec.H.*, XX, 1960, 531-8.

78 **Gottschalk**, L., ed., *Generalization in the Writing of History*, Chicago, 1963. Contains a very good bibliography on historiography, 213-48.

79 **Gras**, N.S.B., *Introduction to Economic History*, 1922.

80 —— 'The rise and development of economic history', *Ec.H.R.*, I, 1927-8, 12-34.

81 **Gunderson**, G., 'The nature of social saving', *Ec.H.R.*, 2nd ser., XXIII, 1970, 207-20. A consideration of the 'new economic history'.

82 **Habakkuk**, H. J., 'Economic history and economic theory', *Daedalus*, 1971, 305-22.

83 **Hale**, J. R., *The Evolution of British Historiography*, 1967. A substantial introductory essay followed by representative extracts.

84 **Hammond**, J. L. See the obituary notice by R. H. Tawney, 'J. L. Hammond, 1872-1949', *Proc.Brit.Acad.*, XLVI, 1960, 267-94.

85 **Hancock**, W. K., 'Economic history at Oxford', 1946. In Harte, ed. (86), listed below.

86 **Harte**, N. B., ed., *The Study of Economic History*, 1971. An extremely useful collection of reprinted inaugural lectures with an introduction by the editor.

87 —— 'Trends in publications on the economic and social history of Great Britain and Ireland', *Ec.H.R.*, 2nd ser., XXX, 1977, 20-41.

88 **Hawke**, G. R., *Economics for Historians*, 1980.

89 **Hayek**, F. A., ed., *Capitalism and the Historians*, 1954.

90 **Heater**, D., 'History and the social sciences'. In Ballard (12), listed above, 134-46.

91 **Heckscher**, E. F., 'A plea for theory in economic history', *Ec. J.Ec.H.Supp.*, I, 1929, 525-34.

92 **Hexter**, J. H., *Doing History*, 1972.

93 —— 'A new framework for social history', in the same author's *Reappraisals in History*, 1961, 14-25.

94 **Hicks**, J., *A Theory of Economic History*, 1969.

95 **Hobsbawm**, E. J., 'Karl Marx's contribution to historiography', in R. Blackburn, ed., *Ideology in Social Science*, 1972, 265-83.

96 —— 'The social function of the past', *P.P.*, 55, 1972, 3-17.

97 —— 'From social history to the history of society' in Flinn and Smout (246), below, 1-22.

98 —— 'The Historians' Group of the Communist Party' in Cornforth (4146), below, 21-48.

99 **Holloway**, S. J. F., 'Sociology and history', *Hist.*, XLVIII, 1963, 154-80.

100 **Hoskins**, W. G., *Local History in England*, 1959, 2nd ed., 1973.

101 **Hughes**, H. S., 'The historian and the social scientist', in A. V. Riasanovsky and B. Riznik, eds., *Generalizations in Historical Writing*, Philadelphia, 1963, 18-59.

102 **Hughes**, J. R. T., 'Fact and theory in economic history', *Expl. Entrepren. H.*, III, 1966, 75-100.

103 —— 'Measuring British economic growth', *J.Ec.H.*, XXIV, 1964, 60-82.

104 **Hunt**, E. H., 'The new economic history', *Hist.*, LIII, 1968, 3-18.

105 **Iggers**, G. G. and Parker, H. T., eds., *International Handbook of Historical Studies*, 1980.

106 **John**, E., 'Some questions on the materialist interpretation of history', *Hist.*, XXXVIII, 1953, 1-10.

107 **Jones**, G. S., 'History: the poverty of empiricism', in R. Blackburn, ed., *Ideology in Social Science*, 1972, 96-118.

108 —— 'From historical sociology to theoretic history', *Brit. J.Soc.*, XXVII, 1976, 295-305.

109 **Jude**, T., 'A clown in regal purple: social history and the historians', *Hist.Workshop*, VII, 1979, 66-94.

110 **Kent**, R. A., *A History of British Empirical Sociology*, 1981. Covers the period from the 1830s, focusing particularly on the contributions of Engels, Mayhew, Booth and the Webbs.

111 **King**, J. E., 'Marx as a historian of economic

thought', *Hist. Pol.Econ.*, XI, 1979, 382-94.

112 **Kuznets**, S., 'Statistics and economic history', *J.Ec.H.*, I, 1941, 26-41.

113 **Landes**, D. S. and Tilly, C., *History as Social Science*, Englewood Cliffs, N. J., 1971.

114 **Laslett**, P., 'The wrong way through the telescope', *Brit. J.Soc.*, XXVII, 1976, 319-42.

115 **Lee**, C. H., *The Quantitative Approach to Economic History*, 1977.

116 **Lennard**, R., 'Agrarian history: some vistas and pitfalls', *Ag.H.R.*, XII, 1964, 83-98.

117 **Lythe**, S. G. E., 'The historian's profession', 1963. In Harte, ed. (86), above.

118 **McClelland**, P. D., *Causal Explanation and Model Building in History, Economics and the New Economic History*, 1975.

119 **Macfarlane**, A., *Reconstructing Historical Communities*, 1977.

120 **McGregor**, O. R., *Social History and Law Reform*, 1981.

121 **Marczewski**, J., 'Quantitative history', *J.Contemp.H.*, III, 1968, 179-92.

122 **Marwick**, A., *The Nature of History*, 1970. 2nd ed. 1981.

123 **Mathias**, P., 'Economic history – direct and oblique'. In Ballard (12), listed above, 76-92.

124 **Meyer**, J. R., 'Economic theory, statistical inference and economic history', *J.Ec.H.*, XVII, 1957, 545-53

125 **Morazé**, C., 'The application of the social sciences to history', *J.Contemp.H.*, III, 1968, 207-16.

126 **Murphy**, G. G. S., 'The "new" history', *Expl.Entrepren.H.*, 2nd ser., II, 1965, 132-46.

127 **North**, D. C., 'The state of economic history', *American Ec.R.*, LV, 1965, *Supplement*, 86-91.

128 —— 'Economic history', *Internat. Encyc.Soc.Sci.*, VI, 1968, 468-74.

129 —— 'Institutional change and economic growth', *J.Ec.H.*, XXXI, 1971, 118-25.

130 —— 'Structure and performance: the task of economic history', *J.Ec.Lit.*, XVI, 1978, 963-78.

131 **Parker**, W. N., 'From old to new to old in economic history', *J.Ec.H.*, XXXI, 1971, 3-14.

132 **Payne**, P. L., 'The uses of business history', *Bus.H.*, V, 1962, 11-21.

133 **Perkin**, H. J., 'What is social history?', *B. John Rylands Lib.*, XXXVI, 1953, 56-74.

134 **Pollard**, S., 'Economic history. A science of Society?', *P.P.*, 30, 1965, 3-22. In Harte, ed. (86), listed above.

135 —— *The Idea of Progress. History and Society*, 1968.

136 **Postan**, M. M., 'The historical method in social science', 1939. In Harte, ed. (86), listed above.

137 —— *Fact and Relevance: Essays on Historical Method*, 1971.

138 —— 'Function and dialectic in economic history', *Ec.H.R.*, 2nd ser., XIV, 1961-2, 397-407. On Postan see the obituary in *Ec.H.R.*, 2nd ser., XXXV, 1982, iv-vi.

139 **Power**, Eileen, 'On medieval history as a social study', 1933. In Harte, ed. (86), listed above.

140 **Powicke**, F. M., 'The economic motive in politics', *Ec.H.R.*, XVI, 1946, 85-92.

141 —— *Modern Historians and the Study of History*, 1955. Includes a study of the Manchester School of historians.

142 **Price**, L. L., 'The position and prospects of the study of economic history', 1908. In Harte, ed. (86), listed above.

143 **Rabb**, T. K., 'The historian and the climatologist', *J.Interdis.H.*, X, 1980, 831-7.

144 **Redlich**, F., 'New and traditional approaches to economic history and their interdependence', *J.Ec.H.*, XXV, 1965, 480-95.

145 —— 'Potentialities and pitfalls in economic history', *Expl.Entrepren.H.*, 2nd ser., VI, 1969, 93-108.

146 **Rogers**, J. E. T., *The Economic Interpretation of History*, 1888.

147 **Roskill**, M., 'History and the uses of photography', *Vict.Studs.*, XXII, 1979, 335-44.

148 **Rostow**, W. W., 'The interrelation of theory and economic history', *J.Ec.H.*, XVII, 1957, 509-23.

149 **Rowney**, D. K. and Graham, J. Q., eds., *Quantitative History: Selected Readings in the Quantitative Analysis of Historical Data*, Homewood, Ill., 1969. Includes sections on 'Social history and social change', 'Historical demography', 'Cliometrics: the new economic history'. Bibliography.

150 **Samuel**, R., 'British marxist historians, 1880-1980', *New Left R.*, CXX, 1980, 21-96.

151 —— ed., *People's History and Socialist Theory*, 1981. A collection of *History Workshop* essays which question and explore the concept of socialist history.

152 **Saville**, J., *Marxism and History*, 1974. Inaugural lecture.

153 **Schofield**, R. S., 'Historical demography: some possibilities and some limitations', *T.R.H.S.*, 5th ser., XXI, 1971, 119-32.

154 **Sée**, H., *The Economic Interpretation of History*, trans. and intro. by M. M. Knight, N. Y., 1929.

155 **Seligman**, E. R. A., *The Economic Interpretation of History*, N. Y., 1902, 2nd ed., 1922.

156 **Shafer**, R. J., *A Guide to Historical Method*, Homewood, Ill., 1969.

157 **Shorter**, E., *The Historian and the Computer: a practical guide*, Englewood Cliffs, N. J., 1971.

158 **Smith**, P., ed., *The Historian and Film*, 1976.

159 **Sombart**, W., 'Economic theory and economic history', *Ec.H.R.*, II, 1929-30, 1-19.

160 **Spiegel**, H. W., 'Theories of economic development: history and classification', *J.H.Ideas*, XVI, 1955, 518-39.

161 **Stephens**, W. B., *Sources for English Local History*, 1973.

162 **Stern**, F., ed., *The Varieties of History from Voltaire to the Present*, Cleveland, Ohio, 1956; London, 1971. A collection of extracts from writings on the nature of history with critical notes and introduction. On economic history Unwin, Clapham and Cochran are represented.

163 **Stone**, L., *The Past and the Present*, 1981. A stimulating collection of essays including a major one on 'History and the social sciences in the twentieth century'.

164 **Supple**, B. E., 'Economic history and economic growth', *J.Ec.H.*, XX, 1960, 548-68.

165 —— 'Economic history in the 1980s: old problems and new directions', *J.Inderdis.H.*, XII, 1981-2, 199-215.

166 **Sutcliffe**, A., 'The condition of urban history in England', *Local H.*, XI, 1975, 278-84.

167 **Swanson**, J. and Williamson, J., 'Explanations and issues; a prospectus for quantitative economic history', *J.Ec.H.*, XXXI, 1971, 43-57.

168 **Tawney**, R. H., 'The study of economic history', 1932. In Harte (86), listed above.

169 —— 'Social history and literature' in Rita Hendon, ed., *The Radical Tradition*, 1966, 191-219. On Tawney see Court (46), listed above, and:

170 **Stone**, L., in *P.P.*, 21, 1962, 73-7;

171 **Ashton**, T. S., in *Proc.Brit.Acad.*, XLVIII, 1963, 461-82;

172 **Chambers**, J. D., 'The Tawney Tradition', *Ec.H.R.*, 2nd ser., XXIV, 1971, 355-69; and

173 **Winter**, J. M., and Joslin, D. M., eds., *R. H. Tawney's Commonplace Book*, 1972. Deals with the years 1912-14.

174 **Temin**, P., ed., *New Economic History*, 1973.

175 —— 'General equilibrium models in economic history', *J.Ec.H.*, XXI, 1971, 58-75.

176 —— 'The future of "new economic history"', *J.Interdis.H.*, XII, 1981-2, 179-197.

177 **Thomas**, K., 'History and anthropology', *P.P.*, 24, 1963, 3-24.

178 **Thompson**, E. P., 'On history, sociology and historical relevance', *Brit. J.Soc.*, XXVII, 1976, 387-402.

179 —— *The Poverty of Theory*, 1978.

180 **Thompson**, F. M. L., 'Agricultural history', *Hist.*, XLVIII, 1963, 28-33.

181 **Thompson**, P., *The Voice of the Past: Oral History*, 1978.

182 **Trevor-Roper**, H. R., 'The past and the present; history and sociology', *P.P.*, 42, 1969, 3-17.

183 **Tuma**, E. H., *Economic History and the Social Sciences*, 1971.

184 **Tunzelmann**, G. N. von, 'The new economic history: an econometric appraisal', *Expl.Entrepren.H.*, 2nd ser., V, 1968, 175-200.

185 **Unwin**, G., *Studies in Economic History: The Collected Papers of George Unwin*, with an introductory memoir by R. H. Tawney, 1927. Part One of the book is taken up with papers on 'The Study and teaching of economic history'. On Unwin see also:

186 **Daniels**, G. W., *George Unwin. A Memorial Lecture*, 1926.

187 **Uselding**, P. J., 'Business history and the history of technology', *Bus.H.R.*, LIV, 1980, 443-52.

188 **Vicinus**, Martha, 'The Study of Victorian Popular Culture', *Vict.Studs.*, XVIII, 1975, 473-83.

189 **Webb**, S. and Beatrice, *Methods of Social Study*, 1932.

190 **Wilson**, B. R., 'Sociological methods in the study of history', *T.R.H.S.*, 5th ser., XXI, 1971, 101-18.

191 **Wilson**, C., 'History in special and in general'. In Wilson (1232), listed below, 201-16.

192 **Winter**, J. M., 'The economic and social history of war', in Winter (251), below, 1-10.

193 **Wrigley**, E. A., 'The prospects for population history', *J.Interdis.H.*, XII, 1981-2, 207-20.

194 **Youngson**, A. J., 'Progress and the individual in economic history', 1959. In Harte, ed. (86), listed above.

GENERAL WORKS

(a) BIBLIOGRAPHIES

195 **Bellot**, H. H. and Milne, A. T., eds., *Writings on British History, 1901-33*, 5 vols., 1968.

196 **Creaton**, H. J., ed., *Writings on British History, 1958-9*, 1977.

197 —— *Writings on British History, 1962-4*, 1979.

198 —— *Writings on British History 1965-6*, 1981.

199 **Denman**, D. R., Switzer, J. F. Q. and Sawyer, O. H. M., eds., *Bibliography of Rural Land Economy and Landownership, 1900-57. A Full List of the Works relating to the British Isles and Selected Works from the U.S. and Western Europe*, 1958.

200 **Elton**, G. R., *Modern Historians on British History, 1485-1945. A Critical Bibliography, 1945-69*, 1970.

201 —— ed., *Annual Bibliography of British and Irish History*, 1976-

202 **Frewer**, L. B., ed., *Bibliography of Historical Writings Published in Great Britain and the Empire 1940-45*. 1947.

203 **Furber**, E. C., ed., *Changing Views on British History: Essays on Historical Writing Since 1939*, Cambridge, Mass., 1966.

204 **Kellaway**, W., *Bibliography of Historical Works Issued in the U.K., 1957-60*, 1962. Reprinted 1969.

205 **Lancaster**, Joan C., ed., *Bibliography of Works Issued in the U.K., 1946-56*, 1957.

206 **Milne**, A. T., ed., *Writings on British History, 1934-45*, 8 vols., 1937-60.

207 **Munro**, D. J., ed., *Writings on British History, 1946-8*, 1973.

208 —— *Writings on British History, 1949-51*, 1975.

209 **Philpin**, C. H. E. and Creaton, H. J., eds., *Writings on British History, 1960-61*, 1978.

210 **Sims**, J. M. and Jacob, P. M., eds., *Writings on British History, 1955-57*, 1977.

(b) SOURCE MATERIAL

211 **Bland**, A. E., Brown, P. A. and Tawney, R. H., eds., *English Economic History. Select Documents*, 1914. Several times reprinted. Covers the period 1000 to 1846.

212 **Clapp**, B. W., Fisher, H. E. S. and Jurica, A. R. J., eds., *Documents in English Economic History*. I: *1000-1760*, 1977; II: *England since 1760*, 1976.

213 **Flinn**, M. W., ed., *Readings in Economic History*, 1964.

(c) GENERAL SURVEYS

214 **Barley**, M. W., *The House and Home*, 1963. (A volume in J. Simmons, ed., *Visual History of Modern Britain*.)

215 **Buckatzch**, E. J., 'The geographical distribution of wealth in England, 1086-1843', *Ec.H.R.*, 2nd ser., III, 1951, 180-202.

216 **Burstall**, A. F., *History of Mechanical Engineering*, 1963. A survey from prehistoric to modern times.

217 **Chaloner**, W. H. and Musson, A. E., *Industry and Technology*, 1963. (A volume in J. Simmons, ed., *Visual History of Modern Britain*.)

218 **Clapham**, J. H., *Concise Economic History of Britain from the Earliest Times to 1750*, 1949.

219 **Cunningham**, W., *The Growth of English Industry and Commerce*, 1882, 6th ed., 3 vols., 1915-17.

220 **Darby**, H. C., ed., *Historical Geography of England Before A.D. 1800*, 1936, new ed., 1973.

221 **Dobb**, M., *Studies in the Development of Capitalism*, 1946.

222 **Dodgshon**, R. A. and Butlin, R. A., eds., *An Historical Geography of England and Wales*, 1978. Extends from prehistoric times to 1900, partly chronological, partly thematic in coverage.

223 **Flinn**, M. W., *An Economic and Social History of Britain, 1066-1939*, 1961.

224 **Green**, J. R., *Short History of the English People*, ed. Mrs J. R. Green and Kate Norgate, 4 vols., 1902. Valuable illustrations.

225 **Harding**, A., *A Social History of English Law*, 1966.

226 **Hechter**, M., *Internal Colonialism. The Celtic Fringe in British National Development, 1536-1966*, 1975.

227 **Higgs**, J., *The Land*, 1964. (A volume in J. Simmons, ed., *Visual History of Modern Britain*.)

228 **Hoskins**, W. G., *The Making of the English Landscape*, 1955.

229 **Jenkins**, R., *Links in the History of Engineering and Technology from Tudor Times*, 1936. A useful collection of miscellaneous papers.

230 **King**, P., *The Development of the English Economy to 1750*, 1971. A useful textbook with extended bibliography.

231 **Laslett**, P., ed., *Household and Family in Past Time*, 1972.

232 **Lipson**, E., *Economic History of England*. I: *The Middle Ages*, 1915, 12th ed., 1962. II and III: *The Age of Mercantilism*, 1931, 6th ed., 1961.

233 **Martin**, G, H., *The Town*, 1961. (A volume in J. Simmons, ed., *Visual History of Modern Britain*.)

234 **Murphy**, B., *A History of the British Economy, 1066-1970*, 1973.

235 **Musson**, A. E., *The Growth of British Industry*, 1978. Surveys the period 1500-1939.

236 **Pollard**, S., and Crossley, D. W., *The Wealth of Britain 1085-1966*, 1968. A valuable, one-volume survey of English economic history. Good bibliography.

237 **Rostow**, W. W., *The Stages of Economic Growth*, 1960. 2nd ed. 1971.

238 **Simmons**, J., *Transport*, 1962. (A volume in J. Simmons, ed., *Visual History of Modern Britain*.)

239 **Stenton**, Doris M., *The Englishwoman in History*, 1957.

240 **Trevelyan**, G. M., *Illustrated English Social History*, 4 vols., 1949-52.

241 **Wallerstein**, I., *The Modern World System. I: Capitalist Agriculture and the Origins of the European World Economy in the Sixteenth Century*, N. Y., 1974.

242 —— *The Modern World System. II: Mercantilism and the Consolidation of the European World Economy, 1600-1750*, 1980.

243 —— *The Capitalist World Economy*, 1979.

Elaborates some of the implications of his 'World System' perspective.

244 **Zupco**, R. E., *A Dictionary of English Weights and Measures from Anglo-Saxon Times to the Nineteenth Century*, Madison, Milwaukee, 1968.

(d) COLLECTIONS OF ESSAYS

245 **Carus-Wilson**, Eleanora M., ed., *Essays in Economic History*, 3 vols., 1954-62. A reprint collection of important articles. Indispensable.

246 **Flinn**, M. W. and Smout, T. C., eds., *Essays in Social History*, 1974.

247 **Floud**, R., ed., *Essays in Quantitative Economic History*, 1974. An extensive collection of articles which range from the fourteenth to the twentieth century.

248 **McGrath**, P. and Cannon, J. eds., *Essays in Bristol and Gloucestershire History*, 1976. Includes chapters on Bristol under the Normans, economic projects in the Vale of Tewkesbury in the early seventeenth century, the Gloucestershire spas, and the economic development of Bristol in the nineteenth century.

249 **Minchinton**, W. E., ed., *Essays in Agrarian History*, 2 vols., 1968. Covers both the medieval and modern periods.

250 **Winter**, J. M., ed., *History and Society. Essays by R. H. Tawney*, 1978. Includes a long introduction, four of Tawney's most important essays, and six shorter reviews and revaluations.

251 —— *War and Economic Development. Essays in Memory of David Joslin*, 1975.

ENGLAND
1066-1300

GENERAL WORKS

(a) BIBLIOGRAPHIES

252 **Altschul**, M., ed., *Bibliographical Handbooks: Anglo-Norman England, 1066-1154*, 1969. A useful compilation covering all aspects of the period.

253 **Bonser**, W., ed., *An Anglo-Saxon and Celtic Bibliography, 450-1087*, 1957.

254 **Graves**, E. B., ed., *A Bibliography of English History to 1485*, 1975. A revised and expanded version of Gross, C., *The Sources and Literature of English History*, 1900, 2nd ed., 1915.

255 **Hall**, H., ed., *Select Bibliography for the Study, Sources and Literature of English Medieval Economic History*, 1914.

(b) SOURCES

256 **Bagley**, J. J., *Historical Interpretation: Sources of English Medieval History, 1066-1540*, 1965.

257 **Douglas**, D. C. and Greenaway, G. W., eds., *English Historical Documents, 1042-1189*, 1955.

258 **Hennings**, Margaret, A., ed., *England under Henry III, 1216-72*, 1924. Section Four, 249-69, is on social and economic aspects of the period.

259 **Rothwell**, H., ed., *English Historical Documents. III: 1189-1327*, 1975. Economic history is not well represented in this selection.

260 **Stenton**, F. M., ed., *Documents Illustrative of the Social and Economic History of the Danelaw*, 1920.

(c) GENERAL WORKS ON THE MEDIEVAL ENGLISH ECONOMY AND ON POST-CONQUEST SOCIETY

261 **Baker**, T., *The Normans*, 1966.

262 **Barlow**, F., *The Feudal Kingdom of England, 1042-1216*, 1955, 2nd ed., 1962.

263 —— *William I and the Norman Conquest*, 1965.

264 **Barraclough**, G., ed., *Social Life in Early England*, 1960. A varied collection of essays originally issued as Hist.Ass. pamphlets.

265 **Barrow**, G. W. S., *Feudal Britain: The Completion of the Medieval Kingdoms, 1066-1314*, 1956. More attention than usual is given to Wales, Scotland and Ireland.

266 **Bloch**, M., *Feudal Society*, 2 vols., Paris, 1939-40, English trans., 1960. For background.

267 **Brooke**, C. N. L., *From Alfred to Henry III, 871-1272*, 1961.

268 **Brown**, R. A., *The Norman Conquest*, 1969.

269 —— *The Origins of English Feudalism*, 1973.

270 **Chevalier**, C. T., ed., *The Norman Conquest*, 1966. Includes essays by Whitelock and Barlow.

271 **Coulton**, G. G., *Social Life in Britain from the Conquest to the Reformation*, 1918, 2nd ed., 1938.

272 —— *Medieval Panorama*, 1938.

273 —— *Medieval Village, Manor and Monastery*, 1925. Reprinted 1960.

274 **Cronne**, H. A., *The Reign of Stephen, 1135-54*,

1970.
275 **Darlington**, R. R., *The Norman Conquest*, 1963. (Creighton Lecture in History for 1962.) A very useful summary.
276 **Denholm-Young**, N., 'Feudal society in the thirteenth century', *Hist.*, XXIX, 1944, 107-19.
277 **Dickinson**, J. C., *The Great Charter*. Hist.Ass. pamphlet, 1955. A readily accessible text of Magna Carta with notes on its background and significance.
278 **Douglas**, D. C., *William the Conqueror: The Norman Impact upon England*, 1964.
279 —— 'The Norman Conquest and English Feudalism', *Ec.H.R.*, IX, 1938-9, 128-43.
280 **Ganshof**, F., *Feudalism*, English trans., 1952, 3rd ed., N. Y. and London, 1964. For background.
281 **Hollings**, M., 'The survival of the Five Hide unit in the west Midlands', *E.H.R.*, LXIII, 1948, 435-87.
282 **Hollister**, C. W., *The Making of England, 55 B.C. to 1399*, Boston, Mass., 1966.
283 —— *The Military Organisation of Norman England*, 1965.
284 —— 'The irony of English Feudalism', *J.Brit.Studs.*, II, 1963, 1-26.
285 —— 'The Norman Conquest and the genesis of English Feudalism', *A.H.R.*, LXVI, 1961, 641-63.
286 —— 'The significance of scutage rates in eleventh and twelfth-century England', *E.H.R.*, LXXV, 1960, 577-88.
287 —— '1066: the "Feudal Revolution" ', *A.H.R.*, LXX, 1968, 708-23.
288 —— 'The Five Hide unit and military obligation', *Speculum*, XXXVI, 1961, 61-74.
289 —— 'The knights of Peterborough and the Anglo-Norman fyrd', *E.H.R.*, LXXVII, 1962, 417-36.
290 —— and Holt, J.C., 'Two comments on the problem of continuity in Anglo-Norman feudalism', *Ec.H.R.*, 2nd ser., XVI, 1963, 104-18.
291 **Holt**, J. C., *Magna Carta*, 1965. A major work on the subject.
292 —— 'The barons and the Great Charter', *E.H.R.*, LXIX, 1955, 1-24.
293 —— 'Feudalism re-visited', *Ec.H.R.*, 2nd ser., XIV, 1961, 333-40.
294 —— 'Politics and property in early medieval England', *P.P.*, 57, 1972, 3-52.
295 **John**, E., 'English feudalism and the structure of Anglo-Saxon society', *B. John Rylands Lib.*, XLVI, 1963, 14-41. For background.
296 **Jones**, R. J., 'Economic organisation and policies in the Middle Ages', *Ec.H.R.*, 2nd ser., XVII,

1965, 570-78. A review article on Postan, Rich and Miller (316), listed below.
297 **Kapelle**, W. E., *The Norman Conquest of the North. The Region and its Transformation, 1100-1135*, 1979.
298 **King**, E., *England, 1175-1425*, 1979. Includes chapters on population and settlement, lordship and wealth, trade and industry.
299 **Lopez**, R. S., 'Agenda for medieval studies', *J.Ec.H.*, XXXI, 1971, 165-71.
300 **Loyn**, H. R., *Anglo-Saxon England and the Norman Conquest*, 1962. A valuable economic and social history. Good bibliography.
301 —— *The Norman Conquest*, 1965.
302 **McKechnie**, W. S., *Magna Carta: A commentary*, 1905, 2nd ed., 1914. Still a standard authority.
303 **Maitland**, F. W., *Domesday Book and Beyond*, 1897. A classic, but one which is preferably read in the light of a modern introduction. Two recent paperback editions of Maitland's book are available: (1) with an introduction by E. Miller, 1960; (2) with an introduction by B. D. Lyon, N. Y., 1966.
304 **Matthew**, D. J. A., *The Norman Conquest*, 1966.
305 **Miller**, E. and Hatcher, J., *Medieval England. Rural Society and Economic Change, 1086-1348*, 1978.
306 **Milsom**, S. F. C., *The Legal Framework of English Feudalism*, 1976.
307 **Painter**, S., *Studies in the History of the English Feudal Barony*, Baltimore, 1943.
308 **Platt**, C., *Medieval England. A Social History and Archaeology from the Conquest to A.D. 1600*, 1978. Includes chapters on the Anglo-Norman settlement, economic growth, the Black Death, conspicuous consumption, and reorientation under the Tudors.
309 **Poole**, A. L., *From Domesday Book to Magna Carta, 1087-1216*, 1951, 2nd ed., 1955. Good bibliography.
310 —— *Obligations of Society in the Twelfth and Thirteenth Centuries*, 1946.
311 —— ed., *Medieval England*, 2 vols., 1958.
312 **Postan**, M. M., ed., *Cambridge Economic History of Europe (1) The Agrarian Life of the Middle Ages*, 2nd ed., 1966.
313 —— *The Medieval Economy and Society. An Economic History of Britain, 1100-1500*, 1972.
314 —— 'The rise of a money economy', *Ec.H.R.*, XIV, 1944, 123-34. Reprinted in Carus-Wilson, ed. (245), listed above, II, 1-12.

315 —— and Rich, E. E., eds., *Cambridge Economic History of Europe II: Trade and Industry in the Middle Ages*, 1952.

316 ——, Rich, E. E., and Miller, E., eds., *Cambridge Economic History of Europe III: Economic Organization and Policies in the Middle Ages*, 1963.

317 **Pounds**, N. J. G., *An Economic History of Medieval Europe*, 1974. For background.

318 **Powicke**, F. M., *The Thirteenth Century, 1216-1307*, 1953. A useful survey, though hardly a readable one. Good bibliography.

319 **Powicke**, M., *Military Obligation in England: A Study in Liberty and Duty*, 1962.

320 **Roehl**, R., *Patterns and Structure of Demand, 1000-1500*, 1970. (Fontana Economic History of Europe, vol. I, section 3.) For background.

321 **Saunders**, I. J., *Feudal Military Service in England: A study of the Constitutional and Military Powers of the Barones in Medieval England*, 1956.

322 **Sawyer**, P. H., 'The wealth of England in the eleventh century', *T.R.H.S.*, 5th ser., XV, 1965, 145-64. Argues that England was wealthier than often supposed and that the chief source of this wealth was wool.

323 **Sayles**, G. O., *The Medieval Foundations of England*, 1948, 2nd ed., 1950. A well-known textbook.

324 **Southern**, R. W., *The Making of the Middle Ages*, 1953.

325 **Stanley**, M., 'The geographical distribution of wealth in medieval England', *J.H.Geog.*, VI, 1980, 315-24.

326 **Stenton**, Doris M., *English Society in the Early Middle Ages, 1066-1307*, 1951, 4th ed., 1965.

327 —— ed., *Preparatory to Anglo-Saxon England: The Collected Papers of F. M. Stenton*, 1970. A useful collection which includes Stenton's essays on 'Norman London', on 'The development of the castle in England and Wales' and on 'The road system of medieval England'.

328 **Stenton**, F. M., *Anglo-Saxon England, c. 550-1087*, 1943, 3rd ed., 1971. Good bibliography.

329 —— *The First Century of English Feudalism, 1066-1166*, 1932, 2nd ed., 1961.

330 **Tomkieff**, O. G., *Life in Norman England*, 1966.

331 **Vinogradoff**, P., *English Society in the Eleventh Century*, 1908. Reprinted 1968. See also Bean (682), listed below, and Clapham (218), Cunningham (219), Lipson (232) and Pollard and Crossley (236), listed above.

(d) MONOGRAPHS AND REGIONAL STUDIES

332 **Altschul**, M., *A Baronial Family in Medieval England: The Clares, 1217-1314*, Baltimore, 1965.

333 **Darby**, H. C., *The Medieval Fenland*, 1940.

334 —— *Medieval Cambridgeshire*, 1977.

335 **Hoskins**, W. G., 'The wealth of medieval Devon'. In Hoskins and Finberg (1248), listed below, 212-49.

336 **Kermode**, J. I., *Medieval Cheshire*, T.H.S.L.C., CXXVIII, 1979. Includes chapters on manorial demesnes, social mobility, and on relations between the Earl of Chester and the gentry.

337 **Wightman**, W. E., *The Lacy Family in England and Normandy, 1066-1194*, 1966.

338 **Witney**, K. P., *The Jutish Forest. A Study of the Weald of Kent from 450 to 1380*, 1976.

DOMESDAY STUDIES

Although many of the entries in this section could quite logically have been placed in other parts of the bibliography – under *Agriculture*, for example – it has been thought most useful to collect most of them under this heading.

The text of the Domesday Book was printed by the Record Commission as follows:

339 **Ellis**, H., ed., *Libri Censualis vocati Domesday Book Additamenta*, 1816. This contains the texts of the Exon Domesday, the Inquisitio Eliensis and the Winchester and Boldon Book surveys.

340 —— *Libri Censualis vocatus Domesday Book Indices*, 3 vols., 1816-33.

341 **Farley**, A., ed., *Liber Censualis vocatus Domesday Book*, 2 vols., 1783.

342 **Ballard**, A., *The Domesday Boroughs*, 1904.

343 **Bishop**, T. A. M., 'The Norman settlement of

Yorkshire', in R. W. Hunt, W. A. Pantin, and R. W. Southern, eds., *Studies in Medieval History Presented to F. M. Powicke*, 1948, 1-14. Reprinted in Carus-Wilson, ed. (245), listed above, II, 1-11.

344 **Brooks**, F. W., *Domesday Book and the East Riding*, East Yorks.Loc.H.Soc., 1966.

345 **Darby**, H. C., ed., *The Domesday Geography of Eastern England*, 1952, 2nd ed., 1957. The first instalment of a massive historical enterprise.

346 —— *Domesday England*, 1977.

347 —— and Terrett, I. B., eds., *The Domesday Geography of Midland England*, 1954, 2nd ed., 1971.

348 —— and Campbell, E. M., eds., *The Domesday Geography of South-east England*, 1962.

349 —— and Maxwell, I. S., eds., *The Domesday Geography of Northern England*, 1962.

350 —— and Finn, R. W., eds., *The Domesday Geography of South-west England*, 1967.

351 —— 'Domesday woodland', *Ec.H.R.*, 2nd ser., III, 1950-1, 21-43.

352 —— and Versey, G. R., *Domesday Gazetteer*, 1975.

353 **Dodwell**, Barbara, 'The making of the Domesday Survey in Norfolk: the Hundred and a Half of Clacklose', *E.H.R.*, LXXXIV, 1969, 79-84.

354 **Ellis**, H., *A General Introduction to Domesday Book*, 1833. Reprinted 1972.

355 **Finn**, R. W., *The Domesday Inquest and the Making of Domesday Book*, 1961. See also Galbraith (368), listed below.

356 —— *Domesday Studies: The Liber Exoniensis*, 1964.

357 —— *Domesday Studies: The Eastern Countries*, 1967.

358 —— *Domesday Studies: The Norman Conquest and its Effect on the Economy, 1066-86*, 1971.

359 —— 'The immediate sources of the Exchequer Domesday', *B. John Rylands Lib.*, XL, 1958, 47-78.

360 —— 'The making of the Dorset Domesday', *Proc.Dorset Nat.H. & Arch. Soc.*, LXXXI, 1960, 50-7.

361 —— 'The Exeter Domesday and its construction', *B. John Rylands Lib.*, XLI, 1959, 360-87.

362 —— 'The making of the Wiltshire Domesday', *Wilts. Arch. & Nat.H. Mag.*, LII, 1948, 318-27.

363 —— 'Some reflections on the Cambridgeshire Domesday', *Proc. Cambridge Antiq.Soc.*, LIII, for 1959, 29-38.

364 —— 'The teamland of the Domesday Inquest', *E.H.R.*, LXXXIII, 1968, 95-101. A reply to Moore (374), listed below.

365 **Foster**, C. W. and Longay, T., eds., *The Lincolnshire Domesday and the Lindsey Survey* (Linc.Rec.Soc., XIX), 1924.

366 **Fowler**, G. H., *Bedfordshire in 1086*, 1922.

367 **Fraser**, H. M., eds., *The Staffordshire Domesday*, 1936.

368 **Galbraith**, V. H., *The Making of Domesday Book*, 1961.

369 **Harvey**, Sally, 'Royal revenue and Domesday terminology', *Ec.H.R.*, 2nd ser., XX, 1967, 221-8.

370 —— 'Domesday Book and Anglo-Norman governance', *T.R.H.S.*, 5th ser., XXV, 1975, 175-93.

371 **Hoskins**, W. G., 'The highland zone in Domesday Book'. In Hoskins (1246), listed below, 15-52.

372 **Hoyt**, R. S., 'Farm of the manor and community of the vill in Domesday Book', *Speculum*, XXX, 1955, 147-69.

373 **Lennard**, R. V., *Rural England, 1086-1135*, 1959.

374 **Moore**, J. S., 'The Domesday teamland: a reconsideration', *T.R.H.S.*, 5th ser., XIV, 1964, 109-30. See Finn (364), listed above.

375 **Postan**, M. M., 'The Maps of Domesday', *Ec.H.R.*, 2nd ser., VII, 1954, 98-100.

376 **Sawyer**, P. H., 'The "original returns" and Domesday Book', *E.H.R.*, LXX, 1955, 177-97.

377 **Tait**, J., ed., *Domesday Survey of Cheshire*, Chet.Soc., n.s., LXXV, 1916.

POPULATION

(a) GENERAL WORKS

378 **Hallam**, H. E., 'Population density in medieval Fenland', *Ec.H.R.*, 2nd ser., XIV, 1961, 71-81.

379 —— 'Some thirteenth-century censuses', *Ec.H.R.*, 2nd ser., X, 1958, 340-61.

380 —— 'Further observations on the Spalding serf lists', *Ec.H.R.*, 2nd ser., XVI, 1963, 338-50.

381 **Harvey**, J. B., 'Population trends and agricultural developments from the Warwickshire hundred

rolls of 1279', *Ec.H.R.*, 2nd ser., XI, 1958-9, 8-18.

382 **Hoskins**, W. G., 'The population of an English village, 1086-1801. A study of Wigston Magna', *Trans.Leics.Arch.Soc.*, XXXIII, 1957, 15-35. Reprinted in Hoskins (1246), 181-208.

383 **Kealey**, E. J., *Medieval Medicus: A Social History of Anglo-Norman Medicine*, Baltimore, 1982. A scholarly study which approaches its subject by way of art, archaeology, biography, ecclesiology and economics.

384 **Roberts**, B. K., *Rural Settlement in Britain*, 1979.

385 —— 'A study of medieval colonisation in the Forest of Arden, Warwickshire', *Ag.H.R.*, XVI, 1968, 101-13.

386 **Russell**, J. C., *British Medieval Population*, Albuquerque, New Mexico, 1949. The main work on the subject, though its conclusions do not command general assent.

387 —— 'The clerical population of medieval England', *Traditio*, 2, 1944, 177-212.

388 —— 'Recent advances in medieval demography', *Speculum*, XL, 1965, 84-101.

389 —— 'The pre-Plague population of England', *J.Brit.Studs.*, V, 1966, 1-21.

390 —— 'A quantitative approach to medieval population change', *J.Ec.H.*, XXIV, 1964, 1-21.

391 —— *Population in Europe, 500-1500*, (Fontana Economic History of Europe, vol. I, section I), 1969. Useful for the general background.

392 —— 'Demographic limitations of the Spalding serf lists', *Ec.H.R.*, 2nd ser., XV, 1962, 138-44. A comment on Hallam (378), listed above.

393 **Titow**, J. Z., 'Some evidence of the thirteenth-century population increase', *Ec.H.R.*, 2nd ser., XIV, 1961, 218-33. See also Hollingsworth (1290) and Wrigley (1302), listed below.

(b) THE FAMILY

394 **Helmholz**, R. H., *Marriage Litigation in Medieval England*, 1975.

395 **Krause**, J. T., 'The medieval household, large or small?', *Ec.H.R.*, 2nd ser., IX, 1957, 420-32.

396 **Painter**, S., 'The family and the feudal system in twelfth-century England', *Speculum*, XXXV, 1960, 1-16. An important study of family solidarity in this period.

AGRICULTURE AND RURAL SOCIETY

397 **Lamond**, Elizabeth, ed., *Walter of Henley's Husbandry*, 1890. Written in the thirteenth century.

398 **Oschinsky**, Dorothea, ed., *Walter of Henley: and Other Treatises on Estate Management and Accounting*, 1971. On Walter of Henley, see:

399 **Denholm-Young**, N., 'Walter of Henley', *Medievalia et Humanistica*, XV, 1962, 61-8.

400 **McDonald**, D., *Agricultural Writers from Walter of Henley to Arthur Young, 1200-1800*, 1908. For other source material in this field, see Bland, Brown and Tawney (211), listed above, and Titow (433), listed below.

(a) GENERAL

401 **Ashley**, W. J., *The Bread of our Forefathers: An Inquiry in Economic History*, 1928.

402 **Bennett**, M. K., 'British wheat yield per acre for seven centuries', *Ec. J.Ec.Hist.Supp.*, III, 1935, 12-29. Reprinted in Minchinton (249), listed above, I, 53-72.

403 **Beresford**, M. W. and Joseph, J. K.St., *Medieval England. An Aerial Survey*, 1958.

404 **Beveridge**, W. H., 'The yield and price of corn in the Middle Ages', *Ec. J.Ec.H.Supp.*, I, 1927, 155-67. Reprinted in Carus-Wilson, (245), I, 13-25.

405 **Butlin**, R. A., 'Some terms used in agrarian history: a glossary', *Ag.H.R.*, IX, 1961, 98-104.

406 **Coss**, P. R., 'Sir Geoffrey de Langley and the crisis of the knightly class in thirteenth-century England', *P.P.*, 68, 1975, 3-37.

407 **Cronne**, H. A., 'The Royal Forest in the reign of Henry I', in Cronne, Moody and Quinn (1841), listed below, 1-23.

408 **Duby**, G., *Rural Economy and Country Life in the Medieval West*, English trans., 1968.

409 —— *Medieval Agriculture, 900-1500* (Fontana Economic History of Europe, Vol. I, section 5), 1969. For background.

410 **Ernle**, Lord (R. E. Prothero), *English Farming Past and Present*, 1912, 6th ed., 1961, with valuable new introductions by G. E. Fussell and O. R. McGregor. A pioneer work of considerable historiographical interest.

411 **Fussell**, G. E., *Farming Technique from Pre-*

historic to Modern Times, 1966.

412 **Hallam**, H. E., *Rural England, 1066-1272*, 1981.

413 **Homans**, G. C., *English Villagers of the Thirteenth Century*, Harvard, Mass., 1942. Reprinted 1960. An important book.

414 —— 'The rural sociology of medieval England', *P.P.*, 4, 1953, 32-43.

415 —— 'Men and the land in the Middle Ages', *Speculum*, XI, 1936, 338-51.

416 **Hoskins**, W. G., 'Sheep farming in Saxon and medieval England'. In Hoskins (1246), listed below, 1-14.

417 **Hyams**, P. R., *King, Lords and Peasants in Medieval England. The Common Law of Villeinage in the Twelfth and Thirteenth Centuries*, 1980.

418 **Jones**, A., 'Land measurement in England, 1150-1350', *Ag.H.R.*, XXVII, 1979, 10-18.

419 **Kershaw**, I., 'The Great Famine and agrarian crisis in England, 1315-1322', *P.P.*, 59, 1973, 3-50.

420 **Kosminsky**, E. A., *Studies in the Agrarian History of England in the Thirteenth Century*, 1956. The work of a Marxist historian in which the peasantry receive most attention.

421 **Lennard**, R. V., 'Statistics of sheep in medieval England. A question of interpretation', *Ag.H.R.*, VII, 1959, 75-81.

422 **Long**, W. H., 'The low yields of corn in medieval England', *Ec.H.R.*, 2nd ser., XXXII, 1979, 459-69.

423 **Neilson**, Nellie, 'Early English woodland and waste', *J.Ec.H.*, II, 1942, 54-62.

424 **Parain**, C., 'The evolution of agricultural technique'. In Postan (312), listed above, 126-79.

425 **Poole**, A. L., 'Livestock prices in the twelfth century', *E.H.R.*, LV, 1940, 284-95.

426 **Postan**, M. M., *Essays on Medieval Agriculture and General Problems of the Medieval Economy*, 1973.

427 —— 'Medieval agrarian society in its prime: England'. In Postan (312), listed above, 549-632.

428 —— 'Investment in medieval agriculture', *J.Ec.H.*, XXVII, 1967, 576-87. A pioneer article.

429 —— 'Village livestock in the thirteenth century', *Ec.H.R.*, 2nd ser., XV, 1962, 219-49.

430 **Sawyer**, P. H., ed., *Medieval Settlement. Continuity and Change*, 1977.

431 **Seebohm**, M. E., *The Evolution of the English Farm*, 1927, 2nd ed., 1952.

432 **Slicher van Bath**, B. M., *Yield Ratios 810-1820*, Wageningen, 1963.

433 **Titow**, J. Z., *English Rural Society, 1200-1350*, 1969. Half the book consists of documents.

434 —— *Winchester Yields. A Study in Medieval Agricultural Productivity*, 1972. Covers the period 1208-1350.

435 **Young**, C. R., *The Royal Forests of Medieval England*, 1979.

(b) REGIONAL STUDIES

436 **Slade**, C. F., ed., *The Leicestershire Survey, c.1130*, University of Leicester, Department of English Loc.H., Occ. Papers, 7, 1956.

437 **Chibnall**, A. C., *Sherington: Fiefs and Fields of a Buckinghamshire Village*, 1965. A survey from the twelfth to the eighteenth century.

438 **Finberg**, H. P. R., *West Country Historical Studies*, 1969.

439 **Gras**, N. S. B. and E. C., *The Economic and Social History of an English Village (Crawley, Hants), 909-1928*, Cambridge, Mass., 1930. Very well documented.

440 **Hallam**, H. E., *Settlement and Society: A Study of the Early Agrarian History of South Lincolnshire*, 1965. An interesting study which examines land and people in the period between the eleventh century and 1307.

441 **Harvey**, P. D. A., *A Medieval Oxfordshire Village: Cuxham, 1240-1400*, 1965.

442 **Hilton**, R. H., *The Social Structure of Rural Warwickshire in the Middle Ages*, Dugdale Soc.Occ. Papers, IX, 1956.

443 —— *A Medieval Society: the West Midlands at the End of the Thirteenth Century*, 1967.

444 —— 'Medieval agrarian history', *V.C.H. Leics.*, ed. W. G. Hoskins and R. A. McKinley, II, 1954, 145-98.

445 **Hoskins**, W. G., 'The making of the agrarian landscape'. In Hoskins and Finberg (1248), 289-333. A general survey from medieval times to the nineteenth century.

446 **Lennard**, R. V., 'The destruction of woodland in the eastern counties under William the Conqueror', *Ec.H.R.*, XV, 1945, 36-43.

447 **Moore**, J. S., *Laughton: A Study in the Evolution of the Wealden Landscape*, University of Leicester, Department of English Loc.H.Occ. Papers, 19, 1966.

448 **Naughton**, K. S., *The Gentry of Bedfordshire in the Thirteenth and Fourteenth Centuries*, 1976.

449 **Raftis**, J. A., *Assart Data and Land Values. Two Studies in the East Midlands, 1200-1350*, Toronto, 1974.

450 **Ravensdale**, J., *Liable to Floods. Village Land-*

scape on the Edge of the Fens, 450-1850, 1974.

451 **Scott**, Richenda, 'Medieval Agriculture', In *V.C. H. Wilts.*, ed. R. B. Pugh, IV, 1959, 7-42.

452 **Siddle**, D. J., 'The rural economy of medieval Holderness', *Ag.H.R.*, XV, 1967, 40-5.

453 **Sylvester**, Dorothy, *The Rural Landscape of the Welsh Borderland: A Study in Historical Geography*, 1969.

454 **Thomas**, C., 'Thirteenth-century farm economies in North Wales', *Ag.H.R.*, XVI, 1968, 1-14.

455 **Vollans**, E. C., 'The evolution of farm lands in the central Chilterns in the twelfth and thirteenth centuries', *T.I.B.G.*, XXVI, 1959, 197-241. See also Hoskins (1245), listed below.

(c) THE MANOR

456 **Page**, F. M., ed., *Wellingborough Manorial Accounts, A.D. 1258-1323*, Northants. Rec.Soc., 1936.

457 **Redwood**, B. C. and Wilson, A. E., eds., *Custumals of the Sussex Manors of the Archbishops of Canterbury*, Sussex Rec.Soc., LVII, 1957.

458 **Wilson**, A. E., ed., *Custumals of the Manors of Laughton, Willingdon and Goring*, Sussex Rec.Soc., LX, 1961.

459 **Aston**, T. H., 'The origins of the manor in England', *T.R.H.S.*, 5th ser. 1958, 59-83. Reprinted in Minchinton (249), listed above, I, 9-35. An important article which considers the development of the manor in the Anglo-Saxon period and in the years following the Norman Conquest.

460 **Bennett**, H. S., *Life on the English Manor*, 1937.

461 **Bishop**, T. A. M., 'The distribution of manorial demesne in the Vale of Yorkshire', *E.H.R.*, XLIX, 1934, 386-406.

462 **Davenport**, F. G., *The Economic Development of a Norfolk Manor, 1086-1565*, 1906.

463 **Drew**, J. S., 'Manorial accounts of St. Swithun's Priory, Winchester', *E.H.R.*, LXII, 1947, 20-41. Reprinted in Carus-Wilson, ed. (245), listed above, II, 12-30. Covers the period from 1248 to 1400.

464 **Hilton**, R. H., 'Winchcombe Abbey and the Manor of Sherborne'. In Finberg (1241), listed below, 89-113.

465 —— 'Kibworth Harcourt, a Merton College manor in the thirteenth and fourteenth centuries', In Hoskins (1426), listed below, 17-40.

466 **Latham**, L. C., 'The manor and the village'. In Barraclough (264), listed above, 29-50. Originally published as an Hist.Ass. pamphlet.

467 **Levett**, Ada E., *Studies in Manorial History*, 1938. Reprinted 1962.

468 **Stenton**, F. M., *Types of Manorial Structure in the Northern Danelaw*, 1910.

469 **Sylvester**, Dorothy, 'The manor and the Cheshire landscape', *T.L.C.A.S.*, LXX, for 1960, 1961, 1-15.

470 **Ugawa**, K., 'The economic development of some Devon manors in the thirteenth century', *T.Devonshire Assoc.*, XCIV, 1962, 630-83.

471 **Vinogradoff**, P., *The Growth of the Manor*, 1905, 2nd ed., 1911. Book 3, 291-379, covers the feudal period. Needs to be read in the light of Aston (459), listed above. See also Titow (574) below.

(d) LAND TENURE AND THE LAND MARKET

Many titles relevant in this connection are listed in the section *General Works*.

472 **Denman**, D. R., *Origins of Ownership: A Brief History of Land Ownership and Tenure in England from Earliest Times to the modern Era*, 1958.

473 **Homans**, G. C., 'Partible inheritance of villagers' holdings', *Ec.H.R.*, VIII, 1937-8, 48-56.

474 **Hoyt**, R. S., *The Royal Demesne in English Constitutional History, 1066-1272*, Ithaca, N. Y., 1950.

475 **Hyams**, P. R., 'The origins of a peasant land market in England', *Ec.H.R.*, 2nd ser., XXIII, 1970, 18-31.

476 **King**, E., *Peterborough Abbey, 1086-1310. A Study in the Land Market*, 1973.

477 **Roden**, D., 'Inheritance customs and succession to land in the Chiltern hills in the thirteenth and fourteenth centuries', *J.Brit.Studs.*, VII, 1967, 1-11.

(e) ESTATES

478 **Stitt**, F. B., ed., *Lenton Priory Estate Accounts, 1296-1298*, Thoroton Soc.Rec. series, XIX, 1959.

479 **Chibnall**, Marjorie, *The English Lands of the Abbey of Bec*, 1946.

480 **Dyer**, C., *Lords and Peasants in a Changing Society. The Estates of the Bishopric of Worcester, 680-1540*, 1980.

481 **English**, B., *The Lords of Holderness*,

1086-1260, 1980.

482 **Harvey**, Barbara, *Westminster Abbey and its Estates in the Middle Ages*, 1977.

483 **Hilton**, R. H., 'Gloucester Abbey leases of the late thirteenth century', *Birm.Hist. Jnl.*, IV, 1953-4, 1-17.

484 **Lennard**, R. V., 'The demesnes of Glastonbury Abbey in the eleventh and twelfth centuries', *Ec.H.R.*, 2nd ser., VIII, 1956, 355-63. A critique of Postan (488), listed below.

485 **May**, Teresa, 'The estates of the Cobham Family in the later thirteenth century', *Arch.Cant.*, LXXXIV, 1970, 211-29. Presents a profit and loss account of a large lay manor.

486 **Miller**, E., *The Abbey and Bishopric of Ely: The Social History of an Ecclesiastical Estate from the Tenth to the Early Fourteenth Century*, 1951. Reprinted 1969.

487 **Oschinsky**, Dorothea, 'Medieval treatises on estate management', *Ec.H.R.*, 2nd ser., VIII, 1955-6, 296-309. See also Oschinsky (398), listed above.

488 **Postan**, M. M., 'Glastonbury estates in the twelfth century', *Ec.H.R.*, 2nd ser., V, 1953, 358-67. See also Lennard (484), listed above.

489 —— 'Glastonbury estates in the twelfth century: a reply', *Ec.H.R.* 2nd ser., IX, 1957, 106-18. A reply to Lennard (484), listed above.

490 **Raban**, S., *The Estates of Thorney and Crowland. A Study in Medieval Monastic Land Tenure*, 1977.

491 **Stansfield**, J., ed., 'Rent roll of Kirkstall Abbey (1459)', *Thoresby Soc.,Miscellanea* I, 1891, 1-21.

492 **Ward**, J. C., 'The estates of the Clare family, 1066-1317', *B.I.H.R.*, XXXVII, 1964, 114-17.

(f) RENT

493 **Hilton**, R. H., 'Rent and capital formation in feudal society', *International Conference of Economic History*, Aix, 1962, 33-68.

494 **Kosminsky**, E. A., 'The evolution of feudal rent in England from the eleventh to the fifteenth centuries', *P.P.*, 7, 1955, 12-36.

(g) FIELD SYSTEMS

495 **Baker**, A. R. H. and Butlin, R. A., (eds.), *Studies of Field Systems in the British Isles*, 1973. A standard work of reference on the development of British field systems from Anglo-Saxon times to the breakup of the medieval pattern.

496 **Bishop**, T. A. M., 'Assarting and the growth of the open fields', *Ec.H.R.*, VI, 1935, 13-29. Reprinted in Carus-Wilson, ed. (245), listed above, I, 26-40.

497 **Dodgshon**, R. A., *The Origin of British Field Systems*, 1980.

498 **Homans**, G. C., 'The explanation of English regional differences', *P.P.*, 42, 1969, 18-34. A critique of Thirsk (501), listed below in this section.

499 **Pocock**, E. A., 'The first fields in an Oxfordshire village', *Ag.H.R.*, XVI, 1968, 85-100.

500 **Rowley**, T., ed., *The Origins of Open Field Agriculture*, 1981. Ten essays of varying value.

501 **Thirsk**, Joan, 'The common fields', *P.P.*, 29, 1964, 3-25. An important article arguing that the growth of the three-field system was slower and less widespread than often assumed.

502 —— 'The origins of the common fields', *P.P.*, 33, 1966, 142-7. A reply to Titow (503), listed below.

503 **Titow**, J. Z., 'Medieval England and the open-field system', *P.P.*, 32, 1965, 86-102. Takes issue with Thirsk (501), listed above.

(h) PLACE-NAME STUDIES

No attempt is made here to provide a comprehensive list of works on this subject. The reader is referred to Altschul's bibliography (252), listed above, 27-9, for details of the publications of the English Place Name Society. Only three items of a general nature are listed below.

504 **Cameron**, K., *English Place Names*, 1961.

505 **Ekwall**, E., *Studies on English Place Names*, Stockholm, 1936. A work by the leading authority on the subject.

506 **Sawyer**, P. H. 'The place names of Domesday Book', *B. John Rylands Lib.*, XXXVIII, 1956, 483-506.

INDUSTRY

(a) GENERAL

507 **Carus-Wilson**, Eleanora M., 'An industrial revolution of the thirteenth century', *Ec.H.R.*, XI, 1941, 39-60. Reprinted in Carus-Wilson, ed. (245), listed above, I, 41-60. The claims for this industrial revolution rest on evidence relating to water-powered fulling mills.

508 **Salzman**, L. F., *English Industries of the Middle Ages*, 1913, 2nd ed., 1923.

509 **White**, L., *Medieval Technology and Social Change*, 1962. Chapters 2 and 3 on 'The agrarian revolution of the early Middle Ages' and 'The medieval expansion of mechanical power' are useful.

(b) TEXTILES

510 **Carus-Wilson**, Eleanora M., 'The English cloth industry in the late twelfth and early thirteenth centuries', *Ec.H.R.*, XIV, 1944, 32-50.

511 —— 'The woollen industry', in Postan and Rich, eds. (315), listed above, 355-429.

512 **Miller**, E., 'The fortunes of the English textile industry during the thirteenth century'. *Ec.H.R.*, 2nd ser., XVIII, 1965, 64-82.

(c) METALS

513 **Schubert**, H. R., *History of the British Iron and Steel Industry from c.450 B.C. to A.D. 1775*, 1957.

Particularly useful on the technical aspects.

514 **Waites**, B., 'Medieval iron-working in N. E. Yorkshire', *Geography*, XLIX, 1964, 33-43. See also Fell (1601), Gough (1605), Lewis (1616), Raistrick and Jennings (1619) and Straker (1623), listed below.

(d) BUILDING

515 **Colvin**, H. M., ed., *Building Accounts of King Henry III*, 1971.

516 —— ed., *History of the King's Works, I and II, The Middle Ages* (by R. A. Brown, H. M. Colvin and A. J. Taylor), 1963.

517 **Johnson**, H. T., 'Cathedral building and the medieval economy', *Expl.Entrepren.H.*, 2nd ser., IV, 1967, 191-210.

518 **Knoop**, D., and Jones, G. P., 'The English medieval quarry', *Ec.H.R.*, IX, 1939, 17-37. See the section on *Labour* for other titles by Knoop and Jones (559-560). See also Salzman (894), listed below.

(e) MISCELLANEOUS

519 **McDonnell**, J., *Inland Fisheries in Medieval Yorkshire, 1066-1300*, Borthwick Papers, 60, 1981.

520 **Murray**, Kathleen M. E., 'Shipping'. In Poole (311), listed above, I, 168-95.

MONEY, PRICES AND PUBLIC FINANCE

(a) MONEY AND PRICES

521 **Brooke**, G. C., *English Coins from the Seventh Century to the Present Day*, 1932. Reprinted 1966.

522 **Craig**, J., *The Mint. A History of the London Mint from A.D. 287 to 1948*, 1953.

523 **Dolley**, R. H. M., *The Norman Conquest and the English Coinage*, 1966.

524 —— 'Coinage'. In Poole (311), listed above, I, 264-99.

525 **Farmer**, D. L., 'Some price fluctuations in Angevin England', *Ec.H.R.*, 2nd ser., IX, 1956-7, 34-43.

526 —— 'Some grain price movements in thirteenth-century England', *Ec.H.R.*, 2nd ser., X, 1957-8, 207-20.

527 **Feavearyear**, A. E., *The Pound Sterling*, 1931, 2nd ed., revised by E. V. Morgan, 1963.

528 **Harvey**, P. D. A., 'The English inflation 1180-1220', *P.P.*, 61, 1973, 3-30.

529 **Homer**, S., *A History of Interest Rates*, New Brunswick, 1963.

530 **Lloyd**, T. H., *The Movement of Wool Prices in Medieval England*, 1973. Covers the period from the thirteenth to the fifteenth century.

531 **Oman**, C., *The Coinage of England*, 1931.

532 **Rogers**, J. E. T., *A History of Agriculture and*

Prices in England, 6 vols., 1866-1900.
533 —— *Six Centuries of Work and Wages*, 1894. Several times reprinted.
534 **Shaw**, W. A., *The History of Currency, 1252-1894*, 2nd ed., 1896.
535 **Spufford**, P., 'Coinage and currency'. In Postan, Rich and Miller, eds. (316), listed above, 576-602. See also the book by E. H. Phelps Brown listed below (2225).

(b) PUBLIC FINANCE

536 **Johnson**, C., ed., *Dialogus de Scaccario: the Discourse of the Exchequer, by Richard son of Nigel*, 1950.
537 —— *The De Moneta of Nicholas Oresme, and English Mint Documents*, 1956.

538 **Brown**, R. A., 'The Treasury of the later twelfth century'. In J. C. Davies, ed., *Studies Presented to Sir Hilary Jenkinson*, 1957, 35-49.
539 **Davies**, J. C., 'The memoranda rolls of the Exchequer to 1307'. In J. C. Davies, ed., *Studies Presented to Sir Hilary Jenkinson*, 1957, 97-154.
540 **Dowell**, S., *History of Taxes and Taxation in England*, 1884, 2nd ed., 1888. Reprinted, 4 vols., 1965, with a new introduction by A. R. Ilersic. Vol. I.
541 **Kaeuper**, R. W., *Bankers to the Crown. The Riccardi of Lucca and Edward I*, Princeton, N. J., 1973.
542 **Mitchell**, S. K., *Studies in Taxation under John and Henry III*, New Haven, Conn., 1914.
543 —— *Taxation in Medieval England*, ed. S. Painter, New Haven, Conn., 1951.
544 **Poole**, R. L., *The Exchequer in the Twelfth Century*, 1912.
545 **Prestwich**, J. O., 'War and finance in the Anglo-Norman state', *T.R.H.S.*, 5th ser., IV, 1954, 19-44.
546 **Prestwich**, M., 'Edward I's monetary policies and their consequences', *Ec.H.R.*, 2nd ser., XXII, 1969, 406-16.
547 **Roseveare**, H. G., *The Treasury: The Evolution of a British Institution*, 1969.
548 **White**, G. H., 'Financial administration under Henry I', *T.R.H.S.*, 4th ser., VIII, 1925, 56-78.
549 **Whitwell**, R. J., 'Italian bankers and the English Crown', *T.R.H.S.*, n.s., XVII, 1905, 175-233. Deals with the thirteenth century.

LABOUR

550 **Beveridge**, W. H., 'Wages on the Winchester manors', *Ec.H.R.*, VII, 1936, 22-43. Covers the period from the early thirteenth to the mid-fifteenth century.
551 —— 'Westminster wages in the manorial era', *Ec.H.R.*, 2nd ser., VIII, 1955-6, 18-35.
552 **Dodwell**, Barbara, 'The free tenantry of the hundred rolls', *Ec.H.R.*, XIV, 1944, 163-71.
553 —— 'The free peasantry of East Anglia in Domesday', *Norfolk Arch.*, XXVII, 1940, 145-57.
554 **Gray**, H. L., 'The commutation in villein services in England before the Black Death', *E.H.R.*, XXIX, 1914, 625-56.
555 **Hilton**, R. H., 'Peasant movements in England before 1381', *Ec.H.R.*, 2nd ser., II, 1949, 117-36. Reprinted in Carus-Wilson, ed. (245), listed above, II, 73-90.
556 —— 'Freedom and villeinage in England', *P.P.*, 31, 1965, 3-19. This and the previous article are valuable contributions to medieval labour history.
557 —— 'Lord and peasant in Staffordshire in the Middle Ages', *North Staffs. J. Field Studs.*, X, 1970, 1-20.
558 **Jones**, G. R. J., 'The distribution of bond settlements in N. W. Wales', *Welsh H.R.*, 2, 1964, 19-36.
559 **Knoop**, D., and Jones, G. P., *The Medieval Mason*, 1933.
560 —— 'The impressment of masons in the Middle Ages', *Ec.H.R.*, VIII, 1937-8, 57-67.
561 **Kosminsky**, E. A., 'Services and money rents in the thirteenth century', *Ec.H.R.*, V, 1935, 24-45. Reprinted in Carus-Wilson, ed. (245), listed above, II, 31-48. Important.
562 **Lennard**, R. V., 'The economic position of the Domesday villani', *Ec. J.*, LVI, 1946, 244-64.
563 —— 'The economic position of the Domesday sokemen', *Ec. J.*, LVII, 1947, 179-95.
564 —— 'The economic position of the bordars and cottars of Domesday Book', *Ec. J.*, LXI, 1951, 342-71.
565 —— 'The composition of the demesne plough

teams in twelfth-century England', *E.H.R.*, LXXV, 1960, 193-207.

566 —— 'Domesday plough teams: the south-west evidence', *E.H.R.*, LXXX, 1965, 217-33.

567 **Lloyd**, T. H., 'Ploughing services on the demesnes of the Bishop of Worcester in the late thirteenth century', *Birm.Hist. J.*, VIII, 1962, 189-96.

568 **Postan**, M. M., 'The chronology of labour services', *T.R.H.S.*, 4th ser., XX, 1937, 169-93. Reprinted in a revised form in Minchinton (249), listed above, I, 73-91.

569 —— *The Famulus: The Estate Labourer in the Twelfth and Thirteenth Centuries*, supplement to *Ec.H.R.* 1954. Demonstrates the importance of the hired labourer.

570 —— and Titow, J. Z., 'Heriots and prices on Winchester manors', *Ec.H.R.*, 2nd ser., XI, 1959, 392-411.

571 **Richardson**, H. G., 'The medieval plough team', *Hist.*, XXVI, 1942, 287-96.

572 **Shelby**, L. R., 'The role of the master mason in medieval English building', *Speculum*, XXXIX, 1964, 387-403. See also the works by Knoop and Jones (559-60), listed above.

573 **Stenton**, F. M., *The Free Peasantry of the Northern Danelaw*, 1969.

574 **Titow**, J. Z., 'Some differences between manors and their effects on the condition of the peasant in the thirteenth century', *Ag.H.R.*, X, 1962, 1-13. Reprinted in Minchinton, (249), listed above, I, 37-51.

575 **Vinogradoff**, P., *Villeinage in England*, 1892.

576 —— *The Collected Papers of Paul Vinogradoff*, ed. Louise Vinogradoff, 2 vols., 1928. Vol. 1: *Historical*. See also the book by Phelps Brown and Hopkins (2225), listed below.

TOWNS

577 **Gross**, C., *A Bibliography of British Municipal History*, Cambridge, Mass., 1897. Reprinted with a new introduction by G. H. Martin, 1966. The main bibliography for older histories of towns. It is brought up to date in:

578 **Martin**, G. H. and MacIntyre, Sylvia, *A Bibliography of British and Irish Municipal History I: General Works*, 1971. Subsequent volumes will deal with the history of individual cities and boroughs.

(a) SOURCES

579 **Ballard**, A., ed., *British Borough Charters, 1042-1216*, 1913.

580 —— and Tait, J., eds., *British Borough Charters, 1216-1307*, 1923.

581 **Bateson**, Mary, ed., *Records of the Borough of Leicester, 1103-1327*, 1899.

582 —— *Borough Customs*, Selden Soc., XVIII and XXI, 2 vols., 1904-6.

583 **Biddle**, M., ed., *Winchester in the Early Middle Ages. An Edition and Discussion of the Winton Domesday*, 1976.

584 **Le Patourel**, J., *Documents Relating to the Manor and Borough of Leeds, 1066-1400*, Thoresby Soc., 1956.

585 **Martin**, G. H., *The Early Court Rolls of the Borough of Ipswich*, University of Leicester,

Department of English Loc.H., Occ. Papers, 5, 1954.

586 **Palmer**, W. M., ed., *Cambridge Borough Documents*, 1931.

(b) SURVEYS AND MONOGRAPHS

587 **Beresford**, M. W., *New Towns of the Middle Ages: Town Plantation in England, Wales and Gascony*, 1967. An important study of a significant aspect of urban history in the medieval period.

588 **Billson**, C. J., *Medieval Leicester*, 1920.

589 **Brooke**, C. N. L., *London, 800-1216. The Shaping of a City*, 1975.

590 **Carus-Wilson**, Eleanora, 'Towns and Trade'. In Poole (311), listed above, I, 209-63.

591 —— 'The first half century of the borough of Stratford upon Avon', *Ec.H.R.*, 2nd ser., XVIII, 1965, 46-63.

592 **Davis**, R. H. C., *The Early History of Coventry*, Dugdale Soc.Occ. Papers, XXIV, 1976.

593 **Finberg**, H. P. R., 'The genesis of the Gloucestershire towns'. In Finberg (1241), listed below, 52-88.

594 **Fox**, L., 'The early history of Coventry', *Hist.*, XXX, 1945, 21-37.

595 **Hibbert**, A., 'The economic policies of towns'. In Postan, Rich and Miller (316), listed above, 157-229.

596 **Hill**, J. W. F., *Medieval Lincoln*, 1948.

597 **Hollaender**, A. E. J. and Kellaway, W., eds., *Studies in London History Presented to Philip Edmund Jones*, 1969. A festschrift which includes essays on London history from medieval to modern times.

598 **Hoskins**, W. G., 'The origin and rise of Market Harborough', *Trans.Leics.Arch.Soc.*, XXV, 1949, 56-68. Reprinted in Hoskins (1246), listed below, 53-67.

599 **Lobel**, Mary D., *The Borough of Bury St. Edmunds: A Study in the Government and Development of a Monastic Town*, 1935.

600 **Martin**, G. H., 'The English borough in the thirteenth century', *T.R.H.S.*, 5th ser., XIII, 1963, 123-44.

601 **Miller**, E., 'Medieval York. The twelfth and thirteenth centuries'. In *V.C.H. Yorks.*, ed. P. M. Tillot. *The City of York*, 1961, 25-116.

602 **Murray**, Katherine M. E., *The Constitutional History of the Cinque Ports*, 1935.

603 **Platt**, C., *The English Medieval Town*, 1975. Particularly valuable on the topography of medieval towns.

604 **Redford**, A., 'The emergence of Manchester', *Hist.*, XXIV, 1939, 32-49.

605 **Reynolds**, Susan, 'The rulers of London in the twelfth century', *Hist.*, LVII, 1972, 337-57.

606 —— *An Introduction to the History of English Medieval Towns*, 1977. Surveys the period from the fifth to the early sixteenth centuries.

607 **Salter**, H. E., *Medieval Oxford*, 1936.

608 **Simmons**, J., *Leicester Past and Present I: The Ancient Borough*, 1974.

609 **Stenton**, F. M., 'Norman London'. In Barraclough, ed. (264), listed above, 179-207. Originally issued as an Hist.Ass. pamphlet.

610 **Stephenson**, C., *Borough and Town: A Study of Urban Origins in England*, Cambridge, Mass., 1933. Contended that the process of urbanisation was only fully developed in England after 1066.

611 **Tait**, J., *The Medieval English Borough*, 1936. Refuted Stephenson's claims (610). Tait demonstrated the importance of towns in the Anglo-Saxon period.

612 —— *Medieval Manchester and the Beginnings of Lancashire*, 1904.

613 **Urry**, W., *Canterbury under the Angevin Kings*, 1967. A significant contribution to urban studies.

614 **Werveke**, H. van, 'The Rise of the Towns'. In Postan, Rich and Miller (316), listed above, 3-41.

615 **Williams**, G. A., *Medieval London from Commune to Capital*, 1963. A well-documented study of the constitutional and social history of London between c.1200 and 1337.

616 **Young**, C. R., *The English Borough and Royal Administration 1130-1307*, Durham, N. C., 1961.

COMMERCE

617 **Baker**, J. N. L., 'Medieval trade-routes'. In Barraclough, ed. (264), listed above, 224-46.

618 **Brutzkus**, J., 'Trade with eastern Europe, 800-1200', *Ec.H.R.*, XIII, 1943, 31-41. For background.

619 **Carus-Wilson**, Eleanora M., 'The English cloth trade in the late twelfth and early thirteenth centuries', *Ec.H.R.*, XIV, 1944, 32-50.

620 **Davies**, J. C., 'Shipping and trade in Newcastle upon Tyne, 1294-1296', *Arch.Aeliana*, 4th ser., XXXI, 1953, 175-204.

621 **Postan**, M. M., 'The trade of medieval Europe: the north'. In Postan and Rich, eds. (316), listed above, 119-256.

622 **Salzman**, L. F., *English Trade in the Middle Ages*, 1931. See also Carus-Wilson and Coleman (928), Kerling (939) and Postan (949), listed below.

GOVERNMENT

623 **Cam**, Helen M., *Liberties and Communities in Medieval England*, 1944, 2nd ed., corrected, 1963.

624 —— *The Hundred and the Hundred Rolls*, 1930.

625 **Chrimes**, S. B., *Introduction to the Administra-*

tive History of Medieval England, 1952, 3rd ed., 1966.

626 **Hoyt**, R. S., 'Royal taxation and the growth of the realm in medieval England', *Speculum*, XXV, 1950, 36-48.

627 **Miller**, E., 'The economic policies of governments: France and England'. In Postan, Rich and Miller (316), listed above, 290-339.

628 —— 'The state and landed interests in thirteenth century France and England', *T.R.H.S.*, 5th ser., II, 1952, 109-29.

629 **Morris**, W. A., *The Medieval Sheriff to A.D. 1300*, 1927.

630 **Richardson**, H. G. and Sayles, G. O., *The Governance of Medieval England from the Conquest to Magna Carta*, 1963.

631 **Sayles**, G. O., *The King's Parliament of England*, 1975.

THE JEWS IN ENGLAND

632 **Adler**, M., *The Jews of Medieval England*, 1939.

633 **Elman**, P., 'Jewish finance in thirteenth-century England', *Trans. Jewish H.Soc.*, XVI, 1945-51, 89-96.

634 —— 'Economic causes of the expulsion of the Jews in 1290', *Ec.H.R.*, VII, 1936-7, 145-54.

635 **Grayzel**, S., *The Church and the Jews in the Thirteenth Century*, Philadelphia, 1933. Useful for the general background.

636 **Lipman**, V. D., *The Jews of Medieval Ipswich*, Jewish H.Soc., 1967.

637 **Richardson**, H. G., *The English Jewry under the Angevin Kings*, 1960.

638 **Roth**, C., *History of the Jews in England*, 1941.

STANDARDS OF LIVING

639 **Calthrop**, D. C., *English Costume from William I to George IV, 1066-1830*, 1937.

640 **Colvin**, H. M., 'Domestic architecture and town planning'. In Poole (311), listed above, I, 37-97.

641 **Cunnington**, Phillis and Lucas, C., *Occupational Dress in England from the Eleventh Century to 1914*, 1967.

642 **Faulkner**, P. A., 'Domestic planning from the twelfth to the fourteenth century', *Arch. J.*, CXV, 1958, 150-83.

643 **Hassall**, W. O., *How They Lived, 55 B.C.-1485*, 1962.

644 **Holmes**, D. T., Jnr., *Daily Living in the Twelfth Century*, Madison, Wis., 1962.

645 **Labarge**, Margaret W., *A Baronial Household of the Thirteenth Century*, London and N. Y., 1965. Based on the accounts of Eleanor, wife of Simon de Montfort.

646 **Nevinson**, J. C., 'Civil costume'. In Poole (311), listed above, I, 300-13.

647 **Wood**, Margaret E., *Thirteenth-century Domestic Architecture in England*, 1950 (supplement to *Arch. J.*, CV).

COMMUNICATIONS AND INTERNAL TRADE

648 **Britnell**, R. H., 'The proliferation of markets in England, 1200-1349', *Ec.H.R.*, 2nd ser., XXXIV, 1981, 209-21.

649 **Coates**, B. E., 'The origin and distribution of markets and fairs in medieval Derbyshire', *Derbyshire Arch. J.*, LXXXV, 1966, 92-111.

650 **Richardson**, H., *The Medieval Fairs and Markets of York*, Borthwick Papers, 20, 1961.

651 **Stenton**, Doris M., 'Communications'. In Poole (311), listed above, I, 196-208.

652 **Stenton**, F. M., 'The road system in medieval England', *Ec.H.R.*, VII, 1936, 1-21. Reprinted in

Doris M. Stenton, ed., (327), listed above, 234-52.

653 **Tupling**, G. H., 'The origin of markets and fairs in medieval Lancashire', *T.L.C.A.S.*, XLIX, 1933, 75-94.

654 **Verlinden**, O., 'Markets and Fairs'. In Postan, Rich and Miller, eds. (316), listed above, 119-53.

THE MONASTERIES

No attempt is made here to list the printed sources for this subject. The reader is referred to Altschul's bibliography (252), listed above, 49-56.

655 **Constable**, G., *Monastic Tithes from their Origins to the Twelfth Century*, 1964.

656 **Day**, L. J. C., 'The early monastic contribution to medieval farming', *Lincs. Historian*, 5, 1950, 200-14.

657 **Dickinson**, J. C., *Monastic Life in Medieval England*, 1961.

658 **Donkin**, R. A., 'Settlement and depopulation on Cistercian estates during the twelfth and thirteenth centuries, especially in Yorkshire', *B.I.H.R.*, XXXIII, 1960, 141-65.

659 —— 'Cistercian sheep farming and wool sales in the thirteenth century', *Ag.H.R.*, VI, 1958, 2-8.

660 —— 'Cattle on the estates of medieval Cistercian monasteries in England and Wales', *Ec.H.R.*, 2nd ser., XV, 1962, 31-53.

661 —— 'The Cistercian order in medieval England: some conclusions', *T.I.B.G.*, 33, 1963, 181-98.

662 —— *The Cistercian Settlement and the English Royal Forests*, 1960.

663 —— 'The Cistercian Order and the settlement of northern England', *Geog. Rev.*, LIX, 1969, 403-16.

664 **Hill**, B. D., *English Cistercian Monasteries and their Patrons in the Twelfth Century*, Urbana, Illinois, 1968.

665 **Knowles**, D., *The Monastic Order in England: A History of its Development, 943-1216*, 1940, 2nd ed., 1963.

666 —— *The Religious Orders in England*, vol. I, 1948. Covers the period 1216-1340.

667 **Madden**, J. E., 'Business monks, banker monks, bankrupt monks: the English Cistercians in the thirteenth century', *Catholic H.R.*, XLIX, 1963, 341-64.

668 **Matthew**, D., *The Norman Monasteries and their English Possessions*, 1962.

669 **Robinson**, D. M., *The Geography of Augustinian Settlement in Medieval England and Wales*, 1980.

670 **Waites**, B., *Moorland and Vale-land Farming in N. E. Yorkshire: The Monastic Contribution in the Thirteenth and Fourteenth Centuries*, Borthwick Papers, 32, 1967.

671 —— 'The monastic grange as a factor in the settlement of N. E. Yorkshire', *Yorks.Arch. J.*, XL, 1959-62, 627-56.

672 —— 'The monastic settlement of N. E. Yorkshire', *Yorks.Arch. J.*, XL, 1959-62, 478-95.

673 **Wood**, S. M., *English Monasteries and their Patrons in the Thirteenth Century*, 1955.

ENGLAND
1300-1500

GENERAL WORKS

(a) BIBLIOGRAPHIES

674 **Guth**, D. L., ed., *Late Medieval England, 1377-1485. Bibliographical Handbooks*, 1976. See also Graves (254), above.

(b) SOURCES

675 **Du Boulay**, F. R., ed., *Documents Illustrative of Medieval Kentish Society*, Kent Archaeological Society, Kent Records, XVIII, 1964.

676 **Flemming**, Jessie H., ed., *England under the Lancastrians*, 1921.

677 **Gairdner**, J., ed., *The Paston Letters*, 6 vols., 1904. There is a one-volume selection of the *Letters*, ed. N. Davis, 1958.

678 **Hughes**, Dorothy, ed., *Illustrations of Chaucer's England*, 1919.

679 **Myers**, A. R., ed., *English Historical Documents IV: 1327-1485*, 1969. An invaluable collection. See especially Part 4 on economic and social developments, Part 2 on the government of the realm, and Part 3 on the Church and education.

680 **Thornley**, Isobel D., ed., *England under the Yorkists*, 1920.

(c) GENERAL SURVEYS

681 **Baker**, D., ed., *Medieval Women*, 1981.

682 **Bean**, J. M. W., *The Decline of English Feudalism, 1215-1540*, 1968.

683 **Beer**, M., *Early British Economics from the Thirteenth to the Middle of the Eighteenth Century*, 1938. Reprinted 1967.

684 **Bennett**, H. S., *The Pastons and their England*, 1922, 2nd ed., 1932. Reprinted 1968.

685 **Bolton**, J. L., *The Medieval English Economy, 1150-1500*, 1980.

686 **Bradac**, J., 'Czech visitors to fifteenth-century England', *H.Today*, 15, 1965, 320-7.

687 **Bridbury**, A. R., *Economic Growth: England in the Later Middle Ages*, 1962. As its title makes clear, this stimulating little book does not share the traditional view of the period. See also Du Boulay (691), listed below.

688 **Cam**, Helen M., 'The decline and fall of English Feudalism', *Hist.*, XXV, 1940, 216-33.

689 **Carus-Wilson**, Eleanora M., *Medieval Merchant Venturers*, 1954.

690 **Denholm-Young**, N., *The Country Gentry in the Fourteenth Century*, 1969.

691 **Du Boulay**, F. R. H., *An Age of Ambition: English Society in the Late Middle Ages*, 1970. Shares Bridbury's rejection of the traditional view of decline and decay in the later Middle Ages. Good bibliography.

692 —— and Barron, Caroline, M., eds., *The Reign of Richard II*, 1972. A *festschrift* for Professor May McKisack which includes essays by V. H. Galbraith on the Peasants' Revolt and J. A. Tuck on aspects of the patronage system.

693 **Fussell**, G. E., 'Social change but static technology: rural England in the fourteenth century', *Hist.Studs.*, I, 1968, 23-32.

94 **Hanawalt**, Barbara A., *Crime and Conflict in English Communities, 1300-48*, 1979. Explores the incidence of crimes such as homicide and robbery within village communities.

95 —— 'Fur collar crime: the pattern of crime among the fourteenth-century nobility', *J.Soc.H.*, VIII, 1975, 1-17.

96 **Hilton**, R. H., ed., *Peasants, Knights and Heretics. Studies in Medieval English Social History*, 1976.

97 —— *The Transition from Feudalism to Capitalism*, 1976.

98 **Hodgett**, G. A. J., *A Social and Economic History of Medieval Europe*, 1972. For background.

99 **Holmes**, G. A., *The Later Middle Ages, 1272-1485*, 1962.

00 **Jacob**, E. F., *The Fifteenth Century, 1399-1485*, 1961. A comprehensive study. Good bibliography.

01 **Jarrett**, B., *Social Theories of the Middle Ages, 1200-1500*, 1926. Reprinted 1968.

02 **Jusserand**, J. J., *English Wayfaring Life in the Middle Ages*, 1889, 2nd ed., 1920. Several times reprinted. Deals for the most part with the fourteenth century.

03 **Kingsford**, C. L., *Prejudice and Promise in Fifteenth Century England*, 1925. Reprinted 1962.

04 **Lander**, J. R., *Conflict and Stability in Fifteenth Century England*, 1970.

05 —— *Crown and Nobility, 1450-1509*, 1976.

06 **MacFarlane**, K. B., 'Bastard feudalism', *B.I.H.R.*, XX, 1945, 161-80.

07 **McKisack**, May, *The Fourteenth Century 1307-1399*, 1959. Good bibliography.

08 **Miskimin**, H. A., *The Economy of Early Renaissance Europe, 1300-1460*, 1975. For background.

709 **Myers**, A. R., *England in the Late Middle Ages, 1307-1536*, 1952. Reprinted with revisions 1956, 1959.

710 **Postan**, M. M., 'The fifteenth century', *Ec.H.R.*, IX, 1938, 160-7.

711 **Power**, Eileen, *Medieval Women*, 1975.

712 **Raftis**, J. A., 'Social structures in five East Midland villages: a study of possibilities in the use of court roll data', *Ec.H.R.*, 2nd ser., XVIII, 1965, 83-99.

713 **Rawcliffe**, C., *The Staffords, Earls of Stafford and Dukes of Buckingham, 1394-1521*, 1978.

714 **Robinson**, W. C., 'Money, population and economic change in late medieval Europe', *Ec.H.R.*, 2nd ser., XII, 1959, 63-76. For background.

715 **Rosenthal**, J. H., *The Purchase of Paradise*, 1972. An examination of medieval charity highlighting the importance of the self-interest motive.

716 —— *Nobles and Noble Life, 1295-1500*, 1976.

717 **Schofield**, R. S., 'The geographical distribution of wealth in England, 1334-1649', *Ec.H.R.*, 2nd ser., XVIII, 1965, 483-510. Suggests that it was mainly concentrated, as in the twentieth century, in the south-east and Midlands.

718 **Tuck**, J. A., *Richard II and the English Nobility*, 1974.

719 **Ullman**, W., *The Individual and Society in the Middle Ages*, Baltimore, 1966. For background.

720 **Watts**, D. G., 'A model for the early fourteenth century', *Ec.H.R.*, 2nd ser., XX, 1967, 543-7.

721 **Wilkinson**, B., *The Later Middle Ages in England 1216-1485*, 1969. Mainly political in emphasis though social and economic aspects are covered. See also Clapham (218), Cunningham (219), Lipson (232), and Pollard and Crossley (236), all listed above.

POPULATION

(a) SOURCES

2 **Ekwall**, E., ed., *Two Early London Subsidy Rolls*, Lund, 1951.

3 **Erskine**, A. M., ed., *The Devonshire Lay Subsidy of 1332*, Devon and Cornwall Rec.Soc., n.s., XIV, 1969.

4 **Glasscock**, R. E., ed., *The Lay Subsidy of 1334*, 1975.

(b) SECONDARY WORKS

725 **Bean**, J. M. W., 'Plague, population and economic decline in England in the later Middle Ages', *Ec.H.R.*, 2nd ser., XV, 1963, 423-37.

726 **Beresford**, M. W., *Lay Subsidies and Poll Taxes*, 1964.

727 —— 'Dispersed and group settlement in medieval Cornwall', *Ag.H.R.*, XII, 1964, 13-27.

728 **Boucher**, C. E., 'The Black Death in Bristol', *Trans.Bristol and Gloucs.Arch.Soc.*, LX, 1938, 31-46.

729 **Bridbury**, A. R., 'The Black Death', *Ec.H.R.*, 2nd ser., XXVI, 1973, 557-92.

730 —— 'Before the Black Death', *Ec.H.R.*, 2nd ser., XXX, 1977, 393-410.

731 **Creighton**, C., *A History of Epidemics in Britain*, 2 vols., 1891 and 1894, 2nd ed., 1965, with additional material by D. E. C. Eversley, E. A. Underwood and L. Ovenall.

732 **Ekwall**, E., *Studies on the Population of Medieval London*, Stockholm, 1956. Concentrates on the period 1250-1350 and is mainly a detailed study of immigration into the capital.

733 **Fraser**, C. M., 'Population density in medieval fenland', *Ec.H.R.*, 2nd ser., XIV, 1961, 71-81.

734 **Gottfried**, R. S., *Epidemic Disease in Fifteenth-Century England. The Medical Response and the Demographic Consequences*, 1978.

735 **Hanawalt**, Barbara A., 'Childbearing among the lower classes of late medieval England', *J.Interdis.H.*, VIII, 1977, 1-22.

736 **Harvey**, Barbara, 'The population trend in England, 1300-48', *T.R.H.S.*, 5th ser., XVI, 1966, 23-42. Contends that there was no dramatic change during this period.

737 **Hatcher**, J., *Plague, Population and the English Economy, 1348-1530*, 1977.

738 **Helleiner**, K. F., 'Population movements and agrarian depression in the later Middle Ages', *Canadian J.Ec.&Pol. Science*, XV, 1949, 368-77.

739 **Langford**, A. W., 'The Plague in Herefordshire', *Trans. Woolhope Nat.Hist. Field Club*, XXXV, 1956, 146-53.

740 **Levett**, Ada E., 'The Black Death on the St Albans manors'. In Levett (467), listed above, 248-86.

741 —— *The Black Death on the Estates of the See of Winchester*, 1916.

742 **Lucas**, H. S., 'The great European famine, 1315, 1316 and 1317', *Speculum*, V, 1930, 343-77.

743 **McClure**, P., 'Patterns of migration in the late Middle Ages: the evidence of English place name surnames', *Ec.H.R.*, 2nd ser., XXXII, 1979, 167-82.

744 **Mullett**, C. F., *The Bubonic Plague and England: An Essay in the History of Preventi[ve] Medicine*, Lexington, Ky., 1956.

745 **Nohl**, J., *The Black Death: A Chronicle of t[he] Plague Compiled from Contemporary Source[s]*, 1961.

746 **Pelham**, R. A., 'The urban population of Suss[ex] in 1340', *Sussex Arch.Collns.*, LXXVIII, 193[7], 211-23.

747 **Postan**, M. M., 'Some economic evidence [of] declining population in the later Middle Age[s]', *Ec.H.R.*, 2nd ser., II, 1949-50, 221-46.

748 **Raftis**, J. A., 'Changes in an English village af[ter] the Black Death', *Medieval Studs*, XXIX, 196[7], 158-77. Looks at Upwood, Hampshire.

749 **Razi**, Z., *Life, Marriage and Death in [a] Medieval Parish. Economy, Society and Demo[g]raphy in Halesowen, 1270-1400*, 1980.

750 **Robo**, E., 'The Black Death in the Hundred [of] Farnham', *E.H.R.*, XLIV, 1929, 560-72.

751 **Rubin**, S., *Medieval English Medicine*, 197[4].

752 **Russell**, J. C., 'Late medieval population pa[t]terns', *Speculum*, XX, 1945, 157-71.

753 —— 'Effects of pestilence and plague, 1315-8[...]' *Comp.Studs.Soc.&H.*, VIII, 1966, 464-73.

754 **Saltmarsh**, J., 'Plague and economic decline [in] England in the later Middle Ages', *Cambrid[ge] H. J.*, VII, 1941, 23-41.

755 **Scammell**, Jean, 'Freedom and marriage [in] medieval England', *Ec.H.R.*, 2nd ser., XXV[I], 1974, 523-37.

756 **Shrewsbury**, J. F. D., *A History of Bubon[ic] Plague in the British Isles*, 1970.

757 **Talbot**, C. H., *Medicine in Medieval Englan[d]*, 1967.

758 **Thrupp**, Sylvia, 'The problem of replaceme[nt] rates in late medieval English populatio[n]', *Ec.H.R.*, 2nd ser., XVIII, 1965, 101-19. Bas[ed] mainly on court roll data.

759 —— 'Plague effects in medieval Europ[e]', *Comp.Studs.Soc.H.*, VIII, 1966, 474-83.

760 **Ziegler**, P., *The Black Death*, 1969. See al[so] Hoskins (1246), Hollingsworth (1290) and Wrig[ley] (1302), listed below, and Russell (386), list[ed] above.

AGRICULTURE AND RURAL SOCIETY

(a) GENERAL

61 **Ault**, W. O., *The Self-directing Activities of Village Communities in Medieval England*, Boston, Mass., 1952.

62 —— *Open Field Farming in Medieval England*, 1972.

63 —— 'By-laws of gleaning and the problem of harvest', *Ec.H.R.*, 2nd ser., XIV, 1961, 210-17. Deals with the situation in England in the fourteenth century.

64 **Baker**, A. R. H., 'Evidence in the Nonarum Inquisitiones of contracting arable land in the early fourteenth century', *Ec.H.R.*, 2nd ser., XIX, 1966, 518-32.

65 —— 'Some evidence of a reduction in the acreage of cultivated lands in Sussex during the early fourteenth century', *Sussex Arch.Collns.*, CIV, 1966, 1-5.

66 **Beresford**, M. W., 'The Poll Tax and the census of sheep', *Ag.H.R.*, I, 1953, 9-15; *ibid.*, II, 1954, 15-29.

67 **Britnell**, R. H., 'Production for the market on a small fourteenth-century estate', *Ec.H.R.*, 2nd ser., XIX, 1966, 380-7. Deals with Langenhoe, Essex.

68 **Britton**, E., *The Community of the Vill. A Study in the History of the Family and Village Life in Fourteenth-Century England*, 1977.

69 **Dyer**, C., 'A redistribution of incomes in fifteenth-century England', *P.P.*, 39, 1968, 11-33. Explores the relationship between a lord and his tenants as an agency of social and agrarian change in the fifteenth century.

70 **Fussell**, G. E., 'The classical tradition in west European farming: the fourteenth and fifteenth centuries', *Ag.H.R.*, XVII, 1969, 1-8.

71 **Gray**, H. L., 'Incomes from land in England in 1436', *E.H.R.*, XLIX, 1934, 607-39.

72 **Hilton**, R. H., 'The content and sources of English agrarian history before 1500', *Ag.H.R.*, III, 1955, 3-19. See also Thirsk (1416), listed below, a companion article for the later period.

73 —— *The English Peasantry in the Later Middle Ages*, 1975. Provocatively original treatment of the peasantry as a social class.

74 **Hodgett**, G. A. J., *Agrarian England in the Later Middle Ages* (Hist.Ass., Aids for Teachers series, 13), 1966. A useful summary with a bibliographical note.

775 **Hoskins**, W. G., 'Regional farming in England', *Ag.H.R.*, II, 1954, 3-11.

776 **Howell**, Cecily, 'Stability and change, 1300-1700: the socio-economic context of the self-perpetuating family farm in England', *J.Peasant Studs.*, II, 1975, 468-82.

777 **Kosminsky**, E. A., *Studies in the Agrarian History of England in the Thirteenth Century*, 1956.

778 **Maddicott**, J. R., 'The county community and the making of public opinion in fourteenth-century England', *T.R.H.S.*, 5th ser., XXVIII, 1978, 27-43.

779 —— *The English Peasantry and the Demands of the Crown, 1294-1341*, 1975.

780 **Taylor**, E. G. R., 'The Surveyor', *Ec.H.R.*, XVII, 1947, 121-33.

781 **Trow-Smith**, R., *A History of British Livestock Husbandry to 1700*, 1957. See also Bennett (402), Beveridge (404), and Ernle (410), listed above.

(b) REGIONAL STUDIES

782 **Cracknell**, B. E., *Canvey Island: The History of a Marshland Community*, University of Leicester, Department of English Loc.H., Occ. Papers, 12, 1959.

783 **Dyer**, C., *Warwickshire Farming, 1349-1520. Preparations for Agricultural Revolution*, Dugdale Soc.Occ.Papers, XXVII, 1981.

784 **Fisher**, P. and W. B., 'The medieval land surveys of County Durham', *Research Paper No. 2*, University of Durham, 1959.

785 **Glasscock**, R. E., 'The distribution of wealth in East Anglia in the early fourteenth century', *T.I.B.G.*, XXXII, 1963, 113-23.

786 **Halcrow**, Elizabeth M., 'The decline of demesne farming on the estates of Durham cathedral priory', *Ec.H.R.*, 2nd ser., VII, 1955, 345-56.

787 **Hallam**, H. E., 'The agrarian economy of medieval Lincolnshire before the Black Death', *Hist.Studs. Australia & New Zealand*, XI, 1964, 163-69.

788 —— 'The agrarian economy of south Lincolnshire in the mid-fifteenth century', *Nottingham Med.Studs.*, XI, 1967, 86-95.

789 **Hatcher**, J., *Rural Economy and Society in the Duchy of Cornwall, 1300-1500*, 1970.

790 **Hewitt**, H. J., *Medieval Cheshire. An Economic and Social History of Cheshire in the Reigns of the Three Edwards*, Chet.Soc., n.s., 88, 1929.

791 **Hogan**, M. Patricia, 'Medieval villainy. A study in the meaning and control of crime in an English village', *Studs.Med.& Renaiss.H.*, n.s., II, 1979, 121-215.

792 **Lythe**, S. G. E., 'The organisation of drainage and embankment in medieval Holderness', *Yorks.Arch. J.*, XXXIV, 1939, 282-95.

793 **Newton**, K. C., *Thaxted in the Fourteenth Century*, 1960.

794 **Ruston**, A. G., and Witney, D., *Hooton Pagnell: The Agricultural Evolution of a Yorkshire Village*, 1934.

795 **Saul**, N., *Knights and Esquires. The Gloucestershire Gentry in the Fourteenth Century*, 1981.

796 **Smith**, A., 'Regional differences in crop production in medieval Kent', *Arch.Cant.*, LXXVIII, 1964, 147-60.

797 **Smith**, R. B., *Blackburnshire: A Study in Early Lancashire History*, University of Leicester, Department of English Loc.H., Occ. Papers, 15, 1961. The first part of the essay is a general survey of landholding and of the economy of the area in the early fourteenth century.

798 **Spufford**, Margaret, *A Cambridgeshire Community: Chippenham from Settlement to Enclosure*, University of Leicester, Department of English Loc.H., Occ. Papers, 20, 1965.
See also Gras (439), Harvey (441), Hoskins (445) and Postan (312), listed above, and Hoskins (1245), listed below.

(c) **THE MANOR**

799 **Dale**, M. K., ed., *Court Roll of Chalgrave Manor, 1278-1313*, Beds.Hist.Rec.Soc., XXVIII, 1948.

800 **Salzman**, L. F. ed., *Ministers' Accounts of the Manor of Petworth, 1347-53*, Sussex Rec.Soc., LV, 1955.
See also Le Patourel (584), and Bland, Brown and Tawney (211), listed above.

801 **Ault**, W. O., 'Manor court and parish church in fifteenth-century England: a study of English by-laws', *Speculum*, XLII, 1967, 53-67. See the other titles by Ault (761-3), listed above.

802 **Bridbury**, A. R., 'The farming out of manors', *Ec.H.R.*, 2nd ser., XXI, 1978, 503-20.

803 **Hatcher**, J., 'Non-manorialism in medieval Cornwall', *Ag.H.R.*, XVIII, 1970, 1-16.

804 **Lloyd**, E., 'The farm accounts of the manor of Hendon 1316-1416', *Trans. London and Middx.Arch.Soc.*, XXI, 1967, 157-63.

805 **Post**, J. B., 'Some manorial amercements an peasant poverty', *Ec.H.R.*, 2nd ser., XXVII 1975, 304-11.
For other material on this subject, see also Davenpo (462) and Hodgett (724), listed above.

(d) **ESTATE MANAGEMENT**

806 **Denney**, A. H., ed., *The Sibton Abbey Estate Select Documents, 1325-1509*, Suffolk Rec.Soc II, 1960.

807 **Hilton**, R. H., ed., *Ministers' Accounts of th Warwickshire Estates of the Duke of Clarenc 1479-80*, Dugdale Soc., XXI for 1944, 1952.

808 **Bean**, J. M. W., *The Estates of the Percy Fam ily, 1416-1537*, 1958.

809 **Britnell**, R. H., 'Minor landlords in England an medieval agrarian capitalism', *P.P.*, 89, 198(3-22.

810 **Denholm-Young**, N., *Seigneurial Adminis tration in England*, 1937.

811 **Du Boulay**, F. R. H., *The Lordship of Canter bury: An Essay on Medieval Society*, 1966. valuable study of the economic, social, legal an military organisation of the lordship.

812 —— 'Who were farming the English demesnes the end of the Middle Ages?', *Ec.H.R.*, 2nd ser XVII, 1965, 443-55.

813 —— 'A rentier economy in the later Middle Age the archbishopric of Canterbury', *Ec.H.R.*, 2n ser., XVI, 1964, 427-38.

814 **Harvey**, Barbara, 'The leasing of the Abbot Westminster's demesnes in the later Middle Ages *Ec.H.R.*, 2nd ser., XXII, 1969, 17-27.

815 **Hilton**, R. H., *The Economic Development o Some Leicestershire Estates in the Fourteent and Fifteenth Centuries*, 1947.

816 **Holmes**, G. A., *The Estates of the Highe Nobility in Fourteenth-Century England*, 1957

817 **Jack**, I. R., 'Entail and descent: the Hasting inheritance, 1370-1436', *B.I.H.R.*, XXXVIII 1965, 1-19.

818 **Keil**, I., 'Farming on the Dorset estates Glastonbury Abbey in the early fourteenth cen tury', *Proc.Dorset Nat.H. & Arch.Soc.*, LXXX VII, 1966, 234-50.

819 **Kershaw**, I., *Bolton Priory: The Economy of Northern Monastery 1286-1325*, 1973.

820 **Page**, F. M., *The Estates of Crowland Abbey 1934.

821 **Plucknett**, T. F. T., *The Medieval Bailif (Creighton Lecture in History, 1952), 1954.

822 **Raftis**, J. A., *The Estates of Ramsey Abbey: A Study in Economic Growth and Organisation*, Toronto, 1957.

823 **Roberts**, A. K. B., *St George's Chapel, Windsor Castle, 1348-1416. A Study in Early Collegiate Administration*, 1947. Includes a discussion of estate management.

824 **Rosenthal**, J. T., 'The estates and finances of Richard, Duke of York, 1411-60'. In W. M. Bowsky, ed., *Studs.Med.& Renaiss.H.*, II, 1965, 115-204.

825 **Ross**, C., *The Estates and Finances of Richard Beauchamp, Earl of Warwick*, Dugdale Soc.Occ. Papers, XII, 1956.

826 **Searle**, Eleanor, *Lordship and Community. Battle Abbey and its Banlieue 1066-1538*, Toronto, 1974.

827 **Smith**, R. A. L., *Canterbury Cathedral Priory: A Study in Monastic Administration*, 1943.

828 **Wolffe**, B. P., 'The management of English royal estates under the Yorkist kings', *E.H.R.*, LXXI, 1956, 1-27. See also the book by the same author listed below (1463).

829 —— 'Acts of Resumption in the Lancastrian parliaments, 1399-1456', *E.H.R.*, LXXIII, 1958, 583-613.

(e) LAND TENURE

830 **Dodwell**, Barbara, 'Holdings and inheritance in medieval East Anglia', *Ec.H.R.*, 2nd ser., XX, 1967, 53-66.

831 **Faith**, R. J., 'Peasant families and inheritance customs in medieval England', *Ag.H.R.*, XIV, 1966, 77-95.

832 **Pitkin**, D. S., 'Partible inheritance and the open fields', *Ag.H.*, XXXV, 1961, 65-9.

833 **Raftis**, J. A., *Tenure and Mobility: Studies in the Social History of the Medieval English Village*, Toronto, 1964.

834 **Razi**, Z., 'Family, land and the village community in later medieval England', *P.P.*, 93, 1981, 3-36.

(f) FIELD SYSTEMS

835 **Ault**, W. O., 'Open field husbandry and the village community: a study of agrarian by-laws in medieval England', *Trans.American Phil.Soc.*, n.s., LV, 1965.

836 **Baker**, A. R. H., 'Open fields and partible inheritance on a Kent manor', *Ec.H.R.*, 2nd ser., XVII, 1964, 1-23. Looks at the manor of Gillingham in 1285 and 1447.

837 —— 'Observations on the Open Fields. The present position of studies in British field systems', *J.H.Geog.*, V, 1979, 315-26.

838 **Beresford**, M. W., 'Glebe terriers and open fields', *Yorks.Arch. J.*, XXXVII, 1951, 325-68.

839 —— 'Ridge and furrow and the open fields', *Ec.H.R.*, 2nd ser., I, 1948, 34-45.

840 —— 'Lot acres', *Ec.H.R.*, XIII, 1943, 74-9. Discusses the practice of dividing up the arable from the waste by lot.

841 **Butler**, R. M., 'The common lands of the borough of Nottingham', *Trans. Thoroton Soc.*, LIV, 1950, 45-62.

842 **Chapman**, V., 'Open fields in West Cheshire', *T.H.S.L.C.*, 104, 1952, 35-60.

843 **Cromarty**, D., *The Fields of Saffron Walden in 1400*, 1966.

844 **Dahlman**, C. J., *The Open Field System and Beyond*, 1980. Applies the techniques of the 'New Economic History' to the problems surrounding the origins and survival of the open field system.

845 **Finberg**, H. P. R., 'The open field in Devon'. In Hoskins and Finberg (1248), listed below, 265-88.

846 **Harris**, A., *The Open Fields of East Yorkshire*, East Yorks.Loc.Hist.Soc., pamphlet series, 9, 1959.

847 **Hilton**, R. H., 'A study in the pre-history of English enclosure in the fifteenth century'. In *Studi in Onore di Armando Sapori*, Milan, 1957, I, 675-85.

848 **Hoskins**, W. G., and Stamp, L. D., *The Common Lands of England and Wales*, 1963.

849 **Lennard**, R. V., 'The alleged exhaustion of the soil in medieval England', *Ec. J.*, XXXII, 1922, 12-27. Refuted the views put forward by Harriet Bradley in *The Enclosures in England: An Economic Reconstruction*, 1918.

850 **Orwin**, C. S., and Christabel S., *The Open Fields*, 1954, 3rd ed., 1967, with an introduction by Joan Thirsk.

851 **Postgate**, M. R., 'The field systems of Breckland', *Ag.H.R.*, X, 1962, 80-101. Points to the variations occurring in traditional field patterns as a response to local soil conditions.

852 **Roden**, D., 'Field systems in Ibstone: a township of the S. W. Chilterns during the later Middle Ages', *Recs. of Bucks.*, XVIII, 1966, 43-57.

853 —— and Baker, A. R. H., 'Field systems of the Chiltern hills and parts of Kent from the late thirteenth to the early seventeenth century', *T.I.B.G.*, XXXVIII, 1966, 73-88.

854 **Saltmarsh**, J. and Darby, H. C., 'The infield-outfield system on a Norfolk manor' (West Wretham),

Ec. J.Ec.H.Supp., III, 1935, 30-44.

855 **Sylvester**, Dorothy, 'The open fields of Cheshire', *T.H.S.L.C.*, 108, 1956, 1-34.

856 **Youd**, G., 'The common fields of Lancashire', *T.H.S.L.C.*, 113, 1962, 1-42.

(g) DESERTED VILLAGES

857 **Allison**, K. J., Beresford, M. W. and Hurst, J. G., *The Deserted Villages of Northamptonshire*, University of Leicester Department of English Loc.H., Occ. Papers, 18, 1966.

858 —— *The Deserted Villages of Oxfordshire*, University of Leicester, Department of English Loc.H., Occ. Papers, 17, 1965.

859 —— 'The lost villages of Norfolk', *Norfolk Arch.*, XXXI, 1955, 116-62.

860 **Beresford**, M. W., *The Lost Villages of England*, 1954. The main work on the subject. Beresford stresses the medieval stages in the history of deserted villages and rejects an oversimplified monocausal explanation based on sixteenth-century enclosures. Reprinted 1965.

861 —— and Hurst, J. G., eds., *Deserted Medieval Villages*, 1971. Brings together essays on the most recent historical and archaeological work on the subject. Gazetteers of deserted sites are appended.

862 **Dyer**, C., 'Population and agriculture on a Warwickshire manor in the later Middle Ages', *Birm.H. J.*, XI, 1968, 113-27. A local study of a village which was only gradually deserted.

863 —— 'Deserted medieval villages in the West Midlands', *Ec.H.R.*, 2nd ser., XXXV, 1982, 19-34.

864 **Gould**, J. D., 'Mr Beresford and the lost villages', *Ag.H.R.*, III, 1955, 107-13.

865 **Hoskins**, W. G., 'The deserted villages of Leicestershire', in Hoskins (1246), listed below, 67-107.

(h) THE FORESTS

866 **Birrell**, J. R., 'The forest economy of the honour of Tutbury in the fourteenth and fifteenth centuries', *Birm.H. J.*, VIII, 1962, 114-34.

867 **Cantor**, L. M., 'The medieval forests and chases of Staffordshire', *North Staffs. J. Field Studies*, VIII, 1968, 39-53.

868 **Husain**, B. M. C., 'Delamere forest in later medieval times', *T.H.S.L.C.*, 107, 1955, 23-39.

869 **Shaw**, R. C., *The Royal Forest of Lancaster*, 1957.

870 **Taylor**, C. C., 'The pattern of medieval settlement in the Forest of Blackmoor', *Proc.Dorset Nat.H. & Arch.Soc.*, LXXXVII, 1966, 251-4.

871 —— 'Whiteparish: a study of the development of a forest-edge parish', *Wilts.Arch.&Nat.H.Mag.*, LXII, 1967, 79-102.

See also Roberts (385), listed above, and Tupling (1252), listed below.

INDUSTRY

(a) GENERAL

872 **Carus-Wilson**, Eleanora M., 'Evidence of industrial growth on some fifteenth-century manors', *Ec.H.R.*, 2nd ser., XII, 1959, 190-205.

873 **Salzman**, L. F., *English Industries of the Middle Ages*, 1913, 2nd ed., 1923. Covers – *inter al.* – mining, building and cloth-making. Illustrated. See also Chaloner and Musson (217) and White (509), listed above.

(b) INDUSTRIAL ORGANISATION

The literature on individual companies is too enormous to list here. The reader is referred to Kahl's bibliography (1539), and to his introduction to Unwin's *Gilds and Companies of London* (1555), both of which are listed below.

874 **Gross**, C., *The Gild Merchant*, 2 vols., 1890. Reprinted, 1965. Still an important work on the subject.

875 **Hibbert**, F. A., *The Influence and Development of English Gilds, as Illustrated by the History of the Craft Gilds of Shrewsbury*, 1891.

876 **Imray**, Jean M., 'Les Bones Gentes de la Mercerye de Londres: a study of the membership of the medieval Mercers' Company'. In Hollaender and Kellaway (597), listed above, 155-78.

877 **Thrupp**, Sylvia, 'The gilds'. In Postan, Rich and Miller (316), listed above, 230-80.

878 —— 'Medieval gilds reconsidered', *J.Ec.H.*, II, 1942, 164-73.

For source material on this subject, see the useful section on 'Towns and gilds' in Bland, Brown and Tawney (211), listed above, 114-50.

(c) TEXTILES

879 **Gray**, H. L., 'The production and exportation of English woollens in the fourteenth century', *E.H.R.*, XXXIX, 1924, 13-35.

880 **McClenaghan**, B., *The Springs of Lavenham and the Suffolk Cloth Trade in the Fifteenth and Sixteenth Centuries*, 1924.

881 **Power**, Eileen, *The Paycockes of Coggeshall*, 1920. A short study of a family of clothiers.

See also Carus-Wilson (511), listed above. Studies of the wool trade are listed below under *Commerce*, (pp. 30-31).

(d) MINING AND METALLURGY

882 **Giuseppi**, M. S., 'Some fourteenth-century accounts of iron works at Tudely, Kent', *Archaeologia*, LXIV, 1912-13, 145-64.

883 **Lapsley**, G. T., 'The account roll of a fifteenth-century ironmaster', *E.H.R.*, XIV, 1899, 509-28.

884 **Hatcher**, J., *English Tin Production and Trade Before 1550*, 1973.

885 —— and Barker, T. C., *A History of British Pewter*, 1974.

886 **Mott**, R. A., 'English bloomeries, 1329-1589', *J. Iron and Steel Institute*, CXCVIII, 1961, 149-61.

887 **Nef**, J. U., 'Mining and metallurgy in medieval civilisation'. In Postan and Rich (315), listed above, 430-92.

888 **Simpson**, J. B., 'Coal mining by the monks', *Trans. Institute of Mining Engineers*, XXXIX, 1910, 572-98.

889 **Sprandel**, R., 'La Production du fer au moyen-âge', *Annales*, 24ᵉ année, 1969, 305-21.

See also Fell (1601), Gough (1605), Lewis (1616), Nef (1589), listed below, and Schubert (513) and Waites (514), listed above.

(e) SALT

890 **Berry**, E. K., 'The borough of Droitwich and its salt industry, 1215-1700', *Birm.H. J.*, VI, 1957, 39-61.

891 **Hallam**, H. E., 'Salt making in the Lincolnshire fenlands during the Middle Ages', *Lincs. Architectural & Arch.Soc.*, n.s., VIII, 1959-60, 85-112.

892 **Rudkin**, E. H. and Owen, Dorothy M., 'The medieval salt industry in the Lindsey marshland', n.s., VIII, 1959-60, 76-84.

See also Bridbury's book on the salt trade (922), listed below.

(f) MISCELLANEOUS

893 **Harvey**, J., *The Master Builders of the Middle Ages*, 1972.

894 **Salzman**, L. F., *Building in England down to 1540: A Documentary History*, 1952, 3rd ed., 1967.

895 **Saul**, A., 'The herring industry at Great Yarmouth, c.1280-1400', *Norfolk Arch.*, XXXVIII, 1981, 33-43.

896 **Turton**, R. B., *The Alum Farm*, 1938. The alum trade in N. E. Yorkshire.

897 **Veale**, Elspeth M., 'Craftsmen and the economy of London in the fourteenth century'. In Hollaender and Kellaway (597), listed above, 133-51.

898 **Wright**, Jane A., *Brick Building in England from the Middle Ages to 1550*, 1972.

See also Colvin (516), Johnson (517), and Knoop and Jones (559), listed above.

(g) SOURCES OF POWER FOR INDUSTRY

899 **Adams**, J. W. R., *Windmills in Kent*, 1955.

900 **Atkinson**, F., 'The horse as a source of rotary power', *Trans. Newcomen Soc.*, XXXIII, 1962, 31-55.

901 **Dewar**, H. S. L., 'The windmills, watermills and horse mills of Dorset', *Proc.Dorset Nat.H. & Arch.Soc.*, LXXXII, for 1960, 109-32.

902 —— 'The windmills, watermills and horsemills of Dorset – new evidence', *Proc.Dorset Nat.Hist. & Arch.Soc.*, LXXXVI, 1965, 179-81.

903 **Freese**, S., *Windmills and Millwrighting*, 1957. Reprinted 1971.

904 **Pelham**, R. A., *Fulling Mills: A Study of the Application of Water Power to the Woollen Industry*, 1958 (Society for the Protection of Ancient Buildings: Wind and Watermill section, publications, 5).

905 **Pratt**, D., 'The medieval watermills of Denbighshire", *Denbighshire H.Soc.Trans.*, XIII, 1964, 22-37.

906 **Reid**, K. C., 'The watermills of London', *Trans. London and Middx.Arch.Soc.*, n.s., XI, 1954, 227-36.

907 **Wailes**, R., *Windmills in England: A Study of Their Origin, Development and Future*, 1948.

908 —— *The English Windmill*, 1954.

909 ——*Tidemills*, Parts 1 and 2, 1956 (Society for the Protection of Ancient Buildings. Wind and

Watermill section, publications 2-3).

910 **Wilson**, P. N., *Watermills: An Introduction*, 1956 (Society for the Protection of Ancient Build-ings. Wind and Watermill section, publications, 1). See also Chaloner and Musson (217), listed above.

COMMERCE

(a) SOURCES

911 **Cobb**, H. S., ed., *The Local Port Book of Southampton, 1439-40*, Southampton Records Series, V, 1961. See also Foster (913), listed below.

912 **Coleman**, Olive, ed., *The Brokage Book of Southampton, 1443-44*, Southampton Records Series, IV, 1960.

913 **Foster**, B., ed., *The Local Port Book of South-ampton for 1435-6*, Southampton Records Series, VII, 1963. See also Cobb (911), above.

914 **Lister**, J., ed., *The Early Yorkshire Woollen Trade: Extracts from the Hull Customs Rolls and Complete Transcripts of the Ulnagers' Rolls*, Yorks.Arch.Soc.Rec.Ser., LXIV, 1924. Deals with the fourteenth and fifteenth centuries.

915 **Quinn**, D. B., ed., *The Port Books or Local Customs Accounts of Southampton for the Reign of Edward IV, vol. 1: 1469-71. Southampton Rec.Soc.*, XXXVII, 1938.

916 **Sellers**, Maud, ed., *The York Mercers and Mer-chant Adventurers, 1356-1917*, Surtees Soc., CXXIX, 1918.

917 **Warner**, G. F., ed., *The Libelle of Englyshe Policye (1436)*, 1926. A contemporary tract which emphasised the opportunities which English mer-chants were missing in South-west Europe. See the article by Holmes (937), listed below.

918 **Wilson**, K. P., ed., *Chester Customs Accounts, 1301-1565*, Rec.Soc.Lancs. & Ches., CXI, 1969. See the article by Wilson (965), listed below.

(b) GENERAL AND MISCELLANEOUS

919 **Baker**, R. L., 'The establishment of the English wool staple in 1313', *Speculum*, XXXI, 1956, 444-53.

920 **Blake**, J. B., 'The medieval coal trade of N. E. England: some fourteenth-century evidence', *Northern H.*, II, 1967, 1-26.

921 —— 'Medieval smuggling in the N. E. Some fourteenth-century evidence', *Arch.Aeliana*, 4th ser., XLIII, 1965, 243-60. On medieval smuggling, see also Williams (964), listed below.

922 **Bridbury**, A. R., *England and the Salt Trade in the Later Middle Ages*, 1965.

923 **Carus-Wilson**, Eleanora M., 'The ulnage accounts: a criticism', *Ec.H.R.*, II, 1929, 114-23.

924 —— 'Trends in the export of English woollens in the fourteenth century', *Ec.H.R.*, 2nd ser., III, 1950, 162-79.

925 —— 'The effects of the acquisition and of the loss of Gascony on the English wine trade', *B.I.H.R.*, XXI, 1947, 145-54.

926 —— 'The medieval trade of the ports of the Wash', *Med.Arch.*, VI-VII, 1962-3, 182-201.

927 —— *The Overseas Trade of Bristol in the Later Middle Ages*, 1937, 2nd ed., 1967. The later edi-tion contains a supplement to the bibliography.

928 —— and Coleman, Olive, *England's Export Trade, 1275-1547*, 1963.

929 **Childs**, Wendy R., *Anglo-Castilian Trade in the Later Middle Ages*, 1978.

930 **Dulley**, A. J. F., 'The level and port of Pevensey in the Middle Ages', *Sussex Arch.Collns.*, CIV, 1966, 26-45.

931 **Flenley**, R., 'London and foreign merchants in the reign of Henry VI', *E.H.R.*, XXV, 1910, 644-55.

932 **Fraser**, C. M., 'The N. E. coal trade until 1421', *Trans.Durham and Northumberland Architec-tural and Arch.Soc.*, XI, 1962, 209-20.

933 **Fryde**, E. B., *The Wool Accounts of William de la Pole: A Study of Some Aspects of the English Wool Trade at the Start of the Hundred Years War*, St. Anthony's Hall publications, 25, 1964.

934 —— *Some Business Transactions of York Mer-chants 1336-49*, Borthwick Papers, 29, 1966.

935 —— 'Edward III's wool monopoly of 1337: a fourteenth-century trading venture', *Hist.*, XXX-VII, 1952, 8-24.

936 **Girling**, F. A., *English Merchants' Marks: A Field Survey of Marks Used by Merchants and Tradesmen in England Between 1400 and 1700*, 1964.

937 **Holmes**, G. A., 'The Libel of English Policy', *E.H.R.*, LXXVI, 1961, 193-216. See Warner, ed. (917), listed above.

938 **James**, Margaret K., *Studies in the Medieval*

Wine Trade, ed. Elspeth Veale, 1971.

939 **Kerling**, Nellie J. M., *Commercial Relations of Holland and Zeeland with England from the Late Thirteenth Century to the Close of the Middle Ages*, Leiden, 1954.

940 **Kingsford**, C. L., 'The beginnings of English maritime enterprise in the fifteenth century', *Hist.*, XIII, 1928-9, 97-106, 193-203.

941 **Lloyd**, T. H., *The English Wool Trade in the Middle Ages*, 1977. The first full-length treatment of the subject. Looks at the production, internal marketing of and overseas trade in wool. See also Power (954), below.

942 **McCusker**, J. J., Jnr., 'The wine prise and medieval mercantile shipping', *Speculum*, XLI, 1966, 279-96.

943 **Mace**, F. A., 'Devonshire ports in the fourteenth and fifteenth centuries', *T.R.H.S.*, 4th ser., VIII, 1925, 98-126.

944 **Mallett**, M. E., 'Anglo-Florentine commercial relations, 1465-1491', *Ec.H.R.*, 2nd ser., XV, 1962, 250-65.

945 **Martin**, G. H., 'Shipments of wool from Ipswich to Calais, 1399-1402', *J.Trans.H.*, II, 1956, 177-81.

946 **Mollat**, M., 'Anglo-Norman trade in the fifteenth century', *Ec.H.R.*, XVII, 1947, 143-50.

947 **Munro**, J. H. A., *Wool, Cloth and Gold: The Struggle for Bullion in Anglo-Burgundian Trade, 1340-1478*, Brussels and Toronto, 1973.

948 **Palais**, H., 'England's first attempt to break the commercial monopoly of the Hanseatic League, 1377-80', *A.H.R.*, LXIV, 1959, 852-65

949 **Postan**, M. M., *Medieval Trade and Finance*, 1973. Collected essays.

950 —— 'Credit in medieval trade', *Ec.H.R.*, I, 1927-8, 234-61. Reprinted in Carus-Wilson, ed. (245), listed above, I, 61-87.

951 —— 'Italy and the economic development of England in the Middle Ages', *J.Ec.H.*, XI, 1951, 339-46.

952 —— 'The economic and political relations of England and the Hansa from 1400 to 1475', in Power and Postan (955), listed below, 91-153.

953 **Pounds**, N. J. G., 'The ports of Cornwall in the Middle Ages', *Devon and Cornwall Notes and Queries*, XXIII, 1947, 65-73.

954 **Power**, Eileen, *The Wool Trade in English Medieval History*, 1941. An important study of England's major export in the fourteenth and fifteenth centuries.

955 —— and Postan, M. M., *Studies in English Trade in the Fifteenth Century*, 1933. Reprinted 1951.

956 **Richardson**, H., 'Medieval trading restrictions in the N. E.', *Arch.Aeliana*, 4th ser., XXXIX, 1961, 135-50.

957 **Ruddock**, A. A., *Italian Merchants and Shipping in Southampton, 1270-1600*, Southampton Records Series, 1951.

958 —— 'Italian trading fleets in medieval England', *Hist.*, XXIX, 1944, 192-202.

959 —— 'John Day of Bristol and the English voyages across the Atlantic before 1497', *Geog. J.*, CXXII, 1966, 225-32.

960 **Sherbourne**, J. W., *The Port of Bristol in the Middle Ages*. Bristol branch of the Hist.Ass., 1965.

961 **Simon**, A. L., *The History of the Wine Trade in England*, 3 vols., 1906-9.

962 **Veale**, Elspeth M., *The English Fur Trade in the Later Middle Ages*, 1966.

963 **Wee**, W. Van der, *The Growth of the Antwerp Market and the European Economy from the Fourteenth to the Sixteenth Centuries*, 3 vols., The Hague, 1963. An important study of an entrepôt which was growing in significance throughout this period.

964 **Williams**, N., *Contraband Cargoes: Seven Centuries of Smuggling*, 1959.

965 **Wilson**, K. P., 'The port of Chester in the fifteenth century', *T.H.S.L.C.*, 117, 1966, 1-16. See also Wilson's edition of the Chester customs accounts (918), listed above.

966 **Wolff**, P., 'English cloth in Toulouse, 1380-1450', *Ec.H.R.*, 2nd ser., II, 1950, 290-4.

(c) THE MERCANTILE COMMUNITY

967 **Carus-Wilson**, Eleanora M., *The Merchant Adventurers of Bristol in the Fifteenth Century*, 1962.

968 —— 'The origins and early development of the Merchant Adventurers' organisation in London as shown in their own medieval records', *Ec.H.R.*, IV, 1932, 147-76.

969 **James**, Margaret K., 'A London merchant of the fourteenth century', *Ec.H.R.*, 2nd ser., VIII, 1956, 364-76.

970 **Postan**, M. M., 'Partnership in English medieval commerce'. In *Studi in Onore di Armando Sapori*, Milan, 1957, I, 522-49.

971 **Thrupp**, Sylvia, *The Merchant Class of Medieval London*, 1948.

972 **Ward**, G. F., 'The early history of the Merchant Staplers', *E.H.R.*, XXXIII, 1918, 297-319.

PRICES, PUBLIC FINANCE, USURY AND THE ORIGINS OF BANKING

(a) PRICES

973 **Ames**, E., 'The sterling crisis of 1337-39', *J.Ec.H.*, XXV, 1965, 496-522.

974 **Burnett**, J., *History of the Cost of Living*, 1969. A work of popularisation.

975 **Herlitz**, L., 'The medieval theory of the just price', *Scand.Ec.H.R.*, VIII, 1960, 71-76. See also Roover (980), listed below.

976 **Hughes**, A., Crump, C. G. and Johnson, C., 'The debasement of the coinage under Edward III', *Ec. J.*, VII, 1897, 185-97.

977 **Mate**, Mavis, 'High prices in fourteenth-century England: causes and consequences', *Ec.H.R.*, 2nd ser., XXVIII, 1975, 1-16.

978 **Miskimin**, H. A., 'Monetary movements and market structure forces for contraction in fourteenth- and fifteenth-century England', *J.Ec.H.*, XXIX, 1964, 470-90.

979 **Reddaway**, T. F., 'The King's Mint and Exchange in London, 1343-1543', *E.H.R.*, LXXXII, 1967, 1-23.

980 **Roover**, R. de., 'The concept of the just price', *J.E.H.*, XVIII, 1958, 418-34. See Herlitz (975), listed above.

981 **Schreiner**, J., 'Wages and prices in England in the later Middle Ages', *Scand.Ec.H.R.*, II, 1954, 61-73. See also Feavearyear (527), and Thorold Rogers (533), listed above, and Beveridge (1943) and Phelps Brown (2225), listed below.

(b) PUBLIC FINANCE

982 **Bryant**, W. N., 'The financial dealings of Edward III with the county communities, 1330-60', *E.H.R.*, LXXXIII, 1968, 760-71.

983 **Fryde**, E. B., 'Materials for the study of Edward III's credit operations, 1327-48', *B.I.H.R.* XXIII, 1950, 1-30.

984 —— 'Loans to the English Crown, 1328-31' *E.H.R.*, LXIX, 1955, 198-211.

985 **MacFarlane**, K. B., 'Loans to the Lancastrian kings: the problem of inducement', *Cambridge H. J.*, IX, 1947, 51-68.

986 **Mayhew**, N. J. ed., *Edwardian Monetary Affairs, 1279-1344*, 1977.

987 **Ramsay**, J. H., *A History of the Revenues of the Kings of England 1066-1399*, 2 vols., 1925.

988 **Steel**, A., *The Receipt of the Exchequer 1377-1485*, 1954.

989 **Unwin**, G., ed., *Finance and Trade under Edward III*, 1918. Reprinted 1962.

990 **Willard**, J. F., *Parliamentary Taxes on Personal Property, 1290-1334: A Study in Medieval English Financial Administration*, Cambridge Mass., 1934.

See also Dowell (540) and Roseveare (547), listed above.

(c) USURY AND THE ORIGINS OF BANKING

991 **Nelson**, N., *The Idea of Usury*, Princeton N. J., 1949.

992 **Noonan**, J. T., *The Scholastic Analysis of Usury*, Cambridge, Mass., 1957.

993 **Pugh**, R. B., 'Some medieval moneylenders' *Speculum*, XLIII, 1968, 274-89.

994 **Usher**, A. P., 'The origins of banking: the primitive bank of deposit, 1200-1600', *Ec.H.R.*, IV 1932-4, 399-428. See also Powell (2003), listed below.

WAR: ITS IMPACT ON MEDIEVAL SOCIETY AND ECONOMY

995 **Allmand**, C. T., 'War and profit in the late Middle Ages', *H.Today*, 15, 1965, 762-69.

996 **Barnie**, J., *War in Medieval Society*, 1974.

997 **Fowler**, K., ed., *The Hundred Years War*, 1971. A collection of essays.

998 **Gillingham**, J., *The Wars of the Roses. Peace and Conflict in Fifteenth-Century England* 1981.

999 **Goodman**, A., *The Wars of the Roses. Military Activity and English Society, 1452-97*, 1981.

Argues that the probable effect of the wars was to increase local allegiances at the expense of an embryonic nationalism.

1000 **Hale**, J. R., 'War and public opinion in the fifteenth and sixteenth centuries', *P.P.*, 22, 1962, 18-33.

1001 **Haward**, W. I., 'Economic aspects of the Wars of the Roses in East Anglia', *E.H.R.*, XLI, 1926, 170-89.

1002 **Hay**, D., 'The division of the spoils of war in fourteenth-century England', *T.R.H.S.*, 5th ser., IV, 1954, 91-109.

1003 **Hewitt**, H. J., *The Organisation of War under Edward III*, 1966.

1004 **Keen**, M., *The Laws of War in the Late Middle Ages*, 1965.

1005 **Lander**, J. R., *The Wars of the Roses*, 1965.

1006 **MacFarlane**, K. B., 'The investment of Sir John Fastolf's profits in war', *T.R.H.S.*, 5th ser., VII, 1957, 91-116.

1007 —— 'England and the Hundred Years' War', *P.P.*, 22, 1962, 3-13.

1008 **Miller**, E., 'War, taxation and the English economy in the late thirteenth and early fourteenth centuries'. In Winter (251), listed above.

1009 **Nef**, J. U., *War and Human Progress*, Cambridge, Mass., 1950.

1010 **Postan**, M. M., 'Some social consequences of the Hundred Years' War', *Ec.H.R.*, XII, 1942, 7-12.

1011 —— 'The costs of the Hundred Years' War', *P.P.*, 27, 1964, 34-53.

1012 **Sherborne**, J. W., 'The Hundred Years' War: the English navy, shipping and manpower, 1369-89', *P.P.*, 37, 1967, 163-75. Comments on the previous article by Postan.

1013 **Steel**, A., 'The financial background of the Wars of the Roses', *Hist.*, XL, 1955, 18-30.

1014 **Vale**, M. G. A., ed., *War and Chivalry. Warfare and Aristocratic Culture in England, France and Burgundy at the end of the Middle Ages*, 1981.

See also Coleman and John (1181), listed below.

LABOUR

(a) GENERAL AND MISCELLANEOUS

1015 **Cheyney**, E. P., 'The disappearance of English serfdom', *E.H.R.*, XV, 1900, 20-38.

1016 **Clark**, Alice, 'Serfdom on an Essex manor, 1308-78', *E.H.R.*, XX, 1905, 479-83.

1017 **Dale**, M. K., 'The London silkwomen of the fifteenth century', *Ec.H.R.*, IV, 1932-3, 324-35.

1018 **Davenport**, F. G., 'The decay of villeinage in East Anglia', *T.R.H.S.*, n.s., XIV, 1900, 123-42.

1019 **Hatcher**, J., 'English serfdom and villeinage: towards a re-assessment', *P.P.*, 90, 1981, 3-39.

1020 **Hilton**, R. H., *The Decline of Serfdom in Medieval England*, 1969. (Studies in Economic History pamphlet series.) A very useful survey with a bibliographical guide.

1021 **Knoop**, D., and Jones, G. P., 'Masons' wages in medieval England', *Ec. J.Ec.H.Supp.*, II, 1933, 473-99.

1022 **Ritchie**, Nora, 'Labour conditions in Essex in the reign of Richard II', *Ec.H.R.*, IV, 1932-4, 429-51. Reprinted in Carus-Wilson, ed. (245), listed above, II, 91-111.

1023 **Smith**, R. E. F., *The Enserfment of the Russian Peasantry*, 1968. The introduction by R. H.

Hilton and R. E. F. Smith is of general relevance. See also Beveridge (550, 551), listed above.

(c) THE PEASANTS' REVOLT

1024 **Dobson**, R. B., ed., *The Peasants' Revolt of 1381*, 1970. A valuable collection of documents.

1025 **Fryde**, E. B., *The Peasants' Revolt of 1381*, 1981. Hist.Ass. pamphlet.

1026 **Harvey**, Barbara, 'Draft letters patent of manumission and pardon for the men of Somerset in 1381', *E.H.R.*, LXXX, 1965, 89-91.

1027 **Hilton**, R. H., *Bond Men Made Free. Medieval Peasant Movements and the English Rising of 1381*, 1973.

1028 —— and Fagan, H., *The English Rising of 1381*, 1950. A Marxist account.

1029 **Kesteven**, G., *The Peasants' Revolt*, 1964.

1030 **Lyle**, H. M., *The Peasants' Revolt, 1381*, 1950.

1031 **Warren**, W. L., 'The Peasants' Revolt of 1381', *H.Today*, 12, 1962, 845-53.

1032 **Wilkinson**, B., 'The Peasants' Revolt of 1381', *Speculum*, XV, 1940, 12-35. See also Hilton (1019), listed above.

ALIEN IMMIGRANTS IN ENGLAND

1090 **Allmand**, C. T., 'A note on denization in fifteenth-century England', *Medievalia et Humanistica*, XVII, 1966, 127-8.

1091 **Beardwood**, Alice, *Alien Merchants in England, 1350-77, their Legal and Economic Position*, Medieval Academy of America Monographs, 3, Cambridge, Mass., 1931.

1092 —— 'Alien merchants and the English crown in the later fourteenth century', *Ec.H.R.*, II, 1929-30, 229-60.

1093 —— 'Mercantile antecedents of the English naturalisation laws', *Medievalia et Humanistica*, XVI, 1964, 64-77.

1094 **Holmes**, G. A., 'Florentine merchants in England, 1346-1436', *Ec.H.R.*, 2nd ser., XIII, 1960, 193-208.

1095 **Kerling**, Nellie, J. M., 'Aliens in the county of Norfolk, 1436-1485', *Norfolk Arch.*, XXXIII, 1963, 200-15.

1096 **Ruddock**, A. A., 'Alien hosting in Southampton in the fifteenth century', *Ec.H.R.*, XVI, 1946, 30-7.

1097 **Thrupp**, Sylvia, 'A survey of the alien population of England in 1440', *Speculum*, XXXII, 1957, 262-73.

1098 —— 'Aliens in and around London in the fifteenth century'. In Hollaender and Kellaway (597), listed above, 251-72.

1099 **Wilson**, C., 'The immigrant in English history', in *Economic Issues in Immigration* (Readings in Political Economy No. 5, Institute of Economic Affairs), 1970, 3-16. A very general survey. See also Cunningham (1716), listed below.

RELIGION

1100 **Aston**, Margaret, 'Lollardy and Literacy', *Hist.*, LXII, 1977, 347-71.

1101 —— 'Lollardy and sedition, 1381-1431', *P.P.*, 17, 1960, 1-44.

1102 **Gilchrist**, J., *The Church and Economic Activity in the Middle Ages*, 1969.

1103 **Hall**, D. J., *The English Medieval Pilgrimage*, 1965.

1104 **Owen**, Dorothy M., *Church and Society in Medieval Lincolnshire*, 1971.

1105 **Southern**, R. W., *Western Society and the Church in the Middle Ages*, 1970.

1106 **Sumption**, J., *Pilgrimage. An Image of Medieval Religion*, 1975.

1107 **Thompson**, A. H., *The English Clergy and their Organisation in the Later Middle Ages*, 1947.

1108 —— *The Later Lollards, 1414-1520*, 1965.

1109 —— 'Piety and charity in late medieval London', *J.Eccles.H.*, XVI, 1965, 178-95.

1110 **Vale**, M. G. A., *Piety, Charity and Literacy among the Yorkshire Gentry, 1370-1480*, Borthwick Papers, 50, 1976.

1111 **White**, L., *Medieval Religion and Technology. Collected Essays*, Berkeley, Cal., 1978.

THE MONASTERIES

1112 **Postan**, M. M. and Brooke, C. N. L., eds., *Carte Nativorum. A Peterborough Abbey Cartulary of the Fourteenth Century*, Northants. Rec.Soc., XX, 1950.

1113 **Dobson**, R. B., *Durham Priory 1400-1450*, 1973.

1114 **Donnelly**, J. S., 'Changes in the grange economy of English and Welsh Cistercian abbeys, 1300-1540', *Traditio*, X, 1954, 399-458.

1115 **Finberg**, H. P. R., *Tavistock Abbey; A Study in the Social and Economic History of Devon*, 1951, 2nd ed., 1969, with minor corrections.

1116 **Furniss**, D. A., 'The monastic contribution to

medieval medical care: aspects of an earlier welfare state', *J. Royal College of General Practitioners*, LXIX, 1968, 244-50.

1117 **Hockey**, S. T., *Quarr Abbey and its Lands, 1132-1631*, 1970.

1118 **Knowles**, D., *The Religious Orders in England*, vol. II: *The End of the Middle Ages*, 1955. Vol. I (666), listed above, is also relevant for the early part of this period.

1118a **Lindley**, E. S., 'Kingswood Abbey, its lands and mills', *Trans. Bristol and Gloucs. Arch. Soc.*, LXXIII, 1955, 115-91, and *ibid.*, LXXIV, 1956, 36-59.

1119 **Platt**, C., *The Monastic Grange in Medieval England: A Re-assessment*, 1969. An interesting and original study which makes use of the techniques of the archaeologist. See also Cowley (5129), Dickinson (657), and Williams (5130).

EDUCATION AND LEARNING

For source material on this subject, see Sylvester (2441), listed below.

1120 **Cobban**, A. B., *The Medieval Universities: Their Origins and Development*, 1975.

1121 **Emden**, A. B., 'Learning and education'. In Poole (311), listed above, II, 515-40.

1122 **Leach**, A. F., *The Schools of Medieval England*, 1915, 2nd ed., 1916. But see Parry (1129) and Simon (1132), listed below.

1123 **Leff**, G., *Paris and Oxford Universities in the Thirteenth and Fourteenth Centuries: An Institutional and Intellectual History*, 1968.

1124 **Lytle**, G. F., 'Patronage patterns and Oxford colleges, *c.* 1300-*c.*1530' in Stone (2477), below, 111-49.

1125 **McMahon**, C., *Education in Fifteenth-century England*, Baltimore, 1947.

1126 **Moran**, J. H., *Education and Learning in the City of York, 1300-1560*, Borthwick Papers, 55,

1979.

1127 **Orme**, N., *English Schools in the Middle Ages*, 1973.

1128 —— *Education in the West of England, 1066-1548*, 1977.

1129 **Parry**, A. W., *Education in England in the Middle Ages*, 1920. A corrective to Leach, (1122), listed above.

1130 **Rashdall**, H., *The Universities of Europe in the Middle Ages*, eds. F. M. Powicke and A. B. Emden, 3 vols., 1936. Vol. 3 deals with the English universities.

1131 **Robson**, J. A., *Wyclif and the Oxford Schools*, 1961.

1132 **Simon**, Joan, *The Social Origins of English Education*, 1971. A useful exploration of the medieval social background.

1133 **Thompson**, J. W., *The Literacy of the Laity in the Middle Ages*, Berkeley, Calif., 1939.

STANDARDS OF LIVING

1033 **Drummond**, J. C. and Wilbraham, Anne, *The Englishman's Food. A History of Five Centuries of English Diet*, 1939, 2nd ed., revised and enlarged by Dorothy Hollingsworth, 1958.

1034 **Jope**, E. M., 'Cornish houses, 1400-1700'. In E. M. Jope, ed., *Studies in Building History*, 1961, 192-222.

1035 **Mead**, W. E., *The English Medieval Feast*, 1931. Reprinted 1968.

1036 **Newton**, Stella M., *Fashion in the Age of the Black Prince*, 1981.

1037 **Pantin**, W. A., 'Medieval English town house plans', *Medieval Arch.*, VI-VII, for 1962-3, 202-39.

1038 —— 'The merchants' houses and warehouses of King's Lynn', *Medieval Arch.*, VI-VII, for 1962-3, 173-81.

1039 **Thompson**, A. H., 'The English house', in Barraclough, ed. (264), listed above, 139-78.

1040 **Wilson**, C. Anne, *Food and Drink in Britain from the Stone Age to Recent Times*, 1973.

1041 **Wood**, Margaret E., *The English Medieval House*, 1965.

See also Barley (2223), listed below, and Ashley (401), listed above.

GOVERNMENT AND ADMINISTRATION

1042 **Baker**, R. L., *The English Customs Service, 1307-43. A study of Medieval administration*, Trans. American Phil.Soc., n.s., LVI, Part 6, 1966.

1043 **Baldwin**, J. F., *The King's Council*, 1913.

1044 **Booth**, P. H. W., *The Financial Administration of the Lordship and County of Chester, 1272-1377*, Chet.Soc., 1981.

1045 **Chibnall**, A. C., *Early Taxation Returns: Taxation of Personal Property in 1332 and Later*, Bucks.Rec.Soc., XIV, 1966.

1046 **Coleman**, Olive, 'The collectors of customs in London under Richard II'. In Hollaender and Kellaway (597), listed above, 181-94.

1047 **Fryde**, E. B., 'The English farmers of the customs, 1343-51', *T.R.H.S.*, 5th ser., ix, 1959, 1-17.

1048 **Griffiths**, R. A., 'Public and private bureaucracies in England and Wales in the fifteenth century', *T.R.H.S.*, 5th ser., XXX, 1980, 109-30.

1049 **Harriss**, G. L., *King, Parliament and Public Finance in Medieval England to 1369*, 1975.

Concentrates on political theory rather than on the practicalities of finance.

1050 **Hunnisett**, R. F., *The Medieval Coroner*, 1961.

1051 **Lapsley**, G. T., *Crown, Community and Parliament in the Later Middle Ages*, 1951.

1052 **Levett**, Ada E., 'Notes on the Statute of Labourers', *Ec.H.R.*, IV, 1932-4, 77-80.

1053 **Pelham**, R. A., 'The provisioning of the Lincoln parliament of 1301', *Birm.H. J.*, III, 1952, 16-32.

1054 **Prestwich**, M., 'Victualling estimates for English garrisons in Scotland during the early fourteenth century', *E.H.R.*, LXXXII, 1967, 536-43.

1055 **Putnam**, Bertha, *The Enforcement of the Statute of Labourers*, Columbia Studies in History, Economics and Public Law, XXXII, 1908.

1056 **Steel**, A., 'The collectors of the customs at Newcastle upon Tyne in the reign of Richard II'. In J. C. Davies, ed., *Studies Presented to Sir Hilary Jenkinson*, 1957, 390-413.

TOWNS

For fuller bibliographical details, the reader is referred to Gross (577) and to Martin and MacIntyre (578), listed above.

1057 **Dilks**, T. B., ed., *Bridgwater Borough Archives, 1445-68*, Somerset Rec.Soc., LX, 1947.

1058 **Dobson**, R. B., ed., *York City Chamberlains'*

Account Rolls, 1396-1500, Surtees Soc., CXCII, 1980.

1059 **Prestwich**, M., ed., *York Civic Ordinances, 1301*, Borthwick Papers, 49, 1976.

1060 **Weinbaum**, M., ed., *British Borough Charters, 1307-1660*, 1943. For further source material on this subject, see the section on 'Towns and gilds' in Bland, Brown and Tawney (211), listed above.

1061 **Bartlett**, J. N., 'The expansion and decline of York in the later Middle Ages', *Ec.H.R.*, 2nd ser., XII, 1965, 17-33.

1062 **Bridbury**, A. R., 'English provincial towns in the later Middle Ages', *Ec.H.R.*, 2nd ser., XXXIV, 1981, 1-24.

1063 **Carus-Wilson**, Eleanora M., *The Expansion of Exeter at the Close of the Middle Ages*, 1963.

1064 **Cronne**, H. A., *The Borough of Warwick in the Later Middle Ages*, Dugdale Soc.Occ. Papers, 10, 1951.

1065 **Dobson**, R. B., 'Admissions to the Freedom of the City of York in the Later Middle Ages', *Ec.H.R.*, XXVI, 1973, 1-22.

1066 **Dulley**, A. J. F., 'Four Kent towns at the end of the Middle Ages', *Arch.Cantiana*, LXXXI, 1966, 95-108.

1067 **Finberg**, H. P. R., 'The borough of Tavistock'. In Hoskins and Finberg (1248), listed below, 172-97.

1068 **Fowler**, J., *Medieval Sherborne*, 1952.

1069 **Gill**, C., 'Coventry in the fifteenth century'. In Gill, *Studies in Midland History*, 1930, 3-85.

1070 **Green**, Mrs J. R., *Town Life in the Fifteenth Century*, 2 vols., 1894.

1071 **Hilton**, R. H., 'Some problems of urban real property in the Middle Ages'. In Feinstein (2200), listed below, 326-37.

1072 **MacDonall**, K., *Medieval London Suburbs*, 1978.

1073 **Phythian-Adams**, C., *Desolation of a City. Coventry and the Urban Crisis of the Late Middle Ages*, 1979.

1074 **Robertson**, D. W., *Chaucer's London*, N. Y., 1968.

1075 **Rörig**, F., *The Medieval Town*, English trans., 1967. For background.

1076 **Salusbury**, G. T., *Street Life in Medieval England*, 1939.

1077 **Smith**, B. S., *A History of Malvern*, 1964.

1078 **Tout**, T. F., 'The beginnings of a modern capital: London and Westminster in the fourteenth century'. In Tout's *Collected Papers*, III, 1934, 249-75.

1079 **Walker**, V. W., 'Medieval Nottingham: a topographical study', *Trans.Thoroton Soc.*, LXVII, 1963, 28-45.

1080 **Woledge**, G., 'The medieval borough of Leeds', *Thoresby Soc.*, XXXVII, 1945, 288-309.

See also Martin (233), and Williams (615), listed above.

COMMUNICATIONS AND INTERNAL TRADE

(a) INLAND TRANSPORT AND COMMUNICATIONS

1081 **Barley**, M. W., 'Lincolnshire rivers in the Middle Ages', *Lincs.Architectural and Arch.Soc.*, n.s., I, 1940, 1-21.

1082 **Hill**, Mary C., *The King's Messengers, 1199-1377*, 1961.

1083 **Willard**, J. F., 'The use of carts in the fourteenth century', *Hist.*, n.s., XVII, 1932, 246-50.

1084 —— 'Inland transportation in England during the fourteenth century', *Speculum*, I, 1926, 361-74.

(b) MARKETS AND FAIRS

1085 **Addison**, W., *English Fairs and Markets*, 1953.

1086 **Oliver**, J. G., 'Churches and wool: a study of the wool trade in fifteenth-century England', *H.Today*, I, 1951, 33-40.

1087 **Pelham**, R. A., 'The early wool trade in Warwickshire and the rise of the merchant middle class', *Trans. Birmingham Arch.Soc.*, LXIII, for 1939-40, 1944, 41-62.

1088 —— 'The cloth markets of Warwickshire during the later Middle Ages', *Trans.Birmingham Arch.Soc.*, LXVI, for 1945 and 1946, 1950, 31-41.

1089 —— 'The trade relations of Birmingham during the Middle Ages', *Trans.Birmingham Arch.Soc.*, LXII, for 1938, 1943, 32-40.

ENGLAND
1500-1700

GENERAL WORKS

(a) BIBLIOGRAPHIES

1134 **Davies**, G., ed., *Bibliography of British History: Stuart Period 1603-1714*, 1928, 2nd ed., revised by Mary F. Keeler, 1970.

1135 **Grose**, C. L., ed., *A Select Bibliography of British History 1660-1760*, Chicago, 1939. Reprinted N. Y., 1967.

1136 **Levine**, M., ed., *Bibliographical Handbooks: Tudor England 1485-1603*, 1968.

1137 **Morrill**, J. S., *Seventeenth-Century Britain, 1603-1714*, 1980.

1138 **Read**, C., ed., *Bibliography of British History: Tudor Period 1485-1603*, 1933, 2nd ed. 1959.

1139 **Sachse**, W. L., ed., *Bibliographical Handbooks: Restoration England 1660-89*, 1971.

1140 **Walcott**, R., 'The later Stuarts 1660-1714: significant work of the last twenty years (1939-59)', *A.H.R.*, LXVII, 1962, 352-70.

(b) SOURCE MATERIAL

1141 **Beer**, E. S. de, *The Diary of John Evelyn*, 6 vols., 1955.

1142 **Browning**, A., ed., *English Historical Documents, 1660-1714*, 1952. Part 3 on public finance, Part 4 on the Church and Part 5 on local government and social life are particularly useful.

1143 **Burton**, Kathleen M., ed., *A Dialogue between Reginald Pole and Thomas Lepset by Thomas Starkey*, 1948.

1144 **Byrne**, Muriel St. C., ed., *The Lisle Letters*, 6 vols., 1981. Correspondence of the period 1533-42.

1145 **Dewar**, Mary, ed., *A Discourse of the Commonweal of this Realm of England*, Washington, D.C., 1970. A new edition of the work made known by Lamond (1150). The editor argues persuasively that the author of the *Discourse* was Sir Thomas Smith.

1146 **Dunham**, W. H. and Pargellis, S., eds., *Complaint and Reform in England 1436-1714*, N. Y., 1938. A miscellaneous collection of contemporary writings.

1147 **Edelen**, G., ed., *William Harrison's Description of England*, Folger Shakespeare Library, 1968. A new edition of the work better known in the Furnivall edition listed below.

1148 **Emmison**, F. G., *Elizabethan Life. Home, Work and Land*, 1976.

1149 **Furnivall**, F. J., ed., *Harrison's Description of England in Shakespeare's Youth*, New Shakespeare Society, 6th ser., I and VIII, 1877 and 1881.

1150 **Lamond**, Elizabeth, ed., *A Discourse of the Commonweal of this Realm of England*, 1893. See also Dewar (1145), listed above. Lamond attributes the Discourse to John Hales.

1151 **Latham**, R. and Matthews, W. M. eds., *The Diary of Samuel Pepys. A New and Complete Transcription*, 9 vols., 1970-6.

1152 **Macfarlane**, A., ed., *The Diary of Ralph Josselin, 1616-83*, 1976. A mine of information about rural economy and society as well as about religious affairs. See also Macfarlane (1343), below.

1153 **More**, Sir Thomas, *Utopia*. Numerous editions

are available, for example the translation by P. Turner, 1967, and the scholarly edition by E. Surtz and J. H. Hexter, New Haven, Conn., 1965.

1154 **Morris**, C., ed., *The Journeys of Celia Fiennes*, 1947, 3rd ed., 1982.

1155 **Stone**, T. G., ed., *England under the Restoration 1660-1688*, 1923.

1156 **Tawney**, R. H. and Power, Eileen, *Tudor Economic Documents*, 3 vols., 1924. The standard collection.

1157 **Thirsk**, Joan and Cooper, J. P., eds., *Seventeenth-century Economic Documents*, 1972. An invaluable source book. Sections on economic crises, agriculture, industries, inland and coastal trade and communications, overseas trade, finance and the coinage, aliens, wealth, population and land: some contemporary statistics.

1158 **Williams**, C. H., ed., *English Historical Documents, 1485-1558*, 1967. Part 2 on the land, Part 3 on the commonweal, Part 5 on religion and Part 6 on daily life in town and country are particularly useful from the economic and social point of view.

1159 **Williams**, E. N., ed., *A Documentary History of England*, vol. 2: *1559-1931*, 1965. The companion volume to Bagley, listed above, (256).

1160 **Wilson**, J. D., *Life in Shakespeare's England*, 1911. Several times reprinted.

1161 **Wilson**, Thomas, *The State of England, 1600*, ed. F. J. Fisher, *Camden Miscellany*, XVI, 1936. See also Bland, Brown and Tawney (211), Part 2 of which, 231-476, covers the period 1485-1600; and Dunham and Pargellis (1146), listed above.

(c) GENERAL SURVEYS

1162 **Appleby**, Joyce O., *Economic Thought and Ideology in Seventeenth-Century England*, Princeton, N. J., 1978.

1163 **Ashley**, M., *Life in Stuart England*, 1964.

1164 **Aston**, T. H., ed., *Crisis in Europe, 1560-1660*, 1965. A collection of reprinted articles from *P.P.*, several of which are directly concerned with English economic and social history in the period.

1165 **Aylmer**, G. E., 'The meaning and definition of "property" in seventeenth-century England', *P.P.*, 86, 1980, 87-97.

1166 **Bindoff**, S. T., *Tudor England*, 1951. A masterly short survey, useful for social and economic history though the main bias is towards the political aspects of the period.

1167 —— Hurstfield, J., and Williams, C. H., eds., *Elizabethan Government and Society: Essays Presented to Sir John Neale*, 1961.

1168 **Black**, J. B., *The Reign of Elizabeth*, 1936, 2nd ed., 1960. Good bibliography.

1169 **Burke**, P., ed., *Economy and Society in Early Modern Europe. Essays from Annales*, 1971. Includes essays by Braudel, Cipolla and Verlinden. For background.

1170 **Byrne**, Muriel St. C., *Elizabethan Life in Town and County*, 1925, 8th ed., revised, 1961.

1171 **Chalklin**, C. W. and Havinden, M. A., eds., *Rural Change and Urban Growth: Essays in Regional History in Honour of W. G. Hoskins*, 1974.

1172 **Chambers**, J. D., *Population, Economy and Society in Pre-industrial England*, 1972.

1173 **Clark**, G. N., *The Wealth of England from 1496 to 1760*, 1946.

1174 —— *The Later Stuarts, 1660-1714*, 1934, 2nd ed., 1955. Good bibliography.

1175 —— *War and Society in the Seventeenth Century*, 1958.

1176 **Clark**, P., Smith, A. G. R., and Tyacke, N., eds., *The English Commonwealth. Essays in Politics and Society presented to Joel Hurstfield*, 1979.

1177 **Clarkson**, L. A., *The Pre-industrial Economy in England, 1500-1750*, 1971. A concise analysis of the changing structure of the economy in this period.

1178 **Coate**, Mary, *Social Life in Stuart England*, 1924.

1179 **Coleman**, D. C., 'Technology and economic history, 1500-1750', *Ec.H.R.*, 2nd ser., XI, 1958-9, 506-14.

1180 —— *The Economy of England, 1450-1750*, 1977.

1181 —— and John, A. H., eds., *Trade, Government and Economy in Pre-industrial England. Essays presented to F. J. Fisher*, 1976. A wide-ranging collection which includes essays on war and late medieval society, English cereal exports, 1660-1765, the sumptuary laws, urban development in the sixteenth and seventeenth centuries.

1182 **Cooper**, J. P., 'The social distribution of land and men in England, 1436-1700', *Ec.H.R.*, 2nd ser., XX, 1967, 419-40.

1183 **Coward**, B., *The Stuart Age. A History of England, 1603-1714*, 1980. Contains good general surveys of society and the economy in the period 1603-40 and of the co-existence of change and continuity later in the century.

1184 **Davis**, J. C., *Utopia and the Ideal Society. A Study of English Utopian Writing, 1516-1700*,

1981. Includes some discussion of the lesser writers such as Samuel Gott as well as leading figures like More, Bacon, Winstanley, Chamberlen and Bellers.

1185 **De Vries**, J., *The Economy of Europe in an Age of Crisis, 1600-1750*, 1976. For background.

1186 **Dodd**, A. H., *Life in Elizabethan England*, 1961.

1187 **Earle**, P., ed., *Essays in European Economic History, 1500-1800*, 1974.

1188 **Elton**, G. R., *England under the Tudors*, 1955, 2nd ed. 1974. Mainly political and constitutional in bias. Contains a valuable critical bibliography.

1189 **Everitt**, A. M., *Change in the Provinces: The Seventeenth Century*, University of Leicester, Department of English Loc.H.Occ. Papers, 2nd ser., 1, 1969.

1190 **Fisher**, F. J., ed., *Essays in the Economic and Social History of Tudor and Stuart England in Honour of R. H. Tawney*, 1961. An invaluable collection of essays.

1191 —— 'The sixteenth and seventeenth centuries: the dark ages in English economic history?', *Economica*, n.s., XXIV, 1957, 2-18. In Harte, ed. (86), listed above.

1192 **Goring**, J., 'Social change and military decline in mid-Tudor England', *Hist.*, LX, 1975, 185-97.

1193 **Hartwell**, R. M., 'Economic growth in England before the Industrial Revolution: some methodological issues', *J.Ec.H.*, XXIX, 1969, 13-31. In Hartwell (2252), listed below.

1194 **Hill**, C., *The Century of Revolution, 1603-1714*, 1961. 2nd ed. 1981. A stimulating textbook, untypical in its method of separating the narrative and analytical chapters.

1195 —— *Reformation to Industrial Revolution: A Social and Economic History of Britain, 1530-1780*, 1967.

1196 —— *Change and Continuity in Seventeenth-century England*, 1975. A stimulating collection of (mainly reprinted) essays.

1197 **Holderness**, B. A., *Pre-industrial England. Economy and Society, 1500-1750*, 1976.

1198 **Hoskins**, W. G., *The Age of Plunder. The England of Henry VIII, 1500-47*, 1976.

1199 **Hurstfield**, J. and Smith, A. G. R., *Elizabethan People: State and Society*, 1972.

1200 **Ives**, E. W., Knecht, R. J., and Scarisbrick, J. J., eds., *Wealth and Power in Tudor England, Essays presented to S. T. Bindoff*, 1978. A valuable collection which includes essays on 'Cardinal Wolsey and the Common Weal', 'Episcopal Palaces, 1535-1660', 'The East and West in Early

Modern London', and on 'Antwerp and London'.

1201 **Jones**, W. R. D., *The Tudor Commonwealth, 1529-1559*, 1970.

1202 **Jordan**, W. K., *Edward VI: The Young King. The Protectorship of the Duke of Somerset*, 1968. A valuable study of this crucial but neglected period of the sixteenth century.

1203 —— *Edward VI: The Threshold of Power*, 1971. Concludes Jordan's survey of the critical years of the mid-sixteenth century by examining the régime of the Duke of Northumberland.

1204 **Lennard**, R. V., ed., *Englishmen at Rest and Play, 1558-1714*, 1931.

1205 **Letwin**, W., *The Origins of Scientific Economics: English Thought, 1660-1776*, 1963.

1206 **Macfarlane**, A., *The Origins of English Individualism*, 1978. Strident revisionism.

1207 **Mathew**, D., *The Social Structure in Caroline England*, 1948.

1208 —— *The Age of Charles I*, 1951.

1209 **Miskimin**, H. A., 'Agenda for early modern economic history', *J.Ec.H.*, XXXI, 1971, 172-83.

1210 **Moir**, Esther A. L., *The Discovery of Britain: The English Tourists 1540-1840*, 1964.

1211 **Nef**, J. U., 'War and economic progress 1540-1640', *Ec.H.R.*, XII, 1942, 13-38.

1212 **Ogg**, D., *England in the Age of Charles II*, 2 vols., 1934, 2nd ed., 1955. A useful survey of the reign. Good bibliography.

1213 —— *England in the Reigns of James II and William III*, 1955.

1214 **Pennington**, D. H. and Thomas, K., eds., *Puritans and Revolutionaries. Essays in Seventeenth-Century History presented to Christopher Hill*, 1978. The *festschrift* includes important essays on 'The Alehouse and the Alternative Society', 'Puritans and Poor Relief', 'The Puritans and Adultery', and on 'Social Mobility and Business Enterprise in Seventeenth-Century England'.

1215 **Plumb**, J. H., *The Growth of Political Stability in England, 1675-1725*, 1967. A full discussion of the changing social foundations of politics.

1216 **Ramsey**, P., *Tudor Economic Problems*, 1963. The best short introduction to sixteenth-century English economic history.

1217 **Rich**, E. E. and Wilson, C., eds., *Cambridge Economic History of Europe IV: The Economy of Expanding Europe in the Sixteenth and Seventeenth Centuries*, 1967. The contributions are of varying usefulness.

1218 **Rowse**, A. L., *The England of Elizabeth: The Structure of Society*, 1951.

1219 **Russell**, C., *The Crisis of Parliaments: Engl-*

ish History 1509-1660, 1971. Mainly political, although there is some discussion of economic factors.

1220 **Salzman**, L. F., *England in Tudor Times: An Account of its Social Life and Industries*, 1926.

1221 **Seaver**, P. S., ed., *Seventeenth-Century England. Society in an Age of Revolution*, 1976. Reprints essays by Stone, Thirsk, Coleman, and Plumb with an editorial introduction.

1222 **Smith**, A. G. R., ed., *The Reign of James VI and I*, 1973. A collection of essays dealing with various aspects of the reign.

1223 **Stoye**, J. W., *English Travellers Abroad, 1604-67: Their Influence in English Society and Politics*, 1952.

1224 **Supple**, B. E., 'Economic history and economic underdevelopment', *Canadian J.Ec. and Pol.Science*, 27, 1961, 460-78.

1225 **Thirsk**, Joan, *Economic Policy and Projects. The Development of a Consumer Society in Early Modern England*, 1978.

1226 **Thomas**, K., 'Age and authority in early modern England', *Proc.Brit.Acad.*, LXII, 1977, 205-48.

1227 **Thompson**, R., *Women in Stuart England and America. A Comparative Study*, 1974. Examines the status and roles of women in the two countries commenting on the implications of sex ratios for the status of women and on the effects of puritanism.

1228 **Wernham**, R. B., ed., *New Cambridge Modern History III: The Counter-Reformation and the Price Revolution, 1559-1610*, 1968.

1229 **Williams**, P., *Life in Tudor England*, 1964.

1230 **Williamson**, J. A., *The Tudor Age*, 1953. Good on maritime affairs.

1231 **Wilson**, C., *England's Apprenticeship, 1603-1763*, 1965. Good bibliography.

1232 —— *Economic History and the Historian. Collected Essays*, 1969. The main part of this useful book consists of reprints of the author's articles on the seventeenth century.

1233 **Wrightson**, K., *English Society, 1580-1680*, 1982. A systematic, up-to-date social history which stresses the co-existence of change and continuity and the considerable social and local variations. See also Cunningham (219), Lipson (232), Pollard and Crossley (236), and Schofield (717), listed above.

(d) REGIONAL STUDIES

1234 **Beckett**, J. V., *Coal and Tobacco. The Lowthers and the Economic Development of West Cumberland, 1660-1760*, 1981.

1235 **Blanchard**, I., 'Commercial crisis and change: trade and the industrial economy of the North East, 1509-32', *Northern H.*, VIII, 1973, 64-85.

1236 **Bouch**, C. M. L. and Jones, G. P., *A Short Economic and Social History of the Lake Counties, 1500-1830*, 1961.

1237 **Chalklin**, C. W., *Seventeenth-century Kent*, 1965.

1238 **Clark**, P., *English Provincial Society from the Reformation to the Revolution. Religion, Politics, and Society in Kent, 1500-1640*, 1977.

1239 **Durston**, C. G., 'London and the provinces: the association between the capital and the Berkshire gentry of the seventeenth century', *Southern H.*, III, 1981, 39-54.

1240 **Edwards**, A. C., *English History from Essex Sources, 1550-1750*, 1952.

1241 **Finberg**, H. P. R., ed., *Gloucestershire Studies*, 1957.

1242 **Hey**, D., *An English Rural Community: Myddle Under the Tudors and Stuarts*, 1974.

1243 **Hodgett**, G. A. J., *Tudor Lincolnshire*, 1975.

1244 **Holmes**, C., *Seventeenth-Century Lincolnshire*, 1980.

1245 **Hoskins**, W. G., *The Midland Peasant: The Economic and Social History of a Leicestershire Village*, 1957. A study of Wigston Magna.

1246 —— *Provincial England: Essays in Social and Economic History*, 1963.

1247 —— ed., *Essays in Leicestershire History*, 1950.

1248 —— and Finberg, H. P. R., *Devonshire Studies*, 1952.

1249 **James**, M. E., *Family, Lineage, and Civil Society. A Study of Society, Politics and Mentality in the Durham Region 1500-1640*, 1974.

1250 **Rowse**, A. L., *Tudor Cornwall*, 1941, 2nd ed., 1969.

1251 **Styles**, P., *Studies in Seventeenth-Century West Midlands History*, 1978. Includes essays on Worcester, Henley in Arden, Bewdley, and on the social structure of Kineton Hundred in the reign of Charles II.

1252 **Tupling**, G. H., *The Economic History of Rossendale*, Chet.Soc., n.s., 87, 1927.

1253 **Walker**, F., *The Historical Geography of South-West Lancashire before the Industrial Revolution*, Chet.Soc., n.s., 103, 1939.

1254 **Watts**, S. J., *From Border to Middle Shire: Northumberland, 1586-1625*, 1975. Though primarily political, there is a full discussion of the distinctive social and economic environment of this turbulent region.

1255 **Whetter**, J., *Cornwall in the Seventeenth Century. An Economic Survey of Kernow*, 1974.

1256 **Wrightson**, K. and Levine, D., *Poverty and Piety in an English Village. Terling, 1525-1700*, 1979.

(e) FOREIGNERS' VIEWS OF ENGLAND

A useful bibliographical introduction to the subject is:

1257 **Fussell**, G. E., *The Exploration of England: A Select Bibliography of Travel and Topography, 1570-1815*, 1935.

1258 **Ballam**, H. and Lewis, R., eds., *The Visitors' Book: England and the English as Others Have Seen Them, 1500-1950*, 1950.

1259 **Bülow**, G. von, ed., 'Journey through England and Scotland made by Leopold von Wedel in the years 1584 and 1585', *T.R.H.S.*, n.s., IX, 1895, 223-70.

1260 —— 'Diary of the journey of Philip Julius, Duke of Stettin-Pomerania through England in the year 1602', *T.R.H.S.*, n.s., VI, 1897, 1-67.

1261 **Letts**, M., *As the Foreigner Saw Us*, 1935. A survey of foreigners' impressions from c. 1500 to c. 1830. Bibliography, 263-71.

1262 **Malfatti**, C. V., ed., *Two Italian Accounts of Tudor England*, Barcelona, 1953.

1263 **Palmer**, R. E., ed., *French Travellers in England, 1600-1900: Selections From Their Writings*, 1960.

1264 **Rye**, W. B., ed., *England as Seen by Foreigners in the Days of Elizabeth and James I*, 1865. Reprinted 1967.

1265 **Salter**, E. G., *Tudor England Through Venetian Eyes*, 1930.

1266 **Scott**, W. D. R., *German Travellers in England, 1400-1800*, 1953.

1267 **Smith**, E., *Foreign Visitors in England*, 1889.

1268 **Sneyd**, C. A., ed., *A Relation, or Rather a True Account of the Island of England . . . About the Year 1500*, Camden Soc., o.s., XXXVII, 1847.

1269 **Williams**, C., ed., *Thomas Platter's Travels in England, 1599*, 1937.

1270 **Wilson**, F. M., *Strange Island: Britain Through Foreign Eyes, 1395-1940*, 1955. See also Thirsk (1414), listed below, xxix-xxxvi.

POPULATION

(a) SOURCES

1271 **Allison**, K. J., ed., 'An Elizabethan village census', *B.I.H.R.*, XXXVI, 1963, 91-103.

1272 **Cornwall**, J., 'An Elizabethan census', *Recs. of Bucks.*, XVI, 1959, 258-73.

1273 **Faraday**, M. A. (ed.), *The Westmorland Protestation Returns 1641-42*, Cumb. and West.Antiq. and Arch.Soc. Tract Ser., XVII, 1971.

1274 **Glass**, D. V., ed., *London Inhabitants Within the Walls, 1695*, London Rec.Soc., II, 1966.

1275 **King**, Gregory, *Natural and Political Observations Upon the State and Condition of England* (1696), in G. Chalmers, ed., *Estimate of the Comparative Strength of Great Britain*, 1782, new ed., 1802.

1276 **Levine**, D., 'The reliability of parochial registration and the representativeness of family reconstitution', *Pop.Studs.*, XXX, 1976, 107-22.

1277 **Munby**, L., ed., *Hertfordshire Population Statistics, 1563-1801*, 1964.

1278 **Petty**, William, *Political Arithmetick, or a Discourse Concerning the Extent and Value of Lands, People, Buildings, Husbandry, etc.*, 1690. The work is included in E. A. Aitken, ed., *Later Stuart Tracts* (An English Garner), 1903, 1-66.

(b) GENERAL

1279 **Appleby**, A. B., *Famine in Tudor and Stuart England*, 1978. A case study of Cumberland and Westmorland.

1280 **Blanchard**, I., 'Population change, enclosure and the early Tudor economy', *Ec.H.R.*, 2nd ser., XXIII, 1970, 427-45.

1281 **Bonar**, J., *Theories of Population from Raleigh to Arthur Young*, 1931. Reprinted 1966.

1282 **Cornwall**, J., 'English population in the early sixteenth century', *Ec.H.R.*, 2nd ser., XXIII, 1970, 32-44.

1283 **Crawford**, Patricia, 'Attitudes to menstruation in seventeenth-century England', *P.P.*, 91, 1981, 47-73.

1284 **Eccles**, Audrey, *Obstetrics and Gynaecology in Tudor and Stuart England*, 1982.

1285 **Eshleman**, M. K., 'Diet during pregnancy in the sixteenth and seventeenth centuries', *J.H.Medicine & Allied Sciences*, XXX, 1975, 23-39.

1286 **Flinn**, M. W., *The European Demographic System, 1500-1820*, 1981.

1287 **Glass**, D. V. and Eversley, D. E. C., eds., *Population in History*, 1965. An important collection of comparative studies. On English population the book contains 'Two papers on Gregory King' by Professor Glass, 159-220.

1288 **Habakkuk**, H. J., 'The economic history of modern Britain', *J.Ec.H.*, XVIII, 1958, 486-501.

1289 **Hair**, P. E. H., 'Bridal pregnancy in rural England in earlier centuries', *Pop.Studs.*, XX, 1966, 233-43.

1290 **Hollingsworth**, T. H., *Historical Demography*, 1969. A valuable discussion of the present state of historical demography and of the available sources. Excellent bibliography.

1291 —— *Demography of the British Peerage*, Supplement to *Pop.Studs.*, XVIII, 1964.

1292 **Kerridge**, E., 'The returns of the Inquisition of Depopulation', *E.H.R.*, LXX, 1955, 212-28.

1293 **Laslett**, P., *The World We Have Lost*, 1965, 2nd ed., 1971.

1294 —— Oosterveen, Karla, and Smith, R. M., eds., *Bastardy and its Comparative History*, 1980. Includes two chapters on illegitimacy and its context in early modern England.

1295 **Patten**, J., 'The Hearth Taxes 1662-89', *Loc.Pop.Studs.*, 7, 1971, 14-27.

1296 **Quaife**, G. R., *Wanton Wenches and Wayward Wives. Peasants and Illicit Sex in Early Seventeenth Century England*, 1979.

1297 **Schnucker**, R. V., 'Elizabethan birth control and puritan attitudes', *J.Interdis.H.*, V, 1975, 655-67.

1298 **Spengler**, J. J., 'Demographic factors and early modern economic development', *Daedalus*, XCVII, 1968, 433-46.

1299 **Thirsk**, Joan, *Sources of Information on Population 1500-1760, and Unexplored Sources in Local Records*, 1965.

1300 **Tucker**, G. S. L., 'English pre-industrial population trends', *Ec.H.R.*, XVI, 1963, 205-18.

1301 **Utterström**, G., 'Climatic fluctuations and population problems in early modern history', *Scand.Ec.H.R.*, III, 1955, 3-47.

1302 **Wrigley**, E. A., ed., *An Introduction to English Historical Demography*, 1966.

1303 —— *Population and History*, 1969. Useful general survey. Good bibliography.

1304 —— 'Family limitation in pre-industrial England', *Ec.H.R.*, XIX, 1966, 82-109. An important article using the Colyton evidence.

1305 —— 'Mortality in pre-industrial England: the example of Colyton, Devon, over three centuries', *Daedalus*, XCVII, 1968, 246-80.

See also F. J. Fisher (1950), listed below.

(c) INTERNAL POPULATION MOBILITY AND EMIGRATION

(i) INTERNAL MOBILITY

1306 **Buckatzch**, E. J., 'The constancy of local populations and migration in England before 1800', *Pop.Studs.*, V, 1951-2, 62-9.

1307 —— 'Places of origin of a group of immigrants into Sheffield, 1624-1799', *Ec.H.R.*, 2nd ser., II, 1950, 303-6.

1308 **Clark**, P., 'Migration in England during the late seventeenth and early eighteenth centuries', *P.P.*, 83, 1979, 57-90.

1309 **Cornwall**, J., 'Evidence of population mobility in the seventeenth century', *B.I.H.R.*, XL, 1967, 143-52. Plays down the extent of internal mobility. But the type of source used – the deposition books of an ecclesiastical court – places a strict limit on the force of the argument.

1310 **Patten**, J., *Rural-Urban Migration in Pre-Industrial England*, 1973.

1311 **Pelham**, R. A., 'The immigrant population of Birmingham, 1686-1726', *Trans. Birmingham Arch.Soc.*, LX for 1936, 1940, 45-86.

1312 **Rich**, E. E., 'The population of Elizabethan England', *Ec.H.R.*, 2nd ser., II, 1950, 247-65. Draws attention to the value of muster rolls as a source for the study of population mobility.

1313 **Spufford**, P., 'Population movement in seventeenth-century England', *Loc.Pop.Studs.*, 4, 1970, 41-50.

1314 **Wareing**, J., 'Changes in the geographical distribution of the recruitment of apprentices to the London companies, 1480-1750', *J.H.Geog.*, VI, 1980, 241-50.

(ii) EMIGRATION

1315 **Banks**, C. E. and Morison, S. E., 'Persecution as a factor in emigration', *Proc. Massachusetts Hist.Soc.*, LXIII, 1930, 136-54.

1316 **Bridenbaugh**, C., *Vexed and Troubled Englishmen, 1590-1642*, 1968. An important book.

ated.oducing.

Its footnotes are a mine of information.

1317 **Campbell**, Mildred, 'Of people either too few or too many. The conflict of opinion on population and its relation to emigration'. In W. A. Aiken and B. D. Henning, eds., (2250), listed below, 169-202.

1318 **Crouse**, N. M., 'Causes of the great migration, 1630-40', *New England Quarterly*, V, 1932, 3-36.

1319 **Newton**, A. P., *The Colonizing Activities of English Puritans*, 1914. Reprinted 1966.

1320 **Salerno**, A., 'The social background of seventeenth-century emigration to America', *J.Brit.Studs.*, XIX, 1979, 31-52.

See also Knorr (1837) and Quinn (1841), listed under the section on *Colonisation*.

(d) DISEASE

1321 **Appleby**, A. B., 'Nutrition and disease. The case of London, 1550-1750', *J.Interdis.H.*, VI, 1975, 1-22.

1322 **Bell**, W. G., *The Great Plague in London in 1665*, 1924, 2nd rev. ed., 1951

1323 **Clarkson**, L. A., *Death, Disease and Famine in Pre-Industrial England*, 1975.

1324 **Copeman**, W. S. C., *Doctors and Disease in Tudor Times*, 1960.

1325 **Debus**, A. G., ed., *Medicine in Seventeenth-century England*, Berkeley, Calif., 1974.

1326 **Levy**, H., 'The economic history of sickness and medical benefit before the Puritan Revolution', *Ec.H.R.*, XIII, 1943, 42-57.

1327 —— 'The economic history of sickness and medical benefit since the Puritan Revolution', *Ec.H.R.*, XIV, 1944, 135-60.

1328 **MacDonald**, M., *Mystical Bedlam: Madness, Anxiety, and Healing in Seventeenth-Century England*, 1981. Based principally on the case-notes of an early seventeenth-century Buckinghamshire physician.

1329 **Mullett**, C. F., 'Some neglected aspects of plague medicine in sixteenth-century England', *Scientific Monthly*, 44, 1937, 325-37.

1330 —— 'The plague of 1603 in England', *Annals Med.H.*, n.s., 9, 1937, 230-47.

1331 *The Plague Reconsidered. A New Look at its Origins and Effects in Sixteenth and Seventeenth Century England*, 1977. Deals primarily with the local history of plague with useful chapters on Bristol, Colyton and Eyam.

1332 **Roberts**, R. S., 'The personnel and practice of medicine in Tudor and Stuart England, Parts 1 and 2', *Medical H.*, 6, 1962, 363-82, *ibid.*, 8, 1964, 217-34.

1333 **Slack**, P. A., 'The disappearance of plague: an alternative view', *Ec.H.R.*, 2nd ser., XXXIV, 1981, 469-76.

1334 **Webster**, C., ed., *Health, Medicine and Mortality in the Sixteenth Century*, 1979.

1335 **Wilshore**, J. E. O., 'Plague in Leicester, 1558-1665', *Trans.Leics.Arch.Soc.*, XLIV, for 1968-9, 1970, 45-71.

1336 **Wilson**, F. P., *The Plague in Shakespeare's London*, 1927.

(e) THE FAMILY

1337 **Anderson**, M., *Approaches to the History of the Western Family, 1500-1914*, 1980.

1338 **Carlton**, C., 'The widow's tale: male myths and female reality in sixteenth- and seventeenth-century England', *Albion*, X, 1978, 118-27.

1339 **Davies**, Kathleen M., 'The sacred condition of equality: how original were puritan doctrines of marriage?', *Soc.H.*, V, 1977, 563-80. See also Morgan (1345) and Schücking (1347), below.

1340 **Goody**, J., Thirsk, Joan, and Thompson, E. P., eds., *Family and Inheritance. Rural Society in Western Europe, 1200-1800*, 1976. An indispensable volume which includes essays on England by Cecily Howell, Margaret Spufford, Joan Thirsk, J. P. Cooper and E. P. Thompson.

1341 **Laslett**, P., *Family Life and Illicit Love in Earlier Generations*, 1977.

1342 **Levine**, D., *Family Formation in an Age of Nascent Capitalism*, 1977.

1343 **Macfarlane**, A., *The Family Life of Ralph Josselin, a Seventeenth-century Clergyman: An Essay in Historical Anthropology*, 1970. See also (1152), above.

1344 **Michel**, R. H., 'English attitudes towards women, 1640-1700', *Canadian J.H.*, XIII, 1978, 35-60.

1345 **Morgan**, E. S., *The Puritan Family*, Boston, Mass., 1944. Based on New England evidence.

1346 **Powell**, C. L., *English Domestic Relations, 1487-1653*, N. Y., 1917.

1347 **Schücking**, L. L., *The Puritan Family: A Study from the Literary Sources*, 1929, English trans., 1969.

1348 **Slater**, Miriam, 'The weightiest business. Marriage in an upper gentry family in seventeenth-century England', *P.P.*, 72, 1976, 25-54.

1349 **Stone**, L., *The Family, Sex and Marriage in England, 1500-1800*, 1977. See the extended review by C. Hill, *Ec.H.R.*, 2nd ser., XXXI, 1978, 450-63.

1350 **Thirsk**, Joan, 'The family', *P.P.*, 27, 1964, 116-22. A useful review article.

1351 —— 'Younger sons in the seventeenth century', *Hist.*, LIV, 1969, 358-78.

1352 **Wrightson**, K., 'Infanticide in early seventeenth-century England', *Loc.Pop.Studs.*, XV, 1975, 10-22. See also the essay by Malcolmson on this subject in Cockburn (2066), below, also Hill (2390), listed below, ch. 13 on 'The spiritualization of the household', 443-81.

(f) LOCAL AND REGIONAL STUDIES

1353 **Chalklin**, C. W., 'The Compton Census of 1676: the diocese of Canterbury and Rochester', *Kent Records, A Seventeenth-Century Miscellany*, Kent Arch.Soc., XVII, 1960, 153-83.

1354 **Meekings**, C. A. F., ed., *Dorset Hearth Tax Assessment, 1662-64*, Dorset Nat.H. and Arch.Soc.Occ.Publs., 1951.

1355 —— *Surrey Hearth Tax, 1664*, Surrey Rec.Soc., XVII, 1940.

1356 **Watkins-Pritchard**, W., ed., *Shropshire Hearth Tax Roll of 1672*, Shropshire Arch.Soc., 1949.

1357 **Weinstock**, Maureen, ed., *Hearth Tax Returns, Oxfordshire, 1665*, Oxfordshire Rec.Soc., 1940.

As an introduction to this class of archive material the following can be recommended:

1358 **Howell**, R., 'Short guides to records. 7; Hearth Tax Returns', *Hist.*, XLIX, 1964, 42-5.

1359 **Cornwall**, J., 'A Tudor Domesday. The musters of 1522', *J.Soc. Archivists*, III, 1965, 19-24.

1360 —— 'The people of Rutland in 1522', *Trans.Leics.Arch.Soc.*, XXXVII, 1961-2, 7-28.

1361 **Cowgill**, Ursula M., 'Life and death in the sixteenth century in the city of York', *Pop.Studs.*, XXI, 1967, 56-62.

1362 **Dymond**, D. P., 'Suffolk and the Compton Census of 1676', *Suffolk R.*, III, 1966, 103-18.

1363 **Eversley**, D. E. C., 'A survey of population in an area of Worcestershire, 1660-1850', *Pop.Studs.*, X, 1957, 253-79.

1364 **Finlay**, R., *Population and Metropolis. The Demography of London, 1580-1650*, 1981.

1365 **Glass**, D. V., 'Notes on the demography of London at the end of the seventeenth century', *Daedalus*, XCVII, 1968, 581-92.

1366 **Gould**, J. D., 'The inquisition of depopulation of 1607 in Lincolnshire', *E.H.R.*, LXVII, 1952, 392-6.

1367 **Hodgson**, R. I., *Demographic Trends in County Durham, 1560-1801*, 1978.

1368 **Hoskins**, W. G., 'The population of an English village, 1086-1801: a study of Wigston Magna', in Hoskins (1246), listed above, 181-208.

1369 **Howson**, W. G., 'Plague, poverty and population in parts of N. W. England, 1580-1720', *T.H.S.L.C.*, CXII, 1960, 29-56.

1370 **James**, F. G., 'The population of the diocese of Carlisle in 1676', *Trans.Cumb. and West.Antiq. and Arch.Soc.*, LI, 1951, 137-41.

1371 **Jones**, P. E. and Judges, A. V., 'London's population in the late seventeenth century', *Ec.H.R.*, VI, 1935, 45-63.

1372 **Laslett**, P. and Harrison, J., 'Clayworth and Cogenhoe'. In H. F. Bell and R. L. Ollard, eds., *Historical Essays 1600-1750 presented to David Ogg*, 1962, 157-84. A pioneer English study of population and social structure using seventeenth-century census material.

1373 **McKinley**, R. A., *Norfolk Surnames in the Sixteenth Century*, University of Leicester, Department of English Loc.H., Occ.Papers, 2nd ser., II, 1969.

1374 **Marshall**, Lydia M., *The Rural Population of Bedfordshire, 1671-1921*, Beds.Hist.Rec.Soc., XVI, 1934.

1375 —— 'The levying of the Hearth Tax, 1662-88', *E.H.R.*, LI, 1936, 628-46.

1376 **Morison**, E. J. D., 'The Hearth Tax in Chester', *J.Chester and N.Wales Architectural, Arch. and H.Soc.*, XXXVI, 1946, 31-43.

1377 **Palliser**, D. M., 'Epidemics in Tudor York', *Northern H.*, VII, 1973, 45-63.

1378 **Parker**, L. A., 'Depopulation returns for Leicestershire in 1607', *Trans.Leics.Arch.Soc.*, XXIII, 1947, 231-91.

1379 **Patten**, J., 'Population distribution in Norfolk and Suffolk during the sixteenth and seventeenth centuries', *T.I.B.G.*, LXV, 1975, 45-65.

1380 **Pickard**, R., *The Population and Epidemics of Exeter in Pre-Census Times*, 1947.

1381 **Ralph**, E., and Williams, M. E., *The Inhabitants of Bristol in 1696*, Bristol Rec.Soc., XXV, 1968.

1382 **Rogers**, C. D., *The Lancashire Population Crisis of 1623*, 1975.

1383 **Smith**, C. T., 'Population'. In *V.C.H. Leicestershire*, ed. W. G. Hoskins and R. A. McKinley, III, 1955, 129-75.

1384 **Spufford**, Margaret, 'The significance of the

Cambridgeshire Hearth Tax', *Proc. Cambridge Antiq.Soc.*, LV, 1962, 53-64.

1385 **Styles**, P., 'A census of a Warwickshire village in 1698', *Birm.H.J.*, III, 1951, 33-51.

AGRICULTURE AND RURAL SOCIETY

(a) SOURCES

1386 **Bankes**, Joyce and Kerridge, E., eds., *The Early Records of the Bankes Family at Winstanley*, Chet.Soc., 3rd ser., 21, 1973. Contains the Memoranda book of James Bankes together with accounts and rentals.

1387 **Eyre**, Adam, *A Dyurnall, or Catalogue of all my Accions and Expenses, etc.* In *Yorkshire Diaries*, Surtees Soc., LXV, 1877.

1388 **Fussell**, G. E., ed., *Robert Loder's Farm Accounts 1610-1620*, Camden Soc., 3rd ser., LIII, 1936.

1389 **Hartley**, Dorothy, ed., *Thomas Tusser: His Good Points of Husbandry*, 1931.

1390 **Lodge**, Eleanor, *The Account Book of a Kentish Estate, 1616-1704* (Godminton), 1927.

1391 **Robinson**, C. B., ed., *Rural Economy in Yorkshire in 1641: Being the Farming and Account Books of Henry Best of Elmeswell in the East Riding*, Surtees Soc., XXXIII, 1857.

1392 **Skeat**, W. W., ed., *Fitzherbert's Book of Husbandry*, English Dialect Soc., XIII, 1882.

See also Lamond (1150) and Dewar (1145) listed above. Additional source material will be found in Tawney and Power (1156), listed above, Vol. I, Section 1, 'Agriculture and rural society', 1-90 and Vol. III, section I, 'Enclosures and the countryside', 12-81.

(b) GENERAL WORKS

1393 **Allison**, K. J., 'Flock management in the sixteenth and seventeenth centuries', *Ec.H.R.*, 2nd ser., XI, 1959, 98-112.

1394 **Amherst**, Alicia, *A History of Gardening in England*, 1895, 3rd ed., enlarged, 1910.

1395 **Bridbury**, A. R., 'Sixteenth-century farming', *Ec.H.R.*, 2nd ser., XXVII, 1974, 538-56.

1396 **Butlin**, R. A., *The Transformation of Rural England, c. 1580-1800. A Study in Historical Geography*, 1982. Excellent bibliography, 68-74.

1397 **Cooper**, J. P., 'In search of agrarian capitalism', *P.P.*, 80, 1978, 20-65.

1398 **Fox**, H. S. A. and Butlin, R. A., eds., *Change in the Countryside. Essays on Rural England,*

1500-1900, 1979. A miscellaneous collection which includes essays on enclosure, mechanisation, and farmers' associations.

1399 **Fussell**, G. E., *The English Dairy Farmer, 1500-1900*, 1966.

1400 —— 'Agriculture from the Restoration to Anne', *Ec.H.R.*, IX, 1938-9, 68-74.

1401 —— 'Crop nutrition in Tudor and Stuart England', *Ag.H.R.*, III, 1955, 95-106.

1402 —— 'Crop nutrition in the late Stuart Age, 1660-1714', *Annals of Science*, XIV, 1958, 173-84.

1403 —— and K. R., *The English Countrywoman: A Farmhouse Social History, 1500-1900*, 1953.

1404 —— and K. R., *The English Countryman: His Life and Works, 1500-1900*, 1955.

1405 **Hoskins**, W. G., 'Harvest fluctuations and English economic history, 1480-1619', *Ag.H.R.*, XII, 1964, 28-46, reprinted in Minchinton (249), listed above, I, 93-115.

1406 —— 'Harvest fluctuations and English economic history, 1620-1759', *Ag.H.R.*, XVI, 1968, 13-31. Two useful articles which emphasise the crucial importance of the harvest in the pre-industrial economy.

1407 **Jones**, E. L., ed., *Agriculture and Economic Growth in England, 1650-1815*, 1967. A useful collection of reprinted articles with an introduction and bibliography.

1408 **Kain**, R., 'Tithe as an index of pre-industrial agricultural production', *Ag.H.R.*, XXVII, 1979, 73-81.

1409 **Kerridge**, E., *Agrarian Problems in the Sixteenth Century and After*, 1969. An attack on Tawney (1413), listed below. Half the book consists of documents.

1410 —— *The Farmers of Old England*, 1973.

1411 —— 'Ridge and furrow in agrarian history', *Ec.H.R.*, 2nd ser., IV, 1951, 14-36.

1412 **Lennard**, R. V., 'English agriculture under Charles II', *Ec.H.R.*, IV, 1932, 23-45. Reprinted in Minchinton (249), listed above, I, 161-85.

1413 **Tawney**, R. H., *The Agrarian Problem in the Sixteenth Century*, 1912. Reprinted, N. Y., 1967 with an introduction by Lawrence Stone. A landmark in the writing of agrarian history.

1414 **Thirsk**, Joan, ed., *The Agrarian History of England and Wales IV: 1500-1640*, 1967. Excellent bibliography. Includes chapters on the farming regions, on landowning and labour, agricultural improvement, rural housing, and marketing.

1415 —— ed., *Land Church and People. Essays Presented to Professor H. P. R. Finberg*, 1970. The collection contains an important and wide-ranging article by Dr Thirsk on 'Seventeenth-century agriculture and social change', 148-77, which attempts to place agricultural developments within the framework of the economic crises of the seventeenth century.

1416 —— 'The content and sources of English agrarian history after 1500', *Ag.H.R.*, III, 1955, 66-79.

1417 —— *Horses in Early Modern England: For Service, For Pleasure, For Power*, 1978.

1418 **Webber**, R., *The Early Horticulturalists*, 1968.

See also Barnes (3483) and Russell (2928), listed below, and Trow-Smith (781), listed above.

(c) MISCELLANEOUS

1419 **Chilton**, D., 'Land measurement in the sixteenth century', *Trans.Newcomen Soc.*, XXXI, 1957-9, 111-29.

1420 **Fussell**, G. E., *The Old English Farming Books from Fitzherbert to Tull*, 1947.

1421 —— *The Farmer's Tools, 1500-1900: The History of British Farm Implements, Tools, and Machinery Before the Tractor Came*, 1952.

1422 **Hallam**, H. E., 'Fen by-laws of Spalding and Pinchbeck', *Trans. Lincs. Architectural & Arch.Soc.*, X, 1967, 40-56. Includes the text of by-laws of 1591.

1423 **Hammersley**, G., 'The Crown Woods and their exploitation in the sixteenth and seventeenth centuries', *B.I.H.R.*, XXX, 1957, 136-61.

1424 **Overton**, M., 'Estimating crop yields from probate inventories: an example from East Anglia, 1585-1735', *J.Ec.H.*, XXXIX, 1979, 363-78.

(d) REGIONAL STUDIES

1425 **Havinden**, M. A., ed., *Husbandry and Marketing in the South-West 1500-1800*, 1973.

1426 **Hoskins**, W. G., ed., *Studies in Leicestershire Agrarian History*, 1949.

1427 **Kerridge**, E., 'Agriculture, 1500-1793', *V.C.H.Wilts.*, ed. E. Crittall. IV, 1959, 43-64.

1428 **Pettit**, P. A. J., *The Royal Forests of Northamptonshire: A Study in Their Economy, 1558-1714*, Northants.Rec.Soc., XXIII, 1968.

1429 **Phythian-Adams**, C., *Continuity, Fields, and Fission. The Making of a Midland Parish*, 1978.

1430 **Rodgers**, H. B., 'Land use in Tudor Lancashire', *T.I.B.G.*, XXVII, 1955, 79-98.

1431 **Rollison**, D., 'Property, ideology and popular culture in a Gloucestershire village, 1660-1740', *P.P.*, 93, 1981, 70-97.

1432 **Skipp**, V. H. T., *Crisis and Development. An Ecological Case Study of the Forest of Arden, 1570-1674*, 1978.

1433 **Smith**, R. B., *Land and Politics in the England of Henry VIII*, 1970.

1434 **Spufford**, Margaret, *Contrasting Communities: English Villagers in the Sixteenth and Seventeenth Centuries*, 1974.

1435 **Thirsk**, Joan, *English Peasant Farming: The Agrarian History of Lincolnshire from Tudor to Recent Times*, 1957.

1436 —— 'The Isle of Axholme before Vermuyden', *Ag.H.R.*, I, 1953, 16-28.

1437 —— 'Agrarian history, 1540-1950'. In *V.C.H.Leics.*, ed. W. G. Hoskins and R. A. McKinley, II, 1954, 199-264.

1438 —— 'Horn and thorn in Staffordshire. The economy of a pastoral county', *N.Staffs J. Field Studs.*, IX, 1969, 1-16.

(e) MARKETING

1439 **Bowden**, P. J., *The Wool Trade in Tudor and Stuart England*, 1962.

1440 **Everitt**, A. M., 'The marketing of agricultural produce'. In Thirsk (1414), listed above, 466-592. An important general survey of the subject.

1441 —— 'The food market of the English town, 1660-1760', *Third International Conference on Economic History*, Paris, 1968, 57-71.

1442 **Fisher**, F. J., 'The development of the London food market, 1540-1640', *Ec.H.R.*, V, 1935, 46-64. Reprinted in Carus-Wilson (245), listed above, I, 135-51.

1443 **Gras**, N. S. B., *The Evolution of the English Corn Market*, Cambridge, Mass., 1915.

1444 **Kneisel**, E., 'The evolution of the English corn market', *J.Ec.H.*, XIV, 1954, 46-52.

1445 **Outhwaite**, R. B., 'Dearth and government intervention in English grain markets, 1590-1700', *Ec.H.R.*, 2nd ser., XXXIV, 1981, 389-406.

1446 **Ponko**, V., 'N. S. B. Gras and Elizabethan corn policy: a re-examination of the problem',

Ec.H.R., 2nd ser., XVII, 1964, 24-42. A critique of Gras's book, listed above.

1447 **Skeel**, Caroline A. J., 'The cattle trade between Wales and England from the fifteenth to the nineteenth centuries', *T.R.H.S.*, 4th ser., ix, 1926, 135-58. See also the section on *Communications and internal trade* (pp. 63-4).

(f) THE MANOR

1448 **Kerridge**, E., ed., *Surveys of the Manors of Philip, First Earl of Pembroke, 1631-32*, Wilts.Arch. and Nat.H.Soc., Records Branch, IX, 1953.

1449 **Ellis**, M. J., 'A study in the manorial history of Halifax parish in the sixteenth and early seventeenth centuries', *Yorks.Arch. J.*, XL, 1960-1, 250-64, 420-42.

1450 **Hill**, C., 'Professor Lavrovsky's study of a seventeenth-century manor', *Ec.H.R.*, XVI, 1946, 125-9.

1451 **Leconfield**, Lord, *Petworth Manor in the Seventeenth Century*, 1954.

1452 —— *Sutton and Duncton Manors*, 1956. See See also Davenport (462), and Kerridge (1409), 17-31, listed above.

(g) LANDHOLDING

See also the separate section on *The gentry and their estates* (2114-36).

(i) LANDHOLDING

1453 **Batho**, G. R., 'Landlords in England: noblemen, gentlemen and yeomen'. In Thirsk (1414), listed above, 276-305. A convenient survey.

1454 **Beckett**, J. V., 'English landownership in the later seventeenth and eighteenth centuries: the debate and the problems', *Ec.H.R.*, 2nd ser., XXX, 1977, 567-81.

1455 **Clay**, C., 'The greed of Whig bishops? Church landlords and their lessees, 1660-1760', *P.P.*, 87, 1980, 128-57.

1456 **Cross**, M. Claire, 'The economic problems of the see of York: decline and recovery in the sixteenth century'. In Thirsk (1415), listed above, 64-83.

1457 **Habakkuk**, H. J., 'Economic functions of English landowners in the seventeenth and eighteenth centuries', *Expl.Entrepren.H.*, VI, 1953, 92-102. Reprinted in Minchinton (249), listed above, I, 187-201.

1458 **Thompson**, F. M. L., 'The social distribution of landed property in England since the sixteenth century', *Ec.H.R.*, 2nd ser., XIX, 1966, 505-17. See also Stone (2108), and Campbell (2092), listed below.

(ii) THE CROWN LANDS

1459 **Batho**, G. R., 'Landlords in England: the Crown', in Thirsk (1414), listed above, 256-76.

1460 **Gentles**, I., 'The management of the Crown lands, 1649-60', *Ag.H.R.*, XIX, 1971, 25-41.

1461 —— 'The sales of Crown lands during the English Revolution', *Ec.H.R.*, 2nd ser., XXVI, 1973, 614-35.

1462 **Pugh**, R. B., *The Crown Estate: An Historical Essay*, 1960.

1463 **Wolffe**, B. P., *The Crown Lands, 1461-1536*, 1970. A valuable examination of the subject. Half the book consists of documents.

1464 —— 'Henry VIII's land revenues and chamber finance', *E.H.R.*, LXXIX, 1964, 225-54. Material relating to the disposal of the dissolved monastic lands is listed below in the sections on *The Land market* and on *The dissolution of the monasteries* (p.50).

(h) THE LAND MARKET

1465 **Clay**, C., 'The price of freehold land in the later seventeenth and eighteenth centuries', *Ec.H.R.*, 2nd ser., XXVII, 1974, 173-89.

1466 **Coleman**, D. C., 'London scriveners and the estate market in the later seventeenth century', *Ec.H.R.*, 2nd ser., IV, 1951, 221-30.

1467 **Gentles**, I., 'The sales of bishops' lands in the English Revolution, 1646-60', *E.H.R.*, XCV, 1980, 573-96.

1468 **Habakkuk**, H. J., 'The market for monastic property', *Ec.H.R.*, 2nd ser., X, 1957-8, 362-80. See also the article by Outhwaite (1470), listed below.

1469 —— 'The long-term rate of interest and the price of land in the seventeenth century', *Ec.H.R.*, 2nd ser., V, 1952, 26-45.

1470 **Outhwaite**, R. B., 'The price of Crown land at the turn of the sixteenth century', *Ec.H.R.*, 2nd ser., XX, 1967, 229-40. See also Habakkuk (1468), listed above.

1471 —— 'Who bought Crown lands? The pattern of purchases 1589-1603', *B.I.H.R.*, XLIV, 1971, 18-33.

1472 **Richardson**, W. C., *History of the Court of Augmentations, 1536-1554*, 1962. An authoritative study of the institution which handled the sales of monastic lands.

1473 **Woodward**, G. W. O., 'A speculation in monastic lands', *E.H.R.*, LXXIX, 1964, 778-83.
See also Thirsk (2304), listed below.

(i) RENT

1474 **Kerridge**, E., 'The movement of rent, 1540-1640', *Ec.H.R.*, 2nd ser., VI, 1953, 16-34. Reprinted in Carus-Wilson (245) listed above, II, 208-26.

1475 **Rea**, W. F., 'The rental and accounts of Sir Richard Shireburn, 1571-77', *T.H.S.L.C.*, CX, 1959, 31-57. See also Bowden (1944), listed under *Prices* below (pp. 64-6).

(j) FIELD SYSTEMS AND ENCLOSURES

1476 **Brewer**, J. G., *Enclosures and the Open Fields: A Bibliography*, 1972. Lists 355 items. See also two items by Thirsk (1492), (1493), listed below. For details of tracts and sermons on enclosures, see the list in Read (1138), listed above, 169 *et. seq.*

1477 **Hosford**, W. A., 'An eye witness's account of a seventeenth-century enclosure', *Ec.H.R.*, 2nd ser., IV, 1951, 215-20.

1478 **Leadam**, I. S., ed., *The Domesday of Inclosures, 1517-18*, 2 vols, 1892. The information gathered by Wolsey's commission.

1479 **Baker**, A. R. H., 'Field systems in the Vale of Holmesdale', *Ag.H.R.*, XIV, 1966, 1-24.

1480 ——— 'Howard Levi Gray and English field systems: an evaluation, *Ag.H.*, XXXIX, 1965, 86-91. Gray's book is listed below (1487).

1481 **Beresford**, M. W., 'Habitation versus improvement: the debate on enclosure by agreement'. In Fisher (1190), listed above, 40-69.

1482 **Butlin**, R. A., 'Northumberland field systems', *Ag.H.R.*, XII, 1964, 99-120.

1483 ——— 'Enclosure and improvement in Northumberland in the sixteenth century', *Arch.Aeliana*, 3rd ser., XLV, 1967, 149-60.

1484 **Curtler**, W. H., *The Enclosure and Redistribution of Our Land*, 1920.

1485 **Elliott**, G., 'The system of cultivation and evidence of enclosure in the Cumberland open fields in the sixteenth century', *Trans.Cumb.& West.Antiq.&Arch.Soc.*, n.s., LIX, 1959, 85-104.

1486 **Gay**, E. F., 'Inquisitions of depopulation in 1517 and the Domesday of Inclosures', *T.R.H.S.*,

n.s., XIV, 1900, 231-303.

1487 **Gray**, H. L., *English Field Systems*, Harvard Hist.Studs., XXII, Cambridge, Mass., 1915, reprinted 1959.

1488 **Johnson**, A. H., *The Disappearance of the Small Landowner*, 1909. Reprinted with an introductory note by Joan Thirsk, 1963.

1489 **Leonard**, Elizabeth M., 'The enclosure of common fields in the seventeenth century', *T.R.H.S.*, n.s., xix, 1905, 101-46. Reprinted in Carus-Wilson, (245), listed above, II, 227-56.

1490 **Parker**, L. A., 'The agrarian revolution at Cotesbach (Leics.)'. In Hoskins (1426), listed above, 41-76.

1491 **Tate**, W. E., 'An early record of open-field agriculture in Nottinghamshire', *Trans. Thoroton Soc.*, XLIII, for 1939, 1940, 33-48.

1492 **Thirsk**, Joan, *Tudor Enclosures*, Hist.Ass. pamphlet, 1959.

1493 ——— 'Enclosing and engrossing'. In Thirsk (1414), listed above, 200-55.

1494 **Yelling**, Joyce A., *Common Field and Enclosure in England, 1450-1850*, 1977.
See also Kerridge's article (1292), listed above, and Gonner (2960) and Tate (2965), listed below.

(k) AGRICULTURAL IMPROVEMENTS

1495 **Wood**, E. B., ed., *Rowland Vaughan, His Booke (1610)*, 1897. A seventeenth-century description by a pioneer of the floating of water-meadows.

1496 **Allison**, K. J., 'The sheep-corn husbandry of Norfolk in the sixteenth and seventeenth centuries', *Ag.H.R.*, V, 1957, 12-30.

1497 **Broad**, J., 'Alternate husbandry and permanent pasture in the Midlands, 1650-1800', *Ag.H.R.*, XXVIII, 1980, 77-89.

1498 **Cornwall**, J., 'Agricultural improvement, 1560-1640', *Sussex Arch.Collns.*, XCVIII, 1960, 118-32.

1499 **Darby**, H. C., *The Draining of the Fens*, 1956.

1500 **Fussell**, G. E., 'The Low Countries' influence on English farming', *E.H.R.*, LXXIV, 1959, 611-22.

1501 **Harris**, L. E., *Vermuyden and the Fens*, 1953.

1502 **Havinden**, M. A., 'Agricultural progress in open-field Oxfordshire', *Ag.H.R.*, IX, 1961, 73-83. Reprinted in Minchinton (249), listed above, I, 147-59. Argues against the traditional view that open-field agriculture was backward and static.

1503 ——— 'Lime as a means of agricultural improvement: the Devon example'. In Chalklin and Havinden (1171), listed above, 104-34.

1504 **Hoskins**, W. G., 'The reclamation of the waste in Devon, 1550-1800', *Ec.H.R.*, XIII, 1943, 80-92.

1505 **Kerridge**, E., *The Agricultural Revolution*, 1967. An important and provocative book which argues that the main agricultural innovations belong, not to the eighteenth century, but to the period from about 1560 to 1690. For a balanced criticism of the book, see the review by Joan Thirsk in *Hist.*, LV, 1970, 259-62.

1506 —— 'The sheepfold in Wiltshire and the floating of the water-meadows', *Ec.H.R.*, 2nd ser., VI, 1954, 282-9.

1507 —— 'A reconsideration of some former husbandry practices', *Ag.H.R.*, III, 1955, 26-40.

1508 **Simpson**, A., 'The East Anglian Foldcourse: some queries', *Ag.H.R.*, VI, 1958, 87-96. Comments on the article by Allison (1496), listed above.

1509 **Thirsk**, Joan, 'Farming techniques'. In Thirsk (1414), listed above, 161-99. Dr Thirsk's essay on 'Seventeenth-century agriculture and social change' (1415), listed above, is also very relevant in this connection.

1510 —— 'New crops and their diffusion: tobacco-growing in seventeenth-century England'. In Chalklin and Havinden (1171), listed above, 76-103.

1511 **Williams**, M., *The Draining of the Somerset Levels*, 1970.

1512 **Yelling**, Joyce A., 'The combination and rotation of crops in east Worcestershire, 1540-1660', *Ag.H.R.*, XVII, 1969, 24-43.

(I) THE DISSOLUTION OF THE MONASTERIES

(i) SOURCES

1513 **Hibbert**, F. A., *The Dissolution of the Monasteries, as illustrated by the Suppression of the Religious Houses of Staffordshire*, 1910. Documentary appendices.

1514 **Mellows**, W. T., ed., *The Last Days of Peterborough Monastery*, Northants. Rec.Soc., XII, 1947.

1515 **Purvis**, J. S., *A Selection of Monastic Records and Dissolution Papers*, Yorks.Arch.Soc., Rec.Ser., LXXX, 1931.

1516 **Youings**, Joyce, ed., *Devon Monastic Lands: Calendar of Particulars for Grants, 1536-1558*, Devon and Cornwall Rec.Soc., n.s., I, 1955.

(ii) STUDIES

1517 **Baskerville**, G., *English Monks and the Suppression of the Monasteries*, 1937. Takes a hostile view of the monks.

1518 **Haigh**, C., *The Last Days of the Lancashire Monasteries and Pilgrimage of Grace*, Chet.Soc., 3rd ser., 17, 1969.

1519 **Hodgett**, G. A. J., 'The dissolution of the religious houses in Lincolnshire and the changing structure of society', *Lincs. Architectural and Arch.Soc. Report and Papers*, IV, 1951, 83-99.

1520 **Jack**, Sybil, 'Monastic lands in Leicestershire and their administration on the eve of the Dissolution', *Trans.Leics.Arch.Soc.*, XLI, 1967, 9-40.

1521 **Kew**, J., 'The disposal of crown lands and the Devon land market, 1536-58', *Ag.H.R.*, XVIII, 1970, 93-105.

1522 **Knowles**, D., *The Religious Orders in England III: The Tudor Age*, 1959.

1523 **Oxley**, J. E., *The Reformation in Essex to the Death of Mary*, 1965. Chapters 6 and 7 deal with the Dissolution and its aftermath.

1524 **Savine**, A., *English Monasteries on the Eve of the Dissolution*, Oxford Studs. in Social and Legal History, 1909. An important study based mainly on the *Valor Ecclesiasticus*.

1525 **Snell**, L. S., *The Suppression of the Religious Foundations of Devon and Cornwall*, 1967.

1526 **Swales**, T. H., 'The re-distribution of the monastic lands in Norfolk at the Dissolution. 1: Value, gifts, leases and sales', *Norfolk Arch.*, XXXIV, 1966, 14-44.

1527 **Woodward**, G. W. O., *The Dissolution of the Monasteries*, 1966. A clear and concise survey.

1528 **Youings**, Joyce, 'The terms of the disposal of the Devon monastic lands, 1536-58', *E.H.R.*, LXIX, 1954, 18-38. Reprinted in Minchinton (249), listed above, I, 117-40.

1529 —— 'Landlords in England: the Church'. In Thirsk (1414), listed above, 306-56. A useful exploration of the subject.

See also Finberg (1241), listed above, 265-77, and Richardson (1472), listed above.

INDUSTRY

(a) GENERAL WORKS

530 **Coleman**, D. C., *Industry in Tudor and Stuart England*, 1975. A useful summary of the current state of research.

531 **Jack**, Sybil M., *Trade and Industry in Tudor and Stuart England*, 1977. Partly a collection of documents. Concentrates on the large-scale industries – such as coal and metals – though others, such as textiles and fishing, are included.

532 **Jones**, E. L., 'The agricultural origins of industry', *P.P.*, 40, 1968, 58-71.

533 **Nef**, J. U., 'English and French industry after 1540 in relation to the constitution'. In Conyers Read, ed., *The Constitution Reconsidered*, N. Y., 1938, 79-103.

534 **Sella**, D., *European Industries, 1500-1700*, 1970. Fontana Economic History of Europe, II, Section 5. Useful background.

535 **Thirsk**, Joan, 'Industries in the countryside'. In Fisher, ed. (1190), listed above, 70-88.

(b) INDUSTRIAL GROWTH

536 **Coleman**, D. C., 'Industrial growth and industrial revolutions', *Economica*, n.s., XXIII, 1956, 1-20.

537 **Nef**, J. U., 'The progress of technology and the growth of large-scale industry in Great Britain, 1540-1640', *Ec.H.R.*, V, 1934, 3-24. Reprinted in Carus-Wilson, ed. (245), listed above, I, 88-107. Presents the famous 'Industrial Revolution' thesis.

538 —— 'A comparison of industrial growth in France and England from 1540 to 1640', *J.Pol.Econ.*, XLIV, 1936, 289-317; 505-33; 643-66.

c) INDUSTRIAL ORGANISATION

Histories of individual companies are too numerous to list in full and only a selection is given here. The reader is referred to the following, which provides a comprehensive bibliography of the subject:

539 **Kahl**, W. F., *The Development of the London Livery Companies: a bibliographical essay*, 1960.

540 **Alford**, B. W. E. and Barker, T. C., *A History of the Carpenters' Company*, 1968.

541 **Bindoff**, S. T., 'The making of the Statute of Artificers'. In Bindoff, Hurstfield and Williams, (1167), listed above, 59-94.

1542 **Blagden**, C., *The Stationers' Company: A History, 1403-1959*, 1960. An interesting and well-documented study. Chapters I-II deal with the pre-1700 period.

1543 **Consitt**, F., *The London Weavers' Company, Vol. I: From the Twelfth Century to the Close of the Sixteenth*, 1933.

1544 **Fisher**, F. J., 'Some experiments in company organisation in the early seventeenth century', *Ec.H.R.*, IV, 1932-4, 177-94.

1545 **Foster**, E. R., 'The procedure of the House of Commons against Patents and Monopolies, 1621-24'. In Aiken and Henning eds. (2250), listed below, 57-87.

1546 **Kellett**, J. R., 'The break-down of gild and corporation control over the handicraft and retail trade in London' (in the seventeenth and eighteenth centuries), *Ec.H.R.*, 2nd ser., X, 1958, 381-94.

1547 **Kramer**, Stella, *The English Craft Gilds and the Government*, Columbia University Studies in History, Economics and Public Law, 23, N. Y., 1905.

1548 —— *The English Craft Gilds: Studies in Their Progress and Decline*, N. Y., 1927.

1549 **Marshall**, T. H., 'Capitalism and the decline of the English gilds', *Cambridge H. J.*, III, 1929, 23-33.

1550 **Ramsay**, G. D., 'Industrial laissez-faire and the policy of Cromwell', *Ec.H.R.*, XVI, 1946, 93-110.

1551 **Reddaway**, T. F., 'The Livery Companies of Tudor London', *Hist.*, LI, 1966, 287-99.

1552 —— 'The London Goldsmiths c. 1500', *T.R.H.S.*, 5th ser., XII, 1962, 49-62.

1553 **Thrupp**, Sylvia, *A Short History of the Worshipful Company of Bakers*, 1933.

1554 **Unwin**, G., *Industrial Organisation in the Sixteenth and Seventeenth Centuries*, 1904, new ed., 1957, with an introduction by T. S. Ashton.

1555 —— *The Gilds and Companies of London*, 1908. New ed., 1966.

1556 **Youings**, Joyce, *Tuckers Hall, Exeter: The History of a Provincial City Company Through Five Centuries*, 1968.

See also W. R. Scott (1777), listed below.

(d) INVESTMENT AND ENTREPRENEURSHIP

1557 **Coleman**, D. C., *Sir John Banks, Baronet and*

Businessman: A Study of Business, Politics and Society in Later Stuart England, 1963. Banks (1627-99) was one of the richest businessmen of his day.

1558 **Davies**, K. G., 'Joint stock investment in the later seventeenth century', *Ec.H.R.*, 2nd ser., IV, 1952, 283-301.

1559 **Davis**, R., 'The earnings of capital in the English shipping industry, 1670-1730', *J.Ec.H.*, XVII, 1957, 409-25.

1560 **Gough**, J. W., *Sir Hugh Myddleton: Entrepreneur and Engineer*, 1964. Not a biography of Myddleton (*c.* 1560-1631) but a study of aspects of his career including his part in the New River project.

1561 —— *The Rise of the Entrepreneur*, 1969. Somewhat old-fashioned in approach, but the book usefully gathers together much material on the subject.

1562 —— *The Superlative Prodigall: A Life of Thomas Bushell*, 1932. A case study of entrepreneurship.

1563 **Robertson**, H. M., 'Sir Bevis Bulmer, a large-scale speculator of Elizabethan and Jacobean times', *J.Ec.& Bus.H.*, 4, 1931, 99-120.

1564 **Stone**, L., 'The Nobility in business'. In *The Entrepreneur*, Cambridge, Mass., 1957, 14-21. See also Stone (2108), listed below.

(e) TEXTILES

1565 **Williams**, N. J., 'Two documents concerning the New Draperies', *Ec.H.R.*, 2nd ser., IV, 1952, 353-8.

1566 **Allison**, K. J., 'The Norfolk worsted industries in the sixteenth and seventeenth centuries. 1: The traditional industry', *Yorks.B.*, 12, 1960, 73-83.

1567 —— 'The Norfolk worsted industry in the sixteenth and seventeenth centuries. 2: The New Draperies', *Yorks.B.*, 13, 1961, 61-77.

1568 **Chapman**, S. D., 'The genesis of the British hosiery industry 1600-1750', *Textile H.*, III, 1972, 7-50.

1569 **Coleman**, D. C., 'An innovation and its diffusion: the New Draperies', *Ec.H.R.*, 2nd ser., XXII, 1969, 417-29.

1570 **Elliott**, G., 'The decline of the woollen trade in Cumberland, Westmorland and Northumberland in the late sixteenth century', *Trans.Cumb.& West.Antiq.&Arch.Soc.*, LXI, 1961, 112-19.

1571 **Heaton**, H., *The Yorkshire Woollen and Worsted Industries*, 1920, 2nd ed., 1965. The standard work.

1572 **James**, J., *History of the Worsted Manufactur[e] in England from the Earliest Times*, 1857. Reprinted 1968. Chapters 2-6 deal with the Middl[e] Ages and early modern period.

1573 **Lipson**, E., *The History of the Woollen an[d] Worsted Industries*, 1921. Reprinted 1965.

1574 **Lowe**, N., *The Lancashire Textile Industry i[n] the Sixteenth Century*, Chet.Soc., 3rd ser., 20, 1972.

1575 **Mann**, Julia de L., 'A Wiltshire family o[f] clothiers: George and Hester Wansey, 1683-1714', *Ec.H.R.*, 2nd ser., IX, 1956, 241-53.

1576 **Mendenhall**, T. C., *The Shrewsbury Draper[s] and the Welsh Wool Trade*, 1953.

1577 **Moir**, Esther A. L., 'Benedict Webb, clothier', *Ec.H.R.*, 2nd ser., X, 1957, 256-64.

1578 **Pilgrim**, J. E., 'The rise of the New Draperies i[n] Essex', *Birm.H.J.*, 7, 1959, 36-59.

1579 **Ramsay**, G. D., 'The distribution of the cloth industry in 1561-2', *E.H.R.*, LVII, 1942, 361-9[.]

1580 —— 'The report of the Royal Commission on th[e] clothing industry, 1640', *E.H.R.*, LVII, 1942, 482-93.

1581 —— *The Wiltshire Woollen Industry in th[e] Sixteenth and Seventeenth Centuries*, 1943.

1582 **Tann**, Jennifer, *Gloucestershire Woollen Mills*, 1967. The first three chapters are relevant to thi[s] period. The main part of the book consists of [a] gazetteer of woollen mills in the county.

1583 **Thirsk**, Joan, 'The fantastical folly of fashion the English stocking knitting industry 1500-1700'[.] In Harte and Ponting (3062), listed below, 50-73[.]

1584 **Wadsworth**, A. P. and Mann, Julia de L., *Th[e] Cotton Trade and Industrial Lancashire 1600-1780*, 1931. Reprinted 1965.

See also Bowden (1439), and Thirsk (1635), liste[d] above.

(f) COAL

1585 **Galloway**, R. L., *Annals of Coalmining an[d] the Coal Trade*, 1898, 1904, 2nd ed., with ne[w] introduction by B. F. Duckham, 1970.

1586 —— *A History of Coalmining in Great Br[i]tain*, 1882. Reprinted with bibliographical intr[o]duction by B. F. Duckham, 1969.

1587 **Hopkinson**, G. G., 'The development of th[e] South Yorkshire coalfield, 1500-1775', *Tran[s] Hunter Arch.Soc.*, VII, 1957, 295-319.

1588 **Langton**, J., *Geographical Change and Indus[]trial Revolution. Coalmining in South West La[n]cashire, 1590-1799*, 1979.

589 **Nef**, J. U., *The Rise of the British Coal Industry, 1550-1700*, 2 vols, 1932. Reprinted 1966. The standard work.

590 **Stone**, L., 'An Elizabethan coalmine', *Ec.H.R.*, 2nd ser., III, 1950-1, 97-106. Stone stresses the very modest scale of the undertaking and so questions Nef's claims for an Industrial Revolution in this period.

(g) METALS

591 **Collingwood**, W. G., *Elizabethan Keswick. Extracts from the Original Account Books, 1564-77, of the German Miners in the Archives of Augsburg*, Cumb.&West.Antiq.&Arch.Soc., Tract series, VIII, 1912.

592 **Crossley**, D. W., ed., *Sidney Iron Works Accounts, 1541-73*. Camden Soc., 4th ser., XV, 1975.

593 **France**, R. S. ed., *The Thieveley Lead Mines, 1629-1635*, Rec.Soc.Lancs.&Ches., CII, 1947.

594 **Hoover**, H. and L., eds., *Agricola: De Re Metallica* (1556), 1912.

595 **Schafer**, R. G., ed., *A Selection from the Records of Philip Foley's Stour Valley Ironworks, 1668-74*, Worcs.H.Soc., IX, 1978.

596 **Andrews**, C. B., *The Story of Wortley Iron Works: a record of its History, Traditions and eight centuries of Yorkshire Iron-Making*, 1950, 2nd rev. ed., 1956.

597 **Court**, W. H. B., *The Rise of the Midland Industries, 1600-1838*, 1938. Deals with coal, chemical and glass as well as metals.

598 **Crossley**, D. W., 'The management of a sixteenth-century iron works', *Ec.H.R.*, 2nd ser., XIX, 1966, 273-88.

599 **Donald**, M. B., *Elizabethan Copper*, 1955.

600 —— *Elizabethan Monopolies: The History of the Company of Mineral and Battery Works*, 1961.

601 **Fell**, A., *The Early Iron Industry of Furness and District: an historical and descriptive account from Earliest Times to the end of the eighteenth century*, 1908. Reprinted 1968.

602 **Flinn**, M. W., 'Sir Ambrose Crowley, ironmonger, 1658-1713', *Expl.Entrepren.H.*, V, 1953, 162-80.

603 —— 'The growth of the English iron industry, 1660-1760', *Ec.H.R.*, 2nd ser., XI, 1958, 144-53. Bibliography.

604 —— 'Timber and the advance of technology: a reconsideration', *Annals of Science*, XV, 1959, 109-20. Concludes that the so-called timber famine has been much exaggerated.

1605 **Gough**, J. W., *The Mines of Mendip*, 1930, rev. ed., 1967.

1606 **Hamilton**, H., *The English Brass and Copper Industries to 1800*, 1926. Reprinted with a bibliographical introduction by J. R. Harris, 1967.

1607 **Hammersley**, G., 'The charcoal iron industry and its fuel 1540-1750', *Ec.H.R.*, XXVI, 1973, 593-613.

1608 **Hopkinson**, G. G., 'The charcoal iron industry in the Sheffield region, 1588-1755', *Trans.Hunter Arch.Soc.*, VIII, 1961, 122-51.

1609 **Jenkins**, R., 'Notes on the early history of steelmaking in England', *Trans. Newcomen Soc.*, III, for 1922-3, 1924, 16-40.

1610 —— 'Copper smelting in England: revival at the end of the seventeenth century', *Trans. Newcomen Soc.*, XXIV, for 1943-5, 1949, 73-80.

1611 —— 'Ironfounding in England, 1490-1603', *Trans. Newcomen Soc.*, XIX, for 1938-9, 1940, 35-49.

1612 **Johnson**, B. L. C., 'The Stour Valley iron industry in the late seventeenth century', *Trans. Worcs.Arch.Soc.*, n.s., XXVII, 1950, 35-46.

1613 —— 'The Foley partnerships: the iron industry at the end of the Charcoal era', *Ec.H.R.*, 2nd ser., IV, 1952, 322-40.

1614 —— 'The Iron industry of Cheshire and North Staffordshire, 1688-1712', *Trans.North Staffs. Field Club*, LXXXVIII, 1953-4, 32-55.

1615 —— 'New light on the iron industry in the Forest of Dean', *Trans.Bristol and Gloucester Archaeological Society*, 72, for 1953, 1954, 129-43.

1616 **Lewis**, G. R., *The Stannaries: A Study of the English Tin Miner*, Harvard Economic Series, III, Cambridge, Mass., 1906. See also Hatcher (884), listed above.

1617 **Pelham**, R. A., 'The migration of the iron industry towards Birmingham during the sixteenth century', *Trans.Birm.Arch.Soc.*, 66, 1950, 192-9.

1618 —— 'The establishment of the Willoughby iron works in N. Warwickshire in the sixteenth century', *Birm.H. J.*, 4, 1953, 18-29.

1619 **Raistrick**, A. and Jennings, B., *A History of Leadmining in the Pennines*, 1965.

1620 **Rees**, W., *Industry before the Industrial Revolution*, 2 vols., 1968. Has chapters on coal and metal mining, on the Mines Royal and on the Mineral and Battery works.

1621 **Rowlands**, Marie B., *Masters and Men in the West Midland Metalware Trades before the*

Industrial Revolution, 1975. Usefully comple-
ments Court (1597) by concentrating on the western
part of the metalware region and explores the co-
existence of small-scale industry and agriculture in
this period.

1622 **Smith**, R. S., 'Sir Francis Willoughby's ironworks, 1570-1610', *Renaiss. & Mod.Studs.*, XI,
1967, 90-140.

1623 **Straker**, E., *Wealden Iron*, 1931. Reprinted
1969.

(h) SALT, LEATHER, PAPER AND GLASS

(i) SALT

1624 **Calvert**, A. F., *Salt in Cheshire*, 1915.

1625 **Chaloner**, W. H., 'Salt in Cheshire, 1600-1870',
T.L.C.A.S., LXXI, for 1961, 1963, 58-74.

1626 **Ellis**, Joyce, 'The decline and fall of the Tyneside salt industry, 1660-1710: a re-examination',
Ec.H.R., 2nd ser., XXXIII, 1980, 45-58.

1627 **Laver**, H., 'Salt works in Essex', *Essex R.*, LII,
1943, 184-8.

(ii) LEATHER

1628 **Clarkson**, L. A., 'English economic policy in the
sixteenth and seventeenth centuries: the case of the
leather industry', *B.I.H.R.*, 38, 1965, 149-62.

1629 —— 'The leather crafts in Tudor and Stuart
England', *Ag.H.R.*, XIV, 1966, 23-39.

1630 —— 'The organisation of the English leather
industry in the late sixteenth and seventeenth centuries', *Ec.H.R.*, 2nd ser., XIII, 1960, 245-56.

1631 **Woodward**, D. M., 'The Chester leather industry, 1558-1625', *T.H.S.L.C.*, 119, 1968, 65-112.

(iii) PAPER

1632 **Coleman**, D. C., *The British Paper Industry,
1495-1860: A study in industrial growth*, 1958.
The standard work on the subject.

1633 **Shorter**, A. H., *Paper Mills and Paper Makers in England 1495-1800*, Hilversum, 1957.
Chapter 1 deals with the period 1495-1700. A full
list of known paper mills is given.

(iv) GLASS

1634 **Crossley**, D. W., 'The performance of the glass
industry in sixteenth-century England', *Ec.H.R.*,
XXV, 1972, 421-33.

1635 **Godfrey**, Eleanor S., *The Development of
English Glassmaking, 1560-1640*, 1975.

1636 **Kenyon**, G. H., *The Glass Industry of the
Weald*, 1967.

1637 **Smith**, R. S., 'Glass-making at Wollaton in the

early seventeenth century', *Trans. Thoroton Soc.*,
LXVI, 1963, 24-34.

(i) SHIPPING

1638 **Albion**, R. G., *Forests and Sea Power: The
Timber problem of the Royal Navy, 1652-1862*,
Harvard Economic Studies, 29, Cambridge, Mass.,
1926.

1639 **Barbour**, V., 'Dutch and English merchant
shipping in the seventeenth century', *Ec.H.R.*, II,
1930, 261-90. Reprinted in Carus-Wilson, ed.
(245), listed above, I, 227-53.

1640 **Burwash**, Dorothy, *English Merchant Shipping, 1460-1540*, Toronto, 1947. Reprinted 1969.

1641 **Coleman**, D. C., 'The naval dockyards under
the later Stuarts', *Ec.H.R.*, 2nd ser., VI, 1953,
134-155.

1642 **Davis**, R., *The Rise of the English Shipping
Industry in the Seventeenth and Eighteenth Centuries*, 1962. The standard work.

1643 **Lane**, F. C., 'Tonnages, medieval and modern',
Ec.H.R., 2nd ser., XVII, 1964, 213-33.

1644 **Scammell**, G. V., 'Ship-owning in England,
1450-1550', *T.R.H.S.*, 5th ser., XII, 1962, 105-22.

1645 —— 'English merchant shipping at the end of
the Middle Ages: some East Coast evidence',
Ec.H.R., 2nd ser., XIII, 1960-1, 327-41.

(j) MISCELLANEOUS

1646 **Cheke**, V., *The Story of Cheesemaking in Britain*, 1959.

1647 **Cutting**, C. L., *Fish Saving: A History of
Fish Processing from Ancient to Modern Times*,
1955.

1648 **Jones**, S. R. H., 'The development of needle
manufacturing in the West Midlands before 1750',
Ec.H.R., 2nd ser., XXXi, 1978, 354-68.

1649 **Lloyd**, G. I. H., *The Cutlery Trades: an Historical Essay in the Economics of Small-scale
Production*, 1913. Reprinted 1968.

1650 **Rowlands**, Marie B., 'Industry and Social
change in Staffordshire, 1660-1760', *Lichfield and
S.Staffs.Arch. and H.Soc.*, IX, 1967-8, 37-58.

1651 **Singer**, C. J., *The Earliest Chemical Industry,
an Essay in the Historical Relations of Economics and Technology Illustrated from the Alum
Trade*, 1948. For developments in England, see
182-202.

1652 **Tomlinson**, H., *Guns and Government. The
Ordnance Office under the Later Stuarts*, 1979.
See also Salzman (894), listed above, on the build-
ing industry, and Brace (3404), listed below.

TOWNS

Urban history has a voluminous literature. For a comprehensive guide to older histories of towns, see Gross (577), and Martin and MacIntyre (578), listed above.

(a) GENERAL

653 **Abrams**, P. and Wrigley, E. A., eds., *Towns in Societies. Essays in Economic History and Historical Sociology*, 1978. A highly miscellaneous collection of essays extending from ancient times to 1914. Three are specifically concerned with England in the medieval and early modern periods. There is a general introduction to the theories and problems of the relationship between towns and economic growth and a consolidated bibliography.

654 **Borsay**, P., 'Culture, status and the English urban landscape', *Hist.*, LXVII, 1982, 1-12.

655 —— 'The English urban renaissance: the development of provincial urban culture, c.1680-1760', *Soc.H.*, V, 1977, 581-603.

656 **Clark**, P., ed., *Country Towns in Pre-Industrial England*, 1981. Comprises case studies of Warwick, Ipswich, Winchester and Bath.

657 —— *The Early Modern Town: A Reader*, 1976. A collection of reprinted articles with a substantial introduction.

658 —— and Slack, P., eds., *Crisis and Order in English Towns, 1500-1700: Essays in Urban History*, 1971.

659 —— *English Towns in Transition, 1500-1700*, 1976.

660 **Cornwall**, J., 'English country towns in the 1520s', *Ec.H.R.*, 2nd ser., XV, 1962, 54-69.

661 **Dodd**, A. H., 'Elizabethan towns and cities', *H.Today*, 11, 1961, 136-44.

662 **Dyer**, A. D., 'Growth and decay in English towns, 1500-1700', *Urban H.Yearbook*, 1979, 60-72.

663 **Everitt**, A. M., ed., *Perspectives on English Urban History*, 1973. An interesting collection of essays, including one by the editor on 'The English urban inn, 1560-1760'.

664 **Hoskins**, W. G., 'English provincial towns in the early sixteenth century', *T.R.H.S.*, 5th ser., VI, 1956, 1-19. Reprinted in Hoskins (1246), listed above, 68-85.

665 **Langton**, J., 'Residential patterns in pre-industrial cities: some case studies from seventeenth-century Britain', *T.I.B.G.*, LXV, 1975, 1-27.

1666 **MacInness**, A., *The English Town, 1660-1760*, 1980. Hist.Ass. pamphlet.

1667 **Patten**, J., *English Towns, 1500-1700*, 1978. A geographical approach.

See also Dyos (3791), listed below.

(b) SPECIALISED STUDIES

1668 **Martin**, G. H., ed., *The Royal Charters of Grantham, 1463-1688*, 1963.

1669 **Riden**, P. and Blair, J., eds., *History of Chesterfield. V: Records of the Borough of Chesterfield and Related Documents 1204-1835*, 1980.

1670 **Atkinson**, T., *Elizabethan Winchester*, 1963.

1671 **Brett-James**, N. G., *The Growth of Stuart London*, 1935.

1672 **Clemens**, P. G. E., 'The rise of Liverpool, 1665-1750', *Ec.H.R.*, 2nd ser., XXIX, 1976, 211-25.

1673 **Cook**, A. J., *The Privileged Playgoers of Shakespeare's London, 1576-1642*, Princeton, 1981.

1674 **Davies**, C. Stella, ed., *A History of Macclesfield*, 1961.

1675 **Dickens**, A. G., 'Tudor York'. In *V.C.H.Yorks. The City of York*, ed. P. M. Tillott, 1961, 117-59. See also Forster (1683), listed below.

1676 **Dyer**, A. D., *The City of Worcester in the Sixteenth Century*, 1973.

1677 —— 'The market towns of southern England, 1500-1700', *Southern H.*, I, 1979, 123-34.

1678 —— 'Warwickshire towns under the Tudors and Stuarts', *Warwicks.H.*, III, 1977, 122-34.

1679 **Edie**, C. A., 'New buildings, new taxes and old interests: an urban problem of the 1670s', *J.Brit.Studs.*, VI, 1967, 35-63.

1680 **Evans**, J. T., *Seventeenth-Century Norwich. Politics, Religion and Government, 1620-90*, 1979.

1681 **Fisher**, F. J., 'The development of London as a centre of conspicuous consumption in the sixteenth and seventeenth centuries', *T.R.H.S.*, 4th ser., XXX, 1948, 37-50. Reprinted in Carus-Wilson, ed. (245), listed above, II, 197-207.

1682 —— 'The growth of London', in Ives (2286), listed below, 76-86. See also Fisher's article on the London food market (245), and Wrigley (1707), listed below.

1683 **Forster**, G. C. F., 'York in the seventeenth century'. In *V.C.H. Yorks. The City of York*, ed. P. M. Tillott, 1961, 160-206. See also Dickens (1675), listed above.

1684 **Foster**, F., *The Politics of Stability. A Portrait of the Rulers in Elizabethan London*, 1977.

1685 **François**, Martha E., 'The social and economic development of Halifax, 1558-1640', *Proc.Leeds Phil. and Lit.Soc.*, XI, 1966, 217-80.

1686 **Gill**, C., *History of Birmingham I: Manor and Borough to 1865*, 1952.

1687 **Hill**, J. W. F., *Tudor and Stuart Lincoln*, 1956.

1688 **Holmes**, M., *Elizabethan London*, 1969.

1689 **Hoskins**, W. G., 'An Elizabethan provincial town: Leicester'. In J. H. Plumb, ed., *Studies in Social History*, 1955, 33-67. Reprinted in Hoskins (1246), listed above, 86-114.

1690 **Kerridge**, E., 'Social and economic history of Leicester, 1509-1660'. In *V.C.H., Leics.*, ed. W. G. Hoskins and R. I. McKinley, IV, 1958, 76-109.

1691 **MacCaffrey**, W. T., *Exeter, 1540-1640: The Growth of an English County Town*, Cambridge, Mass., 1958.

1692 **Marshall**, J. D., 'Kendal in the late seventeenth and eighteenth centuries', *Trans.Cumb.& West.Antiq.& Arch.Soc.*, LXXV, 1975, 186-257. Surveys the demographic structure and economic development of the town through this period.

1693 **Myers**, A. R., 'Tudor Chester', *J.Chester Arch.Soc.*, LXIII, 1980, 43-57.

1694 **Palliser**, D. M., *Tudor York*, 1980. Explores the process of decline and recovery in the sixteenth century and analyses the demographic and occupational structure of the city, the distribution of wealth, and the ruling élite.

1695 **Pearl**, Valerie, 'Change and stability in seventeenth-century London', *London J.*, V, 1979, 3-34.

1696 **Pound**, J. F., 'The social and trade structure of Norwich, 1525-75', *P.P.*, 34, 1966, 49-69.

1697 **Reddaway**, T. F., *The Rebuilding of London after the Great Fire*, 1940. Reprinted 1951.

1698 **Rimmer**, W. G., 'The evolution of Leeds to 1700', *Thoresby Society*, 50, Part 2, 1967, 91-129.

1699 **Ripley**, P., 'The economy of the city of Gloucester, 1660-1740', *Trans.Bristol & Gloucs.Arch.Soc.*, XCVIII, 1981, 135-53.

1700 **Roy**, I. and Porter, S., 'The social and economic structure of an early modern suburb: the tithing at Worcester', *B.I.H.R.*, LIII, 1980, 203-17.

1701 **Stephens**, W. B., *Seventeenth-Century Exeter: A Study in Industrial and Commercial Development, 1625-88*, 1958.

1702 —— ed., *A History of Congleton*, 1970.

1703 **Stone**, L., 'The residential development of the West End of London in the seventeenth century', in Barbara C. Malament, ed., *After the Reformation: Essays in Honour of J. H. Hexter*, 1981, 167-212.

1704 **Thirsk**, Joan, 'Stamford in the sixteenth and seventeenth centuries'. In A. Rogers, ed., *The Making of Stamford*, 1965, 58-76.

1705 **Willan**, T. S., *Elizabethan Manchester*, Chet. Soc., 3rd ser., XXVII, 1980. Based principally on wills, inventories and the records of the Court Leet. Particularly strong on the trading and industrial activities of the town.

1706 **Woodhead**, J. R., *The Rulers of London 1660-1689: a Biographical Record of the Aldermen and Common Councilmen of the City of London*, London and Middx.Arch.Soc., 1966.

1707 **Wrigley**, E. A., 'A simple model of London's importance in changing English society and economy, 1650-1750', *P.P.*, 37, 1967, 44-70. An important article.

See also Redford on Manchester (3867), listed below.

ALIEN IMMIGRANTS

(a) DUTCH, HUGUENOTS, GERMANS AND ITALIANS

1708 **Cross**, F. W., ed., *History of the Walloon and Huguenot Church at Canterbury*, Hug.Soc., 1898.

1709 **Kirk**, R. E. G. and E. F., eds., *Returns of Aliens Dwelling in the City and Suburbs of London from the Reign of Henry VIII to that of James I*, Hug.Soc., 4 vols., 1900-1908.

1710 **Moens**, W. J. C., ed., *The Walloons and their Church at Norwich: Their History and Registers 1565-1832*, Hug.Soc., 1888.

1711 —— *Register of Baptisms in the Dutch Church at Colchester from 1645 to 1728*, Hug.Soc., 1905.

712 **Carter**, Alice C., 'The Huguenot contribution to the early years of the Funded Debt, 1694-1714', *Proc.Hug.Soc.*, XIX, 1955, 21-41.

713 **Chitty**, C. W., 'Aliens in England in the sixteenth century', *Race*, VIII, 1966, 129-45.

714 —— 'Aliens in England in the seventeenth century to 1660', *Race* XI, 1969, 189-201.

715 **Coleman**, D. C., 'The early British paper industry and the Huguenots', *Proc.Hug.Soc.*, XIX, 1959, 210-25.

716 **Cunningham**, W., *Alien Immigrants to England*, 1897. Reprinted with a new introduction by C. Wilson, 1969. The best general survey of the period from the late fifteenth to the eighteenth century. The opening and closing sections of the book, however, are less valuable.

717 **Girouard**, M., 'Some alien craftsmen in sixteenth- and seventeenth-century England', *Proc.Hug.Soc.*, XX, 1959, 26-35.

718 **Gwynn**, R. D., 'The arrival of the Huguenot refugees in England, 1680-1705', *Proc.Hug.Soc.*, XXI, for 1969, 1970, 404-36.

719 **Hayward**, J. F., 'The Huguenot gunmakers of London', *Proc.Hug.Soc.*, XX, 1963-4, 649-63.

720 **Holmes**, M., 'Evil May Day 1517: the story of a riot', *H.Today*, 15, 1965, 642-50.

721 **Le Fanu**, W. R., 'Huguenot refugee doctors in England', *Proc.Hug.Soc.*, XIX, 1956, 113-27.

722 **Morant**, Valerie, 'The settlement of Protestant refugees in Maidstone during the sixteenth century', *Ec.H.R.*, 2nd ser., IV, 1951, 210-14.

723 **Murray**, J. J., 'The cultural impact of the Flemish Low Countries on sixteenth and seventeenth-century England', *A.H.R.*, LXII, 1957, 837-54.

724 **Ramsay**, G. D., 'The undoing of the Italian mercantile colony in sixteenth-century London' in Harte and Ponting (3062), 22-49.

725 **Ransome**, D. R., 'The struggle of the Glaziers' Company with foreign glaziers, 1500-1550', *Guildhall Miscellany*, II, 1960, 12-20.

726 **Rye**, W. B., *The Dutch Refugees in Norwich*, 1887.

727 **Scouloudi**, Irene, 'Alien immigration into and alien communities in London, 1558-1640', *Proc.Hug.Soc.*, XVI, 1938, 27-49.

728 **Scoville**, W. C., 'The Huguenots and the diffusion of technology', *J.Pol.Econ.*, LX, 1952, 294-311, 392-411.

729 **Shears**, P. J., 'Huguenot connections with the clockmaking trade in England', *Proc.Hug.Soc.*, XX, 1960, 158-76.

730 **Sheppard**, F. H. W., 'The Huguenots in Spitalfields and Soho', *Proc.Hug.Soc.*, XXI, 1969, 355-65.

731 **Taube**, E., 'German craftsmen in Tudor England', *Ec.J.Ec.H.Supp.*, 3, 1939, 167-78.

732 **Williams**, L., 'Alien immigrants in relation to industry and society in Tudor England', *Proc.Hug.Soc.*, XIX, 1956, 146-69.

733 —— 'The crown and the provincial immigrant communities in Elizabethan England' in H. Hearder and H. Loyn, eds., *British Government and Administration*, 1974, 117-31.

734 **Wyatt**, T., 'Aliens in England before the Huguenots', *Proc.Hug.Soc.*, XIX, 1953, 74-94. See also Consitt (1543), listed above, 33-60, on the Flemish weavers.

(b) JEWS

1735 **Giuseppi**, J. A., 'Sephardic Jews and the early years of the Bank of England', *Trans. Jewish H.Soc.*, XIX, 1960, 53-64.

1736 **Hyamson**, A. M., *The Sephardim of England: a History of the Spanish and Portuguese Jewish Community, 1492-1951*, 1951.

1737 **Osterman**, N., 'The controversy over the proposed readmission of the Jews to England (1655)', *Jewish Soc.Studs.*, III, 1941, 301-28.

1738 **Rubens**, A., 'Portrait of Anglo-Jewry, 1656-1836. 1: The Anglo-Jewish community, source material', *Trans. Jewish H.Soc.*, XIX, 1960, 13-52.

1739 **Samuel**, E. R., 'Portuguese Jews in Jacobean London', *Trans. Jewish H.Soc.*, XVIII, sessions 1953-5, 1958, 171-230.

1740 **Wolf**, L., 'The Jews in Tudor England'. In C. Roth, ed., *Essays in Jewish History*, 1934, 73-90. See also Roth (638), listed above.

COMMERCE AND COLONISATION

1741 **McCulloch**, J. R., ed., *Early English Tracts on Commerce*, 1856. Reprinted 1952. A very valuable collection which includes Lewes Roberts' *The Treasure of Traffike; or, A Discourse of For-*

raigne Trade (1641) and Thomas Mun's *England's Treasure by Forraign Trade* (1664).

1742 **Willan**, T. S., ed., *A Tudor Book of Rates*, 1962.

For other documentary material on this subject, see Bland, Brown and Tawney (211), and Tawney and Power, (1156), II, 1-89, listed above.

(a) GENERAL WORKS

1743 **Bindoff**, S. T., 'The greatness of Antwerp'. In G. R. Elton, ed., *New Cambridge Modern History*, II, 1958, 50-69.

1744 **Bridenbaugh**, C. and Roberta, *No Peace Beyond the Line: The English and the Carribean 1624-1690*, 1972.

1745 **Connell-Smith**, G., *Forerunners of Drake: A Study of English Trade With Spain in the Early Tudor Period*, 1954.

1746 **Cottrell**, P. L. and Aldcroft, D. H., *Shipping, Trade and Commerce. Essays in Memory of Ralph Davis*, 1981. A miscellaneous collection dealing with trade in the Baltic, with Portugal and with Asia, and with shipping and shipbuilding in England and Scotland.

1747 **Davis**, R., *English Overseas Trade 1500-1700*, 1973.

1748 —— 'English foreign trade, 1660-1700', *Ec.H.R.*, 2nd ser., VII, 1954, 150-166. Reprinted in Minchinton (1757), listed below, 99-120.

1749 —— *A Commercial Revolution: English Overseas Trade in the seventeenth and eighteenth Centuries*, Hist.Ass. pamphlet, 1967. A valuable short survey.

1750 **Fisher**, F. J., 'London's export trade in the early seventeenth century', *Ec.H.R.*, 2nd ser., III, 1950, 151-61. Reprinted in Minchinton (1757), listed below, 64-77.

1751 —— 'Commercial trends and policy in sixteenth-century England', *Ec.H.R.*, X, 1940, 95-117. Reprinted in Carus-Wilson, ed., (245), listed above, I, 152-72. A valuable article.

1752 **Friis**, Astrid, *Alderman Cockayne's Project: the commercial policy of England in its main aspects, 1603-25*, Copenhagen, 1927. A useful book. The wider subtitle is justified.

1753 **Gould**, J. D., 'Cloth exports, 1600-1640', *Ec.H.R.*, 2nd ser., XXIV, 1971, 249-52. A comment on W. B. Stephens's article (1763), listed below. See also Stephens's rejoinder, *ibid.*, 253-7.

1754 **Harper**, L. A., *The English Navigation Laws*, N. Y., 1939.

1755 **Kepler**, J. S., 'Fiscal aspects of the English carrying trade during the Thirty Years War', *Ec.H.R.*, 2nd ser., XXV, 1972, 261-83.

1756 **McLachlan**, Jean M. O., *Trade and Peace with Old Spain, 1607-1750*, 1940.

1757 **Minchinton**, W. E., ed., *The Growth of English Overseas Trade in the Seventeenth and Eighteenth Centuries*, 1969. A collection of reprinted articles with a valuable introduction and critical bibliography.

1758 **Price**, J. M., 'Multilateralism and/or bilateralism. The settlement of English trade balance with "the North" c. 1700', *Ec.H.R.*, 2nd ser., XIV, 1961, 254-74.

1759 **Priestley**, M., 'Anglo-French trade and the "unfavourable balance" controversy, 1660-1685', *Ec.H.R.*, 2nd ser., IV, 1951, 37-52.

1760 **Rabb**, T. K., *Enterprise and Empire: Merchant and Gentry investment in the expansion of England, 1575-1630*, Cambridge, Mass., 1967. A computer-based study. Good bibliography.

1761 **Ramsay**, G. D., *English Overseas Trade during the Centuries of Emergence*, 1957. A good survey.

1762 **Ramsey**, P., 'Overseas trade in the reign of Henry VII: the evidence of customs accounts', *Ec.H.R.*, 2nd ser., VI, 1953, 173-82.

1763 **Stephens**, W. B., 'The cloth exports of the provincial ports, 1600-1640', *Ec.H.R.*, 2nd ser., XXII, 1969, 228-48.

1764 **Stone**, L., 'Elizabethan overseas trade', *Ec.H.R.*, 2nd ser., II, 1949, 30-58.

1765 **Supple**, B. E., *Commercial Crisis and Change in England 1600-1642: A Study in the Instability of a Mercantile Economy*, 1959. A very important contribution to seventeenth-century English economic and social history.

1766 **Taylor**, H., 'Trade neutrality and the "English road", 1630-1648', *Ec.H.R.*, 2nd ser., XXV, 1972, 236-60.

1767 **Waters**, D. W., *The Art of Navigation in England in Elizabethan and Early Stuart Times*, 1958.

1768 **Willan**, T. S., *Studies in Elizabethan Foreign Trade*, 1959. An important collection of essays particularly useful for English trade with Morocco. See also Carus-Wilson and Coleman (928), listed above.

(b) ENGLAND AND THE AGE OF DISCOVERY

Many contemporary accounts of voyages of discovery

have been published in modern editions. The reader is referred to the publications of the Hakluyt Society, London.

1769 **Cipolla**, C. M., *Guns and Sails in the Early Phase of European Expansion, 1400-1700*, 1966. A general survey of the European background.

1770 **Parry**, J. H., *The Age of Reconnaissance*, 1963. The best general introduction.

1771 **Scammell**, G. V., 'The New Worlds and Europe in the sixteenth century', *H.J.*, XII, 1969, 389-412.

1772 **Williamson**, J. A., *A Short History of British Expansion*, 1945.

1773 —— *Maritime Enterprise, 1485-1558*, 1913.

(c) TRADING COMPANIES AND THEIR ORGANISATION

1774 **Carr**, C. T., ed., *Select Charters of Trading Companies, 1530-1707*, Selden Soc., XXVIII, 1913. A very useful collection which includes the charters of the Levant, Newfoundland and African Companies (1600, 1610 and 1618 respectively), and also the charters of major industrial undertakings.

1775 **Rich**, E. E., ed., *Hudson's Bay Company Minutes (1671-84)*, 3 vols., 1942-60.

1776 **Davies**, K. G., 'Joint stock investment in the late seventeenth century', *Ec.H.R.*, 2nd ser., IV, 1952, 283-301. Reprinted in Carus-Wilson, ed. (245), listed above, II, 273-90.

1777 **Scott**, W. R., *The Constitution and Finance of English, Scottish and Irish Joint Stock Companies to 1720*, 3 vols., 1910-12. The scope of the work is as follows: volume 1 deals with the general development of the joint stock system to 1720; volume 2 surveys companies for foreign trade, colonization, fishing and mining; volume 3 covers water supply, postal arrangements, street lighting, manufacturing, banking, finance and insurance.

(i) THE MERCHANT ADVENTURERS

1778 **Lingelbach**, W. E., ed., *The Merchant Adventurers of England: Their Laws and Ordinances, With Other Documents*, Philadelphia, 1902.

1779 **McGrath**, P. V., ed., *Records Relating to the Society of Merchant Venturers of Bristol in the Seventeenth Century*, Bristol Rec.Soc., XVII, 1952.

1780 **Wheeler**, J. A., *Treatise of Commerce* (1601), ed. G. B. Hotchkiss, N. Y., 1931. Designed as a defence of the Merchant Adventurers' Company.

1781 **Lingelbach**, W. E., 'The internal organisation of the Merchant Adventurers of England', *T.R.H.S.*, 2nd ser., XVI, 1902, 19-67.

1782 **McGrath**, P. V., *The Merchant Venturers of Bristol*, 1975.

1783 **Unwin**, G., 'The Merchant Adventurers' Company in the reign of Elizabeth'. In Unwin (185), listed above, 133-220.

(ii) THE RUSSIA COMPANY

1784 **Willan**, T. S., *The Muscovy Merchants of 1555*, 1953.

1785 —— *The Early History of the Russia Company, 1553-1603*, 1956. The standard works on the subject.

(iii) THE EASTLAND COMPANY AND TRADE WITH THE BALTIC

1786 **Sellers**, Maud, ed., *The Acts and Ordinances of the Eastland Company of York*, Camden Soc., 3rd ser., XI, 1906.

1787 **Aström**, S. E., *From Stockholm to St. Petersburg: Commercial Factors in the Political Relations between England and Sweden, 1675-1700*, Finnish H.Soc., Studia Historica, II, Helsinki, 1962.

1788 —— *From Cloth to Iron. The Anglo-Baltic Trade in the Late Seventeenth Century. Part One: The Growth, Structure and Organisation of the Trade*, Helsinki, 1963.

1789 —— *From Cloth to Iron: The Anglo-Baltic Trade in the Late Seventeenth Century. Part Two*, Helsinki, 1965.

1790 —— 'The English Navigation Laws and the Baltic trade 1660-1700', *Scand. Ec.H.R.*, VIII, 1960, 3-18.

1791 **Deardorff**, N. R., 'English trade in the Baltic during the reign of Elizabeth', in *Studies in the History of English Commerce in the Tudor Period*, N. Y., 1912.

1792 **Fedorowicz**, J. K., *England's Baltic Trade in the Early Seventeenth Century. A Study in Anglo-Polish Commercial Relations*, 1979.

1793 **Hinton**, R. W. K., *The Eastland Trade and the Commonwealth in the Seventeenth Century*, 1959. The main work on England's trade with the Baltic. See the review article by R. H. Tawney, *Ec.H.R.*, 2nd ser., XII, 1959, 280-82.

1794 **Zins**, H., *England and the Baltic in the Elizabethan Era*, 1972.

(iv) THE LEVANT

1795 **Davis**, R., 'England and the Mediterranean,

1570-1670', in Fisher, ed. (1190), listed above, 117 37.

1796 **Foster**, W., *England's Quest of Eastern Trade*, 1933.

1797 **Horniker**, A. L., 'Anglo-French rivalry in the Levant from 1583 to 1612', *J.M.H.*, XVIII, 1946, 289-305.

1798 **Skilliter**, Susan A., *William Harborne and the Trade with Turkey, 1578-82. A Documentary Study of the first Anglo-Ottoman Relations*, 1977.

1799 **Willan**, T. S., 'Some aspects of English trade with the Levant in the sixteenth century', *E.H.R.*, LXX, 1955, 399-410.

1800 **Wood**, A. C., *A History of the Levant Company*, 1935. Reprinted 1964.

(v) THE EAST INDIA COMPANY

1801 **Stevens**, H., ed., *The Dawn of British Trade to the East Indies as Recorded in the Minutes of the East India Company, 1599-1603*, 1886.

1802 **Bassett**, D. K., 'The trade of the East India Company in the Far East, 1623-1684', *J.Royal Asiatic Society*, 1960, 32-47.

1803 **Chaudhuri**, K. N., *The English East India Company: The Study of an Early Joint Stock Company, 1600-1640*, 1965.

1804 —— *The Trading World of Asia and the English East India Company 1660-1760*, 1978.

1805 —— 'Treasure and trade balances: the East India Company's export trade', *Ec.H.R.*, 2nd ser., XXI, 1968, 480-502.

1806 **Krishna**, B., *Commercial Relations Between India and England, 1601-1757*, 1924.

1807 **Thomas**, P. J., *Mercantilism and the East India Trade*, 1926. Reprinted 1963.

(vi) MISCELLANEOUS

1808 **Davies**, K. G., *The Royal Africa Company*, 1957.

1809 **Preston**, R. A., 'The Laconia Company of 1629: an English attempt to intercept the fur trade', *Canadian H.R.*, XXXI, 1950, 125-44.

1810 **Rich**, E.E., *The History of the Hudson's Bay Company I: 1670-1763*, Hudson's Bay Rec.Soc., 1958.

1811 **Robbins**, W. G., 'The Massachusetts Bay Company: an analysis of motives', *Historian*, XXXII, 1969, 83-98. See also Rose-Troup (1843), listed below.

(d) THE MERCANTILE COMMUNITY

1812 **Ramsay**, G. D., ed., *John Isham: Mercer and Merchant Adventurer. Two Account Books of a London Merchant in the Reign of Elizabeth I*, Northants.Rec.Soc., XXI, 1962.

1813 **Dodd**, A. H., 'Mr Myddleton, the merchant of Tower St.'. In Bindoff, Hurstfield and Williams, eds., (1167), listed above, 249-81.

1814 **Grassby**, R., 'The personal wealth of the business community in seventeenth-century England', *Ec.H.R.*, 2nd ser., XXIII, 1970, 220-34.

1815 —— 'English merchant capitalism in the late seventeenth century: the composition of business fortunes', *P.P.*, 46, 1970, 87-107.

1816 **Hoskins**, W. G., 'The Elizabethan merchants of Exeter'. In Bindoff, Hurstfield and Williams, eds., (1167), listed above, 163-87.

1817 **Lang**, R. G., 'Social origins and social aspirations of Jacobean London merchants', *Ec.H.R.*, 2nd ser., XXVII, 1974, 28-47.

1818 **Ramsey**, P., 'Some Tudor merchants' accounts'. In A. C. Littleton and B. S. Yamey, eds., *Studies in the History of Accounting*, Homewood, Ill., 1956, 185-201.

1819 **Webb**, J., *Great Tooley of Ipswich: A Portrait of an Early Tudor Merchant*, Suffolk Rec.Soc., 1963.

1820 **Winchester**, Barbara, *Tudor Family Portrait*, 1955.

(e) ANGLO-DUTCH COMMERCIAL RELATIONS

1821 **Boxer**, C. R., *The Dutch Seaborne Empire, 1600-1800*, 1965.

1822 —— 'Some second thoughts on the third Anglo-Dutch War, 1672-74', *T.R.H.S.*, 5th ser., XIX, 1969, 67-94.

1823 **Clark**, G. N., *The Dutch Alliance and the War Against French Trade, 1688-1697*, 1923.

1824 **Farnell**, J. E., 'The Navigation Act of 1651, the first Dutch War and the London merchant community', *Ec.H.R.*, 2nd ser., XVI, 1964, 439-54.

1825 **Wilson**, C., *Profit and Power: A Study of England and the Dutch Wars*, 1957. The main work on the subject. For eighteenth-century developments in Anglo-Dutch relations, see (1231), listed above, by the same author.

1826 —— 'Cloth production and international competition in the seventeenth century', *Ec.H.R.*, 2nd ser., XIII, 1960, 209-21. See also Barbour (1639), listed above.

(f) COASTAL TRADE

1827 **Smith**, R. A., *Sea Coal for London: History of the Coal Factors in the London Market*, 1961. Nef (1589), listed above, is also useful on this aspect.
1828 **Willan**, T. S., *The English Coasting Trade, 1600-1750*, 1938. Reprinted with new preface, 1967. The standard work.

(g) SMUGGLING

1829 **Ramsay**, G. D., 'The smugglers' trade: a neglected aspect of English commercial development', *T.R.H.S.*, 5th ser., II, 1952, 131-57.
1830 **Rive**, A., 'A short history of tobacco smuggling', *Ec. J.Ec.H.Supp.*, I, 1929, 554-69.
See also Williams (964), listed above.

(h) COLONIES

1831 **Allen**, D. G., *In English Ways. The Movement of Societies and the Transferal of English Local Law and Custom to Massachusetts Bay in the Seventeenth Century*, Chapel Hill, N. C., 1981.
1832 **Andrews**, C. M., *The Colonial Period of American History*, 4 vols., 1934.
1833 —— *British Committees, Commissions and Councils of Trade and Plantations, 1622-1675*, Baltimore, 1908.
1834 **Bailyn**, B., *The New England Merchants in the Seventeenth Century*, Harvard, Mass., 1955.
1835 **Cell**, G. T., 'The Newfoundland Company: a study of subscribers to a colonizing venture', *William and Mary Quarterly*, XXII, 1965, 611-25.
1836 **Gillespie**, J. E., *The Influence of Overseas Expansion on England to 1700*, Columbia University Studies in History, Economics and Public Law, N. Y., 1920.
1837 **Knorr**, K. E., *British Colonial Theories, 1570-1850*, 1944. Reprinted 1963.
1838 **Lucas**, C. P., *Religion, Colonising and Trade: The Driving Forces of the Old Empire*, 1930.
1839 **Newton**, A. P., *The European Nations in the West Indies*, 1933.
1840 **Quinn**, D. B., 'The first Pilgrims', *William and Mary Quarterly*, 3rd ser., XXIII, 1966, 359-90.
1841 —— 'The failure of Raleigh's American colonies'. In H. A. Cronne, T. W. Moody and D. B. Quinn, eds., *Essays in British and Irish History in Honour of James Eadie Todd*, 1949, 61-85.

1842 **Rose**, J. H., Newton, A. P. and Benians, E. A., eds., *Cambridge History of the British Empire I: The Old Empire from the Beginnings to 1783*, 1929.
1843 **Rose-Troup**, Frances, *The Massachusetts Bay Company and its Predecessors*, 1930.
1844 **Rowse**, A. L., *The Elizabethans and Americans*, 1959.
1845 **Wright**, L. B., *Religion and Empire: The Alliance Between Piety and Commerce in English Expansion, 1558-1625*, Chapel Hill N. C., 1943.

(i) MISCELLANEOUS

1846 **Hinton**, R. W. K., ed., *The Port Books of Boston, 1601-1640*, Lincs.Rec.Soc., L, 1956.
1847 **Vanes**, Jean, ed., *Documents Illustrating the Overseas Trade of Bristol in the Sixteenth Century*, Bristol Rec.Soc., XXI, 1979.
1848 **Jarvis**, R. C., 'Sources for the history of ports', *J.Trans.H.*, III, 1957-8, 76-93.
1849 **Andrews**, K. R., *Elizabethan Privateering. English Privateering During the Spanish War, 1585-1603*, 1964.
1850 **Ashton**, R., 'The parliamentary agitation for free trade in the opening years of the reign of James I', *P.P.*, 38, 1967, 40-55.
1851 **Croft**, Pauline, 'Free trade and the House of Commons 1605-1606', *Ec.H.R.*, 2nd ser., XXVIII, 1975, 17-27.
1852 **Cullen**, L. M., *Anglo-Irish Trade, 1660-1800*, 1968. Extensive bibliography, 221-42. See also Longfield (1866), listed below.
1853 **Davis**, R., *The Trade and Shipping of Hull, 1500-1700*, East Yorks.Loc.H.Soc., pamphlet series, 17, 1964.
1854 **Edler**, F., 'Winchcombe kerseys in Antwerp, 1538-44', *Ec.H.R.*, VII, 1936, 57-62.
1855 **Gould**, J. D., 'The crisis in the export trade, 1586-7', *E.H.R.*, LXXI, 1956, 212-22.
1856 —— 'The trade depression of the early 1620s', *Ec.H.R.*, 2nd ser., VII, 1954, 81-90.
1857 —— 'The trade crisis of the early 1620s and English economic thought', *J.Ec.H.*, XV, 1955, 121-33.
1858 **Gravil**, R., 'Trading to Spain and Portugal, 1670-1700', *Bus.H.*, X, 1968, 69-88.
1859 **Innis**, H. A., *The Cod Fisheries*, 1940. Chapter 3 deals with the Spanish and English fisheries, 1550-1600.
1860 **Jenkins**, J. T., *The Herring and the Herring

Industries, 1927. See 80-90 for some account of Stuart fishery companies.

1861 **Jones**, D. W., 'The "Hallage" receipts of the London cloth markets 1562-c. 1720', *Ec.H.R.*, 2nd ser., XXV, 1972, 567-87.

1862 **Jones**, J. R., 'Some aspects of London mercantile activity during the reign of Queen Elizabeth'. In N. Downes, ed., *Essays in Honour of Conyers Read*, Chicago, Ill., 1953, 186-99.

1863 **Jones**, W. J., 'Elizabethan marine insurance – the judicial undergrowth', *Bus.H.*, II, 1959, 53-66.

1864 **Kepler**, J. S., *The Exchange of Christendom. The International Entrepôt at Dover, 1622-41*, 1976.

1865 **Koenigsberger**, H., 'English merchants in Naples and Sicily in the seventeenth century', *E.H.R.*, LXII, 1947, 304-26.

1866 **Longfield**, Ada K., *Anglo-Irish Trade in the Sixteenth Century*, 1929. See also Cullen (1852), listed above.

1867 **Loomie**, A. J., 'Religion and Elizabethan commerce with Spain', *Cath.H.R.*, 50, 1964, 27-51.

1868 **Lounsbury**, R. G., *The British Fishery at Newfoundland, 1634-1763*, New Haven, Conn., 1934.

1869 **MacInnes**, C. M., *The Early English Tobacco Trade*, 1926.

1870 **McGrath**, P. V., *Merchants and Merchandise in Seventeenth-Century Bristol*, Bristol Rec.Soc., 1955.

1871 **Maloney**, F. X., *The Fur Trade in New England, 1620-1676*, 1931. Reprinted 1967.

1872 **Miller**, L. R., 'New evidence on the shipping and imports of London, 1601-1602', *Quarterly J. of Econ.*, 1927, 740-60.

1873 **Nettels**, C. P., 'England and the Spanish-American trade, 1680-1715', *J.M.H.*, III, 1931,

1-32.

1874 **Parkinson**, C. N., *The Rise of the Port of Liverpool*, 1952.

1875 **Rabb**, T. K., 'Free trade and the gentry in the parliament of 1604', *P.P.*, 40, 1968, 165-73. A rejoinder to Ashton (1850), listed above.

1876 —— 'Sir Edwin Sandys and the Parliament of 1604', *A.H.R.*, LXIX, 1963, 646-70.

1877 **Reynolds**, P., 'Elizabethan traders in Normandy', *J.M.H.*, IX, 1937, 289-303.

1878 **Ruddock**, A. A., 'London capitalists and the decline of Southampton in the early Tudor period', *Ec.H.R.*, 2nd ser., II, 1949, 137-51.

1879 **Stephens**, W. B., 'The overseas trade of Chester in the early seventeenth century', *T.H.S.L.C.*, 120, 1968, 23-34.

1880 —— 'The West Country ports and the struggle for the Newfoundland fisheries in the seventeenth century', *Trans.Devonshire Assoc.*, LXXXVIII, 1956, 90-101.

1881 —— 'The foreign trade of Plymouth and the Cornish ports in the early seventeenth century', *Trans.Devonshire Assoc.*, CI, 1969, 125-37.

1882 **Tawney**, R. H., *Business and Politics in the Reign of James I: Lionel Cranfield as Merchant and Statesman*, 1958.

1883 **Williams**, N., 'England's tobacco trade in the reign of Charles I', *Virginia Magazine of History and Biography*, LXV, 1957, 403-49.

1884 **Woodward**, D. M., *The Trade of Elizabethan Chester*, University of Hull Occ. Papers in Ec. and Soc.H., No. 4, 1970. Deals with the port's overseas, coastal and home trade.

See also Ruddock (957) and van der Wee (963), listed above. For the English customs in this period, see Atton and Holland (2016), listed in the section on *Government policy and administration*.

THE CONCEPT OF MERCANTILISM

1885 **Biltz**, R. C., 'Mercantilist policies and the pattern of world trade, 1500-1750', *J.Ec.H.*, XXVII, 1967, 39-55.

1886 **Coats**, A. W., 'In defence of Heckscher and the idea of Mercantilism', *Scand.Ec.H.R.*, V, 1957, 173-87. See Heckscher (1891) below.

1887 **Coleman**, D. C., ed., *Revisions in Mercantilism*, 1969. A useful collection of reprinted articles, including Coleman's own essay 'Eli Heckscher and the idea of mercantilism', 92-117. Bibliography.

1888 —— 'Mercantilism revisited', *H.J.*, XXIII, 1980, 773-91.

1889 **Grampp**, W. D., 'The liberal elements in English Mercantilism', *Q.J.Econ.*, 66, 1952, 456-501.

1890 **Heaton**, H., 'Heckscher on mercantilism', *J.Pol.Econ.*, 45, 1937, 370-93.

1891 **Heckscher**, E. F., *Mercantilism*, 2 vols. English trans., 1935, 2nd ed., London and N. Y. 1956. A major work though one which has been criticised for its failure to distinguish between economic theory and economic practice. See Coleman (1887), listed above.

1892 —— 'Revisions in economic history: mercantilism', *Ec.H.R.*, VII, 1936-7, 44-54. Reprinted in Coleman (1887), 19-34. Heckscher's second thoughts on the subject.

1893 **Herlitz**, L., 'The concept of mercantilism', *Scand.Ec.H.R.*, XII, 1964, 101-20.

1894 **Hinton**, R. W. K., 'The mercantile system in the time of Mun', *Ec.H.R.*, 2nd ser., VII, 1954-5, 277-90.

1895 **Judges**, A. V., 'The idea of a mercantile state', *T.R.H.S.*, 4th ser., XXI, 1939, 41-70. Reprinted in Coleman (1887), listed above 35-60.

1896 **Magnusson**, L., 'Eli Heckscher, Mercantilism and the favourable balance of trade', *Scand.Ec.H.R.*, XXVI, 1978, 103-27.

1897 **Minchinton**, W. E., ed., *Mercantilism: system or expediency?*, Boston, Mass., 1969. A collection of brief extracts from the main contributions to the debate on the subject.

1898 **Viner**, J., 'Power versus plenty as objectives of foreign policy in the seventeenth and eighteenth centuries', *World Politics*, I, 1948, 1-29. Reprinted in Coleman (1887), listed above, 61-91.

1899 **Wilson**, C., *Mercantilism*, Hist.Ass. pamphlet, 1958.

1900 —— 'The other face of Mercantilism', *T.R.H.S.*, 5th ser., IX, 1959, 81-101, Reprinted in Wilson (1232), listed above, 73-93.

1901 —— 'Mercantilism. Some vicissitudes of an idea', *Ec.H.R.*, 2nd ser., X, 1957, 181-88. Reprinted in Wilson (1232), listed above, 62-72.

1902 —— 'Treasure and trade balances: the Mercantilist problem', *Ec.H.R.*, 2nd ser., II, 1949, 152-61. Reprinted in Wilson (1232), listed above, 48-61.

1903 —— 'Treasure and trade balances: further evidence', *Ec.H.R.*, 2nd ser., IV, 1951, 231-42.

1904 —— 'Trade, society and the state'. In Wilson (1232), listed above, 487-576.

COMMUNICATIONS AND INTERNAL TRADE

For fuller details of the literature of the subject, the reader is referred to the extensive bibliographies contained in Dyos and Aldcroft (3575) and Jackman (3576), listed below.

(a) RIVER NAVIGATION

1905 **Chalklin**, C. W., 'Navigation schemes of the Upper Medway, 1600-1665', *J.Trans.H.*, V, 1961, 105-15.

1906 **Duckham**, B. F., *The Yorkshire Ouse. The History of a River Navigation*, 1967.

1907 **Skempton**, A. W., 'The engineers of the English river navigations, 1620-1760', *Trans. Newcomen Soc.*, XXIX, 1953-5, 24-54.

1908 **Stephens**, W. B., 'The Exeter Lighter Canal, 1566-1698', *J.Trans.H.*, III, 1957, 1-11.

1909 **Summers**, Dorothy, *The Great Ouse: The History of a River Navigation*, 1973.

1910 **Willan**, T. S., *River Navigation in England, 1600-1750*, 1936. Reprinted 1964. The standard work.

1911 —— *The Navigation of the Great Ouse between St Ives and Bedford in the Seventeenth Century*, Beds.Rec.Soc., 1946.

1912 —— 'The navigation of the Thames and Kennet, 1600-1750', *Berks.Arch. J.*, XL, 1936, 144-56.

1913 —— 'Yorkshire river navigation, 1600-1750', *Geog.*, XXII, 1937, 189-99.

1914 —— 'River navigation and trade from the Witham to the Yare, 1600-1750', *Norfolk Arch.*, XXVI, 1938, 296-309.

1915 —— 'The river navigation and trade of the Severn Valley, 1600-1750', *Ec.H.R.*, VIII, 1937-8, 68-79.

1916 **Wood**, A. C., 'The history of the trade and transport on the river Trent', *Trans. Thoroton Soc.*, LIV, 1950, 1-44.

(b) ROADS AND THEIR TRAFFIC

1917 **Austen**, B., *English Provincial Posts, 1633-1840. A Study based on Kent Examples*, 1978.

1918 **Cossons**, A., 'Warwickshire turnpikes', *Trans.Birm.Arch.Soc.*, LXIX, for 1941-2, 1946, 53-100.

1919 **Crofts**, J. E. W., *Packhorse, Waggon and Post: Land Carriage and Communications under the Tudors and Stuarts*, 1967. A rather unsystematic treatment of the subject, based on literary evidence.

1920 **Emmison**, F. G., 'The earliest Turnpike Bill (Biggleswade to Baldock road), 1622', *B.I.H.R.*, XII, 1935, 108-22.

1921 —— '1555 and all that: a milestone in the history of the English road', *Essex R.*, 64, 1955, 15-25.

1922 —— 'Was the highways Act of 1555 a success?', *Essex R.*, 64, 1955, 221-34.

1923 **Fordham**, H. G., *The Road Books and Itineraries of Great Britain, 1570-1850*, 1924.

1924 **Guttery**, D. R., 'Stourbridge market in Tudor times', *Trans.Worcs.Arch.Soc.*, n.s., XXX, 1954, 16-38.

1925 **Parkes**, Joan, *Travel in England in the Seventeenth Century*, 1925. Reprinted 1968.

1926 **Thomson**, Gladys Scott, 'Roads in England and Wales in 1603', *E.H.R.*, XXXIII, 1918, 234-43.

(c) INTERNAL TRADE

See also the section on *Marketing* under *Agriculture*.

1927 **Sachse**, W. L., ed., *The Diary of Roger Lowe of Ashton in Makerfield, Lancs., 1663-4*, 1938.

1928 **Berger**, R. M., 'The development of retail trade in provincial England, c.1550-1700', *J.Ec.H.*, XL, 1980, 123-8.

1929 **Chartres**, J. A., *Internal Trade in England, 1500-1700*, 1977.

1930 —— 'Road carrying in the seventeenth century: myth and reality', *Ec.H.R.*, 2nd ser., XXX, 1977, 73-94.

1931 **Edwards**, P. R., 'The horse trade of Chester in the sixteenth and seventeenth centuries', *J.Ches-ter Arch.Soc.*, LXII, 1980, 91-106.

1932 —— 'The horse trade of the Midlands in the seventeenth century', *Ag.H.R.*, XXVII, 1979, 90-100.

1933 **Hey**, D., *Packmen, Carriers and Packhorse Roads. Trade and Communications in North Derbyshire and South Yorkshire*, 1980.

1934 **Hodgen**, Margaret J., 'Fairs of Elizabethan England', *Ec.Geog.*, XVIII, 1942, 389-400.

1935 **Rodgers**, H. B., 'The market area of Preston in the sixteenth and seventeenth centuries', *Geog.Studs.*, III, 1956, 46-55.

1936 **Simpson**, A., 'Thomas Callum, draper, 1587-1664', *Ec.H.R.*, 2nd ser., XI, 1958, 19-34.

1937 **Tupling**, G. H., 'Lancashire markets in the sixteenth and seventeenth centuries, Parts 1 and 2', *T.L.C.A.S.*, LVIII, 1947, 1-34; *ibid.*, LIX, 1948, 1-34.

1938 **Westerfield**, R. B., *Middlemen in English Business, Particularly between 1660 and 1760*, Trans. Connecticut Academy of Arts and Sciences, XIX, Connecticut, 1915. Reprinted N. Y., 1969.

1939 **Willan**, T. S., *The Inland Trade. Studies in English Internal Trade in the Sixteenth and Seventeenth Centuries*, 1976. Has chapters on the wholesale and retail trades and on the movement of goods by land, river and sea.

1940 **Williams**, N., *Tradesmen in Early Stuart Wiltshire*, Wilts.Arch. and Nat.H.Soc., Records branch, XV, 1960.

See also Everitt (1440-41), Fisher (1442) and Gras (1443), listed above.

PRICES, PUBLIC FINANCE, BANKING AND FINANCIAL DEALINGS

(a) PRICES

1941 **McCulloch**, J. R., ed., *A Select Collection of Scarce and Valuable Tracts on Money (and Metallic Currency)*, 1856. Reprinted 1966.

1942 **Shaw**, W. A., ed., *Select Tracts and Documents Illustrative of English Monetary History, 1626-1730*, 1896. Reprinted 1967. See also the sections on credit and money lending, high prices and the coinage and on taxation in Tawney and Power (1156), listed above, II, 133-245.

1943 **Beveridge**, W. H., *Prices and Wages in England from the Twelfth to the Nineteenth Century I: Prices Tables: The Mercantile Era*, 1939. Reprinted 1966.

1944 **Bowden**, P. J., 'Agricultural prices, farm profits and rents'. In Thirsk (1414), listed above, 593-695. An important 'physical' interpretation of trends in agricultural prices.

1945 **Braudel**, F. P. and Spooner, F., 'Prices in Europe from 1450 to 1750'. In Rich and Wilson, eds. (1217), listed above, 378-486.

1946 **Brenner**, Y. S., 'The inflation of prices in early sixteenth-century England', *Ec.H.R.*, 2nd ser., XIV, 1961, 225-39.

1947 —— 'The inflation of prices in England, 1551-1650', *Ec.H.R.*, XV, 1962, 266-84.

1948 —— 'The price revolution reconsidered: a reply', *Ec.H.R.*, 2nd ser., XVIII, 1965, 392-6. A reply to Gould (1953), listed below.

1949 **Challis**, C. E., *The Tudor Coinage*, 1978. A Comprehensive study dealing with the supply of bullion, with mints and minting, circulation, and the rôle of government.

1950 **Fisher**, F. J., 'Influenza and inflation in Tudor England', *Ec.H.R.*, 2nd ser., XVIII, 1965, 120-29. Argues that a sharp fall in prices in 1558 was possibly the result of an influenza epidemic in the preceding year.

1951 **Gould**, J. D., *The Great Debasement: currency and the economy in mid-Tudor England*, 1970.

1952 —— 'The Royal Mint in the early seventeenth century', *Ec.H.R.*, 2nd ser., V., 1952, 240-8.

1953 —— 'Y. S. Brenner on prices: a comment', *Ec.H.R.*, 2nd ser., XVI, 1963, 351-60.

1954 —— 'The price revolution reconsidered', *Ec.H.R.*, 2nd ser., XVII, 1964, 249-66.

1955 **Hamilton**, E. J., 'American treasure and Andalusian prices, 1503-1660', *J.Ec.& Bus.H.*, I, 1928, 1-35. Related inflation to the influx of specie from the New World.

1956 **Horsefield**, J. K., *British Monetary Experiments, 1650-1710*, 1960.

1957 **Li**, M. H., *The Great Recoinage of 1696-9*, 1963.

1958 **Monroe**, A. E., *Monetary Theory before Adam Smith*, 1923. Reprinted N. Y., 1966.

1959 **Nef**, J. U., 'Prices and industrial capitalism in France and England, 1540-1640', *Ec.H.R.*, VII, 1937, 155-85. Reprinted in Carus-Wilson, ed. (245), listed above, I, 108-34.

1960 **Outhwaite**, R. B., *Inflation in Tudor and Early Stuart England*, 1969. Studies in Economic History series (pamphlet). A valuable summary, with a bibliographical guide to the growing literature of the subject.

1961 **Price**, J. M., 'Notes on some London price currents, 1667-1715', *Ec.H.R.*, 2nd ser., VII, 1954, 240-50.

1962 **Ramsey**, P., ed., *The Price Revolution in Sixteenth-Century England*, 1971. Collects together several key articles.

1963 **Schumpeter**, Elizabeth, 'English prices and public finance, 1660-1682', *Review of Economics and Statistics*, XX, 1938, 21-37.

1964 **Supple**, B. E., 'Currency and commerce in the early seventeenth century', *Ec.H.R.*, 2nd ser., X, 1957, 239-55.

1965 **Taylor**, H., 'Price revolution or price revision? The English and Spanish trade after 1604',

Renaiss. & Mod.Studs., XII, 1968, 5-32.
See also Brown (2225), Burnett (974), Craig (522), Feavearyear (527), Rogers (532) and Shaw (534).

(b) PUBLIC FINANCE: INCOME AND MANAGEMENT

1966 **Richardson**, W. C., ed., *The Report of the Royal Commission of 1552*, Morgantown, Virginia, 1974. An important source for the study of mid-Tudor financial administration.

1967 **Ashton**, R., *The Crown and the Money Market, 1603-40*, 1960.

1968 —— 'Charles I and the City'. In Fisher (1190), listed above, 138-63.

1969 —— 'Revenue farming under the early Stuarts', *Ec.H.R.*, 2nd ser., VIII, 1956, 310-22.

1970 —— 'Deficit finance in the reign of James I', *Ec.H.R.*, 2nd ser., X, 1957, 15-29.

1971 **Aylmer**, G. E., 'The last years of purveyance, 1610-60', *Ec.H.R.*, 2nd ser., X, 1957, 81-93.

1972 —— 'Attempts at administrative reform, 1625-40', *E.H.R.*, LXXII, 1957, 229-59. See also Aylmer (2017-18), below.

1973 **Baxter**, S. B., *The Development of the Treasury, 1660-1702*, 1957.

1974 **Chandaman**, C. D., *The English Public Revenue, 1660-88*, 1975. Has chapters on direct taxation and on customs and excise, the hearth tax, and casual receipts.

1975 **Dietz**, F., *English Government Finance, 1485-1558*, Urbana, Ill., 1920. Reprinted, with corrections, 1964.

1976 —— *English Public Finance, 1558-1641*, N. Y., 1932. Reprinted 1964.

1977 **Elton**, G. R., 'The Elizabethan Exchequer: war in the receipt'. In Bindoff, Hurstfield and Williams (1167), listed above, 213-48.

1978 —— 'Taxation for war and peace in early Tudor England' in Winter (251), 33-48.

1979 **Harriss**, G. L., 'Aids, loans and benevolences', *H. J.*, VI, 1963, 1-19.

1980 —— 'Fictitious loans', *Ec.H.R.*, 2nd ser., VIII, 1955-56, 187-99.

1981 **Hurstfield**, J., *The Queen's Wards: Wardship and Marriage under Elizabeth I*, 1958. A scholarly investigation of the administration of wardships by the Court of Wards.

1982 —— 'The profits of fiscal feudalism', *Ec.H.R.*, 2nd ser., VIII, 1955, 53-61.

1983 **Mayes**, L. R., 'The sale of peerages in early Stuart England', *J.M.H.*, XXIX, 1957, 21-37.

1984 **Richards**, R. D., 'The Exchequer in Cromwellian times', *Ec.J.Ec.H.Supp.*, II, 1931, 213-33.

1985 —— 'The stop of the Exchequer', *Ec.J.Ec.H.Supp.*, II, 1930, 45-62.

1986 **Richardson**, W. C., 'Some financial expedients of Henry VIII', *Ec.H.R.*, 2nd ser., VII, 1954, 33-58.

1987 **Stone**, L., 'The inflation of honours, 1558-1641', *P.P.*, 14, 1958, 45-70.

1988 **Woodworth**, Allegra, 'Purveyance for the royal household in the reign of Queen Elizabeth', *Trans.American Phil.Soc.*, n.s., XXXV, 1945. See also Dickson (3982), listed below. The books by Dowell (540) and Roseveare (547) listed above, are also relevant in this connection. See also the section on Crown Lands listed under *Agriculture and rural society* (p. 48).

(c) BANKING AND FINANCIAL DEALINGS

1989 **Tawney**, R. H., ed. *Thomas Wilson's Discourse on Usury, 1572*, 1925. Reprinted 1962.

1990 **Andréades**, A. M., *History of the Bank of England, 1640-1903*, 1909, 4th ed., with an introduction by P. Einzig, 1966.

1991 **Ashton**, R., 'Usury and high finance in the age of Shakespeare and Jonson', *Renaiss. & Mod.Studs.*, IV, 1960, 14-43.

1992 **Bindoff**, S. T., *The Fame of Sir Thomas Gresham*, 1973.

1993 **Bisschop**, W. R., *The Rise of the London Money Market, 1640-1826*, 1910. Reprinted 1968.

1994 **Buckley**, H., 'Sir Thomas Gresham and the foreign exchanges', *Ec. J.*, XXXIV, 1924, 589-601.

1995 **Ehrenberg**, R., *Capital and Finance in the Age of the Renaissance*, N. Y., 1928.

1996 **Grassby**, R., 'The rate of profit in seventeenth-century England', *E.H.R.*, LXXXIV, 1969, 721-51.

1997 **Holden**, J. M., 'Bills of exchange in the seventeenth century', *Law Quarterly R.*, LXVII, 1951, 230-48.

1998 **Horsefield**, J. K., 'The Bank of England as mentor', *Ec.H.R.*, 2nd ser., II, 1949, 80-108.

1999 **Lane**, N., 'The origins of Lloyd's', *H.Today*, 7, 1957, 848-53.

2000 —— 'The years before the Stock Exchange', *H.Today*, 7, 1957, 760-5.

2001 **Outhwaite**, R. B., 'The trials of foreign borrowing: the English Crown and the Antwerp Money Market in the mid-sixteenth century', *Ec.H.R.*, 2nd ser., XIX, 1966, 289-305.

2002 —— 'Royal borrowing in the reign of Elizabeth I: the Aftermath of Antwerp', *E.H.R.*, LXXXVI, 1971, 251-63.

2003 **Powell**, E. T., *The Evolution of the Money Market, 1385-1915*, 1915. Reprinted 1966.

2004 **Richards**, R. D., *The Early History of Banking in England*, 1928. Reprinted 1958.

2005 —— 'The pioneers of banking in England', *Ec.J.Ec.H.Supp.*, I, 1929, 485-502.

2006 **Roover**, R. de, *Gresham on Foreign Exchange: An Essay on Early English Mercantilism, With the Text of Sir Thomas Gresham's Memorandum for the Understanding of the Exchange*, Cambridge, Mass., 1949. While the book as a whole is of considerable value, the question of the authorship of the *Memorandum* is less clear-cut than is suggested here.

2007 **Rubini**, D., 'Politics and the battle for the banks, 1688-1697', *E.H.R.*, LXXXV, 1970, 693-714.

2008 **Stone**, L., *An Elizabethan: Sir Horatio Palavicino*, 1956. Palavicino was an important source of loans to the crown.

2009 **Tucker**, G. S. L., *Progress and Profits in British Economic Thought, 1650-1850*, 1960. Chapter 2 deals with 'The problem of interest in the seventeenth century'.

2010 **Yamey**, B. S., 'Scientific book-keeping and the rise of capitalism', *Ec.H.R.*, 2nd ser., I, 1948, 99-113.

2011 ——, Edey, H. C. and Thomson, H. W., *Accounting in England and Scotland, 1543-1800*, 1963.

GOVERNMENT POLICY AND ADMINISTRATION

(a) THE CENTRAL GOVERNMENT

2012 **Elton**, G. R., ed., *The Tudor Constitution: Documents and Commentary*, 1960.

2013 **Hughes**, P. L. and Larkin, J. F., eds., *Tudor Royal Proclamations, 1485-1603*, 3 vols., New

Haven and London, 1964-9.

2014 **Kenyon**, J. P., ed., *The Stuart Constitution: Documents and Commentary*, 1966.

2015 **Ashley**, M., *Financial and Commercial Policy under the Cromwellian Protectorate*, 1934, 2nd ed., 1962.

2016 **Atton**, H. and Holland, H. H., *The King's Customs, 1600-1706*, 2 vols., 1908-10. Reprinted 1968.

2017 **Aylmer**, G. E., *The King's Servants: The Civil Service of Charles I, 1625-42*, 1961, 2nd ed., 1974.

2018 —— *The State's Servants. The Civil Service of the English Republic 1649-1660*, 1973.

2019 —— 'From officeholding to civil service: the genesis of modern bureaucracy', *T.R.H.S.*, 5th ser., XXX, 1980, 91-108.

2020 **Baldwin**, F. E., *Sumptuary Legislation and Personal Regulation in England*, Johns Hopkins University Studies in Historical and Political Science, ser. 44, No. 1, Baltimore, 1926.

2021 **Beresford**, M. W., 'The common informer, the penal statutes and economic regulation', *Ec.H.R.*, 2nd ser., X, 1957-8, 221-38.

2022 **Bindoff**, S. T., 'The making of the Statute of Artificers'. In Bindoff, Hurstfield and Williams, ed., (1167), listed above, 59-94.

2023 **Bush**, M. L., *The Government Policy of Protector Somerset*, 1975.

2024 **Colvin**, H. M., 'Castles and government in Tudor England', *E.H.R.*, LXXXIII, 1968, 225-34.

2025 **Cooper**, J. P., 'Economic regulation and the cloth industry in seventeenth-century England', *T.R.H.S.*, 5th ser., XX, 1970, 73-99.

2026 **Davies**, C. S. L., 'The administration of the royal navy under Henry VIII', *E.H.R.*, LXXX, 1966, 268-86.

2027 —— 'Provisions for armies, 1509-60: a study in the effectiveness of early Tudor government', *Ec.H.R.*, 2nd ser., XVII, 1964, 234-48.

2028 **Davis**, R., 'The rise of Protection in England, 1669-1786', *Ec.H.R.*, XIX, 1966, 306-17.

2029 **Elton**, G. R., *Studies in Tudor and Stuart Politics and Government*, 2 vols., 1974.

2030 —— *The Tudor Revolution in Government*, 1953. A controversial study which concentrates on Thomas Cromwell's administrative reforms and argues that they marked the end of the Middle Ages.

2031 —— *Reform and Renewal: Thomas Cromwell and the Commonweal*, 1973.

2032 —— *Policy and Police*, 1972. A study of the enforcement of the Henrician Reformation.

2033 —— *Star Chamber Stories*, 1958.

2034 **Fox**, H. G., *Monopolies and Patents: A Study in the History and Future of the Patent Monopoly*, Toronto and London, 1947.

2035 **Heinze**, R. W., *The Proclamations of the Tudor Kings*, 1976.

2036 **Hughes**, E., *Studies in Administration and Finance, 1558-1825, With Special Reference to the History of Salt Taxation in England*, 1934.

2037 —— 'The English Stamp Duties, 1664-1764', *E.H.R.*, XVI, 1941, 234-64.

2038 **Hurstfield**, J., *Freedom, Corruption and Government in Elizabethan England*, 1973. Collects together the author's essays in this field.

2039 **Nef**, J. U., *Industry and Government in France and England, 1540-1640*, Memoirs American Phil. Soc., XV, Philadelphia, 1940. Reprinted Ithaca, N. Y., 1957.

2040 **Pearce**, B., 'Elizabethan food policy and the armed forces', *Ec.H.R.*, XII, 1942, 39-46.

2041 **Pickthorn**, K., *Early Tudor Government I: Henry VII*, 1934, revised 1949; *II: Henry VIII*, 1934.

2042 **Prestwich**, Menna, 'Diplomacy and trade in the Protectorate', *J.M.H.*, XXII, 1950, 103-21.

2043 **Price**, W. H., *The English Patents of Monopoly*, Boston and Lond., 1906. Documentary appendix.

2044 **Read**, C., 'Tudor economic policy', in R. L. Schuyler and H. Ausubel, eds., *The Making of English History*, N. Y., 1952, 195-201.

2045 **Reid**, Rachel R., *The King's Council in the North*, 1921. Re-issued 1975.

2046 **Riemersma**, J. C., 'Government influence on company organisation in Holland and England, 1550-1650', *J.Ec.H.*, supplement 10, 1950, 31-9.

2047 **Slack**, P. A., 'The Book of Orders: the making of English social policy, 1577-1631', *T.R.H.S.*, 5th ser., XXX, 1980, 1-22.

2048 **Smith**, A. G. R., *The Government of Elizabethan England*, 1967. A brief general survey with a guide to further reading.

2049 **Stone**, L., 'State control in sixteenth-century England', *Ec.H.R.*, XVII, 1947, 103-20.

2050 **Wilson**, C., 'Government policy and private interest in modern English history'. In Wilson (1232), listed above, 129-39.

See also Margaret G. Davies (2190) and A. A. Gomme (3000), listed below.

(b) LOCAL GOVERNMENT

2051 **Barnes**, T. G., *Somerset, 1625-40: A County's*

Government During the 'Personal Rule', 1961.

2052 **Gleason**, J. H., *The Justices of the Peace in England, 1558-1640*, 1969.

2053 **Kent**, J., 'The English village constable, 1580-1642: the nature and dilemmas of the office', *J.Brit.Studs.*, XX, 1981, 26-49.

2054 **Moir**, Esther A. L., *The Justice of the Peace*, 1969.

2055 **Tate**, W. E., *The Parish Chest*, 1946, 3rd ed., 1969. The best introduction to the records of parochial government.

2056 **Trotter**, Eleanor, *Seventeenth-century Life in the Country Parish, With Special Reference to Local Government*, 1919. Reprinted 1968.

2057 **Webb**, S. and Beatrice, *English Local Government*, 11 vols., 1906-29. Reprinted 1963, with new introductions. The Webbs' major work.

2058 **Willcox**, W. B., *Gloucestershire: A Study in Local Government, 1590-1640*, New Haven, Conn., 1940.

LAW AND ORDER

2059 **Allan**, D. G. C., 'The rising in the west, 1628-31', *Ec.H.R.*, 2nd ser., V, 1952, 76-85.

2060 **Beier**, A. L., 'Vagrants and the social order in Elizabethan England', *P.P.*, 64, 1974, 3-29.

2061 **Bellamy**, J., *The Tudor Law of Treason. An Introduction*, 1979.

2062 **Bindoff**, S. T., *Ket's Rebellion, 1549*, Hist.Ass. pamphlet, 1949, reprinted 1968.

2063 **Boynton**, L., *The Elizabethan Militia*, 1966.

2064 **Brewer**, J. and Styles, J., eds., *An Ungovernable People. The English and their Law in the Seventeenth and Eighteenth Centuries*, 1980. A collection of case studies exploring the connections and conflicts between popular justice and the law and its workings.

2065 **Cockburn**, J. S., *A History of English Assizes, 1558-1714*, 1972.

2066 —— ed., *Crime in England, 1550-1800*, 1977. A fascinating collection of eleven essays – many of them local in scope. Excellent critical bibliography.

2067 **Cornwall**, J., *The Revolt of the Peasantry, 1549*, 1977.

2068 **Davies**, C. S. L., 'The Pilgrimage of Grace reconsidered', *P.P.*, 41, 1968, 54-76..

2069 —— 'Les révoltes populaires en Angleterre, 1500-1700', *Annales*, 24e année, 1969, 24-60.

2070 **François**, Martha E., 'Revolts in late medieval and early modern Europe: a spiral model', *J.Interdis.H.*, V, 1974, 19-43.

2071 **Gatrell**, V. A. C., Lenman, B. and Parker, G., eds., *Crime and the Law. The Social History of Crime in Western Europe since 1500*, 1980.

2072 **Gay**, E. F., 'The Midland Revolt and the Inquisitions of Depopulation of 1607', *T.R.H.S.*, n.s., XVIII, 1904, 195-244.

2073 **Harrison**, S. M., *The Pilgrimage of Grace in the Lake Counties, 1536-7*, 1981.

2074 **James**, M. E., 'Obedience and dissent in Henrician England: the Lincolnshire Rebellion, 1536', *P.P.*, 48, 1970, 3-78.

2075 —— 'The concept of order and the Northern Rising of 1569', *P.P.*, 60, 1973, 49-83.

2076 **Kerridge**, E., 'The revolts in Wiltshire against Charles I', *Wilts.Arch. & Nat.H.Mag.*, LVII, 1958-9, 64-75.

2077 **King**, W. J., 'Punishment for bastardy in early seventeenth-century England', *Albion*, X, 1978, 130-51.

2078 —— 'The regulation of alehouses in Stuart Lancashire: an example of discretionary administration of the law', *T.H.S.L.C.*, CXXIX, 1980, 31-46.

2079 **Lindley**, K. J., *Fenland Riots and the English Revolution*, 1982. Looks at the fenmen's resistance to enclosure and draining and relates it to the causes, course and aftermath of the English Revolution.

2080 **MacCulloch**, D., 'Ket's Rebellion in context', *P.P.*, 84, 1979, 36-59.

2081 **Macfarlane**, A., *The Justice and the Mare's Ale. Law and Disorder in Seventeenth-Century England*, 1981. A case study of law and lawbreakers in Westmorland.

2082 **McGurk**, J. J. N., 'The clergy and the militia, 1580-1610', *Hist.*, LX, 1975, 198-210.

2083 **Salgado**, G., *The Elizabethan Underworld*, 1977.

2084 **Samaha**, J., *Law and Order in Historical Perspective: The Case of Elizabethan Essex*, 1974.

2085 **Sharp**, B., *In Contempt of all Authority. Rural Artisans and Riot in the West of England, 1586-1660*, 1980.

2086 **Sharpe**, J. A., *Defamation and Sexual Slander in Early Modern England. The Church Courts at*

York, Borthwick Papers, 58, 1980.

2087 —— 'Domestic homicide in early modern England', *H. J.*, XXIV, 1981, 29-48.

2088 **Veall**, D., *The Popular Movement for Law Reform, 1640-60*, 1970.

2089 **Walter**, J. and Wrightson, K., 'Dearth and the social order in early modern England', *P.P.*, 71, 1976, 22-42.

2090 **Williams**, N., 'The risings in Norfolk, 1569 and 1570', *Norfolk Arch.*, XXXII, 1959, 73-81.

See also Houlbrooke (2391), below.

CLASSES AND SOCIAL GROUPS

(a) GENERAL AND MISCELLANEOUS

2091 **Batho**, G. R., 'The finances of an Elizabethan nobleman: Henry Percy, ninth Earl of Northumberland (1564-1631)', *Ec.H.R.*, 2nd ser., IX, 1957, 433-50.

2092 **Campbell**, Mildred, *The English Yeoman in the Tudor and Early Stuart Age*, New Haven, Conn., 1942. Reprinted 1960. A valuable and well-documented treatment of the subject.

2093 **Cressy**, D., 'Describing the social order of Elizabethan and Stuart England', *Lit.& H.*, III, 1976, 29-44. A critique of Stone (2110), below.

2094 **Davies**, K. G., 'The mess of the middle class', *P.P.*, 22, 1962, 77-83.

2095 **Everitt**, A. M., 'Social mobility in England, 1500-1700', *P.P.*, 33, 1966, 56-73. See also Stone (2110), listed below.

2096 **Grassby**, R., 'Social mobility and business enterprise in seventeenth-century England' in Pennington and Thomas (1214), above, 355-81.

2097 **Habakkuk**, H. J., 'The rise and fall of English landed families, 1600-1800. Parts I, II and III', *T.R.H.S.*, 5th ser., XXIX, 1979, 187-207; XXX, 1980, 199-221; XXXI, 1981, 195-218.

2098 **Hexter**, J. H., 'The myth of the middle class in Tudor England'. In the same author's *Reappraisals in History*, 1961, 71-116.

2099 —— 'The English aristocracy: its crises and the English Revolution', *J.Brit.Studs.*, VIII, 1968, 22-78.

2100 **Hill**, C., 'The many-headed monster in late Tudor and early Stuart political thinking'. In C. H. Carter, ed., *From Renaissance to Counter-Reformation*, 1966, 296-324. Reprinted in Hill (1196), 181-204.

2101 **Holmes**, G. S., 'Gregory King and the social structure of pre-industrial England', *T.R.H.S.*, 5th ser., XXVII, 1977, 41-68.

2102 —— 'The professions and social change in England, 1680-1730', *Proc.Brit.Acad.*, LXV, 1981, 313-54.

2103 **Ives**, E. W., 'The reputation of the common lawyer in English society 1450-1550', *Birm.H. J.*, VII, 1960, 130-61.

2104 **Marshall**, J. D., 'Agrarian wealth and social structure in pre-industrial Cumbria', *Ec.H.R.*, 2nd ser., XXXIII, 1980, 503-21.

2105 **O'Day**, Rosemary, *The English Clergy. The Emergence and Consolidation of a Profession, 1558-1642*, 1979.

2106 **Ross**, D., 'Class privilege in seventeenth-century England', *Hist.*, XXVIII, 1943, 148-55.

2107 **Speck**, W. A., 'Social status in late Stuart England', *P.P.*, 34, 1966, 127-29. A comment on Stone's article on social mobility (2110), listed below.

2108 **Stone**, L., *The Crisis of the Aristocracy, 1558-1641*, 1965. A massive study which not only presents the 'crisis' thesis, but also comprehensively surveys the whole socio-economic setting and activities of the aristocracy. See the review articles on this book by D. C. Coleman in *Hist.*, LI, 1966, 165-78; by R. Ashton in *Ec.H.R.*, 2nd ser., XXII, 308-22; and by A. M. Everitt in *Ag.H.R.*, XVI, 1968, 60-7.

2109 —— *Family and Fortune. Studies in Aristocratic Finance in the Sixteenth and Seventeenth Centuries*, 1973. A series of case studies which supplement Stone's *Crisis of the Aristocracy*.

2110 —— 'Social mobility in England, 1500-1700', *P.P.*, 33, 1966, 16-55. See also Everitt (2095) and Speck (2107), listed above. Stone's book *Social Change and Revolution* (2130), listed below, is also relevant in this connection.

2111 **Styles**, P., 'The social structure of Kineton hundred in the reign of Charles II', *Trans.Birm.Arch.Soc.*, LXXVIII, 1962, 96-117.

2112 **Supple**, B. E., 'Class and social tension: the case of the merchant', in Ives (2286), listed below, 131-43.

2113 **Williams**, G., *The General and Common Sort of People, 1540-1640*, 1977.

(b) THE GENTRY AND THEIR ESTATES

This section is not intended to be self-contained. It should, for example, be seen in conjunction with those on *Landholding* and the *Land market*.

2114 **Phillips**, C. B., ed., *Lowther Family Estate Books, 1617-75*, Surtees Soc., CXCI, 1979.

2115 **Smith**, A. H., Baker, Gillian, and Kenny, R. W., eds., *The Papers of Nathaniel Bacon of Stiffkey. I: 1556-77*, 1979.

2116 **Clay**, C., *Public Finance and Private Wealth. The Career of Sir Stephen Fox, 1627-1716*, 1978.

2117 —— 'Marriage, inheritance and the rise of large estates in England, 1660-1815', *Ec.H.R.*, 2nd ser., XXI, 1968, 503-18.

2118 **Cliffe**, J. T., *The Yorkshire Gentry from the Reformation to the Civil War*, 1969.

2119 **Cooper**, J. P., 'The counting of manors', *Ec.H.R.*, 2nd ser., VIII, 1956, 377-89. A significant contribution to the debate on the gentry which pointed out the statistical errors underlying Tawney's thesis (2132), listed below.

2120 **Cornwall**, J., 'The early Tudor gentry', *Ec.H.R.*, 2nd ser., XVII, 1965, 456-71.

2121 **Finch**, Mary E., *The Wealth of Five Northamptonshire Families*, Northants.Rec.Soc., XIX, 1956. One of the first real attempts to approach the gentry controversy using the method of case-study rather than that of generalisation.

2122 **Hexter**, J. H., 'Storm over the gentry'. In the same author's *Reappraisals in History*, 1961, 117-62. A very good – and witty – summary of the gentry controversy.

2123 **Hoskins**, W. G., 'The estates of the Caroline gentry'. In Hoskins and Finberg, eds., (1248), listed above, 334-65.

2124 **Laslett**, P., 'The gentry of Kent in 1640', *Cambridge H.J.*, IX, 1948, 148-64. See also the book by Everitt (2328), listed below.

2125 **Lavrovsky**, V. M., 'The Great Estate in England from the sixteenth to the eighteenth centuries', *First International Conference of Economic History, Contributions and Communications*, Stockholm, 1960, 353-65

2126 **Levy**, F. J., 'How information spread among the gentry, 1550-1640', *J.Brit.Studs.*, XXI, 1982, 11-34.

2127 **Mousley**, J. E., 'The fortunes of some gentry families of Elizabethan Sussex', *Ec.H.R.*, 2nd ser., XI, 1958, 467-83.

2128 **Roebuck**, P., *Yorkshire Baronets, 1640-1760. Families, Estates and Fortunes*, 1980.

2129 **Simpson**, A., *The Wealth of the Gentry, 1540-1660*, Chicago and Cambridge, 1961.

2130 **Stone**, L., *Social Change and Revolution in England, 1540-1640*, 1965. Summarises the gentry controversy, providing extracts from contemporary sources and from the main contributions to the historical debate. Useful bibliography.

2131 —— 'The fruits of office: the case of Robert Cecil, first Earl of Salisbury, 1596-1612'. In Fisher (1190), listed above, 89-116.

2132 **Tawney**, R. H., 'The rise of the gentry, 1558-1640', *Ec.H.R.*, XI, 1941, 1-38. The famous article which initiated the gentry controversy. See also Tawney's 'Postscript', *Ec.H.R.*, 2nd ser., VII, 1954, 91-7. Both are reprinted in Carus-Wilson, ed., (245), listed above, I, 173-214.

2133 —— 'Harrington's interpretation of his age', *Proc.Brit.Acad.*, XXVII, 1941, 199-223.

2134 **Trevor-Roper**, H. R., *The Gentry, 1540-1640* (*Ec.H.R.* supplements, I), 1953. A vigorous attack on the Tawney thesis, arguing that the 'mere gentry', who lacked access to profitable offices in royal administration and whose income was derived entirely from the land, actually declined during this period.

2135 **Upton**, A. P., *Sir Arthur Ingram, c. 1565-1642: A Study of the Origins of an English Landed Family*, 1961.

2136 **Wood**, A. C., 'The Holles Family', *T.R.H.S.*, 4th ser., XIX, 1936, 145-65.

POOR RELIEF: CHARITY AND THE POOR LAW

For the medieval background, see:

2137 **Clay**, Rotha M., *The Medieval Hospitals of England*, 1909. Reprinted, 1966.

2138 **Tierney**, B., *Medieval Poor Law: A Sketch of Canonical Theory and its Application in England*, Berkeley and Los Angeles, 1959.

2139 **Cutlack**, S. A., ed., *The Gnosall Records, 1679-1837*, Staffs.Rec.Soc., I, 1936.

2140 **Emmison**, F. G., 'The care of the poor in Elizabethan Essex: recently discovered records', *Essex Review*, LXII, 1953, 7-28.

2141 —— 'Poor relief accounts of two rural parishes in Bedfordshire, 1563-98', *Ec.H.R.*, III, 1931, 102-16.

2142 **Fry**, A. Ruth, ed., *John Bellers, 1654-1725: Quaker, Economist and Social Reformer*, 1935. Contains, *inter al.*, extracts from Bellers's *Proposals for Raising a Colledge of Industry* (1696) and from his *Essays about the Poor, Manufacturers, Trade, Plantations and Immorality* (1699).

2143 **Melling**, Elizabeth, ed., *The Poor: A Collection of Examples from Original Sources in the Kent Archives Office from the Sixteenth to the Nineteenth Century*, 1964.

2144 **Salter**, F. R., ed., *Some Early Tracts on Poor Relief*, 1926. Mainly a collection of early European treatises and ordinances, but the text of the English legislation of 1531 and 1536 is included.

2145 **Slack**, P. A., ed., *Poverty in Early Stuart Salisbury*, Wilts.Rec.Soc., XXXI, 1976.

2146 **Tanner**, J. R., ed., *Tudor Constitutional Documents, 1485-1603*, 1922, 2nd ed., 1930. Has a section on vagabonds, beggars and poor relief, 469-95.

2147 **Webb**, J., ed., *Poor Relief in Elizabethan Ipswich*, Suffolk Rec.Soc., IX, 1966. A collection of documents with an introduction.

2148 **Wilkins**, H. J., ed., *Transcription of the Poor Book of the Tithings of Westbury on Trym, Stoke Bishop and Shirehampton from 1656-1698*, 1910. The text of the 1598 act is contained in Williams (1159). See also Bland, Brown and Tawney (211), Elton (2012) and Tawney and Power (1156), listed above, for other source material on this subject.

2149 **Aydelotte**, F., *Elizabethan Rogues and Vagabonds*, 1913. Reprinted 1967.

2150 **Bagley**, J. J. and A. J., *The English Poor Law*,

1968. A short introduction with suggestions for further reading.

2151 **Beier**, A. L., 'Poor relief in Warwickshire, 1630-1660', *P.P.*, 35, 1966, 77-100. Argues that the Civil War did not bring about a general breakdown in poor relief.

2152 —— 'Social problems in Elizabethan London', *J.Interdis.H.*, IX, 1978, 203-21.

2153 **Bittle**, W. G. and Lane, R. I., 'Inflation and philanthropy in England: a re-assessment of W. K. Jordan's data', *Ec.H.R.*, 2nd ser., XXIX, 1976, 203-10. Argues against there being an increase in philanthropy in this period.

2154 **Cannan**, E., *History of Local Rates in England*, 1896, 4th ed., 1927.

2155 **Carlton**, C., *The Court of Orphans*, 1974.

2156 **Davies**, C. S. L., 'Slavery and Protector Somerset: the Vagrancy Act of 1547', *Ec.H.R.*, 2nd ser., XIX, 1966, 533-49.

2157 **Eden**, F. M., *The State of the Poor; or, A History of the Labouring Classes in England from the Conquest to the Present Period*, 3 vols., 1797. Reprinted 1966.

2158 **Elton**, G. R., 'An early Tudor Poor Law', *Ec.H.R.*, 2nd ser., VI, 1953, 55-67.

2159 **Fessler**, A., 'The official attitude towards the sick poor in seventeenth-century Lancashire', *T.H.S.L.C.*, 102, 1951, 85-114.

2160 **Gray**, B. K., *A History of English Philanthropy from the Dissolution of the Monasteries to the Taking of the First Census*, 1905. Reprinted 1967.

2161 **Hampson**, Ethel M., *The Treatment of Poverty in Cambridgeshire, 1597-1834*, 1934. An important regional study.

2162 **Herlan**, R. W., 'Poor relief in London during the English Revolution', *J.Brit.Studs.*, XVIII, 1979, 30-51.

2163 **Hill**, C., 'Puritans and the poor', *P.P.*, 2, 1952, 32-50. Reprinted in Hill (2277), listed below, as 'William Perkins and the poor', 215-38.

2164 —— 'The Poor and the parish'. In Hill (2390), listed below, 259-97.

2165 **Hobson**, J. M., *Some Early and Later Houses of Pity*, 1926.

2166 **James**, Margaret, *Social Problems and Policy During the Puritan Revolution*, 1930. Reprinted 1966.

2167 **Jones**, G. H., *History of the Law of Charity, 1532-1827*, 1969. The first five chapters deal with the pre-1700 period.

2168 **Jones**, G. P., 'The poverty of Cumberland and Westmorland', *Trans.Cumb. and West.Antiq. and Arch.Soc.*, LV, 1956, 198-208.

2169 **Jordan**, W. K., *Philanthropy in England: A study of the Changing Pattern of English Social Aspirations, 1480-1660*, 1959.

2170 —— *The Charities of Rural England, 1480-1660*, 1961.

2171 —— *The Charities of London, 1480-1660*, 1961.

2172 —— *The Social Institutions of Lancashire*, Chet.Soc., 3rd ser., 11, 1962.

2173 —— *Social institutions in Kent, 1480-1660*, Arch.Cant., 75, 1961.

2174 —— *The Forming of the Charitable Institutions of the West of England*, American Philosophical Soc.Trans., n.s., 50, Part 8, Philadelphia, 1960. Altogether, Jordan's work amounts to a monumental study of the patterns of charitable giving in the early modern period. From a quantitative point of view, however, Jordan is less useful, since the Price Rise is not taken into account.

2175 **Judges**, A. V., *The Elizabethan Underworld*, 1930. Reprinted 1965.

2176 **Kiernan**, V. G., 'Puritanism and the poor', *P.P.*, 3, 1953, 45-54. A comment on Hill (2163), listed above.

2177 **Leonard, Elizabeth M.**, *The Early History of English Poor Relief*, 1900. Reprinted 1965. Still the standard work though largely by default.

2178 **Nicholls**, G. and Mackay, T., *A History of the English Poor Law*, 3 vols., 1854, new edition 1898-1904. Reprinted 1968.

2179 **Pearl**, Valerie, 'Social policy in early modern London' in H. Lloyd-Jones, Valerie Pearl and B. Worden, eds., *History and Imagination. Essays in Honour of H. R. Trevor-Roper*, 1981, 115-31.

2180 **Pinchbeck**, Ivy and Hewitt, Margaret, *Children in English Society I: From Tudor Times to the Eighteenth Century*, 1969. Chapters 5-9 are particularly relevant in this connection. Good bibliography.

2181 **Pound**, J. F., *Poverty and Vagrancy in Tudor England*, 1971.

2182 —— 'An Elizabethan census of the poor. The treatment of vagrancy in Norwich, 1570-80', *Birm.H. J.*, VIII, 1962, 135-61.

2183 **Rodgers**, B., *The Battle against Poverty I: From Pauperism to Human Rights*, 1969.

2184 **Slack**, P. A., 'Vagrants and vagrancy in England, 1598-1664', *Ec.H.R.*, 2nd ser., XXVII, 1974, 360-79.

2185 **Steinbicker**, C. R., *Poor Relief in the Sixteenth Century*, Studia Facultas Theologica, Washington, D. C., 1937. A Roman Catholic attempt to show that Catholic countries excelled Protestant in providing for the poor.

2186 **Styles**, P., 'The evolution of the law of Settlement', *Birm.H. J.*, IX, 1963, 33-63.

See also Marshall (4444), the Webbs (4729), Bruce (4760) and Owen (4747), listed below.

LABOUR

2187 **Buckatzsch**, E. J., 'Occupations in the parish registers of Sheffield, 1655-1719', *Ec.H.R.*, 2nd ser., I, 1948-9, 145-50.

2188 **Clark**, Alice, *The Working Life of Women in the Seventeenth Century*, 1919. Reprinted 1968 and 1982 (with a new introduction).

2189 **Coleman**, D. C., 'Labour in the English economy in the seventeenth century', *Ec.H.R.*, 2nd ser., VIII, 1956, 280-95. Reprinted in Carus-Wilson, ed. (245), listed above, II, 291-308. An important and wide-ranging article.

2190 **Davies**, Margaret G., *The Enforcement of English Apprenticeship 1563-1642: A Study in Applied Mercantilism*, Harvard, Mass., 1956. A useful study showing the gulf between the theory and practice of Tudor economic legislation.

2191 **Dunlop**, O. J. and Denham, R. D., *English Apprenticeship and Child Labour*, 1912.

2192 **Everitt**, A. M., 'Farm labourers'. In Thirsk (1414), listed above, 396-465. A very valuable study of a neglected subject.

2193 **Furniss**, E. S., *The Position of the Labourer in a System of Nationalism*, Boston and N. Y., 1920. Reprinted N. Y., 1957.

2194 **Fussell**, G. E., *The English Rural Labourer*, 1949.

2195 **Glass**, D. V., 'Socio-economic status and occupations in the city of London at the end of the seventeenth century'. In Hollaender and Kellaway (597), listed above, 373-89.

ENGLAND 1500-1700

2196 **Gregory**, T. E., 'The economics of employment in England, 1660-1713', *Economica*, I, 1921, 37-51.

2197 **Habakkuk**, H. J., 'La disparition du paysan anglais', *Annales*, 20e année, 1965, 649-63.

2198 **Hart**, C. E., *The Free Miners of the Forest of Dean*, 1953.

2199 **Hasbach**, W., *History of the English Agricultural Labourer*, 1908. Reprinted 1966.

2200 **Hill**, C., 'Pottage for free-born Englishmen: attitudes to wage labour in the sixteenth and seventeenth centuries'. In C. H. Feinstein, ed., *Socialism, Capitalism and Economic Growth*, 1967, 338-50. Reprinted in Hill (1196) above, 219-38. Considers the stigma which was attached to wage labour in the sixteenth and seventeenth centuries and suggests that this helps explain working-class reluctance to enter the early factories of the Industrial Revolution.

2201 **Hole**, Christina, *The English Housewife in the Seventeenth Century*, 1953. See also Clark (2188), listed above in this section.

2202 **Hoskins**, W. G., 'The farm labourer through four centuries'. In Hoskins and Finberg (1248), listed above, 419-41.

2203 **Jenkin**, A. K. H., *The Cornish Miner*, 1927, 3rd ed., 1962.

2204 **Kelsall, R. K.,** *Wage Regulation under the Statute of Artificers*, 1938. The standard work. See Minchinton (2211), listed below.

2205 —— 'A century of wage assessment in Herefordshire', *E.H.R.*, LVII, 1942, 115-19.

2206 —— 'Statute wages during a Yorkshire epidemic 1679-81', *Yorks.Arch. J.*, XXXIV, 1939, 310-19.

2207 **Knoop**, D. and Jones, G. P., *The Sixteenth-century Mason*, 1937.

2208 —— *The London Mason in the Seventeenth Century*, 1935.

2209 —— 'Overtime in the age of Henry VIII', *Ec. J.Ec.H.Supp.*, 3, 1938, 13-20.

2210 **Kussmaul**, Anna S., *Servants in Husbandry in Early Modern England*, 1982.

2211 **Minchinton**, W. E., ed., *Wage Regulation in Pre-industrial England*, 1971. A valuable reprint of the works by Tawney (2214) and Kelsall (2204), with a new introductory essay.

2212 **Norman**, F. A. and Lee, L. G., 'Labour exchanges in the seventeenth century', *Ec. J.Ec.H.Supp.*, 1, 1928, 399-404.

2213 **Ransome**, D. R., 'Artisan dynasties in London and Westminster in the sixteenth century', *Guildhall Miscellany*, II, 1964, 236-47.

2214 **Tawney**, R. H., 'The assessment of wages in England by the justices of the peace', *Vierteljahrschrift für Sozial- und Wirtschaftsgeschichte*, 11, 1913, 307-37, 533-64. See Minchinton (2211), listed above.

2215 —— 'An occupational census of the seventeenth century', *Ec.H.R.*, V., 1934-5, 25-64. Analyses the occupational structure of Gloucestershire as revealed in the muster roll of 1608. Shows the intertwining of agriculture and industry.

2216 **Woodward**, D. M., 'The assessment of wages by justices of the peace, 1563-1813', *Loc.Historian*, VIII, 1969, 293-9.

2217 —— 'The background to the Statute of Artificers: the genesis of labour policy, 1558-63', *Ec.H.R.*, 2nd ser., XXXIII, 1980, 32-44.

See also the book by Phelps Brown and Hopkins (2225) listed below, and Tanner (2146) listed above, who has a section on the regulation of wages and labour, 502-6.

STANDARDS OF LIVING

2218 **Batho**, G. R., ed., *The Household Papers of Henry Percy, Ninth Earl of Northumberland*, Camden Soc., 3rd ser., XCIII, 1962.

2219 **Cash**, M., *Devon Inventories of the Sixteenth and Seventeenth Centuries*, Devon and Cornwall Rec.Soc., n.s., XI, 1966.

2220 **Harland**, J., ed., *The Household and Farm Accounts of the Shuttleworths of Gawthorpe Hall from September 1582 to October 1621*, Chet.Soc., o.s., 35, 41, 43, 46, 1856-8.

2221 **Havinden**, M. A., ed., *Household and Farm Inventories in Oxfordshire, 1550-1590*, 1965.

2222 **Ashmore**, O., 'Household inventories of the Lancashire gentry, 1550-1700', *T.H.S.L.C.*, 110, 1958-9, 59-105.

2223 **Barley**, M. W., *The English Farmhouse and Cottage*, 1961. Well illustrated.

2224 —— 'Rural housing in England'. In Thirsk (1414), listed above, 696-766.

2225 **Brown**, E. H. P. and Hopkins, Sheila V., *A Perspective of Wages and Prices*, 1981. Brings

73

together the well-known articles on the cost of living.

2226 **Cunnington**, C. W. and Phillis, *Handbook of English Costume in the sixteenth Century*, 1954, 2nd rev. ed., 1970.

2227 **Emmison**, F. G., *Tudor Food and Pastimes*, 1964.

2228 **Hole**, Christina, *English Home Life, 1500-1800*, 1947.

2229 **Hoskins**, W. G., 'The rebuilding of rural England, 1570-1640', *P.P.*, 4, 1953, 44-59. Reprinted in Hoskins (1246), listed above, 131-48.

2230 **Machin**, R., 'The Great Rebuilding: a reassessment', *P.P.*, 77, 1977, 33-56.

2231 **Mercer**, E., 'The houses of the gentry', *P.P.*, 5, 1954, 11-32.

2232 **Rive**, A., 'The consumption of tobacco since 1600', *Ec. J.Ec.H.Supp.*, I, 1926, 57-75.

2233 **Smith**, J. T., 'The evolution of the English peasant house in the late seventeenth century', *J.Brit.Architectural Ass.*, XXXIII, 1970, 122-47.

2234 **Thomas**, K., 'Work and Leisure in pre-industrial society. Conference paper and discussion', *P.P.*, 29, 1964, 50-66.

2235 **Thomson**, Gladys Scott, *Life in a Noble Household, 1641-1700*, 1937.

2236 **Willan**, T. S., 'Sugar and the Elizabethans'. In Willan (1768), listed above, 313-32.

2237 **Wood-Jones**, R. B., *Traditional Domestic Architecture of the Banbury Region*, 1963.

2238 **Woodward**, D. M., 'Wage rates and living standards in pre-industrial England', *P.P.*, 91, 1981, 28-46.

See also Furnivall (1149), Dover Wilson (1160), Stone (2108) and Campbell (2092), listed above, all of which are relevant in this connection.

CIVIL WAR, INTERREGNUM, RESTORATION AND REVOLUTION, 1640-89

What follows is only a selection – though, it is hoped, a representative one – on the period 1640-89. It should, for example, be seen in conjunction with the sections on *Classes and social groups* and on *Religion*.

(a) SOURCES

2239 **Aylmer**, G. E., ed., *The Levellers in the English Revolution*, 1975. A documentary collection.

2240 **Bamford**, F., ed., *A Royalist's Notebook: the Commonplace Book of Sir John Oglander, Knight*, 1936. The archetype of the grumbling 'mere gentleman'.

2241 **Hill**, C. and Dell, E. M., *The Good Old Cause*, 1949, 2nd ed., 1969.

2242 **James**, Margaret and Weinstock, Maureen, *England During the Interregnum, 1642-60*, 1935.

2243 **Lloyd-Thomas**, J. M., ed., *The Autobiography of Richard Baxter*, 1931. New ed., 1974. Baxter – 1615-91 – was a puritan divine; his autobiography forms a valuable contemporary account of the troubles of the mid-seventeenth century and provides some revealing insights into the line-up of society in the Civil War.

2244 **Macray**, W. D., ed., *Clarendon's History of the Rebellion*, 6 vols, 1888. There is also a one-volume edition of *Selections from Clarendon*, ed.

G. Huehns, 1955. Clarendon's *History* is the classic Royalist account of the Civil War.

2245 **Morrill**, J. S., *The Revolt of the Provinces, 1630-50*, 1976. A useful collection of documents with an excellent introduction pointing out the strength of localism in this period.

2246 **Pocock**, J. G. A., ed., *The Political Works of James Harrington*, 1977. Pride of place is given to *Oceana*, Harrington's 'civil history of property' and subsequently a major element in the 'gentry controversy'.

2247 **Prall**, S. E., ed., *The Puritan Revolution, A Documentary History*, 1969. A well-chosen selection.

2248 **Thirsk**, Joan, ed., *The Restoration*, 1976. A useful sourcebook with an introduction and linking commentary.

2249 **Woodhouse**, A. S. P., ed., *Puritanism and Liberty, Being the Army Debates, 1647-49*, 1938, 3rd ed., 1974.

(b) GENERAL WORKS

2250 **Aiken**, W. A. and Henning, B. D., eds., *Conflict in Stuart England. Essays in honour of Wallace Notestein*, 1960.

2251 **Allan**, D. G. C., 'Politics and the climate of

economic opinion, 1660-88', *Notes and Queries*, n.s., III, 1956, 254-58.

2252 **Ashton**, R., *The City and the Court, 1603-43*, 1979. A study of the economics and politics involved in the interplay between City, Parliament and Court.

2253 —— *The English Civil War. Conservatism and Revolution 1603-49*, 1978. Heavily thematic in treatment with chapters on 'monarchy and society', tradition and innovation', 'centralism and localism', 'gentlemen and bourgeois'.

2254 **Aylmer**, G. E., ed., *The Interregnum: The Quest for Settlement 1646-60*, 1972. Includes an important essay by J. P. Cooper on social and economic policy.

2255 **Brinton**, C., *The Anatomy of Revolution*, N.Y., 1938, 2nd ed., N.Y., 1952, London, 1953.

2256 **Brunton**, D. and Pennington, D. H., *Members of the Long Parliament*, 1954. Reprinted 1968. An analysis – on Namierite lines – of the social composition of the Long Parliament. The book threw doubts on some well-known generalisations about Royalists and Roundheads, but was itself much criticised. See Hill (2277), listed below; and Manning (2291).

2257 **Coates**, W. H., 'An analysis of major conflicts in seventeenth-century England'. In Aiken and Henning (2250), listed above, 15-40.

2258 **Davies**, G., *The Restoration of Charles II, 1658-1660*, 1955.

2259 **Elton**, G. R., 'A high road to Civil War'. In C. H. Carter, ed., *From Renaissance to Counter-Reformation*, 1966, 325-47.

2260 **Engberg**, J., 'Royalist finances during the English Civil War, 1642-46', *Scand.Ec.H.R.*, XIV, 1966, 73-96.

2261 **Everitt**, A. M., 'The county community'. In Ives (2286), listed below.

2262 —— *The Local Community and the Great Rebellion*, Hist.Ass. pamphlet, 1969. See also the two specialised studies by Everitt (2327-8), listed below.

2263 **Firth**, C. H., *The Last Years of the Protectorate, 1656-58*, 2 vols., 1909. A continuation of Gardiner (2267-8), listed below.

2264 **Fletcher**, A., *The Outbreak of the English Civil War*, 1981. A narrative approach placing great stress on the interaction between the centre and the provinces.

2265 **Frank**, J., *The Levellers*, Cambridge, Mass., 1955.

2266 **French**, A., *Charles I and the Puritan Upheaval: A Study of the Causes of the Great Migration*, 1955.

2267 **Gardiner**, S. R., *History of the Great Civil War, 1642-49*, 4 vols., 1893.

2268 —— *History of the Commonwealth and Protectorate*, 4 vols., 1893. Continued by Firth (2263), listed above. As a detailed narrative, Gardiner remains unsuperseded.

2269 **Habakkuk**, H. J., 'Landowners and the Civil War', *Ec.H.R.*, 2nd ser., XVIII, 1965, 130-51. See also Thirsk (2304), listed below.

2270 —— 'Public finance and the sale of confiscated property during the Interregnum', *Ec.H.R.*, 2nd ser., XV, 1962-3, 70-88.

2271 —— 'The Parliamentary army and the crown lands', *Welsh H.R.*, 3, 1966-7, 403-26.

2272 —— 'English landownership, 1680-1740', *Ec.H.R.*, X, 1940, 2-17.

2273 —— 'The Land Settlement and the Restoration of Charles II', *T.R.H.S.*, 5th ser., XXVIII, 1978, 201-22.

2274 **Hammersley**, G., 'The revival of the Forest laws under Charles I', *Hist.*, XLV, 1960, 85-102.

2275 **Hardacre**, P. H., *The Royalists during the Puritan Revolution*, The Hague, 1956.

2276 **Hill**, C., *The English Revolution*, 1940, revised 1955.

2277 —— *Puritanism and Revolution: Studies in the Interpretation of the English Revolution of the Seventeenth Century*, 1958.

2278 —— *The Intellectual Origins of the English Revolution*, 1965.

2279 —— *God's Englishman: Oliver Cromwell and the English Revolution*, 1970.

2280 —— *The World Turned Upside Down. Radical Ideas During the English Revolution*, 1972.

2281 —— *Some Intellectual Consequences of the English Revolution*, 1980.

2282 —— 'Parliament and people in seventeenth-century England', *P.P.*, 92, 1981, 100-24.

2283 **Hirst**, D., *The Representative of the People? Voters and Voting in England under the Early Stuarts*, 1975. Argues that popular involvement in and awareness of politics were greater than commonly supposed.

2284 **Hobsbawm**, E. J., 'The crisis of the seventeenth century', *P.P.*, 5, 6, 1954, 33-53, 44-65. Reprinted in Aston (1164), listed above, 5-58. See also Trevor-Roper (2308), listed below.

2285 **Holiday**, P. G., 'Land sales and repurchases in Yorkshire after the Civil Wars, 1650-1670', *Northern H.*, V, 1970, 67-92.

2286 **Ives**, E. W., ed., *The English Revolution, 1600-1660*, 1968. A useful collection of short essays, originally broadcast talks, with guides to further reading.

2287 **Keeler**, Mary F., *The Long Parliament: A Biographical Study of its Members*, American Phil.Soc., Philadelphia, 1954. See also Brunton and Pennington (2256), listed above.

2288 **Madge**, S. J., *The Domesday of Crown Lands: A Study of the Legislation, Surveys and Sales of Royal Estates Under the Commonwealth*, 1938. See also Thirsk (2304), listed below.

2289 **Manning**, B., ed., *Politics, Religion and the English Civil War*, 1973.

2290 —— *The English People and the English Revolution, 1640-49*, 1976. Looks at the role of the 'middle sort of people' in the towns and of the peasantry in the countryside. Links with Hirst (2283), above.

2291 —— 'The Long Parliament', *P.P.*, 5, 1954, 71-6. See also Keeler (2287), listed above. Comments on Brunton and Pennington (2256), above.

2292 **Mulligan**, Lotte, 'Property and parliamentary politics in the English Civil War, 1642-6', *Hist.Studs.*, XVI, 1975, 341-61.

2293 **Parry**, R. H., ed., *The English Civil War and After, 1642-1658*, 1970.

2294 **Pearl**, Valerie, 'The Royal Independents' in the English Civil War', *T.R.H.S.*, 5th ser., XVIII, 1968, 69-96.

2295 —— 'London's Counter-revolution'. In Aylmer (2254), listed above, 29-56.

2296 **Pennington**, D. H., 'The cost of the English Civil War', *H.Today*, 7, 1958, 126-33.

2297 —— 'The accounts of the Kingdom'. In Fisher (1190), listed above, 182-203.

2298 **Pocock**, J. G. A., ed., *Three British Revolutions, 1641, 1688, 1776*, Princeton, N. J., 1980. A symposium which includes essays by Lawrence Stone on 'The results of the English Revolutions of the seventeenth century', Christopher Hill on 'A bourgeois revolution?', and by Robert Ashton on 'Tradition and innovation in the Great Rebellion'.

2299 **Richardson**, R. C., *The Debate on the English Revolution*, 1977. Surveys the historiography of the English Revolution from the seventeenth century to the present day.

2300 **Russell**, C., ed., *The Origins of the English Civil War*, 1973. Includes essays by Conrad Russell, 'Parliament and the King's finances', and by Penelope Corfield, 'Economic issues and ideologies'.

2301 **Schenk**, W., *The Concern for Social Justice in the Puritan Revolution*, 1948.

2302 **Stone**, L., *The Causes of the English Revolu-*

tion, 1529-1642, 1972. The longest section is on the causes of the Revolution which are sensibly discussed under the headings presuppositions, preconditions, precipitants, and triggers.

2303 **Taylor**, P. A. M., ed., *The Origins of the English Civil War: Conspiracy, Crusade or Class Conflict?*, Boston, Mass., 1960. A collection of extracts.

2304 **Thirsk**, Joan, 'The sale of Royalist lands during the Interregnum', *Ec.H.R.*, 2nd ser., V, 1952, 188-207. Shows that the confiscated lands of royalists were commonly being re-acquired by their former owners before the Restoration.

2305 —— 'The Restoration land settlement', *J.M.H.*, XXVI, 1954, 315-28.

2306 **Trevelyan**, G. M., *England under the Stuarts*, 1904, 12th rev. ed., 1925. An elderly textbook though not without its uses.

2307 **Trevor-Roper**, H. R., 'The social origins of the Great Rebellion', *H.Today*, 5, 1955, 376-82.

2308 —— 'The general crisis of the seventeenth century', *P.P.*, 16, 1959, 31-64. Reprinted in Aston (1164), listed above, 59-96.

2309 **Underdown**, D., *Royalist Conspiracy in England, 1649-1660*, New Haven, Conn., 1960.

2310 —— 'The Independents again', *J.Brit.Studs.*, VIII, 1968, 83-93. Part of a debate on the subject. See Yule (2359), listed below.

2311 —— 'The problem of popular allegiance in the English Civil War', *T.R.H.S.*, 5th ser., XXXI, 69-94.

2312 **Walzer**, M., *The Revolution of the Saints*, 1966. A sociological study which analyses the role of puritan ideology in the English Revolution.

2313 **White**, S. D., *Sir Edward Coke and the Grievances of the Commonwealth*, 1979. Includes a full treatment of the economic grievances which Coke articulated in Parliament.

2314 **Wilson**, C., 'Economics and politics in the seventeenth century', *Hist. J.*, V., 1962, 80-92. Reprinted in Wilson (1232), listed above, 1-21.

2315 **Woolrych**, A., 'The English Revolution: an introduction'. In Ives (2286), listed above, 1-33.

2316 —— 'Puritanism, politics and society'. In *ibid.*, 87-100.

2317 **Yule**, G., *The Independents in the English Civil War*, 1957.

2318 —— 'Independents and revolutionaries', *J.Brit.Studs.*, VII, 1967, 11-32.

2319 **Zagorin**, P., *The Court and the Country. The Beginning of the English Revolution*, 1969. Stresses the constitutional aspect of the Rebellion, but at the same time places it firmly in its socio-economic setting.

2320 —— 'The social interpretation of the English Revolution', *J.Ec.H.*, XIX, 1959, 376-401.

2321 —— 'The English Revolution', *J. World H.*, II, 1955, 667-81.

2322 —— *A History of Political Thought in the English Revolution*, 1954. Has chapters on Harrington, the Levellers, and the Diggers.
See also Stone (2108), above.

(c) REGIONAL STUDIES

2323 **Pennington**, D. H., and Roots, I., *The Committee at Stafford, 1643-45: The Order Book of the Staffordshire County Committee*, 1957.

2324 **Blackwood**, B. G., *The Lancashire Gentry and the Great Rebellion, 1640-60*, 1978. Heavily statistical in its approach to the numbers, distribution, status, allegiance and wealth of the county's gentry.

2325 **Coate**, Mary, *Cornwall in the Great Civil War and Interregnum, 1642-1660*, 1933. Reprinted 1963.

2326 **Dore**, R. N., *The Civil Wars in Cheshire*, 1966.

2327 **Everitt**, A. M., *Suffolk and the Great Rebellion*, Suffolk Rec.Soc., III, 1960.

2328 —— *The Community of Kent and the Great Rebellion, 1640-60*, 1966. See the two shorter and more general works by Everitt on the same subject (2261, 2262), listed above.

2329 **Farrar**, W. J., *The Great Civil War in Shropshire, 1642-49*, 1926.

2330 **Fletcher**, A., *A County Community in Peace and War. Sussex, 1600-60*, 1975.

2331 **Guttery**, D. R., *The Great Civil War in Midland Parishes*, 1950.

2332 **Holmes**, C., *The Eastern Association in the English Civil War*, 1974. An interesting analysis of the interaction between local and national issues.

2333 —— 'The county community in Stuart historiography', *J.Brit.Studs.*, XIX, 1980, 54-73.

2334 **Howell**, R., *Newcastle-upon-Tyne and the Puritan Revolution: A Study of the Civil War in Northern England*, 1967.

2335 **Ketton-Cremer**, R. W., *Norfolk in the Civil War*, 1969. Looks old-fashioned in comparison with Everitt (2328), listed above.

2336 **Leach**, A. L., *The History of the Civil War, 1642-49, in Pembrokeshire and on its Borders*, 1937.

2337 **Lennard**, R. V., *Rural Northamptonshire under the Commonwealth*, Oxford Studies in Social and Legal History, 1916.

2338 **Morrill**, J. S., *Cheshire 1630-1660: County Government and Society During the English Revolution*, 1974.

2339 **Pearl**, Valerie, *London and the Outbreak of the Puritan Revolution*, 1961.

2340 **Phillips**, C. B., 'The Royalist North: the Cumberland and Westmorland gentry 1642-60', *Northern H.*, XIV, 1978, 169-92.

2341 **Sherwood**, R. E., *Civil Strife in the Midlands, 1642-51*, 1974.

2342 **Tupling**, G. H., 'The causes of the Civil War in Lancashire', *T.L.C.A.S.*, LXV, 1955, 1-32.

2343 **Underdown**, D., *Somerset in the Civil War and Interregnum*, 1973.

2344 **Willan**, T. S., 'The parliamentary surveys for the North Riding of Yorkshire', *Yorks.Arch. J.*, XXXI, 1933, 224-89.

2345 **Wood**, A. C., *Nottinghamshire in the Civil War*, 1937.

(d) MISCELLANEOUS

2346 **Berens**, C. H., *The Digger Movement in the Days of the Commonwealth*, 1906. Reprinted 1961.

2347 **Brailsford**, H. N., *The Levellers and the English Revolution*, 1961.

2348 **Cole**, W. A., 'The Quakers and the English Revolution', *P.P.*, 9, 1956, 39-54. Reprinted in Aston (1164), listed above, 341-58.

2349 **Davis**, J. C., 'The Levellers and Democracy', *P.P.*, 40, 1968, 174-80.

2350 **Gordon**, M. Dorothy, 'The collection of Ship Money in the reign of Charles I', *T.R.H.S.*, 3rd ser., 4, 1910, 141-62.

2351 **Gregg**, Pauline, *Free-born John: A Biography of John Lilburne*, 1961.

2352 **Lamont**, W. M., *Marginal Prynne, 1600-1669*, 1963.

2353 **Manning**, B., 'The Levellers'. In Ives (2286), listed above, 144-57. Contains a bibliographical note on the subject.

2354 **Petegorsky**, D. W., *Left-wing Democracy in the English Civil War: A Study of the Social Philosophy of Gerrard Winstanley*, 1940.

2355 **Prall**, S. E., *The Agitation for Law Reform During the Puritan Revolution, 1640-60*, 1966. See Veall (2088), listed above.

2356 **Roy**, I., 'The English Civil War and English Society', in I. Roy and B. Bond, eds., *War and Society: A Yearbook of Military History*, 1975, 24-43.

2357 **Thomas**, K., 'Women and the Civil War sects', *P.P.*, 13, 1958, 42-62. Reprinted in Aston (1164), listed above, 317-40.

2358 —— 'The social origins of Hobbes' political thought'. In K. Brown, ed., *Hobbes Studies*, 1965, 185-236.

2359 **Yule**, G., *The Independents in the Civil War*, Melbourne and Cambridge, 1958.

RELIGION

(a) GENERAL AND MISCELLANEOUS

2360 **Ashton**, R., 'Puritanism and progress', *Ec.H.R.*, 2nd ser., XVII, 1965, 579-87. A review article on Hill (2390), listed below.

2361 **Aveling**, J. H. C., *The Handle and the Axe. The Catholic Recusants in England from Reformation to Emancipation*, 1976.

2362 **Barbour**, H., *The Quakers in Puritan England*, Yale, 1964.

2363 **Bebb**, E. D., *Nonconformity and Social Life, 1660-1800*, 1935.

2364 **Blackwood**, B. G., 'Agrarian unrest and the early Lancashire Quakers', *J. Friends' Hist.Soc.*, LI, 1966, 72-6.

2365 **Bossy**, J., *The English Catholic Community, 1570-1850*, 1976. Particularly good on relations between priests and gentry.

2366 **Bouch**, C. M. L., *Prelates and People of the Lake Counties: A History of the Diocese of Carlisle, 1133-1933*, 1948.

2367 **Breslow**, M. A., *A Mirror of England. English Puritan Views of Foreign Nations, 1618-40*, Cambridge, Mass., 1970.

2368 **Brigden**, Susan, 'Youth and the English Reformation', *P.P.*, 95, 1982, 37-67.

2369 **Capp**, B. S., *The Fifth Monarchy Men*, 1972.

2370 **Cole**, W. A., 'The social origins of the early Friends', *J. Friends' Hist.Soc.*, XLVIII, 1957, 99-118. See also Vann (2409), listed below.

2371 **Collinson**, P., *The Elizabethan Puritan Movement*, 1967. The standard work.

2372 —— 'The beginnings of English Sabbatarianism'. In C. W. Dugmore and C. Duggan, eds., *Studies in Church History*, I, 1964, 207-21.

2373 **Cross**, M. Claire, *The Puritan Earl: The Life of Henry Hastings, Third Earl of Huntingdon, 1536-1595*, 1966. A study of influence and patronage.

2374 —— *Church and People, 1450-1660. The Triumph of the Laity in the English Church*, 1976.

2375 **Curtis**, T. C. and Speck, W. A., 'The Societies for the Reformation of Manners: a case study in the theory and practice of moral reform', *Lit.& H.*, III, 1976, 45-64.

2376 **Dickens**, A. G., *The English Reformation*, 1964.

2377 **Everitt**, A. M., 'Nonconformity in country parishes'. In Joan Thirsk, ed., *Land, Church and People: Essays Presented to Professor H. P. R. Finberg*, 1970, 178-99. An interesting survey which examines the social and economic factors affecting the distribution of nonconformity.

2378 **Haigh**, C., *Reformation and Resistance in Tudor Lancashire*, 1975.

2379 **Hall**, B., 'Puritanism: the problem of definition'. In C. J. Cuming, ed., *Studies in Church History*, II, 1965, 283-96.

2380 **Haller**, W., *The Rise of Puritanism*, N. Y., 1938. A classic work by the doyen of historians of puritanism.

2381 —— *Liberty and Reformation in the Puritan Revolution*, N. Y., 1955. Reprinted 1963.

2382 **Hart**, A. T., *The County Clergy in Elizabethan and Stuart Times*, 1958.

2383 —— *The Man in the Pew*, 1966.

2384 **Havran**, M. J., *The Catholics in Caroline England*, 1962.

2385 **Heal**, Felicity, *Of Prelates and Princes. A Study of the Economic and Social Position of the Tudor Episcopate*, 1980.

2386 —— and O'Day, Rosemary, eds., *Church and Society in England. Henry VIII to James I*, 1977. Includes chapters on the economic problems of the clergy and on the disposal of monastic and chantry lands.

2387 **Heinemann**, Margot, *Puritanism and Theatre. Thomas Middleton and Opposition Drama under the Early Stuarts*, 1980. Argues that the conventional view of puritan hostility to drama is largely a myth.

2388 **Hembry**, Pauline M., *The Bishops of Bath and Wells, 1540-1640: Social and Economic Problems*, 1967.

2389 **Hill**, C., *Economic Problems of the Church from Archbishop Whitgift to the Long Parliament*, 1956.

2390 —— *Society and Puritanism in Pre-revolutionary England*, 1964. This and the previous book are essential reading on the social history of religion in the first half of the seventeenth century.

2391 **Houlbrooke**, R. A., *Church Courts and People during the English Reformation, 1520-70*, 1979.

2392 **Jordan, W. K.**, *The Development of Religious Toleration in England*, 4 vols., 1932-40.

2393 **Knappen**, M. M., *Tudor Puritanism*, Chicago, Ill., 1939. Reprinted 1965. A standard work, which still supplements, and is not made redundant by, Collinson (2371), listed above.

2394 **Leys**, Mary D. R., *Catholics in England, 1559-1829: A Social History*, 1961.

2395 **Lloyd**, A., *Quaker Social History, 1669-1738*, 1950.

2396 **McGrath**, P. V., *Papists and Puritans under Elizabeth I*, 1967. A clear survey with a useful bibliography.

2397 **Morton**, A. L., *The World of the Ranters*, 1971. See also Hill (2280), listed above.

2398 **O'Day**, Rosemary and Heal, Felicity, eds., *Continuity and Change. Personnel and Administration of the Church in England, 1500-1642*, 1976. Several of the chapters deal with economic and social aspects.

2399 —— *Princes and Paupers in the English Church, 1500-1800*, 1981. A collection of essays concerned with the economic foundations of the church in the early modern period and with the chronological, geographical and social variations which they displayed.

2400 **Reay**, B., 'The social origins of early Quakerism', *J. Interdis. H.*, XI, 1980, 55-72.

2401 **Richardson**, R. C., *Puritanism in Northwest England: A Regional Study of the Diocese of Chester to 1642*, 1972. A social approach examining the structure of puritanism in the region and the forces at work within it.

2402 **Schlatter**, R. B., *The Social Ideas of Religious Leaders, 1660-1688*, 1940.

2403 **Seaver**, P. S., *The Puritan Lectureships: The Politics of Religious Dissent, 1560-1662*, Stanford, Calif., 1970.

2404 **Solt**, L. F., *Saints in Arms: Puritanism and Democracy in Cromwell's Army*, Stanford, Calif., 1959.

2405 **Steffan**, T. G., 'The social argument against Enthusiasm, 1650-60', *Studies in English*, 21, 1941, 39-63.

2406 **Trevor-Roper**, H. R., *Religion, the Reformation and Social Change*, 1967.

2407 **Trimble**, W. R., *The Catholic Laity in Elizabethan England*, Cambridge, Mass., 1964.

2408 **Tyacke**, N., 'Puritanism, Arminianism and Counter-Revolution'. In Russell (2300), listed above, 119-43.

2409 **Vann**, R. T., *The Social Development of English Quakerism, 1655-1755*, Harvard, Mass., 1969.

2410 —— 'Quakerism and the social structure in the Interregnum', *P.P.*, 43, 1969, 71-91.

2411 **Watts**, M. R., *The Dissenters from the Reformation to the French Revolution*, 1978.

2412 **Whitaker**, W. B., *Sunday in Tudor and Stuart Times*, 1933.

2413 **Whitney**, Dorothy W., 'London puritanism: the Haberdashers' Company', *Church H.*, XXXII, 1963, 298-321. A case study of the patronage wielded by bodies of merchants and tradesmen.

See also Walzer (2312), listed above.

(b) RELIGION AND ECONOMIC DEVELOPMENT

2414 **Birnbaum**, N., 'Conflicting interpretations of the rise of capitalism: Marx and Weber', *Brit. J. Soc.*, IV, 1953, 125-41.

2415 **Breen**, T. H., 'The non-existent controversy. Puritan and Anglican attitudes to work and wealth, 1600-1640', *Church H.*, XXXV, 1966, 273-87. See also the book by the Georges (2420), listed below.

2416 **Burrell**, S. A., 'Calvinism, capitalism and the middle classes: some afterthoughts on an old problem', *J.M.H.*, 32, 1960, 129-41.

2417 **Fanfani**, A., *Catholicism, Protestantism and Capitalism*, N. Y., 1935.

2418 **Fischoff**, E., 'The Protestant ethic and the spirit of capitalism; the history of a controversy', *Social Research*, XI, 1944, 61-77.

2419 **George**, C. H., 'English Calvinist opinion on usury, 1600-1640', *J.H. Ideas*, XVIII, 1957, 455-74.

2420 —— and Katherine, *The Protestant Mind of the English Reformation, 1570-1640*, Princeton, N. J., 1961. A useful book but by no means wholly convincing in its attempts to play down the distinctiveness of puritanism.

2421 **Green**, R. W., ed., *Protestantism and Capitalism: The Weber Thesis and its Critics*, Boston, Mass., 1959. A collection of extracts from the main contributions to the debate.

2422 **Hill**, C., 'Protestantism and the rise of capitalism', in Fisher, ed. (1190), listed above, 29-39. A stimulating essay by a distinguished defender of the Weber Thesis.

2423 **Hudson**, W. S., 'Puritanism and the spirit of capitalism', *Church H.*, XVIII, 1949, 3-16.

2424 **Kearney**, H. F., 'Puritanism, capitalism and the scientific revolution', *P.P.*, 28, 1964, 81-101.

2425 **Kitch**, M. J., ed., *Capitalism and the Reformation*, 1967. A collection of extracts from contemporary writings and from historians interpretations, with an introduction and bibliography.

2426 **Luethy**, M., 'Once again: Calvinism and capitalism', *Encounter*, XXII, 1964, 26-38.

2427 **Orme**, N., 'The dissolution of the Chantries in Devon, 1546-8', *T.Devonshire Ass.*, CXI, 1979, 75-123.

2428 **Razzell**, P. E., 'The protestant ethic and the spirit of capitalism', *Brit. J.Soc.*, XXVIII, 1977, 17-37.

2429 **Reay**, B., 'Quaker opposition to tithes, 1652-60', *P.P.*, 86, 1980, 98-120.

2430 **Robertson**, H. M., *Aspects of the Rise of Economic Individualism*, 1933. Reprinted N. Y., 1959. A hostile criticism of the Weber thesis.

2431 **Samuelsson**, K., *Religion and Economic Action*, 1961. A more recent attack on the Weber thesis.

2432 **Seaver**, P. S., 'The puritan work ethic revisited', *J.Brit.Studs.*, XIX, 1980, 35-53.

2433 **Sombart**, W., *The Quintessence of Capitalism*, London and N. Y., 1915. The work of one of Weber's earliest opponents.

2434 **Supple**, B. E., 'The great capitalist manhunt', *Bus.H.*, VI, 1963, 48-62.

2435 **Tawney**, R. H., *Religion and the Rise of Capitalism*, 1926. Several times reprinted. A profound and wide-ranging study. One of the masterpieces of English historical writing.

2436 **Thomas**, K., *Religion and the Decline of Magic*, 1971.

2437 **Trevor-Roper**, H. R., 'The bishopric of Durham and the capitalist Reformation', *Durham Univ. J.*, XXXVIII, 1946, 45-58.

2438 **Troeltsch**, E., *The Social Teaching of the Christian Churches*, English trans., 2 vols, 1931. Lent support to the Weber thesis.

2439 **Weber**, M., *The Protestant Ethic and the Spirit of Capitalism*, 1904, English trans., N. Y. and London, 1930. One of the earliest attempts to explore the relationship between reformed religion and economic development. Its publication initiated a controversy amongst historians, economists, sociologists and theologians which has lasted for over sixty years. See also the chapter 'Religion and the social environment' in Thompson (2582), listed below.

EDUCATION AND LEARNING

(a) SCHOOLS, SCHOOLING AND HIGHER EDUCATION

2440 **Cressy**, D., *Education in Tudor and Stuart England*, 1975. Source material with extended commentary.

2441 **Sylvester**, D. W., ed., *Educational Documents, 800-1816*, 1970.

2442 **Turnbull**, G. L., ed., *Hartlib, Dury and Comenius*, 1947. The three most influential foreign intellectuals in the English Revolution.

2443 **Adamson**, J. W., *A Short History of Education*, 1919.

2444 —— *The Illiterate Anglo-Saxon and Other Essays on Education Medieval and Modern*, 1946.

2445 —— 'The extent of literacy in England in the fifteenth and sixteenth centuries: notes and con-

jectures', *The Library*, 4th ser., X, 1929-30, 163-93.

2446 **Axtell**, J. L., 'Education and status in Stuart England: the London physician', *H.Educ. Quarterly*, X, 1970, 141-59.

2447 **Beales**, A. C. F., *Education under Penalty: English Catholic Education from the Reformation to the Fall of James II*, 1963.

2448 **Bennett**, H. S., *English Books and Readers, 1475-1640*, 3 vols., 1952-70. A scholarly treatment of the subject.

2449 **Brauer**, G. C., *The Education of a Gentleman: Theories of Gentlemanly Education in England, 1660-1775*, N. Y., 1959.

2450 **Brown**, J. H., *Elizabethan Schooldays*, 1933.

2451 **Caspari**, F., *Humanism and the Social Order in Tudor England*, Chicago and Cambridge, 1955.

2452 **Charlton**, K., *Education in Renaissance England*, 1965.

2453 **Conant**, J. B., 'The advancement of learning during the Puritan Commonwealth', *Proc. Massachusetts H.Soc.*, LXVI, for 1936-41, 1942, 3-31.

2454 **Costello**, W. T., *The Scholastic Curriculum at Early Seventeenth-century Cambridge*, Cambridge, Mass., 1958.

2455 **Cressy**, D., 'The social composition of Caius College, Cambridge, 1580-1640', *P.P.*, 47, 1970, 113-15.

2456 —— *Literacy and the Social Order. Reading and Writing in Tudor and Stuart England*, 1980. Combines a general outline of the subject with local case studies. Includes an extended discussion of the available sources and of the necessary research methods.

2457 **Curtis**, M. H., *Oxford and Cambridge in Transition*, 1959. A valuable study of the two universities in the early modern period.

2458 —— 'The alienated intellectuals of early Stuart England', *P.P.*, 23, 1962, 25-43. Reprinted in Aston (1164), listed above, 295-316.

2459 **Graff**, H. J., ed., *Literacy and Social Development in the West*, 1982. A collection of reprinted essays dealing with the period from the eleventh to the twentieth centuries. The essays by Claunchy, Cressy, Spufford and Schofield specifically relate to England.

2460 **Greaves**, R. L., *The Puritan Revolution and Educational Thought*, Princeton N. J., 1969.

2461 **Green**, V. H. H., *The Universities*, 1969. A competent and readable general outline of their development.

2462 **Hexter**, J. H., 'The education of the aristocracy in the Renaissance'. In the same author's *Reappraisals in History*, 1961, 45-70.

2463 **Houston**, R. A., 'The development of literacy: Northern England, 1640-1750', *Ec.H.R.*, 2nd ser., XXXV, 1982, 199-216.

2464 **Howell**, W. S., *Logic and Rhetoric in England, 1500-1700*, Princeton, N. J., 1958.

2465 **Kearney**, H. F., *Scholars and Gentlemen: Universities and Society in Pre-industrial Britain, 1500-1700*, 1970. An important recent addition to the literature on the subject.

2466 **Lawson**, J., *A Town Grammar School Through Six Centuries* (Hull), 1963. One of the best examples of the large crop of local studies.

2467 **McMullen**, N., 'The education of English gentlewomen, 1540-1640', *H.Educ.*, VI, 1977, 87-101.

2468 **Prest**, W. R., *The Inns of Court under Elizabeth I and the Early Stuarts, 1590-1640*, 1972.

2469 —— 'The legal education of the gentry at the Inns of Court, 1560-1640', *P.P.*, 38, 1967, 20-39.

2470 **Schofield**, R. S., 'The measurement of literacy in pre-industrial England'. In J. Goody, ed., *Literacy in Traditional Societies*, 1968, 311-25.

2471 **Seaborne**, M., *The English School, its Architecture and Organisation. I: 1370-1870*, 1971. Vol. 2 of this work is listed below (5038).

2472 **Simon**, B., ed., *Education in Leicestershire, 1540-1940*, 1968.

2473 **Simon**, Joan, *Education and Society in Tudor England*, 1966. Thorough bibliography.

2474 **Spufford**, Margaret, 'The schooling of the peasantry in Cambridgeshire, 1575-1700'. In Joan Thirsk, ed., *Land, Church and People: Essays Presented to Professor H. P. R. Finberg*, 1970, 112-47. An interesting local study of the availability of education facilities and of the extent of literacy. See also Spufford (1434), above.

2475 **Stone**, L., 'The educational revolution in England, 1560-1640', *P.P.*, 28, 1964, 41-80.

2476 —— 'Literacy and education in England, 1640-1900', *P.P.*, 42, 1969, 69-139. These two articles along with Simon (2473), listed above, are essential reading on the history of education in this period.

2477 —— ed., *The University in Society*, 2 vols, Princeton, N. J., 1975. Includes chapters on the size and composition of the student body and on university links with the country opposition to Charles I.

2478 —— ed., *Schooling and Society. Studies in the History of Education*, 1976. Includes essays on book ownership in England, 1560-1640, and on English working-class education.

2479 **Thomas**, K., *Rule and Misrule in the Schools of Early Modern England*, 1976.

2480 **Vincent**, W. A. L., *The State and School Education 1640-1660 in England and Wales*, 1950.

2481 —— *The Grammar Schools. Their Continuing Tradition 1660-1714*, 1969.

2482 **Webster**, C., 'The curriculum of the grammar schools and universities, 1500-1660. A critical view of the literature', *H.Educ.*, IV, 1975, 51-68.

2483 —— *The Great Instauration. Science, Medicine and Reform 1626-1660*, 1976. The central figure in the book is Samuel Hartlib.

2484 —— ed., *The Intellectual Revolution of the Seventeenth Century*, 1975.

2485 **Wright**, L. B., *Middle Class Culture in Elizabethan England*, Chapel Hill, N. C., 1935. Reprinted Washington, D. C., 1958, and in Britain in 1964.

The various books by Professor Jordan on English philanthropy (2169-2174), listed above, are also relevant in this connection. See also Lawson and Silver (5024), listed below.

(b) THE BOOK TRADE AND THE NEWSPAPER PRESS

2486 **Beer**, E. S. de., 'The English newspapers from 1695 to 1702'. In Ragnild Hatton and J. S. Bromley, eds., *William III and Louis XIV: Essays by and for Mark Thomson*, 1968, 117-29.

2487 **Capp**, B. S., *Astrology and the Popular Press. English Almanacs 1500-1800*, 1979. A study of one of the most widely read forms of literature of the time and of its relevance to social, political, intellectual and religious life. See also Spufford (2496), below.

2488 **Clyde**, W. M., *The Struggle for the Freedom of the Press from Caxton to Cromwell*, 1934.

2489 **Dukes**, G., 'The beginnings of the English newspaper', *H.Today*, 4, 1954, 197-204.

2490 **Eisenstein**, E. L., *The Printing Press as an Agent of Change: Communications and Cultural Transformations in Early Modern Europe*, 1979.

2491 **Frank**, J., *The Beginnings of the English Newspaper, 1620-1660*, Cambridge, Mass., 1961.

2492 **Fraser**, P., *The Intelligence of the Secretaries of State and their Monopoly of Licensed News, 1660-1688*, 1956.

2493 **Myers**, R., *The British Book Trade from Caxton to the Present Day*, 1973.

2494 **Rostenberg**, L., *The Minority Press and the English Crown 1558-1625*, Nieuwkoop, 1971.

2495 **Shaaber**, M. A., *Some Forerunners of the Newspaper in England, 1476-1622*, 1929. Reprinted 1966.

2496 **Spufford**, Margaret, *Small Books and Pleasant Histories. Popular Fiction and its Readership in Seventeenth-Century England*, 1981. See also Capp (2487), above.

2497 **Thompson**, R., *Unfit for Modest Ears. A Study of Pornographic, Obscene and Bawdy Works written or published in the Second Half of the Seventeenth Century*, 1979.

2498 **Varley**, F. J., ed., *Mercurius Aulicus*, 1948. Extracts from the Royalist newspaper published at Oxford, 1643-5.

ENGLAND
1700-1970

GENERAL WORKS
1700-1880

(a) BIBLIOGRAPHIES AND STATISTICS

2499 **Armstrong**, W. A., 'Developments in nineteenth-century British social history', *Brit.Book News*, 1975, 765-774.

2500 **Ashton**, T. S., *The Industrial Revolution: A Study in Bibliography*, 1937.

2501 **Black**, R. D. C., *A Catalogue of Pamphlets on Economic Subjects Published between 1750 and 1900 and Now Housed in Irish Libraries*, Belfast, 1969.

2502 **Brown**, Lucy M. and Christie, I. R., eds., *Bibliography of British History, 1789-1851*, 1977.

2503 **Cannery**, Margaret and Knott, D., eds., *Catalogue of Goldsmiths' Library of Economic Literature*, I, 1970.

2504 **Clark**, G. N., *The Idea of the Industrial Revolution*, 1953.

2505 **Deane**, Phyllis and Cole, W. A., *British Economic Growth 1688-1959: Trends and Structure*, 1962, 2nd ed., 1967.

2506 **Hanson**, L. W., ed., *Contemporary Printed Sources for British and Irish Economic History, 1701-1750*, 1963.

2507 **Mitchell**, B. R. and Deane, Phyllis, *Abstract of British Historical Statistics*, 1962. Covers the period from 1697 to the 1950s.

2508 —— and Jones, H. G., *Second Abstract of British Historical Statistics*, 1971.

2509 **Nicholls**, D., ed., *Nineteenth-century Britain, 1815-1914*, 1978.

2510 **Pargellis**, S. and Medley, D. J., eds., *Bibliography of British History: The Eighteenth Century, 1714-89*, 1951.

2511 **Webb**, A. D., ed., *A New Dictionary of Statistics*, 1911.

2512 **Williams**, Judith B., *A Guide to the Printed Materials for English Social and Economic History 1750-1850*, 2 vols., N. Y., 1926.

(b) SOURCES AND DOCUMENTARY COLLECTIONS

2513 **Bastian**, F., 'Defoe's *Tour* and the historian', *H.Today*, 1967, 845-51. A critical estimate.

2514 **Bowditch**, J. and Ramsland, C., eds., *Voices of the Industrial Revolution. Selected Readings from the Liberal Economists and their Critics*, Ann Arbor, Mich., 1961.

2515 **Brown**, A. F. J., ed., *English History from Essex Sources, 1750-1900*, 1952. Useful book of documents on many aspects of economic and social life.

2516 **Cole**, G. D. H., ed., *Defoe's Tour through the Whole Island of Great Britain*, 2 vols., 1927. Another edition with introductions by G. D. H. Cole and D. C. Browning, 1974.

2517 **Harrison**, J. F. C., *Society and Politics in England, 1780-1960: A Selection of Readings and Comments*, 1965. Largely economic in content.

2518 **Harvie**, C., Martin, G. and Scharf, A., *Industrialisation and Culture, 1830-1914*, 1970. Documentary material with comments.

2519 **Pike**, E. R., ed., *Human Documents of Adam Smith's Time*, 1974.

2520 —— *Human Documents of the Industrial Revolution in Britain*, 1966. Editorial comments not well informed and often flippant; the extracts from documents are useful.

2521 —— *Human Documents of the Victorian Golden Age, (1850-75)*, 1967.

2522 **Tames**, R. L., ed., *Documents of the Industrial Revolution, 1750-1850*, 1971. The extracts tend to be short.

2523 **Taylor**, P. A. M., ed., *The Industrial Revolution in Britain: Triumph or Disaster?*, Boston, Mass., 1958, 2nd rev. ed., 1970. A collection of extracts from the writings of famous economic historians and Karl Marx.

2524 **Warburg**, J., ed., *The Industrial Muse: The Industrial Revolution in English Poetry*, 1958.

2525 **Ward**, J. T., ed., *The Age of Change, 1770-1870. Documents in Social History*, 1975.

(c) GENERAL WORKS

2526 **Ashton**, T. S., *The Industrial Revolution, 1760-1830*, 1948.

2527 —— *An Economic History of England: The Eighteenth Century*, 1955.

2528 **Beales**, H. L., *The Industrial Revolution, 1750-1850: An Introductory Essay*, 1928, reissue with new introduction, 1958.

2529 **Best**, G. F. A., *Mid-Victorian Britain, 1851-75*, 1971.

2530 **Bowden**, W., *Industrial Society in England towards the End of the Eighteenth Century*, 1925. 2nd ed. with new introduction and bibliography, 1965.

2531 **Butt**, J. and Clarke, I. F., eds., *The Victorians and Social Protest*, 1973. Contains chapters by H. J. Perkin on land reform and class conflict in Victorian Britain, and J. H. Treble on Irish immigrant attitudes to north of England Chartism. See Hollis (2556), listed below.

2532 **Chaloner**, W. H. and Ratcliffe, B. M., eds., *Trade and Transport. Essays in Economic History in Honour of T. S. Willan*, 1977. A miscellaneous collection which extends chronologically and topically from seventeenth-century Yorkshire cattle droving and Cumbrian ironworks to the 1930s depression in Scotland.

2533 **Chambers**, J. D., *The Workshop of the World: British Economic History from 1820-1880*, 2nd rev. ed., 1968.

2534 **Chapman**, S. D. and Chambers, J. D., *The Beginnings of Industrial Britain*, 1970. Covers the period c. 1700-1830; good illustrations.

2535 **Checkland**, S. G., *The Rise of Industrial Society in England, 1815-1885*, 1964. Valuable for footnote references to theses; good bibliography 413-54.

2536 **Church**, R. A., *The Great Victorian Boom 1850-73*, 1975.

2537 **Clapham**, J. H., *An Economic History of Modern Britain*: Vol. I, *The Early Railway Age 1820-1850*, 1926; Vol. II, *Free Trade and Steel 1850-1886*, 1932; Vol. III, *Machines and National Rivalries (1886-1914) with an Epilogue (1914-29)*, 1938.

2538 **Clark**, G. K., *The Making of Victorian England*, 1962. Covers the period 1830-60.

2539 **Court**, W. H. B., *A Concise Economic History of Britain from 1750 to Recent Times*, 1954.

2540 **Crafts**, N. F. R., 'English economic growth in the eighteenth century. A re-examination of Deane and Cole's estimates', *Ec.H.R.*, 2nd ser., XXIX, 1976, 226-35.

2541 —— 'Industrial Revolution in England and France. Some thoughts on the question "Why was England first?" ', *Ec.H.R.*, XXX, 1977, 429-41.

2542 **Deane**, Phyllis, *The First Industrial Revolution*, 1965. 2nd ed., 1980.

2543 **Earle**, P., *The World of Defoe*, 1976. The best general introduction.

2544 **Flinn**, M. W., *The Origins of the Industrial Revolution*, 1966.

2545 **Floud**, R. and McCloskey, D., eds., *The Economic History of Britain since 1700*. I, 1700-1860, 1981. For Vol. II see (2658), below.

2546 **Halévy**, E., *A History of the English People in 1815*, 1st ed. in 1 vol., 1924, 2nd ed. in 3 vols. 1938. Vol. 2 of 1938 ed. (i.e. Book II of 1st ed.) deals with economic life.

2547 **Hammond**, J. L. and Barbara, *The Rise of Modern Industry*, 1925. Many times reprinted. The 9th ed., 1965, with new introduction by R. M. Hartwell, XV-XXI, should be used.

2548 **Harrison**, J. F. C., *The Early Victorians 1832-51*, 1971.

2549 **Hartwell**, R. M., ed., *The Industrial Revolution*, 1970. A collection of essays.

2550 —— *The Causes of the Industrial Revolution in England*, 1967. A collection of articles on various aspects of the subject by eminent economic historians.

551 —— *The Industrial Revolution*. Hist.Ass. Pamphlet, 1965.

552 —— *The Industrial Revolution and Economic Growth*, 1972. Collected essays.

553 **Hobsbawm**, E. J., *Industry and Empire: An Economic History of Britain*, 1968.

554 —— *The Age of Capital, 1848-75*, 1975.

555 **Hoffmann**, W. G., *British Industry, 1700-1950*, 1955.

556 **Hollis**, Patricia M. (ed.), *Pressure from Without in Early Victorian England*, 1974. See also Butt and Clarke (2531), listed above.

557 **Jarrett**, D., *England in the Age of Hogarth*, 1975.

558 **Jones**, E. L. and Mingay, G. E., *Land, Labour and Population in the Industrial Revolution: Essays Presented to J. D. Chambers*, 1967.

559 **Klingender**, F. D., *Art and the Industrial Revolution*, 1947. 2nd rev. and enlarged ed., 1968, by Sir Arthur Elton.

60 **Kovacevic**, I., *Fact into Fiction. English Literature and the Industrial Scene, 1750-1850*, 1975. See also Sussmann (2579) and Warburg (2524).

61 **Landes**, D. S., *The Unbound Prometheus: Technological Change and Industrial Development in Western Europe from 1750 to the Present*, 1969. Mainly about Britain.

62 **Little**, A. J., *Deceleration in the Eighteenth-Century British Economy*, 1976.

63 **McCloskey**, D., *Enterprise and Trade in Victorian Britain. Essays in Historical Economics*, 1981. Deploys the techniques of the New Economic History to argue that the British economy in the late nineteenth century did not fail.

64 **Mantoux**, P., *The Industrial Revolution in the Eighteenth Century*, 1st English trans., 1928, rev. ed. with fuller bibliography, 1961.

65 **Marshall**, Dorothy, *English People in the Eighteenth Century*, 1956.

66 **Mathias**, P., *The First Industrial Nation*, 1969.

67 —— *The Transformation of England. Essays in the Economic and Social History of England in the Eighteenth Century*, 1979. Useful on the role of science and technology, on the brewing industry, and on taxation and wages.

68 —— and Postan, M. M., eds., *Cambridge Economic History of Europe. VII: The Industrial Economies. Capital, Labour and Enterprise*, 1978.

69 **Melada**, I., *The Captain of Industry in English Fiction, 1821-1871*, Albuquerque, New Mexico, 1970.

2570 **Moffit**, L. W., *England on the Eve of the Industrial Revolution: A Study of Economic and Social Conditions from 1740 to 1760*, 1925.

2571 **O'Brien**, P., *Economic Growth in Britain and France, 1780-1914*, 1978.

2572 **Pawson**, E., *The Early Industrial Revolution. Britain in the Eighteenth Century*, 1979. A geographical perspective.

2573 **Perry**, P. J., *A Geography of Nineteenth-Century Britain*, 1975.

2574 **Porter**, R., *English Society in the Eighteenth Century*, 1982.

2575 **Pressnell**, L. S., ed., *Studies in the Industrial Revolution Presented to T. S. Ashton*, 1960.

2576 **Ratcliffe**, B. M., ed., *Great Britain and her World, 1750-1914. Essays in Honour of W. O. Henderson*, 1975. A varied collection of essays dealing, for instance, with continental influences on British industrialisation, the legal framework of economic growth, and with the Anglo-French commercial treaty of 1860.

2577 **Smart**, W., *Economic Annals of the Nineteenth Century*, 1910-17. Reprinted 1964. Vol. I covers 1801-20, Vol. II, 1821-30. An economic epitome of Hansard's *Parliamentary Debates* and *The Annual Register*.

2578 **Smout**, T. C., ed., *The Search for Wealth and Stability. Essays in Economic and Social History presented to M. W. Flinn*, 1980. A useful, wide-ranging *festschrift* which includes important essays on research and development in British industry over the last century and on the 'property cycle' of the affluent middle class in the early nineteenth century.

2579 **Sussmann**, H. L., *Victorians and the Machine: The Literary Response to Technology*, Cambridge, Mass., 1968. See also Warburg (2524), listed above.

2580 **Tames**, R. L., *Economy and Society in Nineteenth-Century Britain*, 1972.

2581 **Thomis**, M. I., *Responses to Industrialisation. The British Experience, 1780-1850*, 1976. Deals both with contemporary reactions to the process of industrialisation and its consequences, and also with the historiography of the subject.

2582 **Thompson**, A., *The Dynamics of the Industrial Revolution*, 1973. Considers the interaction between the various factors which produced the industrial changes.

2583 **Toynbee**, A., *The Industrial Revolution of the Eighteenth Century in England*, 1884, latest ed., with introductory note by T. S. Ashton, 1968.

2584 **Wiener**, M. J., *English Culture and the Decline of the Industrial Spirit, 1850-1980*, 1981. Looks at some of the paradoxical attitudes to industrialism and the businessman and examines the ways in which these contributed to Britain's economic decline.

2585 **Wrigley**, E. A., ed., *Nineteenth-Century Society. Essays in the Use of Quantitative Methods for the Study of Social Data*, 1972. Chiefly concerned with the problems arising from census material.

2586 **Young**, G. M., *Victorian England: Portrait of an Age*, 1936.

2587 —— *Early Victorian England, 1830-1865*, 2 vols., 1934. Articles by specialists on many aspects of economic and social life.

(d) REGIONAL STUDIES

2588 **Allen**, G. C., *The Industrial Development of Birmingham and the Black Country 1860-1927*, 1929.

2589 **Ashmore**, O., *The Industrial Archaeology of North-West England*, 1982. Largely a gazetteer of sites.

2590 **Aspin**, C., *Lancashire, the First Industrial Society*, 1969.

2591 **Barnsby**, G. J., *Social Conditions in the Black Country, 1800-1900*, 1980.

2592 **Booker**, F., *The Industrial Archaeology of the Tamar Valley*, 1967.

2593 **Buchanan**, R. A. and Cossons, N., *The Industrial Archaeology of the Bristol Region*, 1969.

2594 **Burt**, R., ed., *Industry and Society in the South West*, 1970. Useful for Cornwall during the Industrial Revolution.

2595 **Chambers**, J. D., *The Vale of Trent, 1670-1800: A Regional Study of Economic Change, Ec.H.R. Supp.*, 3, 1957.

2596 **Hall**, P. G., *The Industries of London since 1861*, 1962.

2597 **Harris**, Helen, *The Industrial Archaeology of Dartmoor*, 1968.

2598 **Hudson**, K., *The Industrial Archaeology of Southern England (Hampshire, Wiltshire, Dorset, Somerset and Gloucestershire and the Severn)*, 1965.

2599 **McCord**, N., *North East England. An Economic and Social History*, 1979. Covers the period 1760-1960.

2600 **Marshall**, J. D., *Furness and the Industrial Revolution*, 1958.

2601 —— and Walton, J. K., *The Lake Counties from 1830 to the mid Twentieth Century. A Study in Regional Change*, 1981. Continues from the point at which Bouch and Jones (1236) leave off. Deals with the continued industrialisation of the west coast, the growing emphasis on pasture farming, and with the development of tourism and conservation.

2602 **Nixon**, F., *The Industrial Archaeology of Derbyshire*, 1969.

2603 **Pollard**, S. and Holmes, C., eds., *Essays in the Economic and Social History of South Yorkshire*, 1976. Seventeen essays sectionalised under (1) economic conditions and employment, (2) the radical tradition, (3) housing, and (4) religion and culture.

2604 **Preston**, J. M., *Industrial Medway. An Historical Survey*, 1977.

2605 **Raybould**, T. J., *The Economic Emergence of the Black Country: A Study of the Dudley Estate*, 1973.

2606 **Rowe**, J., *Cornwall in the Age of the Industrial Revolution*, 1953. See also Todd and Laws (2610) listed below.

2607 **Singleton**, F., *The Industrial Revolution in Yorkshire*, 1970.

2608 **Smith**, D. H., *The Industries of Greater London, Being a Survey of the Recent Industrialisation of the Northern and Western Sectors*, 1933. Useful for the period c. 1900-32.

2609 **Smith**, D. M., *The Industrial Archaeology of the East Midlands (Nottinghamshire, Leicestershire and the Adjoining parts of Derbyshire)*, 1965.

2610 **Todd**, A. C. and Laws, P., *The Industrial Archaeology of Cornwall*, 1972. See also Rowe (2606), listed above.

2611 **Trinder**, B., *The Industrial Revolution in Shropshire*, 1973.

(e) FOREIGNERS' IMPRESSIONS

There are numerous accounts of England, Wales and Scotland by foreign observers, from which the following are selected.

2612 **Fussell**, G. E., and Goodman, Constance 'Travel and topography in eighteenth-century England: a bibliography of sources for economic history', *The Library*, 4th ser., X, 1929-30, 84-103.

2613 **Bell**, V., *To Meet Mr. Ellis: Little Gaddesden in the Eighteenth-Century*, 1956. Material on a Hertfordshire village, visited by the Swede Peter Kalm.

2614 **Blouet**, P. (pseud. Max O'Rell), *John Bull and*

his Island, n.d. (1883).

615 **Faucher**, L., *Études sur l'Angleterre*, 2 vols, Paris, 1845.

616 **Fond**, B. Faujas de Saint, *A Journey through England and Scotland to the Hebrides in 1784*, ed. A. Geikie, 2 vols., 1907.

617 **Henderson**, W. O., *Industrial Britain under the Regency: The Diaries of Escher, Bodmer, May and le Gallois, 1814-18*, 1968.

618 —— *J. C. Fischer and his Diary of Industrial England, 1814-1851*, 1966.

619 **Kohl**, J. G., *England and Wales*, 1844. Reprinted 1968 (early 1840s).

620 **Ratcliffe**, B. M. and Chaloner, W. H., eds., *A French Sociologist looks at Britain. Gustave d'Eichthal and British Society in 1828*, 1977.

621 **Raumer**, F., Von, *England in 1835, During a Residence in London and Excursions into the Provinces*, 3 vols, 1836.

2622 —— *England in 1841*, 2 vols., 1842.

2623 **Rochefoucauld**, F. de la, *A Frenchman in England, 1784*, ed. and trans. J. Marchand and S. C. Roberts, 1933.

2624 **Rydberg**, S., *Svenska Studieresor till England under Frihetstiden*, Uppsala, 1951, Swedish travellers in England in the eighteenth century: summaries in English.

2625 **Svedenstierna**, E. T., *Svedenstierna's Tour: Great Britain, 1802-3: The Travel Diary of an Industrial Spy*, ed. M. W. Flinn, trans. E. M. Dellow, 1973.

2626 **Taine**, H., *Taine's Notes on England*, trans. and ed. E. Hyams, 1957, (covers 1860-70).

2627 **Tristan**, *Flora, Promenades dans Londres*, ed. F. Bedarida, Paris, 1978. The fullest edition. *Flora Tristan's London Journal, 1840* (1980) translates much of, but not all, the French original. See also 1257-8, 1261, 1263, 1267, 1270.

1880-1970

(a) BIBLIOGRAPHIES

2628 **Hanham**, H. J., ed., *Bibliography of British History, 1851-1914*, 1976.

2629 **Havighurst**, A., comp., *Bibliographical Handbooks. Modern England, 1901-70*, 1976.

(b) DOCUMENTARY COLLECTIONS

2630 **Breach**, R. W. and Hartwell, R. M., *British Economy and Society, 1870-1970: Documents, Descriptions, Statistics*, 1972.

2631 **British Association**, *Britain in Depression: A Review of British Industries since 1929*, 1935.

2632 —— *Britain in Recovery*, 1938.

2633 **Court**, W. H. B., ed., *British Economic History, 1870-1914: Commentary and Documents*, 1965. Extracts from contemporary and secondary sources with useful bibliographical notes.

2634 **Handcock**, W. D., ed., *English Historical Documents. XII, 2, 1870-1914*, 1977.

2635 **Keating**, P., ed., *Into Unknown England, 1866-1913. Selections from the Social Explorers*, 1976. Includes essays from Booth, Rowntree, Gissing and others.

2636 **Pike**, E. R., *Human Documents of the Age of the Forsytes*, 1969.

2637 —— *Human Documents of the Lloyd George Era*, 1972. Suffers from the same defects as its predecessors.

2638 **Read**, D., *Documents from Edwardian England, 1901-1915*, 1973.

(c) THE CHANGING STRUCTURE OF THE ECONOMY

2639 **Aldcroft**, D. H., ed., *The Development of British Industry and Foreign Competition, 1875-1914*, 1968.

2640 —— *The Inter-War Economy, 1919-1939*, 1970.

2641 —— and Fearon, P., eds., *Economic Growth in Twentieth Century Britain*, 1969. Thirteen articles by various hands with an introduction and bibliographical guide, 233-7.

2642 —— and Richardson, H. W., *The British Economy 1870-1939*, 1969.

2643 **Allen**, G. C., *British Industries and their Organisation*, 2nd ed., 1935, 3rd ed., 1951.

2644 **Armitage**, Susan M. H., *The Politics of Decontrol of Industry: Britain and the United States*, 1969.

2645 **Ashworth**, W., *An Economic History of England, 1870-1939*, 1960.

2646 **Bagwell**, P. S. and Mingay, G. E., *Britain and*

America, 1850-1939. A Study of Economic Change, 1970. See also Holmes (2664).

2647 **Barry**, E. E., *Nationalisation in British Politics*, 1965 (Begins with the 1890s).

2648 **Beales**, H. L., 'The "basic industries" of England, 1850-1914", *Ec.H.R.*, V, 1935, 99-112.

2649 **Beckerman**, W., *The Labour Government's Economic Record*, 1964-1970, 1972.

2650 **Broadway**, F., *State Intervention in British Industry 1964-68*, 1969.

2651 **Buxton**, N. K. and Aldcroft, D. H., eds., *British Industry between the Wars. Instability and Industrial Development, 1919-39*, 1980. A collection of essays covering both the old depressed industries and the new growth areas (motor manufacturing, rayon, etc.).

2652 **Carter**, G. R., *Tendencies towards Industrial Combination*, 1913.

2653 **Chandler**, A. D., 'The growth of the transnational industrial firm in the United States and the United Kingdom: a comparative analysis', *Ec.H.R.*, 2nd ser., XXXIII, 1980, 396-410.

2654 **Chester**, N., *The Nationalisation of British Industry, 1945-51*, 1975.

2655 **Dow**, J. C. R., *The Management of the British Economy, 1945-60*, 1968.

2656 **Feinstein**, C. H., *National Income, Expenditure and Output, 1855-1965*, 1972.

2657 **Fitzgerald**, P., *Industrial Combination in England*, 1927.

2658 **Floud**, R. and McCloskey, D., eds., *The Economic History of Britain since 1700. II: 1860 to the 1970s*, 1981. For vol. I see (2545), above.

2659 **Hannah**, L., *The Rise of the Corporate Economy*, 1976.

2660 —— and Kay, J. A., *Concentration in Modern Industry*, 1977.

2661 **Harlow**, C., *Innovation and Productivity under Nationalisation. The First Thirty Years*, 1977.

2662 **Hart**, P. E. and Clark, R., *Concentration in British Industry, 1935-75. A Study of the Growth, Causes, and Effects of Concentration in British Manufacturing Industries*, 1980.

2663 **Holland**, R. F., 'The Federation of British Industries and the International Economy, 1929-39', *Ec.H.R.*, 2nd ser., XXXIV, 1981, 287-300.

2664 **Holmes**, G. M., *Britain and America. A Comparative Economic History, 1850-1939*, 1976. See also Bagwell and Mingay (2646), above.

2665 **Jones**, G. P. and Pool, A. G., *A Hundred Years of Economic Development in Great Britain,*

1939. Covers the period 1837-1937.

2666 **Kahn**, A. E., *Great Britain in the Wor[ld] Economy*, 1946.

2667 **Kelf-Cohen**, R., *British Nationalisatio[n] 1945-1973*, 1974.

2668 **Kindleberger**, C. P., *Economic Growth [in] France and Britain, 1851-1950*, 1964. One of t[he] few comparative studies; bibliography, 341-66.

2669 **Kirby**, M. W., *The Decline of Briti[sh] Economic Power since 1870*, 1981.

2670 **Lee**, C. H., *Regional Economic Grou[th] in the United Kingdom since the 1880s*, 1971.

2671 —— 'Regional growth and structural change [in] Victorian Britain', *Ec.H.R.*, 2nd ser., XXXI[V,] 1981, 438-52.

2672 **Levine**, A. L., *Industrial Retardation in B[ri-]tain, 1880-1914*, 1967.

2673 **Levy**, H., *Monopolies, Cartels and Trusts [in] British Industry*, 1927.

2674 **Lucas**, A. F., *Industrial Reconstruction a[nd] the Control of Competition: The British Exper[i-]ment*, 1937.

2675 **McCloskey**, D., ed., *Essays on a Matu[re] Economy: Britain after 1840*, 1971. Mainly indu[s-]trial, with a strong bias towards the 'new econom[ic] history', but includes a chapter on agriculture.

2676 **Macrosty**, H. W., *The Trust Movement [in] British Industry*, 1907.

2677 **Nicholas**, S., 'Total factor productivity grow[th] and revision of post-1870 British economic histor[y',] *Ec.H.R.*, 2nd ser., XXXV, 1982, 83-98.

2678 **Phillips**, G. A. and Madocks, R. T., *T[he] Growth of the British Economy, 1918-1968*, 197[ ]

2679 **Pigou**, A. C., *Aspects of British Economic H[is-]tory, 1918-1925*, 1947.

2680 **Plummer**, A., *New British Industries in t[he] Twentieth Century*, 1937.

2681 **Pollard**, S., *The Development of the Brit[ish] Economy, 1914-1967*, 2nd ed., 1969.

2682 **Read**, D., *England, 1868-1914*, 1979.

2683 **Saul**, S. B., *The Myth of the Great Depressi[on,] 1873-1896*, 1969. Excellent bibliography, 56-62[.]

2684 **Saville**, J., ed., 'The British econom[y] 1870-1914', *Yorks B.*, XVII, No. 1, 1965, 1-11[.]

2685 **Skidelsky**, R., ed., *The End of the Keynesi[an] Era*, 1977.

2686 **Stevenson**, J. and Cook, C., *The Slump. So[ci-]ety and Politics during the Depression*, 1977.

2687 **Stewart**, M., *The Jekyll and Hyde Yea[rs.] Politics and Economic Policy since 1964*, 197[ ]

2688 **Warren**, K., *The Geography of British Hea[vy] Industry since 1800*, 1976.

2689 **Williams**, L. J., *Britain and the Wor[ld]*

Economy, 1919-1970, 1971.

2690 **Worswick**, G. D. N. and Tipping, D. G., *Profits in the British Economy 1909-1938*, 1967.

2691 **Youngson**, A. J., *Britain's Economic Growth, 1920-1966*, 2nd ed., 1968.

(d) SOCIAL CONDITIONS

2692 **Beales**, H. L. and Lambert, R. S., *Memoirs of the Unemployed*, 1934.

2693 **Beveridge**, W. H., *Unemployment: A Problem of Industry*, 1st ed., 1909, 2nd ed., with new material, 1930.

2694 **Briggs**, A., ed., *They Saw It Happen: An Anthology of Eye-witnesses' Accounts of Events in British History 1897-1940*, 1962.

2695 **Hannington**, W., *The Problem of the Distressed Areas*, 1937.

2696 —— *A Short History of the Unemployed*, 1938.

2697 —— *Ten Lean Years: An Examination of the Record of the National Government in the Field of Unemployment*, 1940.

2698 —— *Unemployed Struggles, 1919-1936*, 1937.

2699 **Orwell**, G. (Blair, E.), *The Road to Wigan Pier*, 1937.

2700 **Baily**, L. W. A., *Scrapbook for the Twenties*, 1959.

2701 —— *Scrapbook, 1900 to 1914*, 1957.

2702 **Bedarida**, F., *A Social History of England, 1851-1975*, 1979. A lively and perceptive analysis of the principal forces – economic, sociological, political and spiritual – which have moulded English society in the last century.

2703 **Blythe**, R., *The Age of Illusion: England in the Twenties and Thirties, 1919-1940*, 1963.

2704 **Bogdanov**, V. and Skidelsky, R., eds., *The Age of Affluence, 1951-1964*, 1970.

2705 **Bott**, A., *Our Fathers (1870-1900): Manners and Customs of the Ancient Victorians*, n.d. (c.1930).

2706 **Branson**, Noreen, *Britain in the 1920s*, 1976.

2707 —— and Heinemann, Margot, *Britain in the 1930s*, 1971.

2708 **Brown**, K. D., *Labour and Unemployment, 1900-1914*, 1971, bibliography, 203-13. See Harris (2723), listed below.

2709 **Burns**, Eveline, M., *British Unemployment Programs, 1920-1938*, Washington, D. C., 1941.

2710 **Carney**, J. J., *Institutional Change and the Level of Employment: A Study of British Unemployment, 1918-1929*, Coral Gables, Fla., 1956.

2711 **Carr-Saunders**, A. M. and Jones, D. C., *A Survey of the Social Structure of England and Wales*, 1927, 2nd rev. ed., 1937.

2712 —— and Moser, C. A., *A Survey of Social Conditions in England and Wales as illustrated by Statistics*, 1958.

2713 **Clephane**, Irene, *Ourselves, 1900-1930*, 1933.

2714 **Cole**, G. D. H. and Margaret, I., *The Condition of Britain*, 1937.

2715 **Constantine**, S., *Unemployment in Britain between the Wars*, 1980.

2716 **Davison**, R. C., *The Unemployed: Old Policies and New*, 1929.

2717 —— *British Unemployment Policy: The Modern Phase since 1930*, 1938.

2718 **Garside**, W. R., *The Measurement of Unemployment in Great Britain, 1850-1979. Methods and Sources*, 1981.

2719 **Glynn**, S. and Oxborrow, J., *Interwar Britain. A Social and Economic History*, 1976.

2720 **Goldring**, D., *The Nineteen Twenties: A General Survey and some Personal Memories*, 1945.

2721 **Graves**, R. and Hodge, A., *The Long Weekend: A Social History of Great Britain, 1918-1939*, 1941, latest ed., 1971.

2722 **Halsey**, A. H., ed., *Trends in British Society since 1900*, 1972.

2723 **Harris**, José, *Unemployment and Politics: A Study in English Social Policy, 1886-1914*, 1972. Better than Brown (2708), listed above.

2724 **Hopkins**, H., *The New Look. A Social History of the Forties and Fifties in Britain*, 1963. Extensive bibliography, 493-504.

2725 **Hutt**, A., *The Post-War History of the British Working Class*, 1937.

2726 **Hynes**, S., *The Edwardian Turn of Mind*, 1968.

2727 **Lynd**, Helen M., *England in the Eighteen-eighties: Towards a Social Basis for Freedom*, 1945. Reprinted 1968.

2728 **McElwee**, W., *Britain's Locust Years, 1918-1940*, 1962.

2729 **Manton**, Jo, *Mary Carpenter and the Children of the Streets*, 1976.

2730 **Marsh**, D. C., *The Changing Social Structure of England and Wales, 1871-1961*, rev. ed., 1965.

2731 **Marwick**, A., *The Explosion of British Society, 1914-62*, 1963, 2nd ed., 1971.

2732 —— *British Society since 1945*, 1982.

2733 **Montgomery**, J., *The Twenties*, 1st ed., 1957, 2nd rev. ed., 1970.

2734 —— *The Fifties*, 1965.

2735 **Mowat**, C. L., *Britain Between the Wars*,

1918-1940, 1955.

2736 **Muggeridge**, M., *The Thirties: 1930-1940 in Great Britain*, 1940.

2737 **Nowell-Smith**, S., ed., *Edwardian England 1901-1914*, 1964. Chapters on the economy (A. J. Taylor) and domestic life (Marghanita Laski).

2738 **O'Day**, A., ed., *The Edwardian Age. Conflict and Stability, 1900-14*, 1979.

2739 **Raymond**, J., ed., *The Baldwin Age*, 1960. A collection of essays on various topics of the inter-war period.

2740 **Read**, D., *Edwardian England, 1901-15: Society and Politics*, 1973. See also Read (2638), listed above.

2741 **Ryder**, Judith and Silver, H., *Modern English Society. History and Structure, 1850-1970*, 1970. 2nd ed. 1977. Attempts to marry history and sociology.

2742 **Sissons**, M. and French, P., eds., *The Age of Austerity, 1945-51*, 1963.

2743 **Stevenson**, J., *Social Conditions in Britain between the Wars*, 1977. A 'myth-breaking' book.

2744 **Thompson**, P., *The Edwardians. The Re-making of British Society*, 1975.

2745 **Thompson**, Thea, *Edwardian Childhoods*, 1981. Nine oral history case studies of people born between 1892 and 1904.

(e) THE WORLD WARS AND THEIR EFFECTS

2746 **Abrams**, P., 'The failure of social reform, 1918-20', *P.P.*, 24, 1963, 43-64.

2747 **Bowley**, A. L., *Some Economic Consequences of the Great War*, 1930. Mainly the effects on Great Britain.

2748 **Braybon**, Gail, *Women Workers in the First World War: the British Experience*, 1981.

2749 **Calder**, A., *The People's War: Britain 1939-45*, 1969. Critical bibliography, 624-39.

2750 **Fitzgibbon**, C., *The Blitz*, 1970.

2751 **Johnson**, P. B., *Land Fit for Heroes: The Planning of British Reconstruction, 1916-191[*] Chicago, 1968.

2752 **Kohan**, C. M., *Works and Buildings* (Histc of the Second World War), 1952.

2753 **Longmate**, N., *How We Lived Then: A H tory of English Life During the Second Wor War*, 1971.

2754 **Marwick**, A., *Britain in the Century of Tot War*, 1968. Extensive bibliography.

2755 —— *The Deluge: British Society and the Fii World War*, 1965.

2756 —— *The Home Front. The British and t Second World War*, 1978.

2757 —— *Women at War, 1914-18*, 1977.

2758 **Milward**, A. S., *The Economic Effects of t World Wars on Britain*, 1970. Critical bibl graphy, 53-7.

2759 **Mosley**, L., *Backs to the Wall*, 1971. Life London, 1939-45.

2760 **Pelling**, H. M., *Britain and the Second Wor War*, 1970.

2761 **Playne**, Caroline E., *Society at War, 1914-191* 1931.

2762 —— *Britain Holds On, 1917, 1918*, 1933.

2763 **Postan**, M. M., *British War Production* (H tory of the Second World War), 1952.

2764 *Statistical Digest of the War* (History of t Second World War), 1951.

2765 **Winter**, J. M., 'Britain's lost generation of t First World War', *Pop.Studs.*, XXXI, 197 449-66.

2766 —— 'The impact of the First World War civilian health in Britain', *Ec.H.R.*, 2nd se XXX, 1977, 487-503.

2767 —— 'Military fitness and civilian health in B tain during the First World War', *J.Contemp.I* XV, 1980, 211-44.

2768 —— *Socialism and the Challenge of W. Ideas and Politics in Britain, 1912-18*, 1974.

2769 **Woodward**, L., *Great Britain and the War 1914-1918*, 1967. Chapter XII deals with econor matters.

ECONOMIC FLUCTUATIONS

As a brief general introduction, see:

2770 **Morgan**, E. V., *The Study of Prices and the Value of Money*, 1950.

(a) 1700-1800

2771 **Ashton**, T. S., *Economic Fluctuations in England, 1700-1800*, 1959.

(b) 1800-1913

2772 **Aldcroft**, D. H. and Fearon, P., eds., *British Economic Fluctuations, 1790-1939*, 1972.

2773 **Gayer**, A. D., Rostow, W. W. and Schwartz, Anna J., *The Growth and Fluctuation of the British Economy, 1790-1850*, 2 vols., 1953.

2774 **Hughes**, J. R. T., *Fluctuations in Trade, Industry and Finance: A Study of British Economic Development, 1850-1860*, 1960.

2775 **Layton**, W. T. and Crowther, G., *An Introduction to the Study of Prices*, 3rd rev. ed., 1938. Useful charts and tables of prices since 1820.

2776 **Lewis**, W. A., *Growth and Fluctuations, 1870-1914*, 1978.

2777 **Link**, R. G., *English Theories of Economic Fluctuations, 1815-1848*, 1959.

2778 **Matthews**, R. C. O., *A Study in Trade-Cycle History: Economic Fluctuations in Great Britain, 1833-1842*, 1954.

2779 **Rostow**, W. W., *British Economy of the Nineteenth Century*, 1948. A classic treatment.

2780 **Rousseaux**, P., *Les Mouvements de fond de l'économie anglaise, 1800-1913*, Louvain, 1938.

2781 **Tinbergen**, J., *Business Cycles in the U.K., 1870-1914*, Amsterdam, 1951.

2782 **Ward-Perkins**, C. N., 'The commercial crisis of 1847', in Carus-Wilson, ed. (245), listed above, III, 263-79.

(c) 1918-1939

2783 **Alford**, B. W. E., *Depression and Recovery?, British Economic Growth 1918-1939*, 1972.

2784 **Rees**, G., *The Great Slump: Capitalism in Crisis, 1929-33*, 1970.

2785 **Richardson**, H. W., *Economic Recovery in Britain, 1932-39*, 1967.

POPULATION

(a) GENERAL WORKS

2786 **Spengler**, J. J., ed., *Population Problems in the Victorian Age*, 2 vols, 1973. Reprints articles from contemporary periodicals.

2787 **Anderson**, Olive, 'Did suicide increase with industrialisation in Victorian England?' *P.P.*, 86, 1980, 149-73.

2788 **Banks**, J. A., *Prosperity and Parenthood*, 1954. Family limitation among the late nineteenth-century British middle classes.

2789 **Barker**, T. C. and Drake, M., eds., *Population and Society in Britain 1850-1980*, 1982.

2790 **Buer**, M. C., *Health, Wealth and Population in the Early Days of the Industrial Revolution*, 1926. See also Chambers (1172), listed above.

2791 **Connell**, K. H., 'Some unsettled problems in English and Irish population history, 1750-1845', *Irish H.Studs.*, VII, 1951.

2792 **Drake**, M., ed., *Population in Industriali-sation*, 1969. Reprints eight articles on the subject. Good bibliography.

2793 **Dyhouse**, Carol, 'Working-class mothers and infant mortality in England, 1895-1914', *J.Soc.H.*, XII, 1978, 248-67.

2794 **Eversley**, D. E. C., 'Population and economic growth in England before the "Take Off"', *Communications of the First International Conference of Economic History*, Stockholm, Paris, 1960, 457-73.

2795 **Flinn**, M. W., *British Population Growth, 1700-1850*, 1970. The best introduction to the study of this subject; critical bibliography, 59-64; glossary, 65.

2796 **Glass**, D. V., 'Population and population movements in England and Wales, 1700-1850'. In Glass and Eversley, eds., (1287), listed above, 221-46.

2797 —— ed., *Introduction to Malthus*, 1953. Essays, bibliography (84-112) and reprints of two scarce Malthus items.

2798 —— *Numbering the People. The Eighteenth-Century Population Controversy and the Development of Census and Vital Statistics in Britain*, 1973.

2799 **Griffith**, G. T., *Population Problems of the Age of Malthus*, 1926. Reprinted 1967, with new bibliographical introduction, V-XVII, and bibliography of recent work, 277-80.

2800 **Habakkuk**, H. J., 'English population in the eighteenth century'. In Glass and Eversley, eds., (1287), listed above, 269-84.

2801 —— *Population Growth and Economic Development since 1750*, 1971.

2802 **Himes**, N. E., *Medical History of Contraception*, 1st ed., 1936. Reprinted N. Y., 1963.

2803 **Krause**, J. T., 'Changes in English fertility and mortality, 1781-1850', *Ec.H.R.*, 2nd ser., XI, 1958, 52-70.

2804 —— 'Some neglected factors in the English Industrial Revolution'. Reprinted in Drake (2792), listed above, 103-17.

2805 —— 'Some aspects of population change, 1690-1790'. In Jones and Mingay (2558), listed below, 187-205.

2806 —— 'The changing adequacy of English registration, 1690-1837'. In Glass and Eversley, eds., (1287), listed above, 379-93.

2807 **Langer**, W. L., 'The origins of the birth control movement in England in the early nineteenth century', *J.Interdis.H.*, V, 1975, 669-86.

2808 **McKeown**, T. and Brown, R. G., 'Medical evidence related to English population changes in the eighteenth century'. In Glass and Eversley, eds., (1287), listed above, 285-307.

2809 —— and Record, R. G., 'Reasons for the decline of mortality in England and Wales during the nineteenth century', *Pop.Studs.*, XVI, 1962-3, 94-122. Covers mainly the period 1851-1900.

2810 **McLaren**, A., *Birth Control in Nineteenth-Century England*, 1978.

2811 **Marshall**, T. H., 'The population of England and Wales from the Industrial Revolution to the First World War', *Ec.H.R.*, V, 1934, 65-78.

2812 —— 'The population problem during the Industrial Revolution: a note on the present state of the controversy'. In Carus-Wilson, ed., (245), listed above, I, 306-30.

2813 **Mitchison**, Rosalind, *British Population Change since 1860*, 1977.

2814 **Razzell**, P. E., 'Population change in eighteenth-century England: a re-interpretation'. *Ec.H.R.*, 2nd ser., XVIII, 1965, 312-32. Impor-

tance of mass inoculations against smallpox from 1760s.

2815 —— 'Population growth and economic change in eighteenth and early nineteenth-century England and Ireland'. In Jones and Mingay (2558), listed below, 260-81.

2816 —— *Edward Jenner's Cowpox Vaccine. The History of a Medical Myth*, 1977.

2817 —— *The Conquest of Smallpox. The Impact of Inoculation on Smallpox Mortality in Eighteenth-Century Britain*, 1977.

2818 **Sigsworth**, E. M., 'Gateways to death: Medicines, hospitals and mortality, 1700-1850'. In Mathias, ed. (3008), listed below, 97-110.

2819 **Tranter**, N. L., *Population and Industrialization*, 1973. Extracts from British writers on population problems between 1680 and 1967.

2820 —— *Population since the Industrial Revolution: The Case of England and Wales*, 1973.

2821 **Wrigley**, E. A. and Schofield, R. S., *The Population History of England, 1541-1871: A Reconstruction*, 1981. A monumental study which gives detailed statistics of population size and of births, marriages and deaths. The authors stress the importance of nuptiality in determining variations in the long-term rate of population growth.

(b) REGIONAL STUDIES

2822 **Chambers**, J. D., 'Population change in a provincial town: Nottingham, 1700-1800'. See Pressnell (2575), listed above, 97-124.

2823 **Beckwith**, F., 'The population of Leeds during the Industrial Revolution', *Thoresby Soc.*, XII, 1948, 118-96.

2824 **Lawton**, R., 'Population trends in Lancashire and Cheshire from 1801', *T.H.S.L.C.*, CXIV, 1962, 189-213.

2825 —— 'The population of Liverpool in the mid-nineteenth century', *T.H.S.L.C.*, CVII, 1956, 89-120.

2826 **Martin**, J. M., *The Rise in Population in Eighteenth-Century Warwickshire*. Dugdale Soc.Occ.Papers, XXIII, 1976.

2827 **Minchinton**, W. E., ed., *Population and Marketing. Two Studies in the History of the South West*, 1977.

2828 **Sogner**, S., 'Aspects of the demographic situation in seventeen parishes in Shropshire, 1711-1760: an exercise based on parish registers', *Pop.Studs.*, XVII, 1963-4, 126-46.

See also Hoskins (1246), above, 181-208.

(c) INTERNAL MIGRATION

2829 **Cairncross**, A. K., 'Internal migration in Victorian England', *Manchester School*, XVII, 1949, 67-81. Reprinted in Cairncross (3526), listed below, 65-83.

2830 **Redford**, A., *Labour Migration in England 1800-1850*, 1926, 3rd ed. 1976.

2831 **Saville**, J., *Rural Depopulation in England and Wales, 1851-1951*, 1957.

(d) IMMIGRATION

2832 **File**, N. and Power, C., *Black Settlers in Britain 1555-1958*, 1980. See also Shyllon (2843) and Walvin (2844), below.

2833 **Gainer**, B., *The Alien Invasion: The Origins of the Aliens Act of 1905*, 1972.

2834 **Gartner**, L. P., *The Jewish Immigrant in England, 1870-1914*, 1960.

2835 **Gerrard**, J. A., *The English and Immigration, 1880-1910*, 1971.

2836 **Holmes**, C., ed., *Immigrants and Minorities in British Society*, 1978. Includes chapters on the German, Jewish, Irish and Chinese communities.

2837 **Jackson**, J. A., *The Irish in Britain*, 1963.

2838 **Kerr**, Barbara M., 'Irish seasonal migration to Great Britain 1800-38', *Irish Hist.Studs.*, III, 1942, 365-80.

2839 **Lawton**, R., 'Irish immigration to England and Wales in the mid-nineteenth century', *Irish Geog.*, IV, 1959, 35-54.

2840 **Lees**, L. H., *Exiles of Erin. Irish Migrants in Victorian London*, 1979.

2841 **Lorimer**, D. A., *Colour, Class and the Victorians. English Attitudes to the Negro in the Mid-Nineteenth Century*, 1978. See also File and Power (2832), Shyllon (2843) and Walvin (2844).

2842 **Lunn**, K., ed., *Hosts, Immigrants and Minorities. Historical Responses to Newcomers in British Society, 1870-1914*, 1980.

2843 **Shyllon**, F. O., *Black People in Britain, 1555-1833*, 1977. See also File and Power (2832) and Walvin (2844).

2844 **Walvin**, J., *The Black Presence. A Documentary History of the Negro in England, 1555-1860*, 1971. See also File and Power (2832) and Shyllon (2843).

2845 **Williams**, B., *The Making of Manchester Jewry, 1740-1875*, 1976.

(e) EMIGRATION

2846 **Erickson**, Charlotte, ed., *Emigration from Europe 1815-1914, Select Documents*, 1976.

2847 **MacDonagh**, O., ed., *Emigration in the Victorian Age*, 1974. Reprints articles from contemporary periodicals.

2848 **Berthoff**, R. T., *British Immigrants in Industrial America, 1790-1850*, Cambridge, Mass., 1953.

2849 **Bloomfield**, P., *Edward Gibbon Wakefield*, 1961.

2850 **Boston**, R. J., *British Chartists in America*, 1971.

2851 **Carrothers**, W. A., *Emigration from the British Isles, with Special Reference to the Development of the Overseas Dominions*, 1929.

2852 **Coleman**, T., *The Atlantic Passage*, 1972.

2853 **Cowan**, Helen I., *British Emigration to British North America: The First Hundred Years*, 2nd rev. and enlarged ed., Toronto, 1961.

2854 **Dodd**, A. H., *The Character of Early Welsh Emigration to the United States*, 2nd rev. ed., 1967.

2855 **Duncan**, R., 'Case studies in emigration: Cornwall, Gloucestershire and New South Wales, 1877-1886', *Ec.H.R.*, 2nd ser., XVI, 1963, 272-89.

2856 **Erickson**, Charlotte, 'The encouragement of emigration by British trade unions, 1850-1900', *Pop.Studs.*, III, 1949-50, 248-73.

2857 **Hitchins**, F. H., *The Colonial Land and Emigration Commission, 1840-78*, Philadelphia, 1931.

2858 **Johnson**, S. C., *Emigration from the United Kingdom to North America, 1763-1912*, 1913. Reprinted 1966.

2859 **Johnston**, H. J. M., *British Emigration Policy, 1815-1830*, 1972.

2860 **Jones**, M. A., *Destination America*, 1976.

2861 **Taylor**, P. A. M., *Expectations Westwards: The Mormons and the Emigration of their British Converts in the Nineteenth Century*, 1965.

2862 **Thistlethwaite**, F., 'The Atlantic migration of the pottery industry', *Ec.H.R.*, 2nd ser., XI, 1958, 264-78.

2863 **Thomas**, B., *Migration and Economic Growth: A Study of Great Britain and the Atlantic Economy*, 1954.

2864 —— *Migration and Urban Development: A Reappraisal of British and American Long Cycles*, 1972.

(f) MARRIAGE AND THE FAMILY

2865 **Anderson**, M., *Family Structure in Nineteenth-Century Lancashire*, 1971. A sociological study of the impact of urban industrial life on the kinship system of the working classes.

2866 **Anderson**, Olive, 'The incidence of civil marriage in Victorian England and Wales', *P.P.*, 69, 1975, 50-87. See also Floud and Thane (2869) below.

2867 **Banks**, J. A., *Victorian Values: Secularism and the Size of Families*, 1981.

2868 **Constable**, D., *Household Structure in Three English Market Towns*, 1851-71, 1977.

2869 **Floud**, R. and Thane, Pat, 'The incidence of civil marriage in Victorian England and Wales', *P.P.*, 84, 1979, 146-54. See also Anderson (2866), above.

2870 **Gittins**, Diana, *Fair Sex: Family Size and Structure 1900-39*, 1982.

2871 **Levine**, D., 'Illiteracy and family life during the first Industrial Revolution', *J.Soc.H.*, XIV, 1980, 25-44.

2872 **Menefee**, S. P., *Wives for Sale. An Ethnographic Study of British Popular Divorce*, 1981.

2873 **Outhwaite**, R. B., 'Age at marriage in England from the late seventeenth to the nineteenth century', *T.R.H.S.*, 5th ser., XXIII, 1973, 55-70.

2874 **Shorter**, E., *The Making of the Modern Family*, 1976.

2875 **Wohl**, A. S., ed., *The Victorian Family. Structures and Stresses*, 1978.

2904 **Galpin**, W. F., *The Grain Supply of England during the Napoleonic Period*, N. Y., 1925.

2905 **Gould**, J. D., 'Agricultural fluctuations and the English economy in the eighteenth century', *J.Ec.H.*, XX, 1962, 313-33.

2906 **Habakkuk**, H. J., 'Economic functions of English landowners in the seventeenth and eighteenth centuries'. Reprinted in Carus-Wilson, ed., (245), listed above, I, 187-201.

2907 **Horn**, Pamela, *The Rural World, 1780-1850. Social Change in the English Countryside*, 1980.

2908 —— *The Victorian Country Child*, 1974.

2909 —— *William Marshall (1745-1818). The Life and Work of an Agricultural Pioneer*, 1982.

2910 **James**, N. D. G., *A History of English Forestry*, 1982.

2911 **John**, A. H., 'The course of agricultural change 1660-1760', reprinted in Carus-Wilson, ed. (245), listed above, I, 221-53.

2912 —— 'Farming in war-time: 1793-1815'. In Jones and Mingay (2558), listed below, 28-47.

2913 **Jones**, E. L., *The Development of English Agriculture 1815-73*, 1968. Useful pamphlet, with select bibliography, 35-7.

2914 —— *Agriculture and the Industrial Revolu-*

tion, 1974. Collects together the author's essays on agricultural history from the mid-seventeenth to the late nineteenth centuries.

2915 **Kirk**, J. H., *U.K. Agricultural Policy, 1870-1970*, 1979.

2916 **Marshall**, T. H., 'Jethro Tull and the "New Husbandry" of the eighteenth century', *Ec.H.R.*, II, 1929, 41-60.

2917 **Mills**, D. R., *Lord and Peasant in Nineteenth-Century Britain*, 1980. A useful survey of nineteenth-century social structure.

2918 **Mingay**, G. E., 'The agricultural depression 1730-1750', *Ec.H.R.*, 2nd ser., 1956, 323-38.

2919 —— 'The "Agricultural Revolution" in English history: a reconsideration', *Ag.H.*, XXXVII, 1963, 123-33.

2920 —— *Rural Life in Victorian England*, 1977.

2921 —— ed., *The Victorian Countryside*, 2 vols., 1981. Forty-six chapters broadly divided into five sections dealing with (1) the land, (2) agriculture, (3) country towns and country industries, (4) landed society, (5) labouring life.

2922 **Murray**, K. A. H., *Factors affecting the Prices of Livestock in Great Britain: A Preliminary Study*, 1931. Useful statistical summary of the period 1871-1931.

2923 **Orwin**, Christabel S. and Whetham, Edith H., *History of British Agriculture, 1846-1914*, 1964.

2924 **Parker**, R. A. C., *Coke of Norfolk, a financial and agricultural study, 1707-1842*, 1975.

2925 **Pawson**, H. C., *Robert Bakewell, Pioneer Livestock Breeder*, 1957. A disappointing book.

2926 **Perry**, P. J., ed., *British Agriculture, 1873-1914*, 1973 (a collection of essays on various aspects of this historical problem).

2927 —— *British Agriculture in the Great Depression, 1870-1914: An Historical Geography*, 1974.

2928 **Russell**, E. J., *A History of Agricultural Science in Great Britain 1620-1954*, 1966.

2929 —— *British Agricultural Research: Rothamsted*, 1st ed., 1942, 2nd rev. ed., 1946.

2930 **Taylor**, D., 'The English dairy industry, 1860-1930', *Ec.H.R.*, 2nd ser., XXIX, 1976, 585-601.

2931 **Thompson**, F. M. L., 'Landownership and economic growth in England in the eighteenth century'. In *Agrarian Change and Economic Development*, ed. E. L. Jones and S. J. Woolf, 1969, 41-60.

2932 **Trow-Smith**, R., *A History of British Livestock Husbandy 1700-1900*, 1959.

2933 **Vamplew**, W., 'The protection of English cereal producers: the Corn Laws re-assessed', *Ec.H.R.*

2nd ser., XXXIII, 1980, 382-95.

2934 **Wallace**, A. R., *Land Nationalisation*, 1892. Useful bibliography on the land question, 253-6.

2935 **Whetham**, Edith H., ed., *The Agrarian History of England and Wales. VIII: 1914-39*, 1978. Deals comprehensively with the period with chapters on types of farming, marketing, government policies, war-time emergency, scientific innovation, and on landowners and the rest of rural society.

2936 **Wicker**, E. R., 'Jethro Tull, innovator or crank?' *Ag.H.*, XXXI, 1957, 46-8.

2937 **Woodward**, D. M., 'Agricultural revolution in England, 1500-1900: a survey', *Loc.H.*, IX, 1971, 323-33.

AGRICULTURE AND RURAL SOCIETY

(a) BIBLIOGRAPHIES

2876 **Fussell**, G. E., *More Old English Farming Books from Tull to the Board of Agriculture, 1731-1793*, 1950.

2877 **Harvey**, N., ed., *G. E. Fussell: A Bibliography of his Writings on Agricultural History*, 1967. See also Brewer (1476), listed above.

(b) GENERAL WORKS

2878 **Caird**, J., *English Agriculture in 1850-51*, 1852, 2nd ed., 1968 with important new introduction by G. E. Mingay.

2879 **Carter**, H. B., ed., *The Sheep and Wool Correspondence of Sir Joseph Banks, 1781-1820*, 1979.

2880 **Jewell**, A., ed., *Victorian Farming: A Sourcebook*, 3rd ed. 1975. A useful condensation of H. Stephens, *The Book of the Farm*, 3rd ed., 1876.

2881 **Mingay**, G. E., ed., *The Agricultural Revolution. Changes in Agriculture, 1650-1880*, 1977. A documentary collection.

2882 —— *Arthur Young and his Times*, 1975. A sourcebook culled from Young's travel and agricultural writings. The appendix gives a complete list of Young's publications.

2883 **Pyne**, W. H., *Microcosm*, 1806. Reprinted N. Y., 1961. Well-known early nineteenth-century engravings of agriculture and rural labour.

2884 **Abel**, W., *Agricultural Fluctuations in Europe*, 1980.

2885 **Adams**, L. P., *Agricultural Depression and Farm Relief in England 1813-1852*, 1932, new impression, 1965.

2886 **Beckett**, J. V., 'Regional variation and the Agri-Agricultural Depression, 1730-50', *Ec.H.R.*, 2nd ser., XXXV, 1982, 35-51.

2887 **Beer**, M., ed., *The Pioneers of Land Reform: Thomas Spence, William Ogilvie, Thomas Parrie*, 1920.

2888 **Bonser**, K. J., *The Drovers: Who They Were and How They Went. An Epic of the English Countryside*, 1970. For other works on the drovers see Cregeen (5412), Haldane (5482), Colyer (5166), Godwin (5168) and Hughes (5172) below.

2889 **Carter**, H. B., *His Majesty's Spanish Flock*, 1964. The building up of George III's flock of merino sheep.

2890 **Chambers**, J. D. and Mingay, G. E., *The Agricultural Revolution 1750-1880*, 1966.

2891 **Collins**, E. J. T., 'Harvest technology and labour supply in Britain, 1790-1870', *Ec.H.R.*, 2nd ser., XXII, 1969, 453-73.

2892 —— *The Economy of Upland Britain, 1750-1950. An Illustrated Review*, 1978.

2893 **Collins**, K., 'Marx on the English Agricultural Revolution: theory and evidence', *H.& Theory*, VI, 1966, 351-81. Vigorous debunking.

2894 **Crosby**, T. L., *English Farmers and the Politics of Protection, 1815-32*, 1977.

2895 **Dewey**, P. E., 'Food production and policy in the United Kingdom, 1914-18', *T.R.H.S.*, 5th ser., XXX, 1980, 71-89.

2896 **Douglas**, R., *Land, People and Politics. A History of the Land Question in the United Kingdom, 1878-1952*, 1976.

2897 **Drescher**, L., 'The development of agricultural production in Great Britain and Ireland from the early nineteenth century', *Manchester School*, 1955, 153-83. Translation of an attempt to construct an index of agricultural production, first published in 1935.

2898 **Evans**, E. J., *The Contentious Tithe: The Tithe Problem and English Agriculture, 1750-1850*, 1976. A neglected subject.

2899 **Fletcher**, T. W., 'The Great Depression of English Agriculture 1873-96', in Minchinton (249), listed above, II, 239-58.

2900 **Fussell**, G. E., *Jethro Tull: His Influence on Mechanized Agriculture*, 1973. See also Marshall (2916) and Wicker (2936), listed below.

2901 —— 'The size of English cattle in the eighteenth century', *Ag.H.*, III, 1929, 160-81. Criticises the view that the average weight of cattle and sheep increased considerably.

2902 —— and Goodman, Constance, 'Eighteenth-century estimates of sheep and wool production', *Ag.H.*, IV, 1930, 131-51.

2903 —— and Goodman, Constance, 'The eighteenth-century traffic in milk products', *Ec. J.Ec.H.Supp.*, III, 1937, 380-7.

(c) REGIONAL AND LOCAL STUDIES

2938 **Branch-Johnson**, W., *The Carrington Diary, 1797-1810*, 1956. Based on the papers of John Carrington, a Hertfordshire farmer.

2939 **Melling**, Elizabeth, ed., *Kentish Sources III: Aspects of Agriculture and Industry*, 1961. 1-90 deal with Kentish agriculture.

2940 **Tyrer**, F., ed., *The Great Diurnal of Nicholas Blundell of Little Crosby, Lancashire* I: 1702-11, 1968; II: 1712-19, 1970; III: 1720-8, 1972.

2941 **Ambrose**, P., *The Quiet Revolution: Social Changes in a Sussex Village, 1871-1971*, 1974 (Ringmer).

2942 **Ashby**, Mabel K., *Joseph Ashby of Tysoe, 1859-1919: A Study of English Village Life*, 1961.

2943 **Beastall**, T. W., *The Agricultural Revolution in Lincolnshire*, 1978.

2944 **Davey**, B. J., *Ashwell, 1830-1914. The Decline of a Village Community*, 1980.

2945 **Davies**, C. Stella, *The Agricultural History of Cheshire, 1750-1850*, Chet.Soc., 3rd ser., 10, 1960.

2946 **Fletcher**, T. W., 'The agrarian revolution in arable Lancashire', *T.L.C.A.S.*, LXXII, 1965, 93-122.

2947 —— 'Lancashire livestock farming during the Great Depression', in Perry, ed. (2926), listed above.

2948 **Garnett**, F. W., *Westmorland Agriculture, 1800-1900*, 1912.

2949 **Gaut**, R. C., *A History of Worcestershire Agriculture and Rural Evolution*, 1939.

2950 **Grigg**, D. B., *The Agricultural Revolution in South Lincolnshire*, 1966.

2951 **Havinden**, M. A. and others, *Estate Villages: A Study of the Berkshire Villages of Ardington and Lockinge*, 1966. Study in depth of a Victorian landed estate.

2952 **Hoskins**, W. G., ed., *History from the Farm*, 1970. Historical studies of a number of individual farms in Great Britain.

2953 **Kain**, R. and Holt, H., 'Agriculture and land use in Cornwall, c. 1840', *Southern H.*, III, 1981, 139-82.

2954 **Mutch**, A., 'The mechanisation of the harvest in S. W. Lancashire, 1850-1914', *Ag.H.R.*, XXIX, 1981, 125-32.

2955 **Perkins**, J. A., *Sheep Farming in Eighteenth- and Nineteenth-Century Lincolnshire*, 1977.

2956 **Riches**, Naomi, *The Agricultural Revolution in Norfolk*, 1937, 2nd ed., 1967, with bibliographical note.

2957 **Robin**, Jean, *Elmdon: Continuity and Change in a North West Essex Village, 1861-1964*, 1980.

2958 **Ward**, J. T., *East Yorkshire Landed Estates in the Nineteenth Century*, 1967.

2959 **Winter**, G., *A Country Camera, 1844-1914: Rural Life as Depicted in Photographs*, 1966.

(d) ENCLOSURES

2960 **Gonner**, E. C. K., *Common Land and Inclosure*, 1912, 2nd ed. with introduction by G. E. Mingay, 1966.

2961 **Levy**, H., *Large and Small Holdings: A Study of English Agricultural Economics*, 1st ed. 1911, new impression, 1966.

2962 **McCloskey**, D., 'The enclosure of open-fields: preface to the study of its impact on the efficiency of English agriculture in the eighteenth century', *J.Ec.H.*, XXXII, 1972, 15-35.

2963 **Mingay**, G. E., *Enclosure and the Small Farmer in the Age of the Industrial Revolution*, 1968.

2964 **Slater**, G., *The English Peasantry and the Enclosure of the Common Fields*, 1909. Inaccurate.

2965 **Tate**, W. E., *The English Village Community and the Enclosure Movements*, 1967. See in particular Appendix II on the historiography of the enclosure movements.

2966 —— *A Domesday of English Enclosure Acts and Awards* (ed. M. E. Turner), 1978.

2967 **Turner**, M. E., *English Parliamentary Enclosure. Its Historical Geography and Economic History*, 1980. A useful study which provides significant revisions to the statistics and chronology offered by Gonner (2960) and Tate (2965). See also Brewer (1476), listed above.

(e) LANDED SOCIETY

2968 **Bateman**, J., *The Great Landowners of Great Britain and Ireland*, 4th ed., 1883, 5th ed., with introduction by D. Spring, 1971.

2969 **Brodrick**, G. C., *English Land and English Landlords*, 1st ed., 1881. Reprinted 1968.

2970 **Caird**, J., *The Landed Interest and the Supply of Food*, 1st ed., 1878, 5th ed., 1968, with introduction by G. E. Mingay.

2971 **Beastall**, T. W., *A North Country Estate. The Lumleys and Saundersons as Landowners, 1600-1900*, 1975.

2972 **Cannadine**, D., 'Aristocratic indebtedness in the nineteenth century', *Ec.H.R.*, 2nd ser., XXX, 1977, 624-50.

2973 **Clemenson**, H. A., *The English Landed Estate*, 1981.

2974 **McCahill**, M. W., 'Peers, patronage and the Industrial Revolution, 1760-1800', *J.Brit.Studs.*, XVI, 1976, 84-107.

2975 **Martins**, Susanna W., *A Great Estate at Work. The Holkham Estate and its Inhabitants in the Nineteenth Century*, 1980.

2976 **Massey**, D. and Catalano, A., *Capital and Land. Land Ownership in Great Britain*, 1978.

2977 **Mingay**, G. E., *English Landed Society in the Eighteenth Century*, 1963.

2978 —— 'The eighteenth-century land steward'. In Jones and Mingay (2558), listed above, 3-27.

2979 —— *The Gentry. The Rise and Fall of a Ruling Class*, 1976.

2980 **Spring**, D., *The English Landed Estate in the Nineteenth Century: Its Administration*, Baltimore, Md., 1963.

2981 **Thompson**, F. M. L., *English Landed Society in the Nineteenth Century*, 1963. The final chapter deals with the period 1914-39; excellent bibliography.

2982 **Ward**, J. T. and Wilson, R. G., eds., *Land and Industry: The Landed Estate and the Industrial Revolution*, 1971.

(f) FARM LABOURERS

2983 **Barnett**, D. C., 'Allotments and the problem of rural poverty, 1780-1840'. In Jones and Mingay (2558), listed above, 162-83.

2984 **Collins**, E. J. T., 'Migrant labour in British

agriculture in the nineteenth century', *Ec.H.R.*, 2nd ser., XXIX, 1976, 38-59.

2985 **Dunbabin**, J. P. D., *Rural Discontent in Nineteenth-century Britain*, 1973 (with chapters by A. J. Peacock and Pamela Horn).

2986 **Gash**, N., 'Rural unemployment, 1815-34', *Ec.H.R.*, VI, 1935, 90-3.

2987 **Hammond**, J. L. and Barbara, *The Village Labourer, 1760-1832: A Study in the Government of England before the Reform Bill*, 1911. Reprinted, with an introduction by G. E. Mingay, 1978. Well-written, sentimental and misleading; Gonner's book (2960), although dull and difficult to read, is more valuable than the Hammonds' work.

2988 **Hobsbawm**, E. J. and Rudé, G., *Captain Swing*, 1969, 2nd ed., 1973 with new introduction (The agrarian riots of 1830). See bibliography, 367-71.

2989 **Horn**, Pamela L., *Labouring Life in the Victorian Countryside*, 1976. Mainly about the Midlands and South.

2990 **Kerr**, Barbara, M., *Bound to the Soil: A Social History of Dorset, 1750-1918*, 1968.

2991 **Morgan**, D. H., *Harvests and Harvesting, 1840-1900. A Study of the Rural Proletariat*, 1982.

2992 **Newby**, H., *The Deferential Worker. A Study of Farm Workers in East Anglia*, 1977. Though primarily sociological, the book opens with a lengthy section on the historical context.

2993 **Peacock**, A. J., *Bread or Blood: The Agrarian Riots in East Anglia, 1816*, 1965.

2994 **Samuel**, R., ed., *Village Life and Labour*, 1975.

2995 **Snell**, K. D. M., 'Agricultural seasonal unemployment, the standard of living, and women's work in the South and East, 1690-1860', *Ec.H.R.*, 2nd ser., XXXIV, 1981, 407-37.

2996 **Springall**, L. Marion, *Labouring Life in Norfolk Villages, 1834-1914*, 1936. See also Hasbach (2199) and Fussell (2194), listed above.

(g) WILLIAM COBBETT

2997 **Cole**, G. D. H., *The Life of William Cobbett*, 1927. Includes a chapter on Rural Rides by F. E. Green.

2998 **Spater**, G., *William Cobbett: the Poor Man's Friend*, 2 vols, 1982. Based on much new and important material, this is now the definitive biography.

INDUSTRY

(a) SCIENCE AND TECHNOLOGY

2999 **Clark**, G. N., *Science and Social Welfare in the Age of Newton*, 2nd rev. ed., 1949.

3000 **Gomme**, A. A., *Patents of Invention: Origins and Growth of the Patent System in Britain*, 1946.

3001 **Habakkuk**, H. J., *American and British Technology in the Nineteenth Century: The Search for Labour-saving Inventions*, 1962.

3002 **Harris**, J. R., 'Skills, coal and British industry in the eighteenth century', *Hist.*, LXI, 1976, 167-82.

3003 **Hatfield**, H. S., *The Inventor and his World*, 1933, 2nd rev. ed., 1948, with useful bibliography, 242-52.

3004 **Jeremy**, D. J., *Transatlantic Industrial Revolution. The Diffusion of Textile Technologies between Britain and America, 1790-1830*, 1981.

3005 **Kargon**, R., *Science in Victorian Manchester. Enterprise and Expertise*, 1977. Deals with the amateur scientific tradition in Manchester and the emergence of 'civic science' and university science in the second half of the century.

3006 **Lea**, F. M., *Science and Building. A History of the Building Research Station*, 1971.

3007 **MacLeod**, R. and Collins, P., eds., *The Parliament of Science. The British Association for the Advancement of Science, 1831-1981*, 1982.

3008 **Mathias**, P., ed., *Science and Society, 1660-1900*, 1972. Essays by various hands.

3009 **Musson**, A. E., ed., *Science, Technology and Economic Growth in the Eighteenth Century*, 1972. Assembles eight key articles.

3010 **Musson**, A. E., and Robinson, E. H., *Science and Technology in the Industrial Revolution*, 1969. Also contains important material on the rise of the British chemical industry.

3011 **Robinson**, E. H., 'The Lunar Society: its membership and organisation', *Trans. Newcomen Soc.*, XXXV, 1964, 153-77.

3012 **Saul**, S. B., ed., *Technological Change: The United States and Britain in the Nineteenth Century*, 1970. Six essays by H. J. Habakkuk, D. L. Burn and others.

3013 **Schofield**, R. E., *The Lunar Society of Birmingham: A Social History of Provincial Science and Industry in Eighteenth-century England*, 1963.

3014 **Singer**, S., Holmyard, E. J., Wall, A. R., and Williams, T. I., eds., *A History of Technology. The Industrial Revolution, c.1750-c.1850*, 1958. The various sections are very uneven.

3015 **Williams**, T. I., ed., *A History of Technology. The Twentieth Century, c.1900-c.1950.* VI (Part I), VII (Part II), 1978.

3016 **Woodcroft**, B., *Alphabetical List of Patentees of Inventions*, 1854. Reprinted 1969 with new introduction and corrections.

(b) POWER AND LIGHT

(i) WIND AND WATER MILLS

3017 **Bennett**, R. and Elton, J., *History of Corn Milling*, 4 vols., 1898-1904.

3018 **Ellis**, C. M., 'A gazetteer of the water, wind and tide mills of Hampshire', *Proc. Hants. Field Club*, XXV, 1968, 119-40.

3019 **Farriers**, K. G. and Mason, M. G., *The Windmills of Surrey and Inner London*, 1966.

3020 **Hillier**, J., *Old Surrey Watermills*, 1951.

3021 **Norris**, J. H., 'The water-powered corn mills of Cheshire', *T.L.C.A.S.*, LXXV and LXXVI, 1968, 33-71.

3022 **Pelham**, R. A., *The Old Mills of Southampton*, 1963.

3023 **Syson**, L., *British Water Mills*, 1965. Contains a good bibliography.

(ii) THE STEAM ENGINE

3024 **Tann**, Jennifer, ed., *The Selected Papers of Boulton and Watt I: The Engine*, 1981. The first instalment of the published correspondence of the Birmingham firm that took the lead in supplying steam power in the Industrial Revolution.

3025 **Barton**, D. B., *The Cornish Beam Engine*, 1965. 2nd ed., 1966.

3026 **Cardwell**, D. S. L., *Steam Power in the Eighteenth Century*, 1963. The scientific background.

3027 **Cule**, J. E., 'Finance and industry in the eighteenth century: the firm of Boulton and Watt', *Ec. J., Ec.H.Supp.*, IV, 1940, 319-25.

3028 **Dickinson**, H. W., *The Cornish Engine*, 1950.

3029 —— *James Watt, Craftsman and Engineer*, 1935.

3030 —— *Matthew Boulton*, 1936.

3031 —— *A Short History of the Steam Engine*, 1st ed., 1938, 2nd ed., with corrections and new bibliographical introduction by A. E. Musson, 1963.

3032 —— and Jenkins, R., *James Watt and the Steam Engine*, 1927.

3033 —— and Titley, A., *Richard Trevithick: The Engineer and the Man*, 1934.

3034 **Gale**, W. K. V., 'Soho Foundry: Some Facts and Fallacies', *Trans. Newcomen Soc.*, XXXIV, 1963, 73-87.

3035 **Harris**, J. R., 'The employment of steam power in the eighteenth century', *Hist.*, LII, 1967, 133-48.

3036 **Hills**, R. L., *Power in the Industrial Revolution*, 1970.

3037 **Lord**, J., *Capital and Steam Power, 1750-1800*, 1st ed. 1923, 2nd ed., with corrections and bibliographical introduction by W. H. Chaloner, 1966.

3038 **Musson**, A. E., 'Industrial motive power in the United Kingdom, 1800-70', *Ec.H.R.*, 2nd ser., XXIX, 1976, 415-39.

3039 —— and Robinson, E. H., 'The early growth of steam power', *Ec.H.R.*, 2nd ser., XI, 1959, 418-39. Reprinted with additions in Musson and Robinson (3010), listed above.

3040 **Roll**, E., *An Early Experiment in Industrial Organisation: Being a History of the Firm of Boulton & Watt, 1775-1805*, 1930. Reprinted 1968.

3041 **Rolt**, L. T. C., *Thomas Newcomen: The Prehistory of the Steam Engine*, 1963.

3042 **Robinson**, E. H. and Musson, A. E., *James Watt and the Steam Revolution: A Documentary History*, 1969.

3043 **Tunzelmann**, G. N. von, 'Technological diffusion during the Industrial Revolution: the case of the Cornish pumping engine'. In Hartwell, ed. (2549), listed above, 77-98.

3044 —— *Steam Power and British Industrialisation to 1860*, 1978.

3045 **Watkins**, G., *The Stationary Beam Engine*, 1968.

3046 —— *The Textile Mill Engine*, I, 1970, II, 1971.

(iii) LIGHT

1. GENERAL

3047 **O'Dea**, W. T., *The Social History of Lighting*, 1958.

2. GAS

3048 **Chandler**, D. and Lacey, A. D., *The Rise of the Gas Industry in Britain*, 1949.

3049 **Everard**, S., *History of the Gas Light and Coke Company, 1812-1949*, 1949.

3050 **Falkus**, M., 'The British gas industry before 1850', *Ec.H.R.*, 2nd ser., XX, 1967, 494-508.

3051 —— 'The early development of the British gas industry, 1790-1815', *Ec.H.R.*, 2nd ser., XXXV, 1982, 217-34.

3052 **Harris**, S. A., *The Development of Gas Supply on North Merseyside, 1815-1949*, 1956.

3053 **Peebles**, M. W. H., *The Evolution of the Gas Industry*, 1980.

3054 **Williams**, T. I., *A History of the British Gas Industry*, 1981.

3. ELECTRICITY

3055 **Ballin**, H. H., *The Organisation of Electricity Supply in Great Britain*, 1946. Covers the period 1879-1944.

3056 **Byatt**, I. C. R., *The British Electrical Industry, 1875-1914*, 1979.

3057 **Dunsheath**, P., *A History of Electrical Engineering*, 1962.

3058 **Hannah**, L., *Electricity before Nationalisation. A Study of the Development of the Electricity Supply Industry in Britain to 1948*, 1979.

3059 **Hinton**, C., *The Development of Heavy Current Electricity in the United Kingdom*, 1978.

3060 **Parsons**, R. H., *A Short History of the Power Station Industry*, 1939.

3061 **Swale**, W. E., *Forerunners of the North Western Electricity Board*, 1963.

(c) TEXTILES

(i) GENERAL

3062 **Harte**, N. B. and Ponting, K. G., eds., *Textile History and Economic History: Essays in Honour of Miss Julia de Lacy Mann*, 1973. Essays on aspects of the stocking-knitting, wollen, worsted, linen and cotton trades from 1500 to 1867.

(ii) COTTON

3063 **Baines**, E., *History of the Cotton Manufacture in Great Britain*, 1835, 2nd ed., 1966, with bibliographical introduction, 5-14.

3064 **Ellison**, T., *The Cotton Trade of Great Britain: Including a History of the Liverpool Cotton Market*, 1886.

3065 **Political and Economic Planning**, Report on the British Cotton Industry, 1934.

3066 **Aspin**, C., *James Hargreaves and the Spinning Jenny*, 1964.

3067 **Bowker**, B., *Lancashire under the Hammer*,

1928.

3068 **Boyson**, R., *The Ashworth Cotton Enterprise: The Rise and Fall of a Family Firm, 1818-1880*, 1970.

3069 **Bythell**, D., *The Handloom Weavers: A Study in the English Cotton Industry During the Industrial Revolution*, 1969.

3070 **Catling**, H., *The Spinning Mule*, 1970.

3071 **Chapman**, S. D., *The Early Factory Masters: The Transition to the Factory System in the Midlands Textile Industry*, 1967.

3072 —— *The Cotton Industry in the Industrial Revolution*, 1972. Excellent summary.

3073 —— 'Financial restraints on the growth of firms in the cotton industry, 1790-1850', *Ec.H.R.*, 2nd ser., XXXII, 1979, 50-69.

3074 **Chapman**, S. J., *The Lancashire Cotton Industry: A Study in Economic Development*, 1904. Select bibliography, 277-304.

3075 —— and Ashton, T. S., 'The sizes of businesses, mainly in the textile industries', *J.Roy.Stat.Soc.*, LXXVII, Part V, 1914, 469-555.

3076 —— and Kemp, D., 'The war and the textile industries', *J.Roy.Stat.Soc.*, LXXVIII, Part II, 1915, 157-237.

3077 **Clapp**, B. W., *John Owens, Manchester Merchant*, 1965. Covers period 1790-1846.

3078 **Daniels**, G. W., *The Early English Cotton Industry*, 1920.

3079 **Edwards**, M. M., *The Growth of the British Cotton Trade, 1780-1815*, 1967.

3080 **Ellison**, Mary, *Support for Secession: Lancashire and the American Civil War*, Chicago, 1972.

3081 **English**, W., *The Textile Industry: An Account of the Early Inventions of Spinning, Weaving and Knitting Machines*, 1969. Useful glossary of technical terms and bibliography, 225-35.

3082 **Farnie**, D. A., 'The Cotton Famine in Great Britain', in Ratcliffe (2576), 153-78.

3083 —— *The English Cotton Industry and the World Market, 1815-96*, 1979.

3084 **Fitton**, R. S. and Wadsworth, A. P., *The Strutts and the Arkwrights, 1758-1830*, 1958.

3085 **Henderson**, W. O., *The Lancashire Cotton Famine, 1861-1865*, 1934, 2nd rev. and enlarged ed., 1969, with bibliography, 157-94.

3086 **Jenkins**, D. T., 'The cotton industry in Yorkshire, 1780-1900', *Textile H.*, X, 1979, 75-95.

3087 **Jewkes**, J. and Gray, E. M., *Wages and Labour in the Lancashire Cotton Spinning Industry*, 1935.

3088 **Lee**, C. H., *A Cotton Enterprise, 1795-1840: A History of McConnel and Kennedy*, Fine Cotton Spinners, 1972.

3089 **Lloyd-Jones**, R. and Le Roux, A. A., 'The size of firms in the cotton industry: Manchester, 1815-41', *Ec.H.R.*, 2nd ser., XXXIII, 1980, 72-82.

3090 **Muir**, A., *The Kenyon Tradition: The History of James Kenyon and Son, Ltd., 1664-1964*, 1964.

3091 **Pigott**, S. C., *Hollins: A Study of Industry, 1784-1949*, 1949.

3092 **Prest**, J., *The Industrial Revolution in Coventry*, 1960.

3093 **Robson**, R., *The Cotton Industry in Britain*, 1957.

3094 **Sandberg**, L. G., 'American rings and English mules: the role of economic rationality'. In S. B. Saul, ed., *Technological Change: The United States and Britain in the Nineteenth Century*, 1970, 120-40.

3095 —— *Lancashire in Decline: A Study in Entrepreneurship Technology and International Trade*, Columbus, Ohio, 1974.

3096 **Shapiro**, S., *Capital and the Cotton Industry in the Industrial Revolution*, Ithaca, N. Y., 1967.

3097 **Silver**, A., *Manchester Men and Indian Cotton, 1847-1872*, 1966.

3098 **Smelser**, N. J., *Social Change in the Industrial Revolution: An Application of Theory to the Lancashire Cotton Industry, 1770-1840*, 1959. Bibliography, 411-40.

3099 **Tewson**, W. F., *The British Cotton Growing Association: Golden Jubilee, 1904-1954*, 1954.

3100 **Tippett**, L. H. C., *A Portrait of the Lancashire Textile Industry*, 1969. Covers the period 1919-69.

3101 **Unwin**, G., *et al.*, *Samuel Oldknow and the Arkwrights; The Industrial Revolution at Stockport and Marple*, 1924, 2nd rev. ed., 1968.

3102 **Utley**, F., *Lancashire and the Far East*, 1931. See also Bowker (3067) and Sandberg (3095), listed above.

3103 **Wells**, F. A., *Hollins and Viyella: A Study in Business History*, 1968.

(iii) WOOLLENS AND WORSTEDS

3104 **Atkinson**, F., ed., *Some Aspects of the Eighteenth Century Woollen and Worsted Trade in Halifax*, 1956.

3105 **Beckinsale**, R. P., ed., *The Trowbridge Woollen Industry as Illustrated by the Stock Books of John and Thomas Clark, 1804-1824*, 1951.

3106 **Bischoff**, J., *A Comprehensive History of the Woollen and Worsted Manufactures*, 2 vols., 1842. Reprinted 1968.

3107 **Chapman**, S. D., ed., *The Devon Cloth Industry in the Eighteenth Century. Sun Fire Office Inventories of Merchants' and Manufacturers' Property, 1726-70*. Devon & Cornwall Rec.Soc., XXIII, 1978.

3108 **Hudson**, Patricia, ed., *The West Riding Wool Textile Industry. A Catalogue of Business Records from the Sixteenth to the Twentieth Century*, 1975.

3109 **Mann**, Julia de L., ed., *Documents illustrating the Wiltshire Woollen Trades in the Eighteenth Century*, 1964.

3110 **Plummer**, A., *The Witney Blanket Industry: The Records of the Witney Blanket Weavers*, 1934.

3111 **Beckinsale**, R. P., 'The plush industry of Oxfordshire', *Oxoniensia*, XXVIII, 1963, 53-67.

3112 **Clapham**, J. H., 'The transference of the worsted industry from Norfolk to the West Riding', *Ec. J.*, XX, 1910, 195-210.

3113 **Coleman**, D. C., 'Growth and decay during the Industrial Revolution: the case of East Anglia', *Scand.Ec.H.R.*, X, 1962, 115-27.

3114 **Crump**, W. B., *The Leeds Woollen Industry, 1780-1820*, 1931.

3115 —— and Ghorbal, Gertrude, *History of the Huddersfield Woollen Industry*, 1935. Reprinted 1967.

3116 **Hartley**, Marie and Ingilby, Joan, *The Old Hand-knitters of the Yorkshire Dales*, 1951.

3117 **Hunter**, D. M., *The West of England Woollen Industry*, 1910.

3118 **Jenkins**, D. T., *The West Riding Wool Textile Industry, 1770-1835*. A Study of Fixed Capital Formation, 1975.

3119 **Lipson**, E., *A History of Wool and Wool Manufacture*, 1953.

3120 **Mann**, Julia de L., *The Cloth Industry in the West of England, 1640-1880*, 1971.

3121 —— 'Clothiers and weavers in Wiltshire during the eighteenth century'. In Pressnell, ed. (2575), listed above.

3122 **Moir**, Esther, A. L., 'The gentlemen clothiers: a study of the organisation of the Gloucestershire cloth industry, 1750-1835'. In H. P. R. Finberg, (1241),

3123 **Plummer**, A. and Early, R. E., *The Blanket Makers, 1669-1969. A History of Charles Early and Marriot (Witney) Ltd.*, 1969.

3124 **Ponting**, K. G., ed., *Baines's Account of the Woollen Industry of England*, 1970. Text of E. Baines' article on the subject from T. Baines's *Yorkshire Past and Present*, 1875; useful glossary, 145-65, and bibliography, 60-5.

3125 —— *A History of the West of England Cloth Industry*, 1957.

3126 —— *The Woollen Industry of South-West England*, 1971.

3127 **Prichard**, M. F. Lloyd, 'The decline of Norwich', *Ec.H.R.*, 2nd ser., III, 1951, 371-7.

3128 **Rogers**, K., *Wiltshire and Somerset Woollen Mills*, 1976.

3129 **Sigsworth**, E. M., *Black Dyke Mills: A History*, 1958. Contains useful introductory chapters on the development of the worsted industry in the nineteenth century. See also Tann (1582), listed above.

3130 **Wilson**, R. G., *Gentlemen Merchants: The Merchant Community in Leeds, 1700-1830*, 1971. See also James (1572), Jenkins (5115) and Lipson (1573).

(iv) CLOTHING INDUSTRY

3131 **Thomas**, Joan, *A History of the Leeds Clothing Industry*, 1955.

3132 **Wray**, Margaret, *The Women's Outerwear Industry*, 1957.

(v) SILK AND MAN-MADE FIBRES

3133 **Chaloner**, W. H., 'Sir Thomas Lombe (1685-1739) and the British silk industry'. In *People and Industries*, 1963, 8-20.

3134 **Clapham**, J. H., 'The Spitalfields Acts, 1773-1824', *Ec. J.*, XXVI, 1916, 459-71.

3135 **Coleman**, D. C., *Courtaulds: An Economic and Social History*, 3 vols, 1969-80.

3136 **Hertz** (later Hurst), G. B., 'The English silk industry in the eighteenth century', *E.H.R.*, XXIV, 1909, 710-27.

3137 **Warner**, F., *The Silk Industry of the United Kingdom*, 1921.

3138 **Weinstock**, Maureen, 'Portrait of an eighteenth-century Sherborne silk mill owner'. In *Studies in Dorset History*, 1953, 83-102. On rayon see also Buxton and Aldcroft (2651), above.

(vi) LINEN AND FLAX

3139 **Horner**, J., *The Linen Trade of Europe During the Spinning-Wheel Period*, 1920. Contains useful trade statistics.

3140 **Rimmer**, W. G., *Marshalls of Leeds, Flax-Spinners, 1788-1886*, 1960. Excellent bibliography, 327-35.

3141 **Warden**, A. J., *The Linen Trade, Ancient and Modern*, 1864, 3rd impression, 1967.

(vii) HATTING

3142 **Dony**, J. G., *A History of the Straw Hat Industry*, 1942. South Midlands, Essex and Suffolk in the period 1680-1939.

3143 **Giles**, Phyllis M., 'The felt-hatting industry, c. 1500-1800, with particular reference to Lancashire and Cheshire', *T.L.C.A.S.*, LXIX, 1960, 104-32.

(viii) HOSIERY AND LACE

3144 **Felkin**, W., *History of the Machine-wrought Hosiery and Lace Manufactures*, 1867. 2nd ed., with introduction by S. D. Chapman, 1967, v-xxxviii; select bibliography of books, articles and theses since 1867, xxxix-xliii.

3145 **Varley**, D. E., *A History of the Midland Counties Lace Manufacturers' Association, 1915-58*, 1959.

3146 **Wells**, F. A., *The British Hosiery Trade*, 1935; 2nd rev. and enlarged edn., 1972.

(d) IRON AND STEEL

3147 **Bessemer**, H., *Autobiography*, 1905.

3148 **Flinn**, M. W., *The Law Book of the Crowley Iron Works*, Surtees Soc., CLXVII, 1957.

3149 **Griffiths**, S., *Guide to the Iron Trade of Great Britain*, 1873, 2nd ed., with new introduction, 1967.

3150 **John**, A. H., ed., *Minutes Relating to Messrs. Samuel Walker & Co., Rotherham, Iron Founders and Steel Refiners, 1741-1829*, 1951.

3151 **Scrivenor**, H., *History of the Iron Trade*, 1st ed., 1841, 2nd rev. ed., 1854. Reprinted 1967.

3152 **Addis**, J. P., *The Crawshay Dynasty: A Study in Industrial Organisation and Development, 1765-1867*, 1957.

3153 **Andrews**, P. W. S. and Brunner, Elizabeth, *Capital Development in Steel: A Study of the United Steel Companies, Ltd.*, 1951.

3154 **Ashton**, T. S., *An Eighteenth-century Industrialist: Peter Stubs of Warrington, 1756-1806*, 1939, 2nd ed., 1961. See also Dane (3166), below.

3155 —— *Iron and Steel in the Industrial Revolution*, 1st ed., 1924, 2nd rev. ed., 1951, 3rd ed., with new bibliographical introduction, 1963.

3156 **Barraclough**, K. C., 'Early steelmaking in the Sheffield area', *Trans. Hunter Arch. Soc.*, X, 1979, 335-43.

3157 **Birch**, A., *The Economic History of the British Iron and Steel Industry, 1784-1879*, 1967.

3158 —— and Flinn, M. W., 'The English steel industry before 1856 with special reference to the development of the Yorkshire Steel Industry', *Yorks.B.*, VI, 1954, 163-77.

3159 **Boswell**, J., 'Hope, efficiency or public duty? The United Steel Companies and West Cumberland, 1918-39', *Bus.H.*, XXII, 1980, 35-50.

3160 **Burn**, D. L., *The Economic History of Steelmaking, 1867-1939*, 1940, 2nd rev. ed., 1961.

3161 —— *The Steel Industry, 1939-1959*, 1961.

3162 **Butler**, R. F., *The History of Kirkstall Forge Through Seven Centuries, 1200-1945, A.D.*, 1945, 2nd rev. ed., 1954.

3163 **Campbell**, R. H., *Carron Company*, 1961.

3164 **Carr**, J. C., Taplin, W. and Wright, A. E. G., *History of the British Steel Industry*, 1962.

3165 **Chaloner**, W. H., 'Isaac Wilkinson, potfounder'. In Pressnell (2575), listed above.

3166 **Dane**, E. S., *Peter Stubs and the Lancashire Hand Tool Industry*, 1973.

3167 **Elsas**, Madeleine, *Iron in the Making: Dowlais Iron Company Letters, 1782-1860*, 1960.

3168 **Fereday**, R. P., *The Career of Richard Smith 1783-1868*, 1966. (Smith was mineral agent to the Earl of Dudley.)

3169 **Flinn**, M. W., *Men of Iron. The Crowleys in the Early Iron Industry*, 1962. See also Birch and Flinn (3158), above.

3170 **Gale**, W. K. V., *The Black Country Iron Industry: A Technical History*, 1966 (mainly 1700 to 1960s).

3171 —— 'The Bessemer steelmaking process', *Trans. Newcomen Soc.*, XLVI, 1976, 17-24.

3172 —— *The British Iron and Steel Industry: A Technical History*, 1967.

3173 —— *The Coneygre Story*, 1954, (Tipton, Staffordshire).

3174 **Gloag**, J. and Bridgwater, D., *A History of Cast Iron in Architecture*, 1948.

3175 **Hammersley**, G., 'Did it fall or was it pushed? The Foleys and the end of the charcoal iron industry in the eighteenth century', in Smout (2578), 67-90.

3176 **Harris**, A., *Cumberland Iron: The Story of Hodbarrow Mine, 1855-1968*, 1971.

3177 **Hey**, D., *The Rural Metalworkers of the Sheffield Region*, 1972.

3178 **Hyde**, C. K., *Technological Change and the British Iron Industry, 1700-1870*, Princeton, N. J., 1977. Surveys all aspects of ironmaking in a period of gradual, continuous change.

3179 **Johnson**, B. L. C., 'The Midland iron industry in the early eighteenth century: the background to the first successful use of coke in iron smelting',

Bus.H., II, 1960, 67-74.

3180 **McCloskey**, D., *Economic Maturity and Enterpreneurial Decline: British Iron and Steel, 1870-1913*, 1974.

3181 **Minchinton**, W. E., *The British Tinplate Industry: A History*, 1957.

3182 **Mottram**, R. H. and Coote, C., *Through Five Generations: The History of the Butterley Company*, 1950.

3183 **Musgrave**, P. W., *Technical Change, the Labour Force and Education: A Study of the British and German Iron and Steel Industries, 1860-1964*, 1967. Deals mainly with technical education. Should be used with great caution.

3184 **Mutton**, N., 'The Marked Bar Association: Price Regulation in the Black Country Wrought Iron Trade', *W.Midland Studs.*, IX, 1976, 2-8.

3185 **Osborn**, F. M., *The Story of the Mushets*, 1952.

3186 **Page**, R., 'Richard and Edward Knight: ironmasters of Bringewood and Wolverley', *Trans.Woolhope Nat.Field Club*, XLIII, 1979, 7-17.

3187 **Pollard**, S., *Three Centuries of Sheffield Steel: The Story of a Family Business* (Marsh Bros. & Co.), 1954.

3188 **Raistrick**, A., *Dynasty of Ironfounders: The Darbys and Coalbrookdale*, 1953.

3189 —— and Allen, E., 'The South Yorkshire ironmasters, 1690-1750', *Ec.H.R.*, IX, 1939, 168-85.

3190 **Riden**, P., 'The output of the British iron industry before 1870', *Ec.H.R.*, XXX, 1977, 442-59.

3191 —— 'The iron industry' in Church (2536), 63-86.

3192 **Robinson**, P., *The Smiths of Chesterfield: A History of the Griffin Foundry, Brampton, 1775-1833*, 1957.

3193 **Roepke**, H., *Movements of the British Iron and Steel Industry, 1720-1951*, Urbana, Ill., 1956.

3194 **Sanderson**, M., 'The Professor as industrial consultant: Oliver Arnold and the British steel industry, 1900-14', *Ec.H.R.*, 2nd ser., XXXI, 1978, 585-600.

3195 **Stones**, F., *The British Ferrous Wire Industry, 1882-1962*, 1977.

3196 **Trinder**, B., ed., *'The Most Extraordinary District in the World'. Ironbridge and Coalbrookdale*, 1977.

3197 **Warren**, K., *The British Iron and Steel Sheet Industry since 1840*, 1970.

3198 —— 'Iron and Steel' in Buxton and Aldcroft (2651), 103-28. See also Allen (2588), Raybould (2605), and Schubert (513).

(e) COPPER, BRASS AND LEAD

3199 **Leifchild**, J. R., *Cornwall: Its Mines and Miners*, 1853. Reprinted 1968.

3200 **Burt**, R., ed., *Cornish Mining: Essays on the Organisation of the Cornish Mines and the Cornish Mining Economy*, 1969.

3201 **Clough**, R. T., *The Lead Smelting Mills of the Yorkshire Dales: Their Architectural Character, Construction and Place in the European Tradition*, 1962; bibliography, 169-72.

3202 **Day**, Joan, *Bristol Brass: The History of the Industry*, 1973.

3203 **Ford**, T. D. and Nieuwerts, J. H., eds, *Lead Mining in the Peak District*, 1968; bibliography, 123-4.

3204 **Hunt**, C. J., *The Lead Miners of the Northern Pennines in the Eighteenth and Nineteenth Centuries*, 1970.

3205 **Jennings**, B., ed., *A History of Nidderdale*, 1967, 151-61, 266-325.

3206 **Kirkham**, Nellie, *Derbyshire Lead-mining through the Centuries*, 1968.

3207 **O'Neal**, R., *A Bibliography of Derbyshire Lead Mining*, 1961.

3208 **Raistrick**, A., *Miners and Miners of Swaledale*, 1955.

3209 —— *Two Centuries of Industrial Welfare: The London (Quaker) Lead Company, 1692-1905*, 1938.

3210 —— *The Lead Industry of Wensleydale and Swaledale*, 1975.

3211 **Roberts**, R. O., 'Copper and economic growth in Britain, 1729-84', *Nat.Lib.Wales J.*, X, 1957, 1-10.

3212 **Turnbull**, L., *The History of Lead Mining in the North East of England*, 1975. See also Hamilton (1606), Jenkin (2203), and Raistrick and Jennings (1619).

(f) COAL

3213 **Benson**, J., comp., *Bibliography of the British Coal Industry*, 1981.

3214 **Hair**, T. H., *A Series of Views of the Collieries in the Counties of Northumberland and Durham*, 1844, 2nd ed., with new introduction, 1969.

3215 **Holland**, J., *The History and Description of Fossil Fuel, the Collieries and Coal Trade of Great Britain*, 1835, 2nd ed., 1841, new impression, 1968.

3216 **Jevons**, H. S., *The British Coal Trade*, 1915, 2nd ed., with new introduction, 1969.

3217 **Jevons**, W. S., *The Coal Question*, 1865.

3218 **Leifchild**, J. R., *Our Coal and Our Coal Pits, the People in Them and the Scenes around Them*, 2nd ed., 1856, new impression, 1968.

3219 **Lloyd**, A. L. (compiler), *Come all ye Bold Miners: Ballads and Songs of the Coalfields*, 1952.

3220 **Anderson**, D., 'Blundell's Wigan Collieries' (Parts, I, II, III), *T.H.S.L.C.*, CXVI, 1964, 69-115; 117, 1965, 109-43: 119, 1967, 113-79.

3221 **Ashton**, T. S. and Sykes, J., *The Coal Industry of the Eighteenth Century*, 1929, 2nd rev. ed., 1964, with additions to the bibliography, 255-62.

3222 **Atkinson**, F., *The Great Northern Coalfield, 1700-1900. Illustrated Notes on the Durham and Northumberland Coalfield*, 1966.

3223 **Banks**, A. G. and Schofield, R. B., *Brindley at Wet Earth Colliery: An Engineering Study*, 1968. Reconstruction of James Brindley's work at a colliery near Manchester.

3224 **Benson**, J. and Neville, R. G., eds., *Studies in the Yorkshire Coal Industry*, 1976.

3225 **Bulley**, J. A., ' "To Mendip for coal": A Study of the Somerset Coalfield before 1830', *Proc.Somerset Arch.&Nat.H.Soc.*, Part I, XCVII, 1952, 46-78; Part II, XCVIII, 1953, 46-78.

3226 **Bulmer**, M., ed., *Mining and Social Change. Durham County in the Twentieth Century*, 1977.

3227 **Butt**, J., 'Legends of the coal-oil industry, 1847-64', *Expl.Entrepren.H.*, 2nd ser., II, 1964, 16-30.

3228 —— 'Technical change and the growth of the British shale-oil industry, 1680-1870', *Ec.H.R.*, 2nd ser., XVII, 1965, 511-21.

3229 **Buxton**, N. K., *The Economic Development of the British Coal Industry from Industrial Revolution to the Present Day*, 1978.

3230 **Cromar**, P., 'The coal industry on Tyneside 1715-60', *Northern H.*, XIV, 1978, 193-207.

3231 **Down**, C. G. and Warrington, A. J., *The History of the Somerset Coalfield*, 1971.

3232 **Duckham**, B. F. and H., *Great Pit Disasters: Great Britain 1700 to the Present Day*, 1973.

3233 **Fraser-Stephen**, Elspet, *Two Centuries in the London Coal Trade: The Story of Charringtons*, 1950.

3234 **Griffin**, A. R., *Mining in the East Midlands, 1550-1947*, 1971. Deals with production and unionism.

3235 **Hair**, P. E. H., 'The Lancashire collier girl, 1795', *T.H.S.L.C.*, CXX, 1968, 63-86. See also John (4452).

3236 **Hare**, A. E. C., *The Anthracite Coal Industry of the Swansea District*, 1940.

3237 **Hughes**, E., 'The coal trade', in *North Country Life in the Eighteenth Century: The North East, 1700-1750*, 1952, 151-257.

3238 —— 'The collieries' and 'The coal trade'. In *North Country Life in the Eighteenth Century: Cumberland and Westmorland, 1700-1830*, 1965, 133-99.

3239 **Kirby**, M. W., *The British Coalmining Industry, 1870-1946: A Political and Economic History*, 1977.

3240 **Mott**, R. A., 'The London and Newcastle chaldron for measuring coal', *Arch.Aeliana*, 4th ser., XL, 1962, 227-39.

3241 **Sweezy**, P. M., *Monopoly and Competition in the English Coal Trade, 1550-1850*, Cambridge, Mass., 1938.

3242 **Taylor**, A. J., 'The coal industry'. In Aldcroft, ed. (2639), listed above, 37-70.

3243 —— 'Combination in the mid-eighteenth-century coal industry', *T.R.H.S.*, 5th ser., III, 1953, 23-39.

3244 —— 'Labour productivity and technological innovation in the British coal industry, 1850-1914', *Ec.H.R.*, 2nd ser., XIV, 1961, 48-70.

3245 —— 'The third marquis of Londonderry and the north-eastern coal trade', *Durham University J.*, 1955, 21-7.

3246 —— 'The Wigan coalfield in 1851', *T.H.S.L.C.*, 106, 1954, 117-26.

3247 **Walker**, S. F., *Coal Cutting by Machinery in the United Kingdom*, 1902.

3248 **White**, A. W. A., *Men and Mining in Warwickshire*, 1970.

3249 **Wood**, O., 'A Cumberland colliery during the Napoleonic War', *Economica*, XXI, 1954, 54-63. See also Duckham (5446), Lerry (5190), and Morris and Williams (5194).

(g) ENGINEERING

3250 **Pole**, W., ed., *The Life of Sir William Fairbairn, Bart., Partly Written by Himself*, 1st ed., 1877, 2nd ed., 1970 with new introduction by A. E. Musson.

3251 **Sturt**, G. (pseud. George Bourne), *The Wheelwrights' Shop*, 1st ed., 1923. Reprinted 1934, 1948. A business history, Farnham, Surrey.

3252 **Armytage**, W. H. G., *A Social History of Engineering*, 1st ed. 1961, 3rd rev. ed., 1969.

3253 **Baker**, E. C., *Sir William Preece F.R.S. Victorian Engineer Extraordinary*, 1976. Spans the era from railways to radio.

3254 **Boucher**, C. T. G., *James Brindley, Engineer, 1716-1772*, 1968.

3255 —— *John Rennie, 1761-1821: The Life and Work of a Great Engineer*, 1963.

3256 **Bracegirdle**, B. and Miles, Patricia H., *Thomas Telford*, 1973.

3257 **Clements**, P., *Marc Isambard Brunel, 1769-1849*, 1970.

3258 **Dougan**, D., *The Great Gun Maker*, 1971. A biography of Sir William, later Lord, Armstrong.

3259 **Floud**, R., *The British Machine Tool Industry, 1850-1914*, 1976. A quantitative approach which discusses the structure, efficiency and productivity of the industry and its place in international trade.

3260 **Gibb**, A., *The Story of Telford*, 1934. Still valuable on engineering aspects.

3261 **Harris**, T. R., *Arthur Woolf: The Cornish Engineer, 1766-1837*, 1966.

3262 **McNeil**, I., *Joseph Bramah: A Century of Invention, 1749-1851*, 1968.

3263 **Roe**, J. W., *English and American Tool Builders*, New Haven, Conn., 1916.

3264 **Rolt**, L. T. C., *Great Engineers*, 1962. Short studies of A. Darby, T. Newcomen, W. Jessop, M. Murray, H. Maudslay, J. Locke, J. Fowler, B. Baker, R. E. Crompton and F. W. Lanchester.

3265 —— *Thomas Telford*, 1958.

3266 —— *Tools for the Job: A Short History of Machine Tools*, 1965.

3267 —— *Victorian Engineering*, 1970.

3268 —— *Waterloo Ironworks: A History of Taskers of Andover, 1809-1968*, 1969.

3269 **Ruddock**, T., *Arch Bridges and their Builders, 1735-1835*, 1979.

3270 **Saul**, S. B., 'The machine tool industry in Britain to 1914', *Bus.H.*, X, 1968, 22-43.

3271 —— 'The market and the development of the mechanical engineering industries in Britain, 1860-1914', *Ec.H.R.*, 2nd ser., XX, 1967, 111-30.

3272 **Scott**, J. D., *Siemens Brothers, 1858-1958: An Essay in the History of Industry*, 1958.

3273 **Semler**, E. G., ed., *Engineering Heritage*, 2 vols, 1963, 1966. Short biographies of eminent British engineers and industrial innovators.

3274 **Simmons**, J., 'William Jessop, civil engineer'. In *Parish and Empire*, 1952, 146-54.

3275 **Smiles**, S., *The Lives of the Engineers*, 5 vols, 1874.

3276 **Todd**, A. C., *Beyond the Blaze: A Biography of Davies Gilbert*, 1967.

3277 **Wilson**, C. and Reader, W. J., *Men and Machines: A History of D. Napier & Son, Engineers, Limited, 1808-1958*, 1958. See also Burstall (216), above.

(h) CHEMICALS, SOAP AND SALT

3278 **Barker**, T. C., 'Lancashire coal, Cheshire salt and the rise of Liverpool', *T.H.S.L.C.*, CIII, 1951, 83-101.

3279 **Bolitho**, H., *Alfred Mond, First Lord Melchett*, 1933.

3280 **Clow**, A. and Nan L., *The Chemical Revolution: A Contribution to Social Technology*, 1952.

3281 **Cohen**, J. M., *The Life of Ludwig Mond*, 1956.

3282 **Crathorne**, Nancy, *Tennant's Stalk: The Story of the Tennants of the Green*, 1973.

3283 **Fieldhouse**, D. K., *Unilever Overseas. The Anatomy of a Multinational, 1895-1965*, 1978.

3284 **Haber**, L. F., *The Chemical Industry During the Nineteenth Century: A Study of the Economic Aspect of Applied Chemistry in Europe and North America*, 1958.

3285 —— *The Chemical Industry, 1900-1930: International Growth and Technological Change*, 1971.

3286 **Hardie**, D. W. F., *A History of the Chemical Industry in Widnes*, 1950.

3287 —— 'The Macintoshes and the origins of the chemical industry', *Chemistry and Industry*, 1952, 606-13.

3288 —— and Pratt, J. D., *A History of the Modern British Chemical Industry*, 1966.

3289 **Iredale**, D. A., 'John and Thomas Marshall and the Society for improving the British Salt Trade', *Ec.H.R.*, 2nd ser., XX, 1967, 79-93.

3290 —— 'The rise and fall of the Marshalls of Northwich, salt proprietors, 1720-1917', *T.H.S.L.C.*, CXVII, 1965, 59-82.

3291 **Koss**, S. E., *Sir John Brunner, Radical Plutocrat, 1842-1919*, 1970.

3292 **Musson**, A. E., *Enterprise in Soap and Chemicals: Joseph Crosfield and Sons, Ltd., 1815-1865*, 1965. The soap industry in Warrington.

3293 **Padley**, R., 'The beginnings of the British alkali industry', *Birm.H.J.*, III, 1951, 64-78.

3294 **Reader**, W. J., *Imperial Chemical Industries: A History I: The Forerunners, 1870-1926*, 1970. Excellent bibliography, 524-34. II: *The First Quarter Century 1926-52*, 1975.

3295 —— *Fifty Years of Unilever, 1930-80*, 1980.

3296 **Warren**, K., *Chemical Foundations: The Alkali Industry in Britain to 1926*, 1980.

3297 **Wilson**, C., *The History of Unilever: A Study*

in Economic Growth and Social Change, 2 vols, 1954.

3298 —— *Unilever, 1945-1965: Challenge and Response in the Post-war Industrial Revolution*, 1968.

3299 —— *Management and Policy in Large-Scale Enterprise. Lever Brothers and Unilever, 1918-38*, 1977. For other material on the salt industry see Calvert (1624) and Chaloner (1625) above.

(i) POTTERY

3300 **Jewitt**, Ll., *The Wedgwoods: Being a Life of Josiah Wedgwood: With Notices of his Works and their Productions. Memoir of the Wedgwoods and Other Families and a History of the Early Potteries of Staffordshire*, 1865.

3301 **Meteyard**, Eliza, *Life of Josiah Wedgwood from his Private Correspondence*, 2 vols., 1865-66.

3302 **Owen**, H., *The Staffordshire Potter, with a Chapter on the Dangerous Processes in the Potting Industry by the Duchess of Sutherland*, 1901.

3303 **Anon.**, *Some Descriptions of Pottery Making and Working Conditions, 1557-1844*, 1970.

3304 **Barton**, R. M., *A History of the Cornish China-clay Industry*, 1966.

3305 **Bladen**, V. W., 'The Potteries in the Industrial Revolution', *Ec. J.Ec.H.Supp.*, I, 1926, 117-30.

3306 **Finer**, Ann and Savage, G., eds., *The Selected Letters of Josiah Wedgwood*, 1965.

3307 **Hower**, R. M., 'The Wedgwoods: ten generations of potters', *J.Ec. & Bus.H.*, IV, 1932, 281-313; 665-90.

3308 **Mackenzie**, C., *The House of Coalport, 1750-1950*, 1951.

3309 **Rolt**, L. T. C., *Potters' Field: A History of the South Devon Ball Clay Industry*, 1974.

3310 **Thomas**, J., 'The pottery industry and the Industrial Revolution', *Ec. J.Ec.H.Supp.*, III, 1937, 399-414.

3311 —— *The Rise of the Staffordshire Potteries*, 1971.

3312 **Weatherill**, Lorna, *The Pottery Trade and North Staffordshire, 1660-1760*, 1971.

3313 **Whiter**, L., *Spode: A History of the Family, Factory and Wares from 1733 to 1833*, 1970.

(j) GLASS

3314 **Barker**, T. C., *The Glassmakers. Pilkington: The Rise of an International Company, 1826-1976*, 1977. A substantially enlarged and updated version of a business history first published in 1960. Almost half the book is devoted to the period after 1914.

3315 **Harris**, J. R., 'Origins of the St. Helens glass industry', *Northern H.*, III, 1968, 105-17.

(k) RUBBER

3316 **Payne**, P. L., *Rubber and Railways in the Nineteenth Century: A Study of the Spencer Papers*, 1961.

3317 **Schidrowitz**, P., and Dawson, T. R., eds., *History of the Rubber Industry*, 1952.

3318 **Woodruff**, W., *The Rise of the British Rubber Industry During the Nineteenth Century*, 1958.

(l) PAPER

3319 **Reader**, W. J., *Bowater. A History*, 1981. Written to commemorate the centenary of this giant paper-making concern.

3320 **Shorter**, A. H., *Paper Making in the British Isles*, 1971. See Coleman (1632) and Shorter (1633), listed above.

(m) PRINTING AND PUBLISHING

3321 **Briggs**, A., *Essays in the History of Publishing*, 1974. Includes essays on copyright and on the paperback revolution.

3322 **Carter**, H., *A History of the Oxford University Press. I: To the Year 1780*, 1975.

3323 **Clair**, C., *A History of Printing in Britain*, 1965.

3324 **Handover**, P. M., *Printing in London from 1476 to Modern Times*, 1960.

3325 **Hunt**, C. J., *The Book Trade in Northumberland and Durham to 1860*, 1975.

3326 **Plant**, Marjorie, *The English Book Trade*, 1939. Reprinted 1974.

3327 **Roberts**, S. C., *The Evolution of Cambridge Publishing*, 1956.

(n) SHIPPING AND SHIPBUILDING
(i) GENERAL

3328 **Coleman**, T., *The Liners*, 1976.

3329 **Davies**, P. N., *Sir Alfred Jones: Shipping Entrepreneur par excellence*, 1978.

3330 —— *The Trade Makers: Elder Dempster in West Africa, 1852-1972*, 1973.

3331 **Ewart**, E. A. (pseud. Boyd Cable). *A Hundred Year History of the Peninsular and Oriental*

Steam Navigation Company 1837-1937, 1937.

3332 **Fisher**, H. E. S., ed., *West Country Maritime and Social History: Some Essays*, 1980.

3333 **Hyde**, F. E., *Cunard and the North Atlantic*, 1975.

3334 —— *Shipping Enterprise and Management 1830-1939: Harrisons of Liverpool*, 1967.

3335 —— and Harris, J. R., *Blue Funnel: A History of Alfred Holt and Company of Liverpool, 1865-1914*, 1956.

3336 **Jackson**, G., *The Trade and Shipping of Eighteenth-Century Hull*, E.Yorks.Loc.H.Soc., XXI, 1975.

3337 —— *The Whaling Trade*, 1978.

3338 **Jarvis**, R. C., 'Eighteenth-century London shipping'. In Hollaender and Kellaway (597), listed above.

3339 **John**, A. H., *A Liverpool Merchant House, Being the History of Alfred Booth and Company, 1863-1958*, 1959.

3340 **Kirkaldy**, A. W., *British Shipping: Its History, Organisation and Importance*, 1914. Excellent treatment; useful on shipping conferences, Lloyd's Register and marine insurance, bibliography, XIII-XX.

3341 **Lindsay**, W. S., *History of Merchant Shipping*, 4 vols., 1871-6.

3342 **Marriner**, Sheila, *Rathbones of Liverpool, 1845-73*, 1961. The China trade.

3343 —— and Hyde, F. E., *The Senior: John Samuel Swire, 1825-98: Management in Far Eastern Shipping Trade*, 1967.

3344 **Matthews**, K. and Panting, G., eds., *Ships and Shipbuilding in the North Atlantic Region*, 1978.

3345 **Murray**, M., *Union Castle Chronicle, 1853-1953*, 1953.

3346 **Sturmey**, S. G., *British Shipping and World Competition*, 1962.

3347 **Syrett**, D., *Shipping and the American War, 1775-83: A Study of British Transport Organisation*, 1970. See also Buxton (5439), Donnelly (5445), Moss and Hume (5457), listed below.

(ii) PERSONNEL

3348 **Carew**, A., *The Lower Deck of the Royal Navy, 1900-39. Invergordon in Perspective*, 1982.

3349 **Course**, A. G., *The Merchant Navy: A Social History*, 1963.

3350 **Garstin**, C., ed., *Samuel Kelly: An Eighteenth-Century Seaman*, 1925. His travel diary.

3351 **Grandish**, S., *The Manning of the British Navy during the Seven Years' War*, 1980.

3352 **Kemp**, P., *The British Sailor: A Social History of the Lower Deck*, 1971.

3353 **Lewis**, M., *A Social History of the Navy (1793-1815)*, 1960.

3354 **Lloyd**, C., *The Nation and the Navy: A History of Naval Life and Policy*, 2nd rev. ed., 1961.

3355 **Rasor**, E. L., *Reform in the Royal Navy. A Social History of the Lower Deck, 1850-80*, Hamden, Conn., 1977.

(iii) STEAM

3356 **Hughes**, J. R. T. and Reiter, S., 'The first 1945 British steamships', *J.American Stat.Ass.*, 53, 1958, 360-81. See however, *T.L.S.*, 29 September, 13 and 27 October 1966.

3357 **Kennedy**, J., *The History of Steam Navigation*, 1903. Useful for the Liverpool lines.

3358 **Moyse-Bartlett**, H., *From Sail to Steam*, Hist.Ass. pamphlet, 1946.

3359 **Spratt**, H. P., *The Birth of the Steamboat*, 1958.

3360 **Tyler**, D. B., *Steam Conquers the Atlantic*, N. Y., 1939.

(iv) SHIPBUILDING

3361 **Dougan**, D., *The History of North East Shipbuilding*, 1968.

3362 **Jones**, L., *Shipbuilding in Britain, Mainly Between the two World Wars*, 1957. Chapter I is on the nineteenth century, but contains a number of inaccuracies.

3363 **Pollard**, S. and Robertson, P., *The British Shipbuilding Industry, 1870-1914*, Harvard, 1979. A comprehensive history dealing with the organisation and geography of the industry, with labour and labour relations, wages and productivity, and with state intervention.

3364 **Scott**, J. D., *Vickers: A History*, 1962.

3365 **Trebilcock**, C., *The Vickers Brothers. Armaments and Enterprise, 1854-1914*, 1977.

(o) BUILDING

3366 **Bowley**, Marian, *The British Building Industry: Four Studies in Response to Resistance and Change*, 1969. Covers the twentieth century.

3367 —— *Housing and the State, 1919-1944*, 1946.

3368 —— *Innovations in Building Materials*, 1960.

3369 **Brown**, Joyce M., 'W. B. Wilkinson (1819-1902) and his place in the history of reinforced concrete', *Trans.Newcomen Soc.*, XXXIX, 1966-7, 129-42.

3370 **Cooney**, E. W., 'The origins of the Victorian master builders', *Ec.H.R.*, 2nd ser., VIII, 1955-6, 167-76.

3371 —— 'Long waves in building in the British economy of the nineteenth century'. In Aldcroft and Fearon (2641), listed above, 220-35.

3372 **Davey**, N., *Building in Britain: The Growth and Organisation of Building Processes in Britain from Roman times to the Present Day*, 1964.

3373 —— *A History of Building Materials*, 1961.

3374 **Francis**, A. T., *The Cement Industry, 1796-1914. A History*, 1978.

3375 **Habakkuk**, H. J., 'Fluctuations in house-building in Britain and the United States in the nineteenth century'. In Aldcroft and Fearon (2641), listed above, 236-67.

3376 **Hobhouse**, Hermione, *Thomas Cubitt, Master Builder*, 1971.

3377 **Lewis**, J. P., *Building Cycles and Britain's Growth*, 1965. Covers period from 1700 to the present.

3378 **Lloyd**, N., *A History of English Brickwork from Mediaeval Times to the End of the Georgian Period*, 1925.

3379 **Middlemas**, R. K., *The Master Builders: Thomas Brassey; Sir John Aird; Lord Cowdray; Sir John Norton-Griffiths*, 1963.

3380 **Powell**, C. G., *An Economic History of the British Building Industry, 1815-1979*, 1980. A popular approach combining the approaches of the architectural and social historian.

3381 **Richardson**, H. W. and Aldcroft, D. H., *Building in Britain Between the Wars*, 1968.

3382 **Saul**, S. B., 'House building in England, 1890-1914', *Ec.H.R.*, 2nd ser., XV, 1962-3, 119-37.

3383 **Skempton**, A. W., 'Portland cements, 1843-1887', *Trans.Newcomen Soc.*, XXXV, 1964, 117-52.

(p) FISHING

3384 **Dunlop**, T., *The British Fisheries Society, 1786-1893*, 1978.

3385 **Gray**, M., 'Organisation and growth in the East-coast herring fishing, 1800-1885', in Payne (5473), listed below, 187-216.

3386 **Samuel**, A. M., *The Herring: Its Effect on the History of Britain*, 1918.

3387 **Stern**, W., 'Fish supplies for London in the 1760s: an experiment in overland transport', parts I and II, *J.Roy.Soc. Arts*, CXVIII, 1970, 360-5, 430-5. See also Cutting (1647), listed above.

(q) FOOD AND DRINK

3388 **Blackman**, Janet, 'The food supply of an indus-

trial town: a study of Sheffield's public markets, 1780-1900', *Bus.H.*, V, 1963, 82-97.

3389 **Chivers**, K., 'Henry Jones *versus* the Admiralty', *H.Today*, X, 1960, 247-54. The invention of self-raising flour.

3390 **Corley**, T. E. B., *Quaker Enterprise in Biscuits: Huntley and Palmers of Reading, 1822-1972*, 1972.

3391 **Curtis-Bennett**, N., *The Food of the People: Being the History of Industrial Feeding*, 1949.

3392 **Deerr**, N., *The History of Sugar*, 2 vols., 1949-50.

3393 **Forrest**, D. M., *A Hundred Years of Ceylon Tea, 1867-1967*, 1967.

3394 **French**, R. V., *Nineteen Centuries of Drink in England*, 1886.

3395 **Hugill**, A., *Sugar and All That. A History of Tate and Lyle*, 1978.

3396 **Mathias**, P., *The Brewing Industry in England 1700-1830*, 1959.

3397 **Sigsworth**, E. M., *The Brewing Trade During the Industrial Revolution: The Case of Yorkshire*, 1967.

3398 **Stuyvenberg**, J. H. van, ed., *Margarine: An Economic, Social and Scientific History, 1869-1969*, 1969.

3399 **Twining**, S., *The House of Twining, 1706-1956*, 1956. Tea and coffee.

3400 **Vaizey**, J., *The Brewing Industry, 1886-1951: An Economic Study*, 1960.

3401 **Webber**, R., *Covent Garden: Mud Salad Market*, 1969.

(r) MISCELLANEOUS

3402 **Alford**, B. W. E., *W. D. and H. O. Wills and the Development of the U.K. Tobacco Trade, 1786-1965*, 1973.

3403 **Bartlett**, J. N., *Carpeting the Millions. The Growth of Britain's Carpet Industry, c. 1740-1970*, 1978.

3404 **Brace**, H. W., *History of Seed Crushing in Great Britain*, 1960.

3405 **Bythell**, D., *The Sweated Trades: Outwork in Nineteenth-Century Britain*, 1978.

3406 **Chapman**, S. D., *Jesse Boot of Boots the Chemists*, 1974.

3407 **Hogg**, O. F. G., *The Royal Arsenal: its Background, Origin and Subsequent History*, 2 vols., 1963.

3408 **Salaman**, R. A., *Dictionary of Tools used in the Woodworking and Allied Trades, c. 1700-1970*, 1975.

THE FACTORY SYSTEM AND FACTORY LEGISLATION

3409 **Babbage**, C., *On the Economy of Machinery and Manufactures*, 4th enlarged ed., 1835. Reprinted 1963.

3410 **Dodd**, W., *The Factory System Illustrated*, 1st ed. 1842, 3rd ed., with introduction, 1968.

3411 **Fielden**, J., *The Curse of the Factory System*, 1st ed., 1836, 2nd ed., 1969, with introduction by J. T. Ward. The introduction is the best life of J.F.

3412 **Gaskell**, P., *Artisans and Machinery: The Moral and Physical Condition of the Manufacturing Population Considered with Reference to Mechanical Substitutes for Human Labour*, 1836. Reprinted 1968.

3413 —— *The Manufacturing Population of England*, 1833.

3414 **Kydd**, S. H. G., (pseud. 'Alfred') *The History of the Factory Movement*, 2 vols., 1857. Reprinted N. Y., 1966.

3415 **Taylor**, R. W. Cooke, *Introduction to a History of the Factory System*, 1886.

3416 **Taylor**, W. Cooke, *Notes of a Tour in the Manufacturing Districts of Lancashire*, 1841, 2nd ed., 1842, 3rd ed., 1968.

3417 **Ure**, A., *The Philosophy of Manufactures*, 1st ed., 1835, 3rd ed. 1861. Reprint of 1st ed., 1967.

3418 **Wing**, C., *Evils of the Factory System Demonstrated by Parliamentary Evidence*, 1837. Reprinted 1967. A summary of the Parliamentary Papers and debates.

3419 **Blaug**, M., 'The classical economists and the Factory Acts – a re-examination'. In Coats (4628), listed below, 104-22.

3420 **Bready**, J. Wesley, *Lord Shaftesbury and Social-Industrial Progress*, 1926.

3421 **Clarke**, A., *The Effects of the Factory System*, 1899, 4th ed., 1904.

3422 **Cowherd**, R. G., *The Humanitarians and the Ten Hour Movement in England*, Boston, Mass., 1956. Should be used with caution.

3423 **Djang**, T. K., *Factory Inspection in Great Britain*, 1942.

3424 **Driver**, C., Tory Radical: *The Life of Richard Oastler*, N. Y., 1946.

3425 **Hammond**, J. L., and Barbara, *Lord Shaftsbury*, 1923, 4th rev. ed., 1939. Reprinted 1969.

3426 **Henriques**, Ursula R. Q., *The Early Factory Acts and their Enforcement*, Hist.Ass. pamphlet, 1971.

3427 **Hutchins**, B. L., and Harrison, A., *A History of Factory Legislation*, 1903, 2nd rev. ed., 1911, 3rd ed., 1926. Reprinted 1966. Covers the period up to 1910.

3428 **Hutt**, W. H., 'The factory system of the early nineteenth century'. In Hayek, (89), 160-88.

3429 **Joyce**, P., *Work, Society and Politics. The Culture of the Factory in later Victorian England*, 1980. Relates the political power of the factory-owners to their economic and social leadership in the mill towns and explores the different ways in which this élite influenced the culture of their workforce.

3430 **Langenfelt**, G., *The Historic Origin of the Eight Hours' Day*, Stockholm, 1954.

3431 **Lee**, W. R., 'Robert Baker, the first doctor in the factory department' (Part I: 1803-1858; Part II: 1858 onwards), *Brit. J.Indust.Med.*, XXI, 1964, 85-93, 167-79.

3432 **Martin**, Bernice, 'Leonard Horner: a portrait of an inspector of factories', *Internat.R.Soc.H.*, XIV, 1969, 412-43.

3433 **Moseley**, Maboth, *Irascible Genius: A Life of Charles Babbage, Inventor*, 1964.

3434 **Muter**, W. G., *The Buildings of an Industrial Community: Coalbrookdale and Ironbridge*, 1979.

3435 **Richards**, J. M., *The Functional Tradition in Early Industrial Buildings*, 1958.

3436 **Sorenson**, L. R., 'Some classical economists, *laissez-faire* and the Factory Acts', *J.Ec.H.*, XII, 1952, 247-62.

3437 **Tann**, Jennifer, *The Development of the Factory*, 1970.

3438 **Thomas**, M. W., *The Early Factory Legislation: A Study in Legislative and Administrative Evolution*, 1948. Covers the period 1802-53 in some detail.

3439 **Walker**, K. O., 'The classical economists and the factory Acts', *J.Ec.H.*, I, 1941, 168-77. Takes the question to 1833.

3440 **Ward**, J. T., *The Factory Movement, 1830-1855*, 1962.

3441 —— 'The factory movement' (with bibliographical notes). In Ward (4195), listed below, 54-77.

3442 —— 'The Factory Movement in Lancashire,

1830-1855', *T.L.C.A.S.*, LXXV-VI, 1969, 186-210.

3443 —— *The Factory System*, 2 vols., 1970. Documents and commentary.

3444 —— 'Leeds and the Factory Reform Movement', *Thoresby Soc. Miscellany*, 13, Part II, 1961, 87, 118.

3445 —— and Treble, J. J., 'Religion and education in 1843: reaction to the "Factory Education Bill" ', *J.Eccles.H.*, XX, 1969, 79-110.

3446 **Winter**, J., *Industrial Architecture*, 1970. A study of early factories. See also Berg (4623) and Chapman (3071).

OVERSEAS TRADE AND OVERSEAS INVESTMENT

(a) GENERAL AND STATISTICAL

3447 **Clark**, G. N., *Guide to English Commercial Statistics, 1696-1782*, 1938.

3448 **Crowhurst**, P., *The Defence of British Trade 1689-1815*, 1977.

3449 **Davis**, R., 'English foreign trade, 1700-1774', *Ec.H.R.*, 2nd ser., XV, 1962.

3450 —— *The Industrial Revolution and British Overseas Trade*, 1978.

3451 **Ehrman**, J., *The British Government and Commercial Negotiations with Europe, 1783-1793*, 1962.

3452 **Heckscher**, E. F., *The Continental System: An Economic Interpretation*, 1922.

3453 **Henderson**, W. O., 'The Anglo-French Commercial Treaty of 1786', *Ec.H.R.*, 2nd ser., X, 1957, 104-12.

3454 **Hertz** (*later* Hurst), G. B., *The Old Colonial System*, 1905.

3455 **Hoon**, Elizabeth E., *The Organisation of the English Customs System, 1699-1786*, N. Y., 1938.

3456 **Olson**, M., *The Economics of the War-time Shortage: A History of British Food Supplies in the Napoleonic war and in World Wars I and II*, Durham, N. C., 1963.

3457 **Parkinson**, C. N., ed., *The Trade Winds: A Study of British Overseas Trade during the French Wars, 1793-1815*, 1948.

3458 **Schlote**, W., *British Overseas Trade from 1700 to the 1930s*, 1952. English translation of a German book published in 1938; bibliography of books and articles since 1938, v-vi.

3459 **Schumpeter**, Elizabeth, *English Overseas Trade Statistics, 1697-1808*, 1960. With an introduction by T. S. Ashton.

3460 **Schuyler**, R. L., *The Fall of the Old Colonial System: A Study in British Free Trade, 1770-1870*, N. Y., 1945. Useful bibliography, 327-36.

3461 **Sherwig**, J. M., *Guineas and Gunpowder: British Foreign Aid in the Wars with France*, Cambridge, Mass., 1969.

3462 **Taylor**, P. M., *The Projection of Britain. British Overseas Publicity and Propaganda, 1919-39*, 1981.

3463 **Williams**, Judith B., *British Commercial Policy and Trade Expansion, 1750-1850*, 1972.

(b) TRADE WITH SPECIFIC AREAS UP TO 1815

3464 **Price**, J. M., ed., *Joshua Johnson's Letterbook, 1771-4. Letters from a Merchant in London to his Partners in Maryland*, London Rec.Soc., XV, 1979.

3465 **Armytage**, Frances, *The Free Port System in the British West Indies: A Study in Commercial Policy, 1766-1822*, 1953.

3466 **Crouzet**, F., *L'Economie britannique et le blocus continental (1806-13)*, 2 vols., Paris, 1958.

3467 **Davis**, R., *Aleppo and Devonshire Square: English Traders in the Levant in the Eighteenth Century*, 1967.

3468 **Farnie**, D. A., 'The commercial empire of the Atlantic, 1607-1783', *Ec.H.R.*, 2nd ser., XV, 1962, 205-18.

3469 **Fisher**, H. E. S., *The Portugal Trade: A Study of Anglo-Portuguese Commerce, 1700-1770*, 1971. Excellent bibliography, 153-62.

3470 **Gill**, C., *Merchants and Mariners in the Eighteenth Century*, 1961. Based on the papers of Thomas Hall, 1692-1748.

3471 **Kent**, H. S. K., *War and Trade in the Northern Seas. Anglo-Scandinavian Economic Relations in the mid-eighteenth Century*, 1973.

3472 **Marshall**, P. J., *East India Fortunes. The British in Bengal in the Eighteenth Century*, 1976.

3473 **Pares**, R., *Merchants and Planters*, 1960. The anatomy of the colonial trade.

3474 —— *War and Trade in the West Indies, 1739-1763*, 1936. Reprinted 1963.

3475 —— *A West India Fortune*, 1950 (the Pinneys of Bristol).

3476 **Parkinson**, C. N., *Trade in the Eastern Seas, 1793-1813*, 1937.

3477 **Shillington**, V. M. and Chapman, A. B. W., *The Commercial Relations of England and Portugal*, 1907.

3478 **Sutherland**, Lucy S., *A London Merchant, 1695-1774*, (William Braund), 1933. Reprinted 1962.

3479 **Thomsen**, Birgit N., Thomas, B. and Oldham, J. W., *Dansk-Engelsk Samhandel: Et Historisk Rids, 1661-1963*, Aarhus, 1966. An historical sketch of Anglo-Danish trade: long English summary of Danish text.

3480 **Walford**, R., *The British Factory in Lisbon*, Lisbon, 1940.

3481 **Wilson**, C., *Anglo-Dutch Commerce and Finance in the Eighteenth Century*, 1941.

3482 **Yogev**, G., *Diamonds and Coral: Anglo-Dutch Jews and Eighteenth-Century Trade*, 1978.

(c) THE REPEAL OF THE CORN LAWS, THE FREE TRADE ERA AND AFTER

(i) THE REPEAL OF THE CORN LAWS AND THE COMING OF FREE TRADE

3483 **Barnes**, D. G., *A History of the English Corn Laws from 1660-1846*, 1930. Useful statistical tables, 297-302, and excellent bibliography, 303-31.

3484 **Brown**, Lucy M., *The Board of Trade and the Free Trade Movement, 1830-42*, 1958.

3485 **Chaloner**, W. H., 'The agitation against the Corn Laws'. In Ward (4195), 135-48. Bibliographical notes, 149-51.

3486 **Fay**, C. R., *The Corn Laws and Social England*, 1932.

3487 **Grampp**, W. D., *The Manchester School of Economics*, 1960. Good bibliography, 139-49, inferior text.

3488 **Hyde**, F. E., *Mr Gladstone at the Board of Trade*, 1934.

3489 **Imlah**, A. H., 'The fall of protection in Britain'. In D. E. Lee and G. E. McReynolds, eds., *Essays in History and International Relations in Honor of G. H. Blakeslee*, Worcester, Mass., 1949, 306-20.

3490 **McCord**, N., *The Anti-Corn Law League,* *1838-1846*, 1958. Important study based on private papers of Cobden and George Wilson.

3491 **Prentice**, A., *History of the Anti-Corn Law League*, 2 vols., 1853. Reprinted, with new bibliographical introduction 1968.

3492 **Prouty**, R., *The Transformation of the Board of Trade, 1830-1855: A Study of Administrative Reorganization in the Heyday of Laissez-faire*, 1957.

3493 **Read**, D., *Cobden and Bright: A Victorian Political Partnership*, 1967.

(ii) THE FREE TRADE ERA AND AFTER, 1860-1939

3494 **McCord**, N., *Free Trade: Theory and Practice from Adam Smith to Keynes*, 1970. Documents, with commentary.

3495 **Turner**, B., *Free Trade and Protection*, 1971. Documents with commentary.

3496 **Abel**, D., *A History of British Tariffs, 1923-1942*, 1945.

3497 **Beveridge**, W. H., *et al.*, *Tariffs: The Case Examined*, 1931.

3498 **Brown**, B. H., *The Tariff Reform Movement in Great Britain 1881-1895*, N. Y., 1943.

3499 **Dunham**, A. L., *The Anglo-French Treaty of Commerce of 1860 and the Progress of the Industrial Revolution in France*, Ann Arbor, Mich., 1930.

3500 **Hutchinson**, H. J., *Tariff-making and Industrial Reconstruction*, 1965. An account of the work of the Import Duties Advisory Committee.

3501 **McGuire**, E. B., *The British Tariff System*, 1939. Good on technical points of the working of tariffs.

3502 **Richardson**, J. H., *British Economic Foreign Policy*, 1936.

3503 **Saul**, S. B., *Studies in British Overseas Trade, 1870-1914*, 1960.

3504 **Snyder**, R. K., *The Tariff Problem in Great Britain, 1918-1923*, Stanford University Publications in History, Economics and Political Science, V, No. 2, Stanford, Calif., 1944.

(d) TRADE WITH SPECIFIC AREAS AFTER 1815

3505 **Buck**, N. S., *The Development of the Organisation of Anglo-American Trade, 1800-1850*, New Haven, Conn., 1925.

3506 **Greenberg**, M., *British Trade and the Opening of China, 1800-1842*, 1951.

3507 **Hoffman**, R. J. S., *Great Britain and the Ger-*

man Trade Rivalry, 1875-1914, Philadelphia, 1933.

3508 **Hyde**, F. E., *Far Eastern Trade, 1860-1914*, 1973.

3509 **Munting**, R., 'Ransomes in Russia: An English Agricultural Engineering Company's trade with Russia to 1917', *Ec.H.R.*, 2nd ser., XXXI, 1978, 257-69.

3510 **Platt**, D. C. M., *Latin America and British Trade, 1806-1914*, 1972. Deals with the nature of Latin American markets, the changing pattern of British investment and with the extent of foreign competition.

3511 **Redford**, A., *et al.*, *Manchester Merchants and Foreign Trade 1794-1858*, 1934.

3512 —— and Clapp, B. W., *Manchester Merchants and Foreign Trade*, II: *1850-1939*, 1956.

3513 **Steeds**, D. and Nish, I., *China, Japan and Nineteenth-Century Britain*, 1977.

3514 **Tolley**, B. H., *Liverpool and the American Cotton Trade*, 1978.

(e) THE SLAVE TRADE

3515 **Ashton**, T. S., ed., *Letters of a West African Trader, Edward Grace, 1767-70*, 1950.

3516 **Anstey**, R., *The Atlantic Slave Trade and British Abolition, 1710-1810*, 1975.

3517 **Coupland**, R. G., *The British Anti-Slavery Movement*, 1933, 2nd ed., with new introduction, 1964.

3518 **Klein**, H. S., *The Middle Passage. Comparative Studies in the Atlantic Slave Trade*, 1978.

3519 **Mackenzie-Grieve**, Averil, *The Last Years of the English Slave Trade. Liverpool, 1750-1807*, 1941. Reprinted with corrections 1968.

3520 **Mellor**, G. R., *British Imperial Trusteeship, 1783-1850*, 1951.

3521 **Merritt**, J. E., 'The triangular trade', *Bus.H.*, III, 1960, 1-7.

3522 **Temperley**, H., *British Antislavery, 1833-1870*, 1972.

3523 **Williams**, E., *Capitalism and Slavery*, Chapel Hill, N. C., 1944.

3524 —— *British Historians and the West Indies*, 1966. Attempts to rebut Coupland (3517) and Mellor (3520), listed above.

3525 **Williams**, G., *Liverpool Privateers and Letters of Marque with an Account of the Liverpool Slave Trade*, 1897. Reprinted 1966.

(f) OVERSEAS INVESTMENT

3526 **Cairncross**, A. K., *Home and Foreign Investment 1870-1913: Studies in Capital Accumulation*, 1953.

3527 **Cottrell**, P. L., *British Overseas Investment in the Nineteenth Century*, 1975.

3528 **Feis**, H., *Europe, the World's Banker 1870-1914*. New Haven, Conn., 1930. Sections on British overseas investments.

3529 **Hall**, A. R., ed., *The Export of Capital from Britain 1870-1914*, 1969. A collection of articles.

3530 **Jenks**, L. H., *The Migration of British Capital to 1875*, 1927.

3531 **Jones**, C. A., 'Great capitalists and the direction of British overseas investment in the late nineteenth century: the case of Argentina', *Bus.H.*, XXII, 1980, 152-69.

3532 **Paterson**, D. G., *British Direct Investment in Canada, 1890-1914*, 1976.

3533 **Perkins**, E. J., *Financing Anglo-American Trade. The House of Brown, 1800-80*, 1976.

(g) IMPERIALISM

3534 **Ambirajan**, S., *Classical Political Economy and British Policy in India*, 1978.

3535 **Barber**, W. J., *British Economic Thought and India, 1600-1858*, 1975.

3536 **Bartlett**, C. J., ed., *Britain Pre-eminent: Studies in British World Influence in the Nineteenth Century*, 1969. Essays by various authors.

3537 **Blaug**, M., *Economic Theory in Retrospect*, 2nd rev. ed., 1968. Pages 261-71 contain the best short refutation of the theories of Marx and Lenin on imperialism.

3538 **Bodelsen**, C. A. G., *Studies in Mid-Victorian Imperialism*, Copenhagen, 1924; new impression, London, 1960.

3539 **Bolt**, Christine, *Victorian Attitudes to Race*, 1970.

3540 **Cain**, P. J., *Economic Foundations of British Overseas Expansion, 1815-1914*, 1980.

3541 —— 'J. A. Hobson, Cobdenism and the radical theory of economic imperialism, 1898-1914', *Ec.H.R.*, XXXI, 1978, 565-84.

3542 **Chamberlain**, M. E., *The New Imperialism*, 1970. A useful Hist.Ass. pamphlet on the period 1870-1914, with bibliography, 43-6.

3543 **Drummond**, I. A., *British Economic Policy and the Empire, 1919-1939*, 1972. Contains useful extracts from original documents.

3544 —— *Imperial Economic Policy, 1917-39*, 1974.

3545 **Fieldhouse**, D. K., *Economics and Empire 1830-1914*, 1973.

3546 **Fuchs**, C. J., *The Trade Policy of Great Britain and her Colonies since 1860*, 1905. English translation of a book first published in 1893.

3547 **Galbraith**, J. S., *Crown and Charter. The Early Years of the British South Africa Company*, 1975.

3548 **Gillard**, D., *The Struggle for Asia, 1828-1914. A Study of British and Russian Imperialism*, 1977.

3549 **Hobson**, J. A., *Imperialism: A Study*, 1902, 3rd rev. ed., 1938. Once influential, but now largely of historiographical interest; written in the shadow of the Boer War, 1899-1902.

3550 **Hyam**, R., *Britain's Imperial Century, 1815-1914. A Study of Empire and Expansion*, 1976. Looks at the foundations, dynamics and controls of British imperialism. Particularly useful on the cultural ramifications.

3551 —— and Martin, G., *Reappraisals in British Imperial History*, 1975.

3552 **Hynes**, W. G., *The Economics of Empire. Britain, Africa and the New Imperialism, 1870-95*, 1979.

3553 **Imlah**, A. H., *Economic Elements in the Pax Britannica: Studies in British Foreign Trade in the Nineteenth Century*, Cambridge, Mass., 1958.

3554 **Kent**, Marion, *Oil and Empire. British Policy and Mesopotamian Oil, 1900-20*, 1976.

3555 **Kesner**, R. M., 'Builders of empire: the role of the crown agents in imperial development, 1880-1914', *J. Imperial and Commonwealth H.*, V, 1977, 310-30.

3556 **Koebner**, R. and Schmidt, H. D., *Imperialism: The Story and Significance of a Political Word, 1840-1960*, 1964.

3557 **Lewis**, W. R., ed., *Imperialism. The Robinson and Gallagher Controversy*, 1976.

3558 **Meredith**, D., 'The British government and colonial economic policy, 1919-39', *Ec.H.R.*, 2nd ser., XXVIII, 1975, 484-99.

3559 **Platt**, D. C. M., *Finance, Trade and Politics in British Foreign Policy, 1815-1914*, 1968. The standard work; excellent bibliography, 418-33.

3560 —— ed., *Business Imperialism, 1840-1930*, 1977. Looks at the operations of British firms trading in South America.

3561 **Porter**, B., *Critics of Empire. British Radical Attitudes to Colonialism in Africa, 1895-1914*, 1968.

3562 **Ratcliffe**, B. M., 'Commerce and empire. Manchester merchants and West Africa, 1873-1905', *J. Imperial & Commonwealth H.*, VII, 1979, 293-320.

3563 **Rendell**, W., *The History of the Commonwealth Development Corporation, 1948-72*, 1976.

3564 **Semmel**, B., *Imperialism and Social Reform: English Social-Imperial Thought 1895-1914*, 1960.

3565 —— *The Rise of Free Trade Imperialism: Classical Political Economy, the Empire of Free Trade and Imperialism, 1750-1850*, 1970.

3566 **Shaw**, A. G. L., ed., *Great Britain and her Colonies, 1815-1865*, 1970. A collection of articles.

3567 **Tomlinson**, B. R., *The Political Economy of the Raj, 1914-47. The Economics of Decolonisation in India*, 1979.

3568 **Varga**, E. and Mendelson, L., eds., *New Data for V. I. Lenin's 'Imperialism: the Highest Stage of Capitalism'*, n.d. (1939).

3569 **Winks**, R. W., *British Imperialism: Gold, God, Glory*, N. Y., 1966. Extracts from the literature on British Imperialism.

3570 **Wolff**, R. D., *The Economics of Colonialism: Britain and Kenya, 1870-1930*, New Haven, Conn., 1975.

INTERNAL TRANSPORT, THE COASTING TRADE AND PORTS

Note: for books and articles on river navigation, see 1905-16 above.

(a) GENERAL

3571 **Aldcroft**, D. H., *British Transport since 1914*, 1975.

3572 —— *Studies in British Transport History, 1870-1914*, 1974.

3573 **Bagwell**, P. S., *The Transport Revolution from 1770*, 1974.

3574 **Barker**, T. C., and Savage, C. I., *An Economic History of Transport in Britain*, 3rd rev. ed., 1974.

3575 **Dyos**, H. J. and Aldcroft, D. H., *British Transport: An Economic Survey from the Seventeenth Century to the Twentieth*, 1969. Excellent bibliography, 401-38.

3576 **Jackman**, W. T., *The Development of Transportation in Modern England*, 1916, 2 vols., 2nd rev. ed., with new bibliographical introduction, 1962, 3rd ed., 1966.

3577 **Pratt**, E. A., *A History of Inland Transport and Communication in England*, 1912.

3578 **Sherrington**, C. E. R., *One Hundred Years of Inland Transport in Great Britain*, 1934. Reprinted 1970.

(b) ROADS

3579 **Ballen**, Dorothy, *Bibliography of Roads and Roadmaking in the United Kingdom*, 1914.

3580 **Albert**, W. A., *The Turnpike Road System in England, 1663-1840*, 1971. The indispensable work on the subject.

3581 **Austen**, B., 'The impact of the mail coach on public coach services in the East and West, 1784-1840', *J.Trans.H.*, 3rd ser., II, 1981, 25-38.

3582 **Copeland**, J., *Roads and Their Traffic, 1750-1850*, 1968. Unsatisfactory.

3583 **Earle**, J. B. F., *A Century of Road Materials: The History of the Roadstone Division of Tarmac Ltd.*, 1971.

3584 **Everitt**, A. M., 'Country carriers in the nineteenth century', *J.Trans.H.*, new ser., III, 1976, 179-202.

3585 **Freeman**, M. J., 'Road transport in the Industrial Revolution: an interim re-assessment', *J.Hist.Geog.*, VI, 1980, 17-28.

3586 **Jeffreys**, R., *The King's Highway: An Historical and Autobiographical Record of the Developments of the Past Sixty Years*, 1949.

3587 **Pawson**, E., *Transport and Economy. The Turnpike Roads of Eighteenth-Century Britain*, 1977.

3588 —— *The Turnpike Trusts of the Eighteenth Century. A Study of Innovation and Diffusion*, 1976. See also Albert (3580), above.

3589 **Reader**, W. J., *Macadam: The Macadam Family and the Turnpike Roads 1798-1861*, 1980.

3590 **Turnbull**, G. L., 'Provincial road carrying in the eighteenth century', *J.Trans.H.*, new ser., IV, 1977, 17-39.

3591 —— *Traffic and Transport. An Economic History of Pickfords*, 1979.

3592 **Williams**, L. A., *Road Transport in Cumbria in the Nineteenth Century*, 1974.

3593 **Woodforde**, J., *History of the Bicycle*, 1970.

(c) THE COASTING TRADE

3594 **Read**, A., *The Coastwise Trade of the United Kingdom, Past and Present and its Possibilities*, 1925. See Willan (1828), listed above.

(d) PORTS AND THEIR TRADE

3595 **Craig**, R. and Jarvis, R. C., eds., *Liverpool Registry of Merchant Ships*, Chet.Soc., 3rd ser., 15, 1967.

3596 **Jarvis**, R. C., *Customs Letter Books of the Port of Liverpool, 1711-1813*, Chet.Soc., 3rd ser., 6, 1954.

3597 **Minchinton**, W. E., *The Trade of Bristol in the Eighteenth Century*, Bristol Rec.Soc., XX, 1957.

3598 **Andrews**, J. H., 'Two problems in the interpretation of the port books', *Ec.H.R.*, 2nd ser., IX, 1956, 119-22.

3599 —— 'The port of Chichester and the grain trade, 1650-1750', *Sussex Arch.Collns.*, XCII, 1954, 93-105.

3600 —— 'The Thanet seaports 1650-1750', *Arch.Cant.*, LXVI, 1953, 37-44.

3601 —— 'The trade of the port of Faversham, 1650-1750', *Arch.Cant.*, LXIX, 1955, 125-31.

3602 **Clark**, E. A. G., *The Ports of the Exe Estuary, 1660-1860: A Study in Historical Geography*, 1960.

3603 **Craig**, R., 'Shipping and shipbuilding in the port of Chester in the eighteenth and early nineteenth centuries', *T.H.S.L.C.*, CXVI, 1964, 39-68.

3604 **Hyde**, F. E., *Liverpool and the Mersey: An Economic History of a Port, 1700-1970*, 1971. See also Parkinson (1874) listed above and Harris (3839) listed below.

3605 **Swann**, D., 'The pace and progress of port investment in England 1660-1830', *Yorks.B.*, XII, 1960, 32-44.

(e) CANALS

3606 **Phillips**, J., *A General History of Inland Navigation*, Reprint of 5th ed., 1805, with introduction by C. Hadfield, 1970.

3607 **Priestley**, J., *Historical Account of the Navigable Rivers, Canals, and Railways throughout Great Britain*, 1831. Reprinted, with introduction by W. H. Chaloner, 1967.

3608 **Barker**, T. C., 'The Sankey Navigation', *T.H.S.L.C.*, 1948, 121-55. The first eighteenth-century canal in Great Britain, 1755-57.

3609 **Broadbridge**, S. R., *The Birmingham Canal*

Navigations I (1768-1846), 1974.

3610 **Farnie**, D. A., *The Manchester Ship Canal and the Rise of the Port of Manchester, 1894-1975*, 1980.

3611 **Hadfield**, C., *British Canals: An Illustrated History*, 1950, 2nd ed., rev. and enlarged, 1959.

3612 —— *The Canals of South Wales and the Border*, 1960.

3613 —— *The Canals of the West Midlands*, 1966, 2nd rev. ed., 1969.

3614 —— *The Canals of the East Midlands*, 1966.

3615 —— *The Canals of Yorkshire and North-East England*, 2 vols., 1972-3.

3616 —— and Biddle, G., *The Canals of North-West England*, 2 vols., 1970.

3617 **Malet**, H., *Bridgewater, the Canal Duke, 1763-1803*, 1977.

3618 **Mather**, F. C., *After the Canal Duke: A Study of the Industrial estates Administered by the Trustees of the Third Duke of Bridgewater in the Age of Railway Building, 1825-1872*, 1970. See also Richards, E. (5427) listed below.

3619 **Patterson**, A. T., 'The making of the Leicestershire canals, 1766-1814', *Trans.Leics.Arch.Soc.*, XXVII, 1951, 1-35.

3620 **Porteous**, J. D., *Canal Ports. The Urban Achievement of the Canal Age*, 1977. Based largely on case studies of Runcorn, Stourport, Ellesmere Port and Goole.

3621 **Rolt**, L. T. C., *The Inland Waterways of England*, 1950.

3622 **Ward**, J. R., *The Finance of Canal Building in Eighteenth-century England*, 1974.

(f) POSTAL HISTORY AND TELECOMMUNICATIONS

3623 **Baldwin**, F. G. C., *The History of the Telephone in the United Kingdom*, 1925.

3624 **Clear**, C. R., *John Palmer (of Bath), Mail Coach Pioneer*, 1955.

3625 **Ellis**, K. L., *The Post Office in the Eighteenth Century: A Study in Administrative History*, 1958.

3626 **Hemmeon**, J. C., *The History of the British Post Office*, Cambridge, Mass., 1912.

3627 **Hill**, R. and Hill, G. B., *The Life of Sir Rowland Hill . . . and the History of Penny Postage*, 2 vols., 1880.

3628 **Kieve**, J. L., *The Electric Telegraph: A Social and Economic History*, 1973.

3629 **Robertson**, J. H., *The Story of the Telephone: A History of the Telecommunications Industry*

of Britain, 1948.

3630 **Robinson**, H., *The British Post Office: A History*, Princeton, N. J., 1948.

3631 **Staff**, F., *The Penny Post, 1680-1918*, 1964.

3632 **Vale**, E., *The Mail Coach Men of the Late Eighteenth Century*, 1960.

(g) RAILWAYS
(i) BIBLIOGRAPHIES

3633 **Bryant**, E. T., *Railways: A Reader's Guide*, 1968.

3634 **Ottley**, G., *A Bibliography of British Railway History*, 1965.

3635 **Peddie**, R. A., *Railway Literature, 1556-1830, a Handlist*, 1931.

(ii) CONTEMPORARY ACCOUNTS

3636 **Acworth**, W., *The Railways of England*, 1st ed., 1889, 5th and best ed., 1900.

3637 **Chattaway**, E. D., *Railways: their capital and dividends*, 1855-6.

3638 **Dorsey**, E. B., *English and American Railroads Compared*, 1887.

3639 **Francis**, J., *A History of the English Railway*, 2 vols., 1852. Reprinted 1968.

3640 **Galt**, W., *Railway Reform: its importance and practicability*, 1865.

3641 **Lardner**, D., *Railway Economy. A Treatise on the New Art of Transport*, 1850.

3642 **Simmons**, E. J., *Memoirs of a Station Master (1879)*, ed. J. Simmons, 1974.

3643 **Simmons**, J., ed., *The Birth of the Great Western Railway. Extracts from the Diary and Correspondence of George Henry Gibbs*, 1971. Shows at first hand the activities of a major promoter and director.

3644 —— *The Railway Traveller's Handy Book*, 1971. An assortment of hints, suggestions and advice first published in 1862.

3645 **Spencer**, H., *Railway Morals and Railway Policy*, 1855.

3646 **Williams**, F. S., *Our Iron Roads*, 1852.

(iii) GENERAL WORKS

3647 **Aldcroft**, D. H., *British Railways in Transition: The Economic Problems of Britain's Railways since 1914*, 1968.

3648 —— 'The efficiency and enterprise of British railways, 1870-1914', *Expl.Entrepren.H.*, 2nd ser., V, 1968, 157-74.

3649 **Alderman**, G., *The Railway Interest*, 1972. Examines the growth of the railway lobby in the

E

nineteenth century.

3650 **Bagwell**, P. S., *The Railway Clearing House in the British Economy, 1844-1922*, 1968.

3651 **Baxter**, B., *Stone Blocks and Iron Rails*, 1966. Deals with the pre-steam railway.

3652 **Bell**, R., *History of the British Railways during the War, 1939-45*, 1946.

3653 **Bonavia**, M. R., *Railway Policy between the Wars*, 1981. Focuses attention on railway management and compares the managers' own assessment of their policies with the historians' verdicts.

3654 **Broadbridge**, S. R., *Studies in Railway Expansion and the Capital Market in England, 1825-1873*, 1970. Deals mainly with the finances on the Lancashire & Yorkshire Railway Company.

3655 **Cain**, P., 'Private enterprise or public utility? Output, pricing and investment on English and Welsh railways, 1870-1914', *J.Trans.H.*, 3rd ser., I, 1980, 9-28.

3656 **Campbell**, C. D., *British Railways in Boom and Depression: An Essay in Trade Fluctuations and Their Effects, 1878-1930*, 1932.

3657 **Cleveland-Stevens**, C., *English Railways: Their Development and Relation to the State*, 1915.

3658 **Ellis**, C. H., *British Railway History: An Outline from the Accession of William IV to the Nationalisation of Railways*, 2 vols., 1954-59. The two volumes divide at 1876-7.

3659 **Gourvish**, T. R., *Railways and the British Economy, 1830-1914*, 1980.

3660 —— 'The performance of British railway management after 1860; the railways of Forbes and Watkins', *Bus.H.*, XX, 1978, 186-200.

3661 **Hawke**, G. R., *Railways and Economic Growth in England and Wales, 1840-1870*, 1970. The first large-scale attempt to apply the methods of the 'new economic history' to a British subject.

3662 **Irving**, R. J., 'The efficiency and enterprise of British railways, 1870-1914: an alternative hypothesis', *Ec.H.R.*, 2nd ser., XXXI, 1978, 46-66.

3663 **Lewin**, H. G., *Early British Railways: A Short History of Their Origin and Development, 1801-1844*, 1925.

3664 —— *The Railway Mania and its Aftermath, 1845-1852*, 1936.

3665 **Lewis**, M. J. T., *Early Wooden Railways*, 1970.

3666 **Marshall**, C. F. D., *A History of British Railways down to the Year 1830*, 1938, 2nd rev. ed., 1971.

3667 **Mitchell**, B. R., 'The coming of the railway and

United Kingdom economic growth' in Reed (3671) listed below, 13-32.

3668 **Parris**, H., *Government and the Railways in Nineteenth-Century Britain*, 1965.

3669 **Perkin**, H. J., *The Age of the Railway*, 1970. Social and economic effects, c. 1780-1914.

3670 **Pratt**, E. A., *British Railways and the Great War*, 2 vols., 1921.

3671 **Reed**, M. C., ed., *Railways in the Victorian Economy: Studies in Finance and Economic Growth*, 1969.

3672 —— *Investment in Railways in Britain, 1820-44*, 1975. A detailed analysis of the shareholders of eleven railway companies.

3673 **Robbins**, M. R., *The Railway Age*, 1962. An analytical study with useful 'Notes on Sources', 199-212.

3674 **Schivelbusch**, W., *The Railway Journey. Trains and Travel in the Nineteenth Century*, 1980.

3675 **Simmons**, J., *The Railways of Britain: An Historical Introduction*, 1961, 2nd ed., 1969. Includes a useful chapter 'Literature and Maps'.

3676 —— *The Railway in England and Wales, 1830-1914. I: The System and its Working*, 1978.

(iv) RAILWAY BIOGRAPHIES

3677 **Gooch**, D., *The Diaries of Sir Daniel Gooch*, 1892, reprinted 1962.

3678 **Gourvish**, T. R., *Mark Huish and the London and North Western Railway*, 1972. Exhaustive survey of a general manager.

3679 —— 'A British business élite: the chief executive managers of the railway industry, 1850-1922', *Bus.H.R.*, XLVII, 1973, 00-00.

3680 **Lambert**, R. S., *The Railway King, 1800-71: A Study of George Hudson and the Business Morals of his Time*, 1934.

3681 **Marshall**, J. D., *A Biographical Dictionary of Railway Engineers*, 1978.

3682 **Pease**, A., ed., *The Diaries of Edward Pease, the Father of English Railways*, 1907. The leading promoter in the early days of railways.

3683 **Rolt**, L. T. C., *George and Robert Stephenson: The Railway Revolution*, 1960.

3684 —— *Isambard Kingdom Brunel: A Biography*, 1957.

3685 **Webster**, N. W., *Joseph Locke: A Railway Revolutionary*, 1971. A neglected contemporary of the Stephensons.

(v) LOCOMOTIVES

3686 **Ahrons**, E. L., *The British Steam Railway*

Locomotive, 1825-1925, 1927.

87 Anon., *History of the North British Loco-motive Co.*, 1953.

88 **Clark**, E. K., *Kitson's of Leeds*, 1938.

89 **Kidner**, R. W., *The Early History of the Locomotive, 1804-1876*, 1956.

90 **Marshall**, C. F. D., *A History of Railway Locomotives down to the end of the Year 1831*, 1953.

91 **Warren**, J. G. H., *A Century of Locomotive Building by Robert Stephenson and Company 1823-1923*, 1923. An account of the Stephensons' works at Newcastle upon Tyne.

(vi) INDIVIDUAL LINES AND REGIONAL STUDIES

The histories of individual lines are now so numerous – and of such varying quality – that it would be impossible here to list them all. A selection only is given below. For a fuller list see Ottley (3634) above.

92 **Allen**, C. J., *The Great Eastern Railway*, 4th ed., 1967.

93 **Barker**, T. C., and Robbins, R. M., *A History of London Transport: Passenger Travel and the Development of the Metropolis*, Vol. I, 1963, vol. II, 1974.

94 **Barnes**, E. G., *The Rise of the Midland Railway, 1844-74*, 1966.

95 **Carlson**, R. E., *The Liverpool and Manchester Railway Project, 1821-1831*, 1969.

96 **Channon**, G., 'The Great Western Railway under the British Railways Act of 1921', *Bus.H.R.*, LV, 1981, 188-216.

97 **Christiansen**, R., *A Regional History of the Railways of Great Britain. VII: The West Midlands*, 1973.

98 **Dow**, G., *Great Central*, 3 vols., 1959-65.

99 **Irving**, R. J., *The North Eastern Railway Company, 1870-1914. An Economic History*, 1976.

00 **MacDermot**, E. T., *History of the Great Western Railways*, 3 vols., 1964.

01 **Robbins**, R. M., 'Transport and Suburban Development in Middlesex down to 1914', *Trans.London & Middx.Arch.Soc.*, XXIX, 1978, 129-36.

02 **Thomas**, R. H. G., *The Liverpool and Manchester Railway*, 1980.

03 **Webster**, N. W., *Britain's First Trunk Line: The Grand Junction Railway*, 1972.

(h) MOTOR TRANSPORT

04 **Church**, R. A., *Herbert Austin. The British*

Motor Car Industry to 1941, 1979.

3705 **Cornwell**, E. L., *Commercial Road Vehicles*, 1960. Emphasis on technical history.

3706 **Dunnett**, P. J. S., *The Decline of the British Motor Industry. The Effects of Government Policy, 1945-79*, 1980.

3707 **Hibbs**, J., *A History of British Bus Services*, 1970.

3708 —— ed., *The Omnibus: Readings in the History of Road Passenger Transport*, 1971.

3709 **Holding**, D., *A History of British Bus Services. The North-East*, 1979.

3710 **Knockolds**, H., *Lucas: The First Hundred Years*, 2 vols., 1976-8.

3711 **Lloyd**, I., *Rolls Royce. I: The Growth of a Firm. II: The Merlin at War. III: The Years of Endeavour*, 3 vols., 1979.

3712 **Maxcy**, G. and Silbertson, A., *The British Motor Industry*, 1959.

3713 **Overy**, R. J., *William Morris, Viscount Nuffield*, 1976.

3714 **Perkin**, H. J., *The Age of the Automobile*, 1976. A general survey which emphasises the social implications of the coming of the motor car for patterns of leisure and community life.

3715 **Plowden**, W., *The Motor Car and Politics, 1896-1970*, 1971. Contains an up-to-date bibliography, 421-4.

3716 **Saul**, S. B., 'The motor industry in Britain to 1914', *Bus.H.*, V, 1962, 23-44. See Aldcroft (3571) and Dyos and Aldcroft (3575), above.

(i) THE CHANNEL TUNNEL

3717 **Slater**, H., Barnett, C., and Geneau, R. H., *The Channel Tunnel*, 1958; bibliography, 205-6.

3718 **Whiteside**, T., *The Tunnel under the Channel*, 1962.

(j) AIR TRAVEL

3719 **Aldcroft**, D. H., 'Britain's internal airways: the pioneer stage of the 1930s', *Bus.H.*, VI, 1964, 113-23.

3720 **Brooks**, P. W., 'A short history of London's airports', *J.Trans.H.*, III, 1957, 12-22.

3721 **Gardner**, C., *British Aircraft Corporation: A History*, 1981.

3722 **Higham**, R., *Britain's Imperial Air Routes, 1918-39*, 1960.

3723 **Pudney**, J., *The Seven Skies: A Study of B.O.A.C. and its Forerunners since 1919*, 1959. See also Dyos and Aldcroft (3575), above.

HOME MARKET, INCLUDING SHOPPING AND THE CO-OPERATIVE MOVEMENT

(a) DEVELOPMENTS TO 1850

3724 **Marshall**, J. D., ed., *The Autobiography of William Stout of Lancaster, 1665-1752*, 1967.

3725 **Adburgham**, Alison, *Shopping in Style. London from the Restoration to Edwardian Elegance*, 1979.

3726 **Alexander**, D., *Retailing in England during the Industrial Revolution*, 1970.

3727 **Atkins**, P. J., 'The retail milk trade in London, c. 1790-1914', *Ec.H.R.*, 2nd ser., XXXIII, 1980, 522-37.

3728 **Chapman**, S. D., 'British marketing enterprise: the changing roles of merchants, manufacturers and financiers, 1700-1860', *Bus.H.R.*, LIII, 1979, 205-34.

3729 **Davis**, Dorothy, *A History of Shopping*, 1965.

3730 **Eversley**, D. E. C., 'The home market and economic growth in England 1750-80'. In Jones and Mingay (2558), listed above, 206-59.

3731 **Gilboy**, Elizabeth W., 'Demand as a factor in the Industrial Revolution', in A. H. Cole, ed., *Facts and Factors in Economic History*, Cambridge, Mass., 1932. Reprinted in Hartwell, ed. (2550), listed above, 121-38.

3732 **McKendrick**, N., 'Home demand and economic growth: a new view of the role of women and children in the Industrial Revolution' in McKendrick ed., *Historical Perspectives*, 1974, 152-210.

3733 —— Brewer, J., and Plumb, J. H., *The Birth of a Consumer Society: The Commercialisation of Eighteenth-Century England*, 1982.

3734 **Mokyr**, J., 'Demand *versus* supply in the Industrial Revolution', *J.Ec.H.*, XXXVII, 1977, 981-1008.

3735 **Robinson**, E. H., 'Eighteenth-century commerce and fashion: Matthew Boulton's marketing techniques', *Ec.H.R.*, 2nd ser., XVI, 1963, 39-60.

3736 **Scola**, R., 'Food markets and shops in Manchester, 1700-1870', *J.H.Geog.*, I, 1975, 153-68.

3737 **Wilian**, T. S., *An Eighteenth-century Shopkeeper: Abraham Dent of Kirkby Stephen*, 1970.

(b) CO-OPERATION

3738 **Barou**, N. I., ed., *The Co-operative Movement in Labour Britain*, 1948.

3739 **Carr-Saunders**, A. M., Florence, P. Sargant, and Peers, R., eds., *Consumers' Co-operation Great Britain*, 1933, 3rd rev. ed., 1942.

3740 **Cole**, G. D. H., *A Century of Co-operatio* 1945. A history of the co-operative movement Great Britain and Ireland.

3741 **Flanagan**, D., *1869-1969: The Centenary Sto* of the Co-operative Union of Great Britain a Ireland, 1969.

3742 **Holyoake**, G. J., *The History of Co-operatio* 2 vols., 1875-79, 2nd rev. ed., 2 vols., 1906.

3743 **Mercer**, T. W., ed., *Dr William King and t Co-operator, 1828-1830*, 1922. Reprinted 1947.

3744 **Musson**, A. E., 'The ideology of early operation in Lancashire and Cheshire *T.L.C.A.S.*, LXVIII, 1959, 117-38. Reprinted Musson (4300), listed below.

3745 **Pollard**, S., 'Nineteenth century co-operatio from community-building to shopkeeping'. Briggs and Saville (4138), listed below, 74-112.

3746 **Redfern**, P., *The Story of the C.W.S.: t Jubilee History of the Co-operative Wholesa Society Ltd., 1863-1913*, 1913.

3747 —— *The New History of the C.W.S.*, 1938

3748 **Richardson**, W., *The C.W.S. in War a Peace, 1939-76*, 1977.

3749 **Webb**, Catherine, ed., *Industrial C operation: The Story of a Peaceful Revoluti Being an Account of the History, Theory a Practice of the Co-operative Movement in Gr Britain*, 2nd ed., 1906.

(c) DEVELOPMENTS SINCE 1850

3750 **Adburgham**, Alison, *Shops and Shoppi 1800-1914: Where and in What Manner t Well-Dressed Englishwoman Bought h Clothes*, 1964.

3751 **Briggs**, A., *Friends of the People. The Cen nary History of Lewis's*, 1956.

3752 **Corina**, M., *Fine Silks and Oak Counte Debenham, 1778-1978*, 1978.

3753 —— *Pile it High, Sell it Cheap. The Auth ised Biography of Sir John Cohen, Founder Tesco*, 1971.

3754 **Fraser**, W. H., *The Coming of the Mass M ket, 1850-1914*, 1981.

3755 **Grether**, E. T., *Resale Price Maintenance Great Britain*, University of California Pu cations in Economics, XI (for 1932-5), 1942.

56 **Harrison**, G. and Mitchell, F. C., *The Home Market: A Handbook of Statistics*, 1936, 2nd rev. ed., 1939.

57 **Jefferys**, J. B., *Retail Trading in Britain, 1850-1950*, 1954.

58 **Lambert**, R. S., *The Universal Provider: A Study of William Whiteley and the Rise of the London Department Store*, 1938.

59 **Mathias**, P., *Retailing Revolution: A History of Multiple Retailing in the Food Trades, Based on the Allied Suppliers Group of Companies*, 1967. Useful bibliography, 402-5. A history of the group built up around Maypole, Home and Colonial, and Lipton.

60 **Pound**, R., *Selfridge: A Biography*, 1960.

61 **Rees**, G., *St Michael: A History of Marks and Spencer*, 1969.

62 **Willcock**, H. D., ed., *Browns and Chester: Portrait of a Shop 1780-1946*, 1946.

(d) ADVERTISING

3763 **Darwin**, B., *The Dickens Advertiser*, 1930. A collection of the advertisements in the original parts of Dickens's novels.

3764 **Elliott**, Blanche B., *A History of English Advertising*, 1962.

3765 **Field**, E., *Advertising: The Forgotten Years*, 1959. The inter-war period.

3766 **Mills**, G. H. S., *There is a Tide*, 1954. Life of Sir William Crawford (1878-1950), pioneer of modern advertising: some details about general advertising history.

3767 **Sampson**, H., *A History of Advertising from the Earliest Times*, 1875.

3768 **Treasure**, J., *History of British Advertising Agencies, 1875-1939*, 1977.

3769 **Turner**, E. S., *The Shocking History of Advertising*, 1952.

3770 **Vries**, L. de, *Victorian Advertisements*, 1968.

BUSINESS HISTORY

71 **Barker**, T. C. *et al.*, *Business History*, 2nd rev. ed., 1971. Useful bibliography, 27-32.

72 **Bellamy**, Joyce, ed., *Yorkshire Business Histories: A Bibliography*, 1970.

73 **Cain**, L. P. and Uselding, P. J., eds., *Business Enterprise and Economic Change*, Athens, Ohio, 1973.

74 **Hannah**, L., ed., *Management Strategy and Business Development. A Historical and Comparative Study*, 1976. Deals with the British tobacco, glass, petroleum, pharmaceutical, electrical and service industries.

75 **Horrocks**, S., ed., *Lancashire Business Histories*, 1971. Part III of *The Lancashire Bibliography* (in progress).

76 **Marriner**, Sheila, ed., *Business and Businessmen: Studies in Business, Economic and Accounting History*, 1978. A miscellaneous collection which includes essays on marine insurance, business management, steel technology, and the use of company financial statements as a historical source.

3777 **Prais**, S. J., *The Evolution of Giant Firms in Britain*, 1976.

3778 **Supple**, B. E., ed., *Essays in British Business History*, 1977. Includes essays on the hardware, rayon and motor industries, and on the development of insurance services.

3779 **Tucker**, K. A., ed., *Business History*, 1977. Reprints twenty essays arranged under the following headings: (1) Aims and Methods in Business History; (2) Entrepreneurs, the firm and industrial structure; (3) Techniques of business management and organisation.

3780 **Williams**, P. L., *The Emergence of the Theory of the Firm from Adam Smith to Alfred Marshall*, 1979.

URBAN HISTORY

(a) GENERAL WORKS

31 **Sutcliffe**, A., ed., *The History of Urban and* *Regional Planning*, 1981. A bibliography on planners and planning in different countries and cities.

3782 **Ashworth**, W., *The Genesis of Modern British Town Planning: A Study in the Economic and Social History of the Nineteenth and Twentieth Centuries*, 1954. Excellent bibliography.

3783 **Briggs**, A., *Victorian Cities*, 1963, 2nd rev. ed., 1968. Includes London, Manchester, Leeds, Birmingham and Middlesborough.

3784 **Cannadine**, D., *Lords and Landlords. The Aristocracy and the Towns, 1774-1967*, 1980. A valuable study which deals with the aristocratic contribution to urban development both in general terms and by way of two case studies of Edgbaston and Eastbourne.

3785 —— ed., *Patricians, Power and Politics in Nineteenth-Century Towns*, 1982. Has chapters on the development of Cardiff, Dudley, Southport and Bournemouth.

3786 —— 'The Victorian cities: how different?', *Soc.H.*, IV, 1977, 457-482.

3787 **Chalklin**, C. W., *The Provincial Towns of Georgian England: A Study of the Building Process 1740-1820*, 1974.

3788 **Clapham**, J. H. and Mary H., 'Life in the new towns'. In G. M. Young, ed., *Early Victorian England, 1830-1865*, 1934, I, 227-44.

3789 **Coleman**, B. I., *The Idea of the City in Nineteenth Century Britain*, 1973. A collection of documents with useful commentary, and good bibliography, 235-8.

3790 **Cunningham**, C., *Victorian and Edwardian Town Halls*, 1981. Discusses the financial, organisational, architectural and symbolic aspects of civic buildings.

3791 **Dyos**, H. J., ed., *The Study of Urban History*, 1968. The best introduction to the subject.

3792 —— and Wolff, M., *The Victorian City: Images and Reality*, 2 vols., 1973.

3793 **Fraser**, D., ed., *Municipal Reform and the Industrial City*, 1981. Has substantial chapters on Manchester, Leeds and Bradford.

3794 —— *Power and Authority in the Victorian City*, 1979. A general discussion exemplified with case studies of Liverpool, Leeds, Birmingham, Bristol, Leicester, Bradford and Sheffield.

3795 **Hartley**, Dorothy, *Water in England*, 1964.

3796 **Hennock**, E. P., *Fit and Proper Persons. Ideal and Reality in Nineteenth-Century Urban Government*, 1973.

3797 **Keith-Lucas**, B., *Unreformed Local Government, 1800-35*, 1980.

3798 —— and Richards, P. G., *A History of Local Government in the Twentieth Century*, 1978.

3799 **Kellett**, J. R., *The Impact of Railways on Victorian Cities*, 1969.

3800 —— 'Municipal socialism, enterprise, and trading in the Victorian city', *Urban H.Yearbook* 1978, 36-45.

3801 **Laski**, H. J., Jennings, W. I. and Robson, A., eds., *A Century of Municipal Progress 1835-1935*, 1935. Published to mark the centenary of the Municipal Corporations Act, 1835.

3802 **Lipman**, V. D., *Local Government Areas 1834-1945*, 1949.

3803 **Mottram**, R. H., 'Town Life'. In G. M. Young, ed., *Early Victorian England 1830-1865*, 1934, 155-233.

3804 **Offer**, A., *Property and Politics, 1870-1914. Landownership, Law and Urban Development in England*, 1981.

3805 **Pfautz**, H., *Charles Booth on the City*, Chicago, 1967.

3806 **Sigsworth**, E. M., ed., *Ports and Resorts in the Regions*, 1982. Fifteen essays weighted particularly towards the North.

3807 **Sutcliffe**, A., *Towards the Planned City. Germany, Britain, the United States and France 1780-1914*, 1981. Concentrates particularly on Germany and stresses its importance as a pioneer of the urban extension plan.

3808 —— ed., *British Town Planning: The Formative Years*, 1981. Includes chapters on suburban planning, housing and town planning in Manchester before 1914, and on the emergence of the town planning profession.

3809 **Thompson**, F. M. L., ed., *The Rise of Suburbia*, 1981. Has chapters on Bromley, Bexley, outer West London, and Leeds. See also Everitt (1606) and Porteous (3620).

(b) INDIVIDUAL TOWNS AND CITIES

3810 **Armstrong**, W. A., *Stability and Change in an English County Town: A Social Study of York 1801-51*, 1974. See also Feinstein (3829) and Rowntree (3872-3), below.

3811 **Aspden**, J. C., *A Municipal History of Eastbourne, 1938-74*, 1979.

3812 **Bailey**, F. A., *History of Southport*, 1955.

3813 **Barker**, T. C. and Harris, J. R., *A Merseyside Town in the Industrial Revolution: St Helens 1750-1900*, 1954.

3814 **Bateson**, H., *A Centenary History of Oldham*, 1949. Largely a chronicle; little historical understanding.

3815 **Brown**, A. F. J., *Colchester, 1815-1914*, 19

3816 **Bush**, G., ed., *Bristol and its Municipal Government, 1820-51*, Bristol Rec.Soc., XXIX, 1976. See also Little (3852) and Minchinton (3855), below.

3817 **Carson**, R., *A Short History of Middlesborough*, 1977.

3818 **Carter**, G. A., *et al.*, *Warrington Hundred*, 1947. A short history of the town from prehistoric times to 1947.

3819 **Chaloner**, W. H., *The Social and Economic Development of Crewe, 1780-1923*, 1950.

3820 **Chandler**, G., *Liverpool*, 1957. A badly arranged chronicle. See also Harris (3839), Lawton (2825), and White (3890).

3821 **Childs**, W. M., *The Town of Reading During the Early Part of the Nineteenth Century*, 1910. See also Hinton (3843) below.

3822 **Church**, R. A., *Economic and Social Change in a Midland Town: Victorian Nottingham, 1815-1900*, 1966.

3823 **Daysh**, G. H. J., ed., *A Survey of Whitby and the Surrounding areas*, 1958. Contains much historical information.

3824 **Dickinson**, H. W., *Water Supply of Greater London*, 1954.

3825 **Dyos**, H. J., *Victorian Suburb: A Study of the Growth of Camberwell*, 1961.

3826 —— 'The slums of Victorian London', *Vict. Studs.*, XI, 1967-8, 5-40. On London, see also (3836, 3847, 3849-50, 3856, 3862, 3870, 3875-6, 3884, 3887, 3891-2).

3827 **Ede**, J. F., *History of Wednesbury*, 1962.

3828 **Elliot, M.**, *Victorian Leicester*, 1979. See also Greaves (3837), Patterson (3864), and Simmons (3879), below.

3829 **Feinstein**, C. H., ed., *York, 1831-1981. 150 Years of Scientific Endeavour and Social Change*, 1981. See also Armstrong (3810), above, and Rowntree (3872-3), below.

3830 **Fieldhouse**, R., and Jennings, B., *A History of Richmond and Swaledale*, 1978.

3831 **Foster**, D., 'Poulton le Fylde: a nineteenth-century market town', *T.H.S.L.C.*, CXXVII, 1978, 91-108.

3832 **Fraser**, D., ed., *A History of Modern Leeds*, 1980. A comprehensive history concentrating on post-1750 economic, social and political developments. See also Wilson (3130), above.

3833 **Gill**, C. and Briggs, A., *History of Birmingham*, 2 vols., 1952, vol. I: *Manor and Borough to 1865*; vol. II: *Borough and City 1865 to 1938*. See also Stephens (3883), below.

3834 **Gillett**, E., *A History of Grimsby*, 1973.

3835 —— and Macmahon, M. A., *A History of Hull*, 1980. See also Jackson (3848), below.

3836 **George**, M. Dorothy, *London Life in the Eighteenth Century*, 1925, 3rd corrected ed., 1951. On London see also (3825-6, 3847, 3849-50, 3856, 3862, 3870, 3875-6, 3884, 3887, 3891-2).

3837 **Greaves**, R. W., *The Corporation of Leicester, 1689-1836*, 1st ed., 1939, 2nd ed., 1969. See also Elliot (3828), Patterson (3864), and Simmons (3879).

3838 **Grinsell**, L. V., *et al.*, *Studies in the History of Swindon*, 1950.

3839 **Harris**, J. R., ed., *Liverpool and Merseyside*, 1969. See also Chandler (3820), Lawton (2825), and White (3890).

3840 **Heape**, R. G., *Buxton under the Dukes of Devonshire*, 1948.

3841 **Hill**, J. W. F., *Georgian Lincoln*, 1966.

3842 —— *Victorian Lincoln*, 1975.

3843 **Hinton**, M., *A History of the Town of Reading*, 1954; bibliography, 166-8.

3844 **Homeshaw**, E. J., *The Corporation of the Borough and Foreign of Walsall*, 1960.

3845 **Hoskins**, W. G., *Industry, Trade and People in Exeter, 1688-1800, with Special Reference to the Serge Industry*, 1935.

3846 **Hunt**, Edith M., *The History of Ware*, 1946. Reprinted 1949.

3847 **Jackson**, A. A., *Semi-detached London*, 1973. See also (3891).

3848 **Jackson**, G., *Hull in the Eighteenth Century: A Study in Economic and Social History*, 1971. See also Gillett and Macmahon (3835).

3849 **Jenkins**, S., *Landlords to London. The Story of a Capital and its Growth*, 1975.

3850 **Jones**, G. S., *Outcast London*, 1972. See also Dyos (3826).

3851 **Kennedy**, M., *Portrait of Manchester*, 1970. The best one-volume treatment. See also Redford (3867), Stewart (3885), and Vigier (3889).

3852 **Little**, B., *The City and County of Bristol: A Study in Atlantic Civilisation*, 1954. See also Bush (3816) and Minchinton (3855).

3853 **Lowerson**, J., ed., *Cliftonville, Hove. A Victorian Suburb*, 1977.

3854 **Mason**, F., *Wolverhampton. The Town Commissioners, 1777-1848*, 1977.

3855 **Minchinton**, W. E., 'Bristol: metropolis of the west in the eighteenth century', *T.R.H.S.*, 5th ser., 4, 1954, 69-89. See also Bush (3816) and Little (3852).

3856 **Mingay**, G. E., *Georgian London*, 1975. See also George (3836) and Rudé (3875).

3857 **Money**, J., *Experience and Identity. Birmingham and the West Midlands, 1760-1800*, 1977. The centre of interest is politics but there is a full discussion of the social and economic community and its cultural provision.

3858 **Morgan**, J. B. and Peberdy, P., eds., *Collected Essays on Southampton*, 1968. Aspects of civic history from Anglo-Saxon times to the present.

3859 **Musgrave**, C., *Life in Brighton*, 1970.

3860 **Neale**, R. S., *Bath, 1680-1850. A Social History*, 1981. Looks at patterns in consumption, production and social consciousness.

3861 **Newton**, R., *Victorian Exeter, 1837-1914*, 1968. See also Hoskins (3845).

3862 **Olsen**, D. J., *Town Planning in London: The Eighteenth and Nineteenth Centuries*, Yale, 1967.

3863 **Owen**, C. C., *The Development of Industry in Burton upon Trent*, 1978.

3864 **Patterson**, A. T., *Radical Leicester: A History of Leicester, 1780-1850*, 1954. See also Elliot (3828), Greaves (3837), and Simmons (3879).

3865 —— *A History of Southampton, 1700-1914*, vol. I, 1966 (covers 1700-1835); vol. II, 1972 (covers the period 1836-67), vol. III, (1868-1914), 1975.

3866 **Peacock**, S. E., *Borough Government in Portsmouth, 1835-1974*, 1975.

3867 **Redford**, A. and Russell, Ina S., *History of Local Government in Manchester*, 3 vols., 1939-40. See also Kennedy (3851), Stewart (3885), and Vigier (3889).

3868 **Richardson**, K., *Twentieth-century Coventry*, 1972.

3869 **Robbins**, R. M., *Middlesex*, 1953. Covers many aspects of London's economic and social history; good bibliography, 397-417.

3870 **Robson**, W. A., *The Government and Misgovernment of London*, 1939. Contains much historical material mainly from 1835 to date of publication.

3871 **Roebuck**, Janet, *Urban Development in Nineteenth-Century London: Lambeth, Battersea and Wandsworth, 1838-88*, 1979. Concentrates on local government administration.

3872 **Rowntree**, B. S., *Poverty: A Study of Town Life*, 1901. The classic study of York.

3873 —— *Poverty and Progress. A Second Social Survey of York*, 1941.

3874 **Royle**, S. A., 'The development of Coalville, Leicestershire in the nineteenth century', *East Midlands Geog.*, VII, 1978, 32-42.

3875 **Rudé**, G., *The History of London: Hanoverian London, 1714-1808*, 1971.

3876 —— *Paris and London in the Eighteenth Century*, 1970. Concerned mainly with problems of public order and disorder. See also George (3836) and Mingay (3856).

3877 **Schofield**, M. M., *Outlines of an Economic History of Lancaster, 1680-1860*, 2 vols., 1946-51.

3878 **Sheppard**, F. H. W., *London, 1808-70. The Infernal Wen*, 1971.

3879 **Simmons**, J., *Leicester Past and Present. II: The Modern Town*, 1975. Vol. I is listed above (608). On Leicester see also (3828, 3837 and 3864).

3880 **Smith**, J. H. and Simonds, J. V., eds., *New Mills. A Short History including an Analysis of the Census of 1851*, 1977.

3881 **Smith**, V., ed., *The Town Book of Lewes, 1837-1901*, Sussex Rec.Soc., LXX, 1976.

3882 **Spiers**, M., *Victoria Park, Manchester. A Nineteenth-Century Suburb in its Social and Administrative Context*, Chet.Soc., 3rd ser., XXIII, 1976. On Manchester see also (3851, 3867, 3885, 3889).

3883 **Stephens**, W. B., ed., *V.C.H. Warwickshire VII: The City of Birmingham*, 1964.

3884 **Stevenson**, J., ed., *London in the Age of Reform*, 1977. Includes chapters on the city opposition to Walpole and his successors and on the experience of 1848.

3885 **Stewart**, C., *The Stones of Manchester*, 1956. The Victorian buildings of the city. On Manchester see also (3851, 3867, 3889).

3886 **Taylor**, R. P., *Rochdale Retrospect*, 1956. Useful summary; source references, 207-8.

3887 **Thompson**, F. M. L., *Hampstead: Building a Borough, 1650-1964*, 1974. See also Williams (3891).

3888 **Unwin**, R. W., 'Tradition and transition: market towns of the Vale of York, 1660-1830', *Northern H.*, XVII, 1981, 72-116.

3889 **Vigier**, F., *Change and Apathy: Liverpool and Manchester During the Industrial Revolution*, Cambridge, Mass., 1970. On Liverpool see also (3820, 3839, 3890), on Manchester (3851, 3867, 3885).

3890 **White**, B. D., *A History of the Corporation of Liverpool, 1834-1914*, 1951. On Liverpool see also (3820, 3839, 3889).

3891 **Williams**, G. R., *London in the Country: The Growth of Suburbia*, 1975. See also Thompson (3887).

3892 **Winter**, G., *Past Positive: London's Social History Recorded in Photographs*, 1971. Covers period from 1840s to 1914.

3893 **Wood**, R., *West Hartlepool: The Rise and Development of a Victorian New Town*, 1967.

BANKING, CURRENCY AND PUBLIC FINANCE

3894 **Clapham**, J. H., 'Modern bibliography of banking and currency (British Empire) from the fifteenth century to 1815'. In J. G. Van Dillen, *History of the Principal Public Banks*, 1934, 449-56.

3895 **Fetter**, F. W. and Gregory, D., *Monetary and Financial Policy*, 1973. A guide to nineteenth-century Blue Books.

(a) BANKING AND THE LONDON MONEY MARKET

3896 **Anderson**, B. L. and Cottrell, P. L., *Money and Banking in England. The Development of the Banking System, 1694-1914*, 1974.

3897 **Gregory**, T. E., ed., *Select Statutes, Documents and Reports Relating to British Banking, 1832-1928*, 2 vols., 1929, 2nd ed., 1964 (vol. I: 1832-44; vol. II: 1847-1928).

3898 **Acworth**, A. W., *Financial Reconstruction in England, 1815-1822*, 1925.

3899 **Ashton**, T. S. and Sayers, R. S., eds., *Papers in English Monetary History*, 1953.

3900 **Balogh**, T., *Studies in Financial Organisation*, 1947.

3901 **Bolitho**, H. and Peel, D., *The Drummonds of Charing Cross*, 1967.

3902 **Boyle**, A., *Montagu Norman*, 1967.

3903 **Clapham**, J. H., *The Bank of England: A History*, 2 vols., 1944. Reprinted 1958 (Vol. I: 1694-1797, Vol. II: 1797-1914).

3904 **Clay**, H., *Lord Norman*, 1957, especially Chapter VIII on banks and the finance of industry.

3905 **Costigliola**, F. C., 'Anglo-American financial rivalry in the 1920s', *J.Ec.H.*, XXXVII, 1977, 911-34.

3906 **Cramp**, A. B., *Opinion on Bank Rate, 1822-1860*, 1962.

3907 **Dacey**, H. M., *The British Banking Mechanism*, 1951. Outlines the working of the financial system since 1931.

3908 **De Cecco**, M., *Money and Empire. The International Gold Standard, 1890-1914*, 1975.

3909 **Duffy**, I. P. H., 'The discount policy of the Bank of England during the suspension of cash payments, 1797-1821', *Ec.H.R.*, 2nd ser., XXXV, 1982, 67-82.

3910 **Fetter**, F. W., *The Development of British Monetary Orthodoxy, 1797-1875*, Cambridge, Mass., 1965.

3911 **Fletcher**, G. A., *The Discount Houses in London*, 1976.

3912 **Giuseppi**, J. A., *The Bank of England: A History from its Foundation in 1694*, 1966. A much slighter work than Clapham's.

3913 **Goetschin**, P., *L'Evolution du marché monétaire de Londres (1931-1952)*, Geneva and Paris, 1963.

3914 **Goodhart**, C. A. E., *The Business of Banking, 1891-1914*, 1972.

3915 **Grant**, A. T. K., *A Study of the Capital Market in Britain from 1919-1936*, 2nd ed., 1967, of book originally published 1937 under slightly different title.

3916 **Hawtrey**, R. G., *A Century of Bank Rate*, 1938.

3917 **Horsefield**, J. K., 'The origins of the Bank Charter Act, 1844'. In Ashton and Sayers, eds. (3899), listed above, 109-25.

3918 **King**, W. T. C., *The History of the London Discount Market*, 1936.

3919 **Lavington**, E., *The English Capital Market*, 1921. Reprinted 1969.

3920 **Moggridge**, D. E., *The Return to Gold, 1925*, 1969.

3921 —— *British Monetary Policy, 1924-1931: The Norman Conquest of $4.86*, 1972.

3922 **Morgan**, E. V., *The Theory and Practice of Central Banking, 1797-1913*, 1st ed., 1943, 2nd ed., 1965.

3923 —— *Studies in British Financial Policy, 1914-1925*, 1952.

3924 —— and Thomas, W. A., *The Stock Exchange: Its History and Functions*, 1962.

3925 **Nishimura**, S., *The Decline of Inland Bills of Exchange in the London Money Market, 1855-1913*, 1971.

3926 **Pollard**, S., ed., *The Gold Standard and Employment Policies between the wars*, 1970. Seven essays by Keynes, R. S. Sayers and others.

3927 **Pressnell**, L. S., 'Gold reserves, banking reserves and the Baring Crisis of 1890'. In *Essays in Money and Banking in Honour of R. S. Sayers*, eds. C. R. Whittlesey and J. S. G. Wilson, 1968, 167-78.

3928 **Rees**, J. F., *A Short Fiscal and Financial History of England, 1815-1918*, 1921.

3929 **Richards**, R. D., 'The first fifty years of the Bank of England, 1694-1744'. In J. G. van Dillen, *History of the Principal Public Banks*, 1934, 2nd ed., 1964, 201-72.

3930 **Rowland**, B. M., ed., *Balance of Power or Hegemony: The Inter-war Monetary System*, 1976.

3931 **Sayers**, R. S., *The Bank of England, 1891-1944*, 3 vols., 1976. Vol. I takes the study as far as the Macmillan Committee, vol. II covers the years 1931-44, and vol. III consists of appendices.

3932 —— *Central Banking after Bagehot*, 1957.

3933 —— *Gilletts in the London Money Market, 1867-1967*, 1968.

3934 **Sheppard**, D. K., *The Growth and Role of U.K. Financial Institutions, 1880-1962*, 1971.

3935 **Silberling**, N. J., 'Financial and monetary policy in Great Britain during the Napoleonic Wars', *Quarterly J.Economics*, LXXIII, 1924, 145-68.

3936 **Solomon**, R., *The International Monetary System, 1945-76*, 1977.

3937 **Tew**, B., *The Evolution of the International Monetary System, 1945-77*, 1977.

3938 **Thomas**, S. E., *British Banks and the Finance of Industry*, 1931.

3939 **Thornton**, H., *An Enquiry into the Nature and Effects of the Paper Credit of Great Britain*, 1802, ed. F. A. Hayek, 1939, 2nd ed., 1962.

3940 **Truptil**, R. J., *British Banks and the London Money Market*, 1936.

3941 **Whale**, P. B., 'A retrospective view of the Bank Charter Act, 1844'. In Ashton and Sayers, eds. (3899), listed above, 126-31.

3942 **Wood**, E., *English Theories of Central Banking Control, 1819-1858, With Some Account of Contemporary Procedure*, Cambridge, Mass., 1939. See also Andréades (1990) and Bisschop (1993), above.

(b) THE EXCHANGE EQUALISATION ACCOUNT

3943 **Hall**, N. F., *The Exchange Equalization Account*, 1935.

3944 **Waight**, L., *The History and Mechanism of the Exchange Equalisation Account*, 1939.

(c) COUNTRY BANKING
(i) GENERAL WORKS

3945 **Gillett**, W., *History of the Clearing for Country Bankers' Cheques and Notes*, 1925.

3946 **Horne**, H. O., *A History of Savings Banks*, 1947.

3947 **Moss**, D. J., 'The Bank of England and the country banks: Birmingham, 1827-33', *Ec.H.R.*, 2nd ser., XXXIV, 1981, 540-53.

3948 **Pressnell**, L. S., *Country Banking in the Industrial Revolution*, 1956.

3949 **Sykes**, J., *The Amalgamation Movement in English Banking*, 1926.

3950 **Thomas**, S. E., *The Rise and Growth of Joint Stock Banking*, 2 vols., 1934.

(ii) REGIONAL AND LOCAL STUDIES

3951 **Allman**, A. H., *et al.*, *Williams Deacon's, 1771-1970*, 1971.

3952 **Ashton**, T. S., 'The bill of exchange and private banks in Lancashire, 1790-1830'. In Ashton and Sayers, eds. (3899), listed above, 37-50.

3953 **Bidwell**, W. H., *Annals of an East Anglian Bank*, 1900.

3954 **Cave**, C. H., *A History of Banking in Bristol from 1750 to 1899*, 1899.

3955 **Chandler**, G., *Four Centuries of Banking, as Illustrated by the Bankers, Customers, and Staff Associated with the Constituent Banks of Martins Bank Ltd.*, 2 vols., 1964-8. Vol. I: *The Grasshopper and the Liver-Bird—Liverpool and London* Vol. II: *The Northern Constituent Banks*.

3956 **Christy**, M., 'The history of banks and banking in Essex', *J.Institute of Bankers*, XXVII, 1906, 319-30.

3957 **Crick**, W. F. and Wadsworth, J. E., *A Hundred Years of Joint Stock Banking*, 1936. A history of the Midland Bank.

3958 **Grindon**, L. H., *Manchester Banks and Bankers*, 1st ed., 1877, 2nd ed., 1878.

3959 **Hoare**, H. P. R., *Hoare's Bank: A Record 1673-1932*, 1932.

3960 **Hughes**, J., *Liverpool Banks and Bankers* 1916.

3961 **Hyde**, F. E. *et al.*, 'The port of Liverpool and the crisis of 1793', *Economica*, n.s., XVIII, 1951, 363-78.

3962 **Leader**, R. E., *The Sheffield Banking Company Ltd.*, 1916.

3963 **Leighton-Boyce**, J. A. S. L., *Smiths the Bankers [of Nottingham] 1658-1958*, 1958.

3964 **Matthews**, P. W. and Tuke, A. W., *A History of Barclays Bank Ltd.*, 1928.

3965 **Perkins**, M., *Dudley Tradesmen's Tokens and History of Dudley Banks, Bankers and Bank Notes*, 1905.

3966 **Phillips**, M., *A History of Banks, Bankers and Banking in Northumberland, Durham and North Yorkshire*, 1894.

3967 **Roth**, H. L., *The Genesis of Banking in Halifax*, 1914.

3968 **Saunders**, P. T., *Stuckey's Bank*, 1926. A famous Somerset bank.

3969 **Sayers**, R. S., *Lloyds Bank in the History of English Banking*, 1957.

3970 **Smith**, T. J., *Banks and Bankers of Leek*, 1891.

3971 **Taylor**, Audrey M., *Gilletts, Bankers at Banbury and Oxford: A Study in Local Economic History*, 1964.

See (5209-11) on Welsh banking, (5477-9) on Scottish banking, and (5760-8) on Irish banking.

(c) CURRENCY

3972 **Cannan**, E., ed., *The Paper Pound of 1797-1821: A Reprint of the Bullion Report* (of 1810), 1919, 2nd ed., 1925, 3rd ed., with new introduction by B. A. Corry, 1969.

3973 **Tooke**, T., *An Inquiry into the Currency Principle*, 2nd ed., 1844. Reprinted 1959.

3974 **Chaloner**, W. H., 'Currency problems of the British Empire, 1814-1914', in Ratcliffe (2576), 179-208.

3975 **Coppieters**, E., *English Bank Note Circulation, 1694-1954*, The Hague, 1955.

3976 **Dalton**, R. and Hamer, S. H., *The Provincial Token Coinage of the Eighteenth Century*, 4 vols., 1910-18. Reissued in one vol., 1967.

3977 **Davis**, W. J., *The Nineteenth-Century Token Coinage of Great Britain and Ireland*, 1904, 2nd ed., 1969.

3978 **Graham**, W., *The One Pound Note in the History of Banking in Great Britain*, 1911.

3979 **Holden**, J. M., *The History of Negotiable Instruments in English Law*, 1955.

3980 **Mathias**, P., *English Trade Tokens: The Industrial Revolution Illustrated*, 1962.

(e) PUBLIC FINANCE
(i) THE NATIONAL DEBT

3981 **Carter**, Alice C., *The English Public Debt in the Eighteenth Century*, 1968.

3982 **Dickson**, P. G. M., *The Financial Revolution in England: A Study in the Development of Public Credit, 1688-1756*, 1967.

3983 **Hargreaves**, E. L., *The National Debt*, 1930, 2nd ed., 1966.

(ii) THE SOUTH SEA BUBBLE

3984 **Carswell**, J., *The South Sea Bubble*, 1960.

3985 **Sperling**, J. G., *The South Sea Company: An Historical Essay and Bibliographical Finding List*, Boston, Mass., 1962.

(iii) TAXES

3986 **Kennedy**, W., *English Taxation, 1640-1799: An Essay on Policy and Opinion*, 1913, 2nd ed., 1964.

3987 **Langford**, P., *The Excise Crisis. Society and Politics in the Age of Walpole*, 1975.

3988 **Mathias**, P. and O'Brien, P., 'Taxation in Britain, 1715-1810', *J.Europ.Ec.H.*, V, 1976, 601-50. See also Dowell (540), listed above.

1. INCOME TAX

3989 **Farnsworth**, A., *Addington, Author of the Modern Income Tax*, 1951.

3990 **Hope-Jones**, A., *Income Tax in the Napoleonic Wars*, 1939.

3991 **Sabine**, B. E. V., *A History of Income Tax*, 1966. Covers the modern period.

3992 **Shehab**, F. A., *Progressive Taxation: A Study of the Progressive Principle in the British Income Tax*, 1953.

2. LAND TAX

3993 **Ward**, W. R., *The English Land Tax in the Eighteenth Century*, 1953.

3. SALT TAX

See Hughes (2036), above.

(iv) ADMINISTRATION AND BUDGETARY CONTROL

3994 **Baker**, N., *Government and Contractors: The British Treasury and War Supplies, 1775-1783*, 1971.

3995 **Binney**, J. E. D., *British Public Finance and Administration, 1774-1792*, 1958.

3996 **Hicks**, Ursula K., *British Public Finances: Their Structure and Development, 1880-1952*, 1954.

3997 —— *The Finance of British Government, 1920-36*, 1938.

3998 **Hirst**, F. W., *Gladstone as Financier and Economist*, 1931.

3999 —— and Allen, J. E., *British War Budgets*, 1926. Goes up to the budget of 1924.

4000 **Howson**, Susan, *Domestic Monetary Management in Great Britain, 1919-38*, 1975.

4001 **Keynes**, M., ed., *Essays on John Maynard Keynes*, 1975.

4002 **Kirkcaldy**, A. W., *British Finance During and After the War, 1914-21*, 1921.

4003 **Mallet**, B., *British Budgets, 1887-88 to 1912-13*, 1913.

4004 —— and George, C. O., *British Budgets: Sec-*

ond Series, *1913-14 to 1920-21*, 1929.

4005 —— and George, C. O., *British Budgets: Third Series, 1921-22 to 1932-33*, 1933.

4006 **Middleton**, R., 'The constant employment budget balance and British budgetary policy, 1929-39', *Ec.H.R.*, 2nd ser., XXXIV, 1981, 266-86.

4007 **Minsky**, H. P., *John Maynard Keynes*, 1976.

4008 **Moggridge**, D. E., *Keynes*, 1976.

4009 **Morgan**, B., *Monetarists and Keynesians. Their Contribution to Monetary Theory*, 1978.

4010 **Morton**, W. A., *British Finance, 1930-1940*, Madison, Wis., 1943.

4011 **Murray**, B. K., *The People's Budget, 1909-10*,

1980.

4012 **Nevin**, E., *The Mechanism of Cheap Money: A Study of British Monetary Policy, 1931-39*, 1955.

4013 **Patinkin**, D., *Keynes's Monetary Thought. A Study of its Development*, 1976.

4014 **Roseveare**, H. G., *The Treasury, 1660-1870. The Foundations of Control*, 1973. A volume in the *Historical Problems: Studies and Documents* series.

4015 **Sabine**, B. E. V., *British Budgets in Peace and War, 1932-1945*, 1970.

4016 **Sayers**, R. S., *Financial Policy, 1939-45*, 1956. Part of the British official civil history of the war.

ACCOUNTANCY

4017 **Brown**, R., ed., *A History of Accounting and Accountants*, 1905, 2nd ed., 1968. Particularly valuable for Scotland.

4018 **Jones**, E., *Accountancy and the British Economy, 1840-1980. The Evolution of Ernst and Whinney*, 1982.

4019 **Littleton**, A. C. and Yamey, B. S., *Studies in*

the History of Accounting, 1956. Contains a number of articles on various aspects of British accountancy history.

4020 **Stacey**, N. A. H., *English Accountancy: A Study in Social and Economic History, 1800-1954*, 1954. See also Yamey, Edey, and Thomson (2011), listed above.

INSURANCE

4021 **Cockerell**, H. A. L. and Green, E., *The British Insurance Business, 1547-1970. An Introduction and Guide to Historical Records in the United Kingdom*, 1976.

4022 **Dickson**, P. G. M., *The Sun Insurance Office, 1710-1960: The History of Two Hundred and Fifty Years of British Insurance*, 1960.

4023 **Drew**, B., *The London Assurance: A Second Chronicle*, 1949. Much enlarged version of a 'first chronicle' published in 1927.

4024 **Garnett**, R. G., *A Century of Co-operative Insurance: The Co-operative Insurance Society 1867-1967*, 1968.

4025 **Morrah**, D., *A History of Industrial Life Assurance*, 1955.

4026 **Supple**, B. E., *The Royal Exchange Assurance: A History of British Insurance*, 1970. The best treatment of the subject.

4027 **Withers**, H., *Pioneers of British Life Assurance*, 1951.

BUILDING SOCIETIES

4028 **Bacon**, R. K., *The Life of Sir Enoch Hill: The Romance of the Modern Building Society*, 1934.

4029 **Bellman**, H., *The Thrifty Three Millions: A Study of the Building Society Movement and the*

Story of the Abbey Road Society, 1935.

4030 **Clearly**, E. J., *The Building Society Movement*, 1965. The best general history.

4031 **Hobson**, O. R., *A Hundred Years of the*

Halifax: The History of the Halifax Building Society, 1853-1953, 1953.

4032 **Mansbridge**, A., *Brick upon Brick*, 1934. History of the Co-operative Permanent Building Society from 1884.

4033 **Price**, S. J., *Building Societies: Their Origins and History*, 1958.

4034 —— *From Queen to Queen: The Centenary History of the Temperance Permanent Building Society, 1854-1954*, 1954.

CAPITAL FORMATION

4035 **Anderson**, B. L., ed., *Capital Accumulation in the Industrial Revolution*, 1974. Selected readings from Adam Smith to Giffen.

4036 **Cottrell**, P. L., *Industrial Finance, 1830-1914. The Finance and Organisation of English Manufacturing Industry*, 1980. Deals with the development of company law, with shares and shareholders, private companies and public combines, and with the role of the banks.

4037 **Crouzet**, F., intro. and ed., *Capital Formation in the Industrial Revolution*, 1972. A symposium of essays by various hands.

4038 **Higgins**, J. P. R. and Pollard, S., eds., *Aspects of Capital Investment in Great Britain, 1750-1850*: A Preliminary Survey, 1971.

4039 **Minchinton**, W. E., ed., *Capital Formation in South-West England*, 1978.

4040 **Pollard**, S., 'Fixed capital in the industrial revolution in Britain', *J.Ec.H.*, XXIV, 1964.

4041 **Thomas**, W. A., *The Provincial Stock Exchanges*, 1973. Mainly 1800-1914.

4042 —— *The Finance of British Industry, 1918-76*, 1978. Deals, inter al., with internal funding, the capital market, the banks and industry, and with the public corporations.

JOINT STOCK COMPANIES

4043 **Campbell**, R. H., 'The law and the joint-stock company in Scotland'. In Payne (5473), 136-51.

4044 **Cooke**, C. A., *Corporation, Trust and Company: An Essay in Legal History*, 1950.

4045 **Du Bois**, A. B., *The English Business Company After the Bubble Act, 1720-1800*, N. Y., 1938.

4046 **Evans**, G. H., *British Corporation Finance, 1775-1800*, Baltimore, 1936. The evolution of the preference share in the canal age.

4047 **Formoy**, R. R., *Historical Foundations of Modern Company Law*, 1923.

4048 **Hunt, B. C.**, *The Development of the Business Corporation in England, 1800-1867*, Cambridge, Mass., 1936.

4049 **Jefferys**, J. B., 'The denomination and character of shares, 1855-1885'. In Carus-Wilson, ed. (245), listed above, I, 344-57.

4050 **Shannon**, H. A., 'The coming of general limited liability'. In Carus-Wilson, ed., (245), listed above, I, 358-79.

4051 —— 'The first five thousand limited companies and their duration', *Ec. J., Ec.H.Supp.*, II, 1932, 396-424.

4052 —— 'The limited companies of 1866-1883'. In Carus-Wilson, ed. (245), listed above, I, 380-405.

4053 **Tyson**, R. E., 'William Marcroft (1822-94) and the limited liability movement in Oldham', *T.L.C.A.S.*, LXXX, 1980, 60-80.

4054 **Welbourne**, E., 'Bankruptcy before the era of Victorian reform', *Cambridge H. J.*, IV, 1932, 51-62.

CLASSES AND SOCIAL GROUPS

(a) GENERAL WORKS

4055 **Briggs**, A., 'The language of "class" in early nineteenth-century England', in Briggs and Saville (4138), below, I, 43-73.

4056 —— 'The language of "mass" and "masses" in nineteenth-century England', in Martin & Rubinstein (4161), below, 62-83.

4057 **Cannadine**, D., 'The theory and practice of the English leisure classes' (Review article), H.J., XXI, 1978, 445-67.

4058 **Donajgrodzki**, A. P., ed., *Social Control in Nineteenth-Century Britain*, 1977. See also Thompson (4067), below.

4059 **Gloversmith**, F., ed., *Class, Culture and Social Change. A New View of the 1930s*, 1980.

4060 **Hardy**, D., *Alternative Communities in Nineteenth-Century England*, 1979.

4061 **Mabey**, R., ed., *Class: A Symposium*, 1967.

4062 **Marwick**, A., *Class: Image and Reality in Britain, France and the U.S.A. since 1930*, 1980.

4063 **Morris**, R. J., *Class and Class Consciousness in the Industrial Revolution*, 1979. A general introduction with useful select bibliography.

4064 **Neale**, R. S., *Class in English History, 1680-1850*, 1981. Rehearses the author's well-known five-class model of English society and explores the theoretical and empirical problems involved in defining class and class consciousness.

4065 **Perkin**, H. J., *The Origins of Modern English Society 1780-1880*, 1969. Principally concerned with class and class consciousness and their relation to the Industrial Revolution and its consequences.

4066 —— *The Structured Crowd. Essays in English Social History*, 1981. A curiously titled miscellany of essays. 'Land reform and class conflict in Victorian Britain' is the most substantial.

4067 **Thompson**, F. M. L., 'Social control in Victorian Britain', *Ec.H.R.*, 2nd ser., XXXIV, 1981, 189-208. See also Donajgrodzki (4058), above.

4068 **Wade**, J., *History of the Middle and Working Classes*, 1833. Reprinted N. Y., 1966.

(b) THE ENTREPRENEURIAL AND PROFESSIONAL MIDDLE CLASSES

4069 **Aldcroft**, D. H., 'British industry and foreign competition, 1875-1914'. In Aldcroft (2639), listed above, 11-36.

4070 **Armytage**, W. H. G., *The Rise of the Technocrats: A Social History*, 1965. Contains important material on connections between British industrialists and scientists.

4071 **Arnstein**, W. L., 'The myth of the triumphant Victorian middle class', *Historian*, XXXVII, 1975, 205-21.

4072 **Baker**, M., *The Rise of the Victorian Actor*, 1978.

4073 **Beresford**, M. W., *The Leeds Chambers of Commerce*, 1951.

4074 **Bradley**, I., *The English Middle Classes are Alive and Kicking*, 1982. See also Lewis and Maude (4088), below.

4075 **Burnley**, J., *Fortunes Made in Business*, 3 vols., 1884-6.

4076 **Campbell**, R. H. and Wilson, R. G., eds., *Entrepreneurship in Britain, 1750-1939*, 1975.

4077 **Carr-Saunders**, A. M., and Wilson, P., *The Professions*, 1933.

4078 **Checkland**, S. G., *The Gladstones. A Family Biography, 1764-1851*, 1971.

4079 **Crossick**, G., ed., *The Lower Middle Class in Britain, 1870-1914*, 1976. Includes chapters on values, politics, religion, culture and housing.

4080 **Duman**, D., 'The creation and diffusion of a professional ideology in nineteenth-century England', *Soc.R.*, XXVII, XXVII, 1979, 113-38. See also Perkin (4065), above.

4081 **Erickson**, Charlotte, *British Industrialists: Steel and Hosiery, 1850-1950*, 1959.

4082 **Green**, E., *Debtors to their Profession. A History of the Institute of Bankers, 1879-1979*, 1979.

4083 **Gross**, J., *The Rise and Fall of the Man of Letters. Aspects of English Literary Life since 1800*, 1969.

4084 **Harries-Jenkins**, G., *The Army in Victorian Society*, 1977.

4085 **Hartwell**, R. M., 'Business management in England during the period of early industrialization: inducements and obstacles'. In Hartwell, ed., (2549), listed above, 28-41.

4086 **Heeney**, B., *A Different Kind of Gentleman. Parish Clergy as Professional Men in Early and Mid-Victorian England*, 1977.

4087 **Howe**, E., *The British Federation of Master Printers, 1900-1950*, 1950.

4088 **Lewis**, R. and Maude, A., *The English Middle Classes*, 1949. See also Bradley (4074), above.

4089 **Mackay**, T., ed., *The Autobiography of*

Samuel Smiles, LL.D., 1905.

4090 **Mayer**, A. J., 'The lower middle class as historical problem', *J.M.H.*, XLVII, 1975, 409-36.

4091 **Minchinton**, W. E., 'The merchants of Bristol in the eighteenth century', *Sociétés et Groupes Sociaux en Aquitaine et en Angleterre*, Bordeaux, 1979.

4092 **Munford**, W. A., *A History of the Library Association, 1877-1977*, 1977.

4093 **Parry**, N. and J., *The Rise of the Medical Profession. A Study of Collective Social Mobility*, 1976.

4094 **Payne**, P. L., *British Entrepreneurship in the Nineteenth Century*, 1974.

4095 **Perkin**, H. J., *Key Profession: The History of the Association of University Teachers*, 1969.

4096 **Pollard**, S., *The Genesis of Modern Management: A Study of the Industrial Revolution in Great Britain*, 1965.

4097 **Reader**, W. J., *Professional Men: The Rise of the Professional Classes in Nineteenth-century England*, 1966.

4098 **Robson**, R., *The Attorney in Eighteenth-century England*, 1959.

4099 **Rubinstein**, W. D., *Men of Property*, 1981. Surveys the propertied elite from the Industrial Revolution. Packed with statistical tables.

4100 —— 'The Victorian middle class: wealth, occupation and geography', *Ec.H.R.*, 2nd ser., XXX, 1977, 582-601.

4101 **Schwarz**, L. D., 'Social class and social geography: the middle classes in London at the end of the eighteenth century', *Soc.H.*, VII, 1982, 167-86.

4102 **Skelly**, A. R., *The Victorian Army at Home*, 1977. See also Harries-Jenkins (4084), above.

4103 **Smiles**, Aileen, *Samuel Smiles and his Surroundings*, 1956. See also (4105).

4104 **Thompson**, F. M. L., *Chartered Surveyors: The Growth of a Profession*, 1968. With the exception of the first two chapters the book is concerned with developments after 1700.

4105 **Travers**, T. H. E., 'Samuel Smiles and the origins of Self Help: reform and the new enlightenment', *Albion*, IX, 1977, 161-87. See also (4103).

4106 **Tropp**, A., *The School Teachers: The Growth of the Teaching Profession in England and Wales from 1800 to the Present Day*, 1957. On the gentry and aristocracy see the section on landed society, (pp. 93-7), above.

(c) THE WORKING CLASS

(i) BIBLIOGRAPHICAL STUDIES, DICTIONARIES AND STATISTICS

4107 **Bain**, G. S. and Woolven, Gillian B., comps., *A Bibliography of British Industrial Relations, 1880-1970*, 1979.

4108 **Bellamy**, Joyce and Saville, J., eds., *Dictionary of Labour Biography*, I, 1972; II, 1974. III, 1976; IV, 1977; V, 1979.

4109 **Department of Labour and Productivity**, *British Labour Statistics: Historical Abstract, 1886-1968*, 1971.

4110 **Lee**, C. H., *British Regional Employment Statistics, 1841-1971*, 1979.

4111 **Maehl**, W. H., ' "Jerusalem deferred": recent writing in the history of the British labour movement', *J.M.H.*, 41, 1969, 335-67.

4112 **Mowat**, C. L., 'The history of the Labour Party: the Coles, the Webbs, and some others', *J.M.H.*, 23, 1951, 146-53.

4113 **Wolfe**, W., 'A century of books on the history of Socialism in Britain. Part I: before 1950. Part II: after 1850', *Brit.Studs.Monitor*, X, 1 & 2, 1980, 46-65; X, 3, 1981, 18-46.

(ii) DOCUMENTARY COLLECTIONS AND CONTEMPORARY WORKS

4114 **Bray**, J. F., *A Voyage from Utopia*, ed. M. F. Lloyd-Pritchard, 1957.

4115 —— *Labour's Wrongs and Labour's Remedy*, 1839. Reprinted 1931.

4116 **Coats**, A. W., ed., *Poverty in the Victorian Age*, 4 vols, 1974. Reprints articles from contemporary periodicals.

4117 **Cole**, G. D. H., and Filson, A. W., *British Working Class Movements: Select Documents, 1789-1875*, 1951. Reprinted 1965.

4118 **Hobsbawm**, E. J., ed., *Labour's Turning Point ... 1880-1900: Extracts from Contemporary Sources*, 1948.

4119 **Hodgskin**, T., *Labour Defended Against the Claims of Capital*, 1825. Reprinted 1922 and 1964, with introduction by G. D. H. Cole.

4120 **Hollis**, Patricia M., ed., *Class and Conflict in Nineteenth-century England, 1815-50*, 1973. A collection of documents largely from Radical sources; guides to further reading are unsatisfactory.

4121 **Jefferys**, J. B., ed., *Labour's Formative Years ... 1849-1879: Extracts from Contemporary Sources*, 1948.

4122 **Mayhew**, H., *London Labour and the London*

Poor, 1st ed. in 3 vols., *1851*, 2nd enlarged ed. in 4 vols., *1861-2*, new impression, 1967.

4123 —— *The Street Trader's Lot – London, 1851*, (ed. S. Rubinstein), 1947.

4124 ——*Mayhew's London, Being Selections from London Labour and the London Poor*, ed. P. Quennell, 1969.

4125 —— *London's Underworld: Selections from London Labour and the London Poor*, ed. P. Quennell, 1969.

4126 —— *The Unknown Mayhew: Selections from the Morning Chronicle, 1849-50*, eds. E. P. Thompson and Eileen Yeo, 1971. On Mayhew see:

4127 **Hughes**, J. R. T., 'Henry Mayhew's London', *J.Ec.H.*, XXIX, 1969, 526-36.

4128 **Humpherys**, Anne, *Travels into the Poor Man's Country. The Work of Henry Mayhew*, 1980.

4129 **Thompson**, E. P., 'The political education of Henry Mayhew', *Vict.Studs.*, XI, 1967-8, 41-62.

4130 **Morris**, M., ed., *From Cobbett to the Chartists ... 1815-1848: Extracts from Contemporary Sources*, 1948.

4131 **Wrigley**, C. J., ed., *The Working Classes in the Victorian Age. Debates on the Issue from Nineteenth-Century Critical Journals*, 4 vols., 1973.

(iii) SOCIALIST THEORIES AND THEORISTS

4132 **Beales**, H. L., *The Early English Socialists*, 1933.

4133 **Beer**, M., *A History of British Socialism*, 2 vols., 1919, 2nd rev. and enlarged ed., in 1 vol., 1940.

4134 **Gray**, A., *The Socialist Tradition: Moses to Lenin*, 3rd rev. impression, 1948. 'The pre-Marxians', 262-96.

4135 **Halévy**, E., *Thomas Hodgskin*, trans. and ed. A. J. Taylor, 1956.

4136 **Kimball**, Janet, *The Economic Doctrines of John Gray, 1799-1883*, Washington, D. C., 1948.

4137 **Pankhurst**, R. K. P., *William Thompson, 1775-1833: Britain's Pioneer Socialist, Feminist and Co-operator*, 1954.

(iv) GENERAL WORKS

4138 **Briggs**, A. and Saville, J., eds., *Essays in Labour History: In Memory of G. D. H. Cole*, 1960; rev. ed., 1967. Includes essays on the language of 'class', on the nineteenth-century Co-operative Movement, and on wages and workloads.

4139 —— *Essays in Labour History, 1886-1923*, 1971. Includes essays on the Triple Industrial Alliance, on Clydeside, and on the foundation of the Co-operative Party.

4140 —— *Essays in Labour History. III: 1918-39*, 1977. The collection includes essays on the T.U.C. in 1926, and on the non-political trade union movement.

4141 **Brown**, K. D., *The English Labour Movement, 1700-1851*, 1982.

4142 ——, ed., *Essays in Anti-Labour History. Responses to the Rise of Labour in Britain*, 1974. Includes essays on the New Liberalism, the Anti-Socialist Union, and on the Charity Organisation Society.

4143 **Calhoun**, C., *The Question of Class Struggle. Social Foundations of Popular Radicalism in the Industrial Revolution*, 1982.

4144 **Church**, R. A. and Chapman, S. D., 'Gravenor Henson and the making of the English working class', in Jones and Mingay (2558), above, 131-61.

4145 **Cole**, G. D. H. and Postgate, R., *The Common People, 1746-1946*, 1946.

4146 **Cornforth**, M., ed., *Rebels and their Causes: Essays in Honour of A. L. Morton*, 1978. Includes essays on 'Lollards to Levellers', 'Robert Owen and the Family', and on the nineteenth-century working class.

4147 **Day**, C., 'The distribution of industrial occupations in England 1841-1861', *Trans. Connecticut Academy of Arts and Sciences*, XXVIII, 1927, 79-235.

4148 **Donnelly**, F. K., 'Ideology and early English working-class history: Edward Thompson and his critics', *Soc.H.*, I, 1976, 219-38.

4149 **Engels**, F., *The Condition of the Working Class in England* (originally published in 1845), trans. and ed. by W. O. Henderson and W. H. Chaloner, 1958, 2nd rev. ed., 1971. Another edition ed. E. J. Hobsbawm, 1969. On Engels, see: Henderson (4154) and Marcus (4160), below.

4150 **Foster**, J., *Class Struggle and the Industrial Revolution: Early Industrial Capitalism in Three English Towns* (Oldham, Northampton and South Shields), 1974.

4151 **Hammond**, J. L. and Barbara, *The Skilled Labourer, 1760-1832*, 1919. Last reprinted 1965. The best of the 'labourer' trilogy.

4152 —— *The Town Labourer, 1760-1832: The New Civilisation*, 1917. Reprinted with an introduction by J. Rule, 1978.

4153 **Hearn**, F., *Domination, Legitimation and Resistance: The Incorporation of the Nineteenth-Century English Working Class*, Westport, Conn., 1978. Heavily sociological and theoretical treatment. Contains an extended historiographical discussion of the competing explanations of the nineteenth-century emergence of the working class.

4154 **Henderson**, W. O., *The Life of Friedrich Engels*, 2 vols., 1976.

4155 **Humphries**, S., *Hooligans or Rebels? An Oral History of Working-Class Childhood and Youth, 1889-1913*, 1982.

4156 **Kiernan**, V. G., 'Working class and nation in nineteenth-century Britain' in Cornforth (4146), above, 123-40.

4157 **Kynaston**, D., *King Labour. The British Working Class, 1850-1914*, 1976.

4158 **Maccoby**, S., *English Radicalism*, 6 vols., 1935-61. I: *1762-1785*; II: *1786-1832*, 1955; III: *1832-1852*, 1935; IV: *1853-1886*, 1938; V: *1886-1914*, 1953; VI: *The End?*, 1961.

4159 **Malcolmson**, R. W., *Life and Labour in England, 1700-80*, 1981.

4160 **Marcus**, S., *Engels, Manchester and the Working Class*, 1974.

4161 **Martin**, D. E. and Rubinstein, D., eds., *Ideology and the Labour Movement. Essays presented to John Saville*, 1979. The collection includes essays on the language of 'class', working-class women and the reform of family law, and on the post Second World War government's policy of social welfare.

4162 **Meacham**, S., *A Life Apart. The English Working Class, 1890-1914*, 1977.

4163 **Richards**, P., 'The state and early industrial capitalism: the case of the handloom weavers', *P.P.*, 83, 1979, 91-115.

4164 **Rule**, J. G., *The Experience of Labour in Eighteenth-Century Industry*, 1981. Concentrates on adult male labour outside the factory, and has sections on wages, apprenticeship and industrial relations.

4165 **Saville**, J., ed., *Democracy and the Labour Movement*, 1955.

4166 **Stearns**, P. N., *Lives of Labour. Work in a Maturing Industrial Society*, 1975.

4167 **Tholfsen**, T., *Working-class Radicalism in Mid-Victorian England*, 1976. Suggests that after Chartism, the radical tradition was preserved in a working-class sub-culture.

4168 **Thomis**, M. I., *The Town Labourer and the Industrial Revolution*, 1974.

4169 **Thompson**, E. P., *The Making of the English Working Class*, 1963, 2nd ed., with critical appendix, 916-39. A major contribution to 'history from

below'. By attempting to present the working-class – and by that the author chiefly means the artisans – in the light of their own experience, Thompson seeks to rescue them from 'the enormous condescension of posterity'.

4170 —— 'The moral economy of the crowd in eighteenth-century England', *P.P.*, 50, 1971, 76-136.

4171 **Vincent**, D., 'Love and death and the nineteenth-century working class', *Soc.H.*, V, 1980, 223-47.

4172 **Weisser**, H., *British Working-Class Movements and Europe, 1815-48*, 1976.

4173 **Williams**, G. A., *Artisans and Sans Culottes. Popular Movements in France and Britain during the French Revolution*, 1968.

4174 **Winstanley**, M., *Life in Kent at the Turn of the Century*, 1978. An oral history which examines both urban and rural life and also the working patterns of Kentish fishermen.

(v) MISCELLANEOUS

4175 **Hanson**, H., *The Canal Boatmen, 1760-1914*, 1975.

4176 **Prior**, Mary, *Fisher Row: Fishermen, Bargemen and Canal Boatmen in Oxford, 1500-1900*, 1981.

4177 **Stern**, W., *The Porters of London*, 1960.

(vi) LUDDISM AND POPULAR DISTURBANCES
1. LUDDISM

4178 **Hobsbawm**, E. J., 'The Machine breakers', in Hobsbawm, (4287) listed below.

4179 **Munby**, L. M., ed., *The Luddites and Other Essays*, 1971. Contributions by Marxist historians.

4180 **Peel**, F., *The Risings of the Luddites, Chartists and Plugdrawers*, 1880, 4th ed., with new introduction, 1968.

4181 **Thomis**, M. I., *The Luddites*, 1970.

4182 —— ed., *Luddism in Nottinghamshire*, 1972. A collection of documents of 1811-16 with short introduction.

2. POPULAR DISTURBANCES

4183 **Divine**, D., *Mutiny at Invergordon*, 1970. Includes new material, badly handled.

4184 **Dugan**, J., *The Great Mutiny, Spithead and the Nore, 1797*, 1966. See Gill (4186) and Manwaring and Dobrée (4187), listed below.

4185 **Edwards**, K., *The Mutiny at Invergordon*, 1937. See also 3348 above.

4186 **Gill**, C., *The Naval Mutinies of 1797*, 1913. See Dugan (4184), listed above, and Manwaring (4187), listed below.

4187 **Manwaring**, G. E. and Dobrée, B., *The Floating Republic: An Account of the Mutinies at Spithead and the Nore in 1797*, 1935. See also Dugan (4184) and Gill (4186), listed above.

4188 **Read**, D., *Peterloo: The 'Massacre' and its Background*, 2nd ed., 1973. See also Walmsley (4194), listed below.

4189 **Rose**, A. G., 'The Plug Riots of 1842 in Lancashire and Cheshire', *T.L.C.A.S.*, LXVII, 1958, 75-112.

4190 **Rudé**, G., *The Crowd in History, 1730-1848: A Study of Popular Disturbances in France and England*, N. Y., 1964.

4191 **Shelton**, W. J., *English Hunger and Industrial Disorders*, 1973. Confined to the 1760s.

4192 **Stevenson**, J., and Quinault, R., *Popular Protest and Public Order: Six Studies in British History, 1790-1920*, 1975.

4193 **Thomis**, M. I., *Politics and Society in Nottingham 1785-1835*, 1969.

4194 **Walmsley**, R., *Peterloo: The Case Reopened*, 1969. See also Read (4188), listed above, and Mather (4225), listed below.

4195 **Ward**, J. T., ed., *Popular Movements c. 1830-1850*, 1970. Includes chapters on the factory movement, the anti-New Poor Law agitation, trade unionism, Chartism, the agitation against the Corn Laws, and the public health movement. See also the section on *Law and Order* (p.147), below.

(vii) OWENISM AND UTOPIANISM

4196 **Owen**, R., *The Life of Robert Owen written by Himself*, vol. I, 1857. Reprinted 1971 with an introduction by J. Butt. A reprint of both volumes of the first edition (1857 and 1858) was issued in 1967.

4197 —— *A New View of Society and other Writings*, ed. J. Butt, 1974.

4198 —— *A New View of Society and Report to the County of Lanark*, ed. with introduction by V. A. C. Gatrell, 1969.

4199 —— *A New View of Society*, ed. with introduction by J. Saville, Clifton, N. J., 1972.

4200 **Armytage**, W. H. G., *Heavens Below: Utopian Experiments in England 1560-1960*. 1961. Includes Scotland, Wales and Ireland.

4201 **Butt**, J. ed., *Robert Owen, Prince of Cotton Spinners*, 1971. Essays in honour of Owen's 200th anniversary.

4202 **Cole**, G. D. H., *The Life of Robert Owen*, 1925, 3rd ed., 1965, with new introduction by Margaret I. Cole.

4203 **Cole**, Margaret I., *Robert Owen of New Lanark*, 1953.

4204 **Garnett**, R. G., *Co-operation and the Owenite Socialist Communities in Britain, 1825-45*, 1972.

4205 **Goodwin**, B., *Social Science and Utopia: Nineteenth-Century Models of Social Harmony*, 1978.

4206 **Harrison**, J. F. C., *Robert Owen and the Owenites in Britain and America: the Quest for the New Moral World*, 1969. Detailed bibliography, 263-369.

4207 —— *The Second Coming. Popular Millenarianism, 1780-1850*, 1979.

4208 **Morton**, A. L., *The Life and Ideas of Robert Owen*, 1962. A Marxist view with extracts from Owen's writings.

4209 **Podmore**, F., *The Life of Robert Owen*, 2 vols., 1906. Reprint in 1 vol., 1923.

4210 **Pollard**, S. and Salt, J., eds., *Robert Owen: Prophet of the Poor*, 1971. Essays in honour of Owen's 200th anniversary.

(viii) CHARTISM

I. GENERAL WORKS

4211 **Harrison**, J. F. C. and Thompson, Dorothy, *Bibliography of the Chartist Movement, 1837-1976*, 1977.

4212 **Gammage**, R. G., *History of the Chartist Movement*, 1854, 2nd ed., 1895, reprinted 1969 with introduction by J. Saville, 4-66.

4213 **Mather**, F. C., ed., *Chartism and Society. An Anthology of Documents*, 1980.

4214 **Thompson**, Dorothy, *The Early Chartists*, 1971. Covers the period 1837-41 only; documents, with commentary.

4215 **Cullen**, M., 'The Chartists and education', *New Zealand J.H.*, X, 1976, 162-77.

4216 **Dolléans**, E., *Le Chartisme, 1831-1848*, 2nd rev. ed., Paris, 1949.

4217 **Faulkner**, H. U., *Chartism and the Churches*, 1st ed., 1916. Reprinted 1970.

4218 **Hadfield**, Alice M., *The Chartist Land Company*, 1970.

4219 **Hammond**, J. L. and Barbara, *The Age of the Chartists, 1832-1854: A Study of Discontent*, 1930.

4220 **Haraszti**, Eva H., *Chartism*, 1978.

4221 **Harrison**, B., 'Teetotal Chartism', *Hist.*, 58, 1973, 193-217.

4222 **Hovell**, M., *The Chartist Movement*, 1918, 3rd ed., 1966, 4th ed., 1970, with bibliographical additions (iii-ix, 318) which give details of literature up to 1970.

4223 **Jones**, D., *Chartism and the Chartists*, 1975. Extensive bibliography.

4224 **MacAskill**, Joy, 'The Chartist Land Plan'. In Briggs, ed. (4232), listed below, 304-41.

4225 **Mather**, F. C., *Public Order in the Age of the Chartists*, 1959.

4226 —— *Chartism*, Hist.Assoc. pamphlet, 1965, 3rd rev. ed., 1974. Sums up research since 1925.

4227 **Rosenblatt**, F. F., *The Chartist Movement in its Social and Economic Aspects*, 1916. Reprinted 1967.

4228 **Slosson**, P. W., *The Decline of the Chartist Movement*, 1916. Reprinted 1967.

4229 **Ward**, J. T., *Chartism*, 1973.

4230 **West**, J., *History of Chartism*, 1920.

4231 **Yeo**, Eileen, 'Christianity in Chartist struggle, 1838-42', *P.P.*, 91, 1981, 109-39. For Christian Socialism see p.153.

2. REGIONAL STUDIES

4232 **Briggs**, A., ed., *Chartist Studies*, 1959. Mainly essays on local aspects of the movement.

4233 **Cannon**, J., *The Chartists in Bristol*, 1964.

4234 **Goodway**, D., *London Chartism, 1838-48*, 1982.

4235 **Howell**, G., *A History of the London Working Men's Association from 1836 to 1850*, new ed., 1972.

4236 **Peacock**, A. J., *Bradford Chartism, 1838-1840*, 1969.

4237 **Rowe**, D. J., ed., *London Radicalism, 1830-1843: A Selection from the Papers of Francis Place*, London Rec.Soc., 1970. See also Thale (4317) and Wallas (4250), listed below.

4238 **Wilson**, A., *The Chartist Movement in Scotland*, 1970.

4239 **Wright**, L. C., *Scottish Chartism*, 1953.

3. BIOGRAPHIES

4240 **Cole**, G. D. H., *Chartist Portraits*, 1941, 2nd ed., 1965. Useful bibliography of Chartist literature, 359-66.

4241 **Conklin**, R. J., *Thomas Cooper the Chartist (1805-1892)*, Manila, 1935.

4242 **Epstein**, J. and Thompson, Dorothy, eds., *The Chartist Experience: Studies in Working-class Radicalism and Culture, 1830-60*, 1982.

4243 **Harrison**, B. and Hollis, Patricia M., eds., *Robert Lowery, Radical and Chartist*, 1979.

4244 **Kirby**, R. G. and Musson, A. E., *The Voice of the People: John Doherty, 1798-1854, Trade Unionist, Radical and Factory Reformer*, 1975.

4245 **Plummer**, A., *Bronterre: A Political Biogra-*

phy of Bronterre O'Brien, 1801-1864, 1971.

4246 **Read**, D., and Glasgow, E. L. H., *Feargus O'Connor, Irishman and Chartist*, 1961.

4247 **Saville**, J., ed., *Ernest Jones, Chartist: Selections from the Writing and Speeches of Ernest Jones . . .*, 1952.

4248 **Schoyen**, A. R., *The Chartist Challenge: A Portrait of George Julian Harney*, 1958.

4249 **Smith**, F. B., *Radical Artisan: William James Linton, 1812-1897*, 1973.

4250 **Wallas**, G., *The Life of Francis Place*, 4th ed., 1951. See also Thale (4317), listed below, and Rowe (4237), listed above.

4251 **Williams**, D., *John Frost: A Study in Chartism*, 1939. Reprinted 1969.

(ix) FRIENDLY SOCIETIES, ETC.

4252 **Baernreither**, J. M., *English Associations of Working Men*, 1889.

4253 **Fuller**, Margaret, D., *West Country Friendly Societies*, 1964.

4254 **Gosden**, P. H. J. H., *The Friendly Societies in England, 1815-75*, 1961.

4255 —— *Self-Help: Voluntary Associations in the Nineteenth Century*, 1973.

4256 **Holyoake**, G. J., *Self Help a Hundred Years Ago*, 2nd ed., 1890. Essays on the history of English social reform movements.

(ix) TRADE UNIONISM AND LABOUR

1. GENERAL WORKS

4257 **Smith**, H., *The British Labour Movement to 1970: A Bibliography*, 1981.

4258 **Aspinall**, A., ed., *The Early English Trade Unions: Documents from the Home Office Papers in the Public Record Office*, 1949. Covers the period 1791-1825.

4259 **Bailey**, W. M., *Trade Union Documents: Compiled and Edited with an Introduction*, 1929. Documents and extracts ranging from 1841 to 1928 but mostly 1913-28.

4260 **Coates**, K. and Topham, T., *Workers' Control: A Book of Readings and Witnesses for Workers' Control*, 1970. Documents and extracts from books relative to anarchosyndicalism in the British labour movement from 1910 to 1969.

4261 **Frow**, Ruth and E. and Katanka, M., *Strikes: A Documentary History*, 1971. Collection of contemporary or near-contemporary accounts of strikes in Britain, 1812-1926.

4262 **Howell**, G., *Trade Unionism Old and New.* Reprint of 4th ed., 1907, with introduction by F.

M. Leventhal, 1973.

4263 **Pollard**, S., ed., *The Sheffield Outrages: Report Presented to the Trades Union Commissioners in 1867*, 1971.

4264 **Robertson**, N. and Sams, K. I., *British Trade Unionism: Select Documents*, 2 vols., 1972.

4265 **Saville**, J., ed., *Working Conditions of the Victorian Age*, 1974. Reprints articles from contemporary periodicals.

4266 **Ward**, J. T. and Fraser, W. H., eds., *Workers and Employers. Documents on Trade Unions and Industrial Relations since the Early Eighteenth Century*, 1980.

4267 **Bagwell**, P. S., *Industrial Relations*, 1974. Guide to British Parliamentary Papers on this subject.

4268 **Barou**, N. I., *British Trade Unions*, 1947.

4269 **Bienefield**, M. A., *Working Hours in British Industry. An Economic History*, 1972. Deals with the period from 1820 and covers all major branches of industrial labour.

4270 **Browne**, H., *The Rise of British Trade Unionism, 1818-1914*, 1979.

4271 **Burgess**, K., *The Origins of British Industrial Relations: The Nineteenth-Century Experience*, 1975.

4272 —— *The Challenge of Labour. Shaping British Society, 1850-1930*, 1980.

4273 **Clegg**, H. A., Fox, A. and Thompson, A. F., *A History of British Trade Unions since 1889*, I (1889-1910), 1964.

4274 **Clinton**, A., *Trade Union Rank and File. Trades Councils in Britain, 1900-40*, 1977.

4275 **Cole**, G. D. H., *Attempts at General Union: A Study in British Trade Union History, 1818-1834*, 1953. Should be used with caution; many inaccuracies.

4276 **Cronin**, J. E., *Industrial Conflict in Modern Britain*, 1979. Deals with the period from the 1880s to c. 1970.

4277 **Cruikshank**, Marjorie, *Children and Industry. Juvenile Work and Welfare in the North West, 1800-1900*, 1981.

4278 **Dobson**, C. R., *Masters and Journeymen. A Pre-history of Industrial Conflict, 1717-1800*, 1980.

4279 **Fraser**, W. H., *Trade Unions and Society: The Struggle for Acceptance, 1850-1880*, 1974.

4280 **Frow**, Ruth and E. and Katanka, M., *The History of British Trade Unionism: A Select Bibliography*, Hist.Ass., 1969. Extremely useful, and should be used to supplement this section.

4281 **George**, M. Dorothy, 'The Combination Laws reconsidered', *Ec. J.Ec.H.Supp.*, I, 1927, 214-2[...] Essential for any real understanding of the lav[...] relating to early trade unions.

4282 —— 'The Combination Laws', *Ec.H.R.*, V[...] 1936, 172-8. See remarks on previous entry.

4283 **Goodrich**, C. L., *The Frontier of Control: Study in British Workshop Politics*, 1920. 2[...] rev. ed., 1975, with new foreword by R. Hyma[...]

4284 **Gupta**, P. S., *Imperialism and the Britis[...] Labour Movement, 1914-64*, 1975.

4285 **Hedges**, R. Y., and Winterbottom, A., *T[...] Legal History of Trade Unionism*, 1930.

4286 **Hinton**, J., *The First Shop Stewards' Mov[...] ment*, 1973. See also Pribicevic (4302), liste[...] below.

4287 **Hobsbawm**, E. J., *Labouring Men: Studies [...] the History of Labour*, 1964. Reprints eightee[...] articles on working-class subjects.

4288 —— 'General labour unions in Britai[...] 1889-1914'. In Hobsbawm (4287), listed abov[...] 179-203.

4289 **Hopkins**, E., 'Working hours and conditio[...] during the Industrial Revolution: a re-appraisa[...] *Ec.H.R.*, 2nd ser., XXXV, 1982, 52-66.

4290 **Hunt**, E. H., *British Labour Histor[...] 1815-1914*, 1981. A comprehensive, judiciou[...] study which explores the labour market, income[...] and consumption, and the whole spectrum [...] working-class movements.

4291 **Jenkins**, M., *The General Strike of 1842*, 1980[...]

4292 **Knowles**, K. G. J. C., *Strikes: A Study [...] Industrial Conflict, with Special Reference t[...] British Experience between 1911 and 1947*, 1952[...]

4293 **Leeson**, R. A., *Strike. A Live Histor[...] 1887-1971*, 1973. Covers 150 strikes in twent[...] major industries from the strikers' point of view[...]

4294 —— *Travelling Brothers: The Six Centurie[...] Road from Craft Fellowship to Trade Unionism[...]* 1979. A study of the tramping system.

4295 **Lovell**, J., *British Trade Unions, 1875-1933[...]* 1977.

4296 **McCord**, N., *Strikes*, 1980. A brief survey[...] with chapters on the 1871 engineers' strikes and o[...] 1926.

4297 **Macdonald**, D. F., *The State and the Trad[...] Unions*, 1960.

4298 **Middlemas**, R. K., *Politics in Industrial Soc[...] ety. The Experience of the British System sinc[...] 1911*, 1979. A study of the politics of industria[...] relations.

4299 **Musson**, A. E., *British Trade Unions[...] 1800-1875*, 1972. Excellent bibliography.

4300 —— *Trade Union and Social History*, 1974[...]

Collected essays.

301 **Orton**, W. A., *Labour in Transition: A survey of British Industrial History since 1914*, 1921.

302 **Pribicevic**, B., *The Shop Stewards' Movement and Workers' Control, 1910-1922*, 1959. See also Hinton (4286), listed above.

303 **Sharp**, I. G., *Industrial Conciliation and Arbitration in Great Britain*, 1950.

304 **Trades Union Congress**, *Seventy Years of Trade Unionism*, 1938.

305 **Webb**, S. and Beatrice, *The History of Trade Unionism*, 1894 (bibliography), 2nd enlarged ed., 1920 (no bibliography).

306 **Wrigley**, C. J., *The Government and Industrial Relations, 1910-21*, 1980.

2. WORKING-CLASS AUTOBIOGRAPHIES

307 **Bamford**, S., *The Autobiography of Samuel Bamford*, ed., W. H. Chaloner, 2 vols., 1967.

308 **Burnett**, J., ed., *Useful Toil: Autobiographies of Working People from the 1820s to the 1920s*, 1974.

309 **Carter**, T., *Memoirs of a Working Man*, 1846.

310 **Chancellor**, Valerie E., ed., *Master and Artisan in Victorian England: The Diary of William Andrews and the Autobiography of William Gutteridge*, 1969.

311 **Herbert**, G., *Shoemaker's Window: Recollection of Banbury Before the Railway Age*, 1972.

312 **Holloway**, J., ed., *The Journals of Two Poor Dissenters, 1786-1880*, 1970. A bricklayer and baker named Swan.

313 **Hopkinson**, J., *Memoirs of a Victorian Cabinet Maker*, 1968, ed. Jocelyne B. Goodman.

314 **Lovett**, W., *The Life and Struggles of William Lovett*, 1876, 2nd ed., introduction by R. H. Tawney, 1920.

315 **Smith**, C. M., *The Working Man's Way in the World*, ed. E. Howe, 1968.

316 **Somerville**, A., *The Autobiography of a Working Man*, 1848, 2nd ed., ed. J. Carswell, 1951.

317 **Thale**, Mary, ed., *The Autobiography of Francis Place*, (*1771-1854*), 1972. See also Rowe (4237) and Wallas (4250), listed above.

318 **Thomson**, C., *The Autobiography of an Artisan*, 1847.

319 **Vincent**, D., *Bread, Knowledge and Freedom: A Study of Nineteenth-Century Working-Class Autobiography*, 1981. A useful analysis of this substantial body of source material. Working-class family life and the pursuit of knowledge receive particular attention.

3. THE LABOUR ARISTOCRACY

4320 **Banks**, J. A., 'Imperialism and the aristocracy of labour'. In *Marxist Sociology in Action*, 1970, 218-37.

4321 **Chaloner**, W. H., *The Skilled Artisan During the Industrial Revolution, 1750-1850*, 1969.

4322 **Gray**, R., *The Aristocracy of Labour in Nineteenth-Century Britain, 1850-1914*, 1981.

4323 **Hobsbawm**, E. J., 'The labour aristocracy in nineteenth-century Britain'. In Hobsbawm (4287), listed above, 272-315.

4324 —— 'The tramping artisan'. In Hobsbawm (4287), listed above, 34-63.

4325 **Moorhouse**, H. F., 'The marxist theory of the labour aristocracy', *Soc.H.*, III, 1978, 61-82.

4326 **More**, C., *Skill and the English Working Class, 1870-1914*, 1980. Considers the nature of technology in various industries the growth of technical education and the implications for the labour aristocracy.

4327 **Pelling**, H. M., 'The concept of the labour aristocracy'. In *Popular Politics and Society in Late Victorian Britain*, 1968, 37-61.

4328 **Price**, R., *An Imperial War and the British Working Class: Working Class Attitudes and Reactions to the Boer War, 1899-1902*, 1972.

4. THE T.U.C., THE LABOUR PARTY, THE I.L.P. AND THE FABIAN SOCIETY

4329 **Bealey**, F. and Pelling, H. M., *Labour and Politics, 1900-1906: A History of the Labour Representation Committee*, 1958.

4330 **Birch**, L., ed., *The History of the Trades Union Congress, 1868-1968*, 1968.

4331 **Brand**, C. F., 'The conversion of British trade unions to political action', *A.H.R.*, XXX, 1924, 251-70.

4332 **Brown**, E. H. P., *The Growth of British Industrial Relations from the Standpoint of 1906-14*, 1959.

4333 **Cole**, G. D. H., 'Some notes on British trade unionism in the third quarter of the nineteenth century'. In Carus-Wilson, ed. (245), listed above, 144, III, 202-21.

4334 **Davis**, W. J., *The British Trades Union Congress: History and Recollections*, 2 vols., 1910, 1916.

4335 **Dowse**, R. E., *Left in the Centre*, 1966. History of the Independent Labour Party.

4336 **Duffy**, A. E. P., 'New Unionism in Britain, 1889-90: a reappraisal', *Ec.H.R.*, 2nd ser., XIV, 1961, 306-19.

4337 **Frow**, E. and Katanka, M., *1868: Year of the Unions*, 1968.

4338 **Garbati**, J., 'British trade unionism in the mid-Victorian era', *University of Toronto Quarterly*, XX, 1950-51, 69-84.

4339 **Gillespie**, F. E., *Labor and Politics in England, 1850-1867*, Durham, N. C., 1927.

4340 **Harrison**, M., *Trade Unions and the Labour Party since 1945*, 1960.

4341 **Harrison**, R., *Before the Socialists: Studies in Labour and Politics, 1861-1881*, 1965.

4342 **Leventhal**, F. M., *Respectable Radical: George Howell and Victorian Working-class Politics*, 1971.

4343 **London Trades Council**, *The First Annual Trades Union Directory of the United Kingdom*, 1861. Reprinted 1968.

4344 **Lovell**, J. and Roberts, B. C., *A Short History of the T.U.C.*, 1968.

4345 **McBriar**, A. M., *Fabian Socialism and English Politics, 1884-1918*, 1962. Excellent bibliography, 350-74.

4346 **McKenzie**, N., ed., *The Letters of Sidney and Beatrice Webb*, 3 vols., 1978.

4347 —— *Socialism and Society. A New View of the Webb Partnership*, 1978.

4348 —— and Jeanne, *The First Fabians*, 1977.

4349 **McKibbin**, R., *The Evolution of the Labour Party, 1910-1924*, 1975.

4350 **Musson**, A. E., *The Congress of 1868: The Origins and Establishment of the Trades Union Congress*, 1955, 2nd rev. ed., 1968.

4351 **National Association for the Promotion of Social Science**, *Trades' Societies and Strikes*, 1860. Reprinted 1968.

4352 **Pease**, E. R., *The History of the Fabian Society*, 1918, 3rd ed., 1963.

4353 **Pelling**, H. M., *A Short History of the Labour Party*, 1961, 3rd rev. ed., 1968. Useful guides to further reading at each end of each chapter.

4354 —— *The Origins of the Labour Party, 1880-1900*, 1954, 2nd ed., 1965, with excellent bibliographical essay, 234-45.

4355 —— *Social Geography of British Elections 1885-1910*, 1967.

4356 **Poirier**, P. P., *The Advent of the Labour Party*, 1958. History of the Labour Representation Committee.

4357 Roberts, B. C., *The Trades Union Congress, 1868-1921*, 1958.

4358 **Webb**, S. and Beatrice, *Our Partnership*, 1948.

5. HISTORIES OF UNIONISM IN PARTICULAR INDUSTRIES

AGRICULTURE

4359 **Dunbabin**, J. P. D., 'The "Revolt of the Field" the agricultural labourers' movement in the 1870s *P.P.*, 26, 1963, 68-97, (see also *P.P.*, 27, 196 109-13 for further discussion). See also Dunbab (2985), listed above.

4360 **Edwards**, G., *From Crow-scaring to Westmi ster: An Autobiography*, 1922, 2nd ed., 1957.

4361 **Fussell**, G. E., *From Tolpuddle to T.U.C.: Century of Farm Labourers' Politics*, 1948.

4362 **Green**, F. E., *A History of the Englis Agricultural Labourer, 1870-1920*, 1920. Main about agricultural trade unionism.

4363 **Groves**, R., *Sharpen the Sickle! The Histo of the Farm Workers' Union*, 1949.

4364 **Horn**, Pamela L., *Joseph Arch (1826-1919 the Farm Workers' Leader*, 1971. A model bi graphy with abundant documentation.

4365 **Marlow**, Joyce, *The Tolpuddle Martyrs*, 197 See also Trades Union Congress (4368), list below.

4366 **Russell**, R. C., *The 'Revolt of the Field' Lincs.: The Origins and Early History of Far Workers' Trade Unions*, 1956.

4367 **Selley**, E., *Village Trade Unions in Two Ce turies*, 1919.

4368 **Trades Union Congress**, *The Book of the Ma tyrs of Tolpuddle*, 1934. See also Marlow (4365 listed above.

ENGINEERING AND METALWORKERS

4369 **Allen**, E., Clarke, J. F., McCord, N., and Row D. J., eds, *The North-East Engineers' Strikes 1871*, 1971.

4370 **Fyrth**, H. J., and Collins, H., *The Found Workers: A Trade Union History*, 1959.

4371 **Jefferys**, J. B., *The Story of the Enginee 1800-1945*, 1946. The Amalgamated Society Engineers and the Amalgamated Engineerin Union.

4372 **Kidd**, A. T., *History of the Tin-Plate Wor ers' and Sheet-Metal Workers' and Brazier Societies*, 1949.

4373 **Mortimer**, J. E., *A History of the Associatio of Engineering and Shipbuilding Draughtsme 1960.

4374 —— *History of the Boilermakers' Society, 1834-1906*, 1973.

4375 **Owen**, J., *Ironmen: Short History of th National Union of Blastfurnacemen, 1878-193*

1935, 2nd rev. ed., 1953.

4376 **Pugh**, A., *Men of Steel, by One of Them: A Chronicle of Eighty-eight Years of Trade Unionism*, 1952.

BUILDERS AND WOODWORKERS

4377 **Connelly**, T. J., *The Woodworkers, 1860-1960*, 1960.

4378 **French**, J. O., *Plumbers in Unity: History of the Plumbing Trades Union, 1865-1965*, 1965.

4379 **Higenbottam**, S., *Our Society's History*, 1939. The Amalgamated Society of Woodworkers.

4380 **Hilton**, W. S., *Foes to Tyranny: A History of the Amalgamated Union of Building Trade Workers*, 1963.

4381 **Newman**, J. R., *The N.A.O.P. Heritage: A Short Historical Review of the Development of the National Association of Operative Plasterers 1860-1960*, 1961.

4382 **Postgate**, R. W., *The Builders' History*, 1923.

4383 **Price**, R., *Masters, Unions and Men. Work Control in Building and the Rise of Labour, 1830-1914*, 1980.

RAILWAY LABOUR

4384 **Hudson**, K., *Working to Rule: Railway Workshop Rules: A Study of Industrial Discipline*, 1970.

4385 **Williams**, A., *Life in a Railway Factory*, 1915. Reprinted with a new introduction, 1969. Deals with the Swindon works.

4386 **Bagwell**, P. S., *The Railwaymen: the History of the National Union of Railwaymen*, 1963. Vol. II: *The Beeching Era and After*, 1982.

4387 **Coleman**, T., *The Railway Navvies*, 1965, 2nd rev. ed., 1968. Excellent guide to sources and selected bibliography, 238-46 of 2nd ed.

4388 **Kingsford**, P. W., *Victorian Railwaymen: The Emergence and Growth of Railway Labour, 1830-1870*, 1970.

4389 **Lewis**, R. A., 'Edwin Chadwick and the railway labourers', *Ec.H.R.*, 2nd ser., III, 1950, 107-18.

4390 **McKenna**, F., *The Railway Workers, 1840-1970*, 1980.

4391 **McKillop**, N., *The Lighted Flame: A History of the Associated Society of Locomotive Engineers and Firemen*, 1950.

COAL MINING

4392 **Arnot**, R. P., *The Miners: A History of the Miners' Federation of Great Britain, 1889-1910*, 1949.

4393 —— *The Miners: Years of Struggle: A History*

of the Miners' Federation of Great Britain from 1910 onwards, 1953.

4394 —— *The Miners in Crisis and War: A History of the Miners' Federation of Great Britain from 1930 onwards*, 1961.

4395 **Benson**, J., *British Coalminers in the Nineteenth Century: A Social History*, 1980. Has chapters on the miner at work, on earnings, domestic life, and on community and recreation.

4396 **Challinor**, R., *The Lancashire and Cheshire Miners*, 1972. A study in trade union history from the 1840s onwards.

4397 —— and Ripley, B., *The Miners Association: A Trade Union in the age of the Chartists*, 1969.

4398 **Daunton**, M. J., 'Down the pit: work in the Great Northern and South Wales coalfields, 1870-1914', *Ec.H.R.*, 2nd ser., XXXIV, 1981, 578-97.

4399 **Garside**, W. R., *The Durham Miners, 1919-60*, 1971.

4400 **Gregory**, R., *The Miners and British Politics, 1906-14*, 1968.

4401 **Griffin**, A. R., *The Miners of Nottinghamshire A History of the Nottinghamshire Miners' Association*, I, 1956.

4402 —— *The Miners of Nottinghamshire, 1914-1944: A History of the Nottinghamshire Miners' Union*, II, 1962.

4403 **McCormick**, B. J., *Industrial Relations in the Coal Industry*, 1979.

4404 **Machin**, F., *The Yorkshire Miners: A History*, I, 1958.

4405 **Samuel**, R., ed., *Miners, Quarrymen, and Salt Workers*, 1977. Has two chapters on the Durham miners. Slate quarrymen, Cheshire saltworkers, and mineral workers receive attention in the rest of the volume.

4406 **Taylor**, A. J., 'The Miners' Association of Great Britain and Ireland, 1842-48 . . .'. *Economica*, XXII, 1955, 45-60.

4407 **Webb**, S., *The Story of the Durham Miners, 1662-1921*, 1921.

4408 **Welbourne**, E., *The Miners' Unions of Northumberland and Durham*, 1923.

4409 **Williams**, J. E., *The Derbyshire Miners: A Study in Industrial and Social History*, 1962.

PRINTING AND PUBLISHING

4410 **Bundock**, C. J., *The National Union of Journalists: A Jubilee History, 1907-1957*, 1957.

4411 **Healey**, H. A. H. (pseud. T. N. Shane), *Passed for Press: A Centenary History of the Associa-*

tion of the Correctors of the Press, 1954.

4412 **Howe**, E., ed., *The London Compositor: Documents Relating to Wages, Working Conditions and Customs of the London Printing Trade, 1785-1900*, 1947.

4413 —— and Waite, H. H., *The London Society of Compositors: A Centenary History*, 1948.

4414 —— and Child, J., *The Society of London Bookbinders, 1780-1951*, 1952.

4415 **Moran**, J., *Natsopa Seventy-five Years: The National Society of Operative Printers and Assistants, 1889-1964*, 1964.

4416 **Musson**, A. E., *The Typographical Association: Origins and History up to 1949*, 1954.

WHITE-COLLAR AND SERVICE WORKERS

4417 **Anderson**, G., *Victorian Clerks*, 1976. Deals with their status, work conditions and salaries, and with their involvement in voluntary associations, trade unions and commercial education.

4418 **Bain**, G. S., *The Growth of White Collar Unionism*, 1970.

4419 **Hoffman**, P. C., *They also Serve: The Story of the Shop Worker*, 1950. See also Whitaker (4426), listed below.

4420 **Hughes**, F., *By Hand and Brain: The story of the Clerical and Administrative Workers' Union*, 1953.

4421 **Humphreys**, B. V., *Clerical Unions in the Civil Service*, 1958.

4422 **Radford**, F. H., *'Fetch the Engine . . .': The Official History of the Fire Brigades Union*, 1951.

4423 **Reynolds**, G. W., and Judge, A., *The Night the Police Went on Strike*, 1969.

4424 **Spoor**, A., *White-collar Union: Sixty Years of N.A.L.G.O.*, 1967. National Association of Local Government Officers.

4425 **Swift**, H. G., *A History of Postal Agitation from Fifty Years Ago till the Present Day*, 1900, 2nd ed., 1929.

4426 **Whitaker**, W. B., *Victorian and Edwardian Shopworkers: The Struggle to Obtain Better Conditions and a Half-holiday*, 1973.

COTTON UNIONS

4427 **Hopwood**, E., *A History of the Lancashire Cotton Industry and the Amalgamated Weavers' Association*, 1969.

4428 **Turner**, H. A., *Trade Union Growth Structure and Policy: A Comparative Study of the Cotton Unions*, 1962.

4429 **White**, J. L., *The Limits of Trade Union Mili-*

tancy. The Lancashire Textile Workers, 1910-14, Westport, Conn., 1978.

DOCKERS

4430 **Brown**, R., *Waterfront Organisation In Hull, 1870-1900*, 1972.

4431 **Lovell**, J., *Stevedores and Dockers*, 1969. London waterside unionism c. 1870-1914.

4432 **Pedlar**, Ann (pseud. Stafford), *A Match to Fire the Thames*, 1961. The London match-girls, dockers and gas workers' strikes of 1888-9.

4433 **Smith**, H. L., and Nash, V., *The Story of the Dockers' Strike*, 1889.

FOOTWEAR AND CLOTHING

4434 **Cuthbert**, N. H., *The Lace Makers' Society: A Study of Trade Unionism in the British Lace Industry, 1760-1960*, 1960.

4435 **Fox**, A., *A History of the National Union of Boot and Shoe Operatives, 1874-1957*, 1958.

4436 **Galton**, F. W., ed., *Select Documents, Illustrating the History of Trade Unionism. I: The Tailoring Trade*, 1896.

4437 **Kiddier**, W., *The Old Trade Unions: From Unprinted Records of the Brushmakers*, 1930, 2nd ed., 1932.

4438 **Stewart**, Margaret and Hunter, L., *The Needle is Threaded: The History of an Industry.* (National Union of Tailors and Garment Workers.) 1964.

MISCELLANEOUS

4439 **Hyman**, R., *The Workers' Union*, 1971.

6. DOMESTIC SERVICE

4440 **Gathorne-Hardy**, J., *The Rise and Fall of the English Nanny*, 1972.

4441 **Hecht**, Jean J., *The Domestic Servant Class in Eighteenth-Century England*, 1956.

4442 **Horn**, Pamela L., *The Rise and Fall of the Victorian Servant*, 1975. A general survey of recruitment to domestic service, conditions and pay, and employer-servant relations.

4443 **McBride**, Theresa M., *The Domestic Revolution. The Modernisation of Household Service in England and France, 1820-1920*, 1976.

4444 **Marshall**, Dorothy, *The English Domestic Servant in History*, 1949. (Hist.Ass. pamphlet.)

4445 **Simon**, Daphne, 'Master and servant'. In Saville, ed. (4165), listed above, 160-200. The historical development of the laws affecting employers and employed in mid-nineteenth century England.

4446 **Waterson**, M., *The Servants' Hall. A Domes-*

tic History of Erddig, 1980. Makes full use of the portraits and other records relating to servants in this country house near Wrexham.

7. OTHER CATEGORIES OF FEMALE EMPLOYMENT

4447 **Boston**, S., *Women Workers and the Trade Union Movement*, 1980.

4448 **Burman**, S., ed., *Fit Work for Women*, 1979.

4449 **Davies**, R., *Women and Work*, 1975.

4450 **Ferguson**, N. A., 'Women's work: employment opportunities and economic roles, 1918-39', *Albion*, VII, 1975, 55-68.

4451 **Hewitt**, Margaret, *Wives and Mothers in Victorian Industry*, 1958.

4452 **John**, Angela V., *By the Sweat of their Brow. Women Workers at Victorian Coal Mines*, 1980.

4453 **Neff**, Wanda F., *Victorian Working Women: An Historical and Literary Study of Women in British Industries and Professions, 1832-1850*, 1929, 2nd ed., 1966.

4454 **Pinchbeck**, Ivy, *Women Workers and the Industrial Revolution, 1750-1850*, 1930.

4456 **Soldon**, N. C., *Women in British Trade Unions, 1874-1976*, 1978.

4457 **White**, Rosemary, *Social Change and the Development of the Nursing Profession: A Study of the Poor Law Nursing Service, 1848-1948*, 1978.

8. LOCAL STUDIES

4458 **Barnsby**, G. J., *The Working-Class Movement in the Black Country, 1750-1867*, 1977.

4459 **Bennett**, A., *Oldham Trades and Labour Council . . . 1867-1967*, 1967.

4460 **Corbett**, J., *The Birmingham Trades Council, 1866-1966*, 1966.

4461 **Crossick**, G., *An Artisan Elite in Victorian Society: Kentish London, 1840-80*, 1978.

4462 **Cullen**, M. J., 'The 1887 survey of the London working class', *Internat.R.Soc.H.*, XX, 1975, 48-60.

4463 **Dutton**, H. I. and King, J. E., *Ten Per Cent and No Surrender. The Preston Strike, 1853-4*, 1981.

4464 **Hambling**, W., *A Short History of the Liverpool Trades Council 1848-1948*, 1948.

4465 **Hone**, J. Ann, *For the Cause of Truth. Radicalism in London 1796-1821*, 1982.

4466 **Large**, D. and Whitfield, R., *The Bristol Trades Council, 1873-1973*, 1973.

4467 **Pollard**, S., *A History of Labour in Sheffield*, 1959.

4468 **Prothero**, I. T., *Artisans and Politics in Early Nineteenth-Century London*, 1978.

4469 **Tate**, G. K., *London Trades Council, 1860-1950: A History*, 1950.

4470 **Warburton**, W. H., *The History of Trade Union Organisation in the North Staffordshire Poteries*, 1931.

9. WAGES

4471 **Brown**, E. H. P. and Browne, Margaret H., *A Century of Pay*, 1968.

4472 **Dorfman**, G. A., *Wage Politics in Britain, 1945-67*, 1974.

4473 **Hilton**, G. W., *The Truck System, Including a History of the British Truck Acts, 1465-1960*, 1960.

4474 **Hines**, A. G., 'Trade unions and wage inflation in the United Kingdom, 1893-1961', *R.Economic Studs.*, XXXI, 1964, 221-52.

4475 **Hobsbawm**, E. J., 'Custom, wages and workload', in Hobsbawm (4287), listed above.

4476 **Hunt**, E. H., *Regional Wage Variations in Britain, 1850-1914*, 1973.

4477 **Lipsey**, R. G., 'The relation between unemployment and the rate of change of money wage rates in the United Kingdom 1862-1957: a further analysis', *Economica*, XXVII, 1960, 1-31.

4478 **Phillips**, A. W., 'The relation between unemployment and the rate of change of money wages in the United Kingdom, 1861-1957', *Economica*, XXV, 1958, 283-99.

4479 **Routh**, G., *Occupational Pay in Great Britain, 1906-60*, 1965.

10. THE GENERAL STRIKE OF 1926

4480 **Blaxland**, G., *J.H. Thomas: A Life for Unity*, 1964, 179-203.

4481 **Bullock**, A., *The Life and Times of Ernest Bevin*, I, 1960, 248-390.

4482 **Clegg**, H. A., 'Some consequences of the General Strike', *Proc.Manchester Stat.Soc.*, 1954, 1-29.

4483 **Crook**, W. H., *The General Strike: A Study Of Labour's Tragic Weapon in Theory and Practice*, Chapel Hill, N. C., 1931, 233-495.

4484 —— *Communism and the General Strike*, 1960.

4485 **Farman**, C., *The General Strike*, 1973.

4486 **Glasgow**, G., *General Strikes and Road Transport, Being an Account of the Road Transport Organisation Prepared by the British Government to Meet National Emergencies*, 1926.

4487 **Hills**, R. I., *The General Strike in York, 1926*, Borthwick Papers, 57, 1980.

4488 **Hughes**, M., ed., *Cartoons from the General Strike*, 1968.

4489 **Martin**, K., *The British Public and the General Strike*, 1926.

4490 **Mason**, A., *The General Strike in the North East*, 1970.

4491 **Morris**, Margaret, *The General Strike*, 1976.

4492 **Phillips**, G. A., *The General Strike. The Politics of Industrial Conflict*, 1976.

4493 **Renshaw**, P., *The General Strike*, 1975.

4494 **Simon**, J., *Three Speeches on the General Strike*, 1926.

4495 **Sitwell**, O., 'The General Strike' In *Laughter in the Next Room*, 1949, 199-243.

4496 **Skelley**, G., ed., *The General Strike*, 1976.

4497 **Symons**, J., *The General Strike: A Historical Portrait*, 1957.

II. THE COMMUNIST PARTY

4498 **Collins**, H., and Abramsky, C., *Karl Marx and the British Labour Movement: The Years of the First International*, 1965.

4499 **Holton**, R., *British Syndicalism, 1900-14. Myths and Realities*, 1976.

4500 **Klugmann**, J., *History of the Communist Party of Great Britain*, Vol. I (*1919-1924*), 1968. Vol. II (*1925-1927: The General Strike*), 1969.

4501 **MacFarlane**, L. J., *The British Communist Party: Its Origin and Development until 1929*, 1966.

4502 **MacIntyre**, S., *Little Moscows: Communism and Working-Class Militancy in Inter-War Britain*, 1980.

4503 **Martin**, R., *Communism and the British Trade Unions, 1924-1933: A Study of the National Minority Movement*, 1969.

4504 **Pelling**, H. M., *The British Communist Party: A Historical Profile*, 1958.

(d) **THE WOMAN QUESTION**

4505 **Barrow**, M., ed., *Women, 1870-1928*, 1981. A select guide to printed and archival sources in the U.K.

4506 **Mitchell**, G., ed., *The Hard Way Up: The Autobiography of Hannah Mitchell, Suffragette and Rebel*, 1968.

4507 **Pankhurst**, E. Sylvia, *The Suffragette Movement. An Intimate Account of Persons and Ideals*, 1931.

4508 **Adam**, R., *Woman's Place, 1910-75*, 1975.

4509 **Banks**, J. A. and Olive, *Feminism and Family Planning in Victorian England*, 1964.

4510 **Basch**, F., *Relative Creatures: Victorian Women in Society and the Novel, 1837-67*, 1975.

4511 **Bell**, E. M., *Octavia Hill. A Biography*, 1942.

4512 **Bott**, A. and Clephane, Irene, *Our Mothers . . Late Victorian Women, 1870-1900*, 1932.

4513 **Branca**, Patricia, *Silent Sisterhood: Middle-Class Women in the Victorian Home*, 1975.

4514 **Burston**, Joan N., *Victorian Education and the Ideal of Womanhood*, 1980.

4515 **Crow**, D., *The Victorian Woman*, 1971.

4516 —— *The Edwardian Woman*, 1978.

4517 **Delamont**, S. and Duffin, L., eds., *The Nineteenth-Century Woman: Her Cultural and Physical World*, 1978.

4518 **Dunbar**, Janet, *The Early Victorian Woman: Some Aspects of Her Life, 1837-1857*, 1953.

4519 **Dyhouse**, Carol, *Girls Growing up in Late Victorian and Edwardian England*, 1981.

4520 **Fletcher**, Sheila, *Feminists and Bureaucrats: A Study in the Development of Girls' Education in the Nineteenth Century*, 1980.

4521 **Fulford**, R., *Votes for Women: The Story of a Struggle*, 1957, 2nd ed., 1958. Good bibliographical appendix, 273-83.

4522 **Harrison**, B., *Separate Spheres: The Opposition to Women's Suffrage in Britain*, 1978.

4523 **Hellerstein**, Erna O., Hume, L. P. and Offen, Karen M., eds., *Victorian Women: A Documentary Account of Women's Lives in Nineteenth-Century England, France, and the United States*, 1981.

4524 **Holcombe**, Lee, *Victorian Ladies at Work: Middle-class Working Women in England and Wales, 1850-1914*, 1974.

4525 **Hollis**, Patricia M., *Women in Public, 1850-1900: Documents of the Victorian Women's Movement*, 1979.

4526 **McGregor**, O. R., *Divorce in England: A Centenary Study*, 1957.

4527 **MacWilliams-Tullberg**, Rita, *Women at Cambridge*, 1975.

4528 **Mitchell**, D., *The Fighting Pankhursts: A Study of Tenacity*, 1967. Select bibliography, 341-4.

4529 **Newton**, Stella M., *Health, Art and Reason. Dress Reformers of the Nineteenth Century*, 1975. Explores feminist attacks on the tyranny of fashion.

4530 **O'Neill**, W., *The Woman Movement in Britain and America*, 1969.

4531 **Pedersen**, Joyce S., 'Schoolmistresses and headmistresses: elites and education in nineteenth-century England', *J.Brit.Studs.*, XV, 1975, 135-62.

4532 **Prochaska**, F. K., *Women and Philanthropy in Nineteenth-Century England*, 1980.

4533 **Purvis**, June, 'Separate spheres and inequality in the education of working-class women, 1854-1900', *H.Educ.*, X, 1981, 227-43.

4534 **Rees**, B., *The Victorian Lady*, 1977.

4535 **Rosen**, A., *Rise Up Women. The Militant Campaign of the Women's Social and Political Union, 1903-14*, 1974.

4536 **Rover**, Constance, *Women's Suffrage and Party Politics in Great Britain, 1866-1914*, 1967.

4537 —— *Love, Morals and The Feminists*, 1970.

4538 **Vicinus**, Martha, ed., *Suffer and Be Still. Women in the Victorian Age*, Bloomington, Ind., 1972. Discusses the social position and sexuality of Victorian women.

4539 —— *A Widening Sphere. Changing Roles of Victorian Women*, Bloomington, Ind., 1977.

STANDARDS OF LIVING

a) HOUSING

4540 **Wall**, R., ed., *Slum Conditions in London and Dublin*, 1974. Reprints articles from the *Journal of the Royal Statistical Society*.

4541 **Brunskill**, R. W., *Illustrated Handbook of Vernacular Architecture*, 1970. Excellent bibliography, 212-24.

4542 **Burnett**, J., *A Social History of Housing, 1815-1970*, 1978.

4543 **Chadwick**, G. F., *The Works of Sir Joseph Paxton, 1803-1865*, 1961.

4544 **Chapman**, S. D., ed., *The History of Working-Class Housing: A Symposium*, 1971.

4545 **Chesher**, V. M. and F. J., *The Cornishman's House: An Introduction to the History of Traditional Domestic Architecture in Cornwall*, 1968.

4546 **Cook**, O. and Smith, E., *English Cottages and Farmhouses*, 1954.

4547 —— *The English House through Seven Centuries*, 1968; bibliography, 313-16.

4548 **Clifton-Taylor**, A., *The Pattern of English Building*, 1962; bibliography, 343-7.

4549 **Dunbar**, J. G., *The Historic Architecture of Scotland*, 1966.

4550 **Dutton**, R., *The Victorian Home: Some Aspects of Nineteenth-century Taste and Manners*, 1954.

4551 **Eden**, P. M., *Small Houses in England, 1520-1820: Towards a Classification*, 1969.

4552 **Fletcher**, V., *Chimney Pots and Stacks: An Introduction to Their History, Variety and Identification*, 1968.

4553 **Forrester**, H., *The Smaller Queen Anne and Georgian House, 1700-1840*, 1964.

4554 **Gauldie**, Enid M., *Cruel Habitations: A History of Working-class Housing, 1780-1918*, 1974.

4555 **Girouard**, M., *Life in the English Country House. A Social and Architectural History*, New Haven, Conn., 1978.

4556 —— *The Victorian Country House*, 1979.

4557 **Gloag**, J., *The English Tradition in Architecture*, 1963; bibliography, 241-7.

4558 —— *Victorian Comfort: A Social History of Design from 1830-1900*, 1961. Should be used with caution.

4559 —— *Victorian Taste: Some Social Aspects of Architecture and Industrial Design, from 1820 to 1900*, 1962; bibliography, 159-65.

4560 **Goodhart-Rendel**, H. S., *English Architecture since the Regency: An Interpretation*, 1953.

4561 **Hadfield**, M., *Landscape with Trees*, 1967; bibliography, 186-92.

4562 **Hartley**, Marie and Ingilby, Joan, *Life and Tradition in the Yorkshire Dales*, 1968.

4563 **Henderson**, A., *The Family House in England*, 1964.

4564 **Hitchcock**, H.-R., *Architecture, Nineteenth and Twentieth Centuries*, 1958; bibliography, 473-83.

4565 **Hussey**, C., *English Country Houses: Early Georgian, 1715-1760*, 1955.

4566 —— *English Country Houses: Mid-Georgian, 1760-1800*, 1956.

4567 —— *English Country Houses: Late Georgian, 1800-1840*, 1958.

4568 —— *English Gardens and Landscapes 1700-1750*, 1967.

4569 **Iredale**, D., *This Old House*, 1968.

4570 **Jenkins**, F., *Architect and Patron*, 1961.

4571 **Jones**, S. R., *English Village Homes and Country Buildings*, 1936.

4572 **Kerr**, Barbara, *Dorset Cottages*, Dorset Monographs, 4, 1965.

4573 **Lees-Milne**, J., *English Country Houses: Baroque, 1685-1715*, 1970.

4574 **Lloyd**, N., *A History of the English House from Primitive Times to the Victorian Period*, 1931.

4575 **Melling**, J., ed., *Housing, Social Policy and the State*, 1980.

4576 **Potter**, M. and A., 'The changing shape of things'; *Houses, Being a Record of the Changes in Construction, Style and Plan of the Smaller English Home from Medieval Times to Present Day*, 1948.

4577 **Pritchard**, R. M., *Housing and the Spatial Structure of the City. Residential Mobility and the Housing Market in an English City since the Industrial Revolution*, 1976. A case study of Leicester.

4578 **Roberts**, E., 'Working-class housing in Barrow and Lancaster, 1880-1930', *T.H.S.L.C.*, CXXVII, 1977, 109-32.

4579 **Rubinstein**, D., ed., *Victorian Homes*, 1974. A source collection dealing with the homes of all classes of Victorians.

4580 **Simpson**, M. A. and Lloyd, T., eds., *Middle-Class Housing in Britain*, 1976.

4581 **Summerson**, J., *Architecture in Britain, 1530-1830*, 1953, 4th ed., 1963; bibliography, 363-70.

4582 —— *Heavenly Mansions and Other Essays on Architecture*, 1949.

4583 —— *The London Building World of the 1860s*, 1974.

4584 **Swenarton**, M., *Homes Fit for Heroes. The Politics and Architecture of Early State Housing in Britain*, 1981. Deals with the housing legislation which followed the First World War.

4585 **Tarn**, J. N., *Working-class Housing in Nineteenth Century Britain*, 1971.

4586 —— *Five Per Cent Philanthropy: An Account of Housing in Urban Areas, 1840-1914*, 1974.

4587 **Wohl**, A. S., *The Eternal Slum. Housing and Social Policy in Victorian London*, 1977.

4588 **Woodforde**, J., *The Truth about Cottages*, 1969.

(b) FOOD AND DRINK

4589 **Barker**, T. C., McKenzie, J. C. and Yudkin, J., *Our Changing Fare: Two Hundred Years of British Food Habits*, 1966. Contains chapters on marketing, bread, meat, fish and fruit consumption and Scots diet, with detailed references.

4590 —— Oddy, D. J. and Yudkin, J., *The Dietary Surveys of Dr Edward Smith, 1862-3: A New Assessment*, 1970.

4591 —— and Yudkin, J., eds., *Fish in Britain: Trends in its Supply, Distribution and Consumption During the Past Two Centuries*, 1971.

4592 **Burnett**, J., *Plenty and Want: A Social History of Diet in England from 1815 to the Present Day*, 1966.

4593 **Chaloner**, W. H., 'Trends in fish consumption', in Barker *et al.* (4589), listed above, 94-114.

4594 **Crawford**, W. and Broadley, H., *The People's Food*, 1938.

4595 **Filby**, F. A., *History of Food Adulteration and Analysis*, 1934.

4596 **Johnston**, J., *A Hundred Years Eating. Food, Drink, and the Daily Diet in Britain since the late Nineteenth Century*, 1977.

4597 **Morris**, Helen, *Portrait of a Chef: The Life of Alexis Soyer*, 1938.

4598 **Oddy**, D. J. and Miller, D. S., eds., *The Making of the Modern British Diet*, 1976. Eighteen essays grouped under three main headings: supply, consumption, and nutritional evaluation.

4599 **Palmer**, A., *Movable Feasts*, 1952. Reprinted 1953. Changing English mealtimes.

4600 **Salaman**, R. N., *The History and Social Influence of the Potato*, 1949.

4601 **Unwin**, Jane C., ed., *The Hungry Forties, or Life under the Bread Tax*, 1904. See also Ashley (401), Drummond and Wilbraham (1033), Wilson (1040) and Cheke (1646), listed above.

(c) THE STANDARD OF LIVING CONTROVERSY

4602 **Ashton**, T. S., 'The standard of life of the workers in England, 1790-1830'. In Hayek, ed. (89), listed above, 127-59.

4603 —— Changes in standards of comfort in eighteenth-century England', *Proc.Brit.Acad.*, XLI, 1955, 171-87.

4604 **Barnsby**, G. J., 'The Standard of living in the Black Country during the nineteenth century', *Ec.H.R.*, 2nd Ser., XXIV, 1971, 220-33.

4605 **Chaloner**, W. H., *The Hungry Forties*, Hist.Ass. pamphlet, 1957, 3rd rev. ed., 1963.

4606 **Collier**, Frances, *The Family Economy of the Working Classes in the Cotton Industry, 1784-1833*, 1964.

4607 **Gilboy**, Elizabeth, W., *Wages in Eighteenth-Century England*, Cambridge, Mass., 1934.

4608 —— 'The cost of living and real wages in eighteenth-century England', *Review of Economic Statistics*, XVIII, 1936, 134-43.

4609 **Hartwell**, R. M., 'Interpretations of the Industrial Revolution in England', *J.Ec.H.*, XIX, 1959, 229-49.

4610 —— 'The standard of living controversy: a summary'. In Hartwell, ed., (2549), listed above, 167-79.

4611 —— 'The rising standard of living in England, 1800-1850'. In Hartwell (2552), listed above, 313-45.

4612 **Hobsbawm**, E. J., 'The British standard of living, 1790-1850', *Ec.H.R.*, 2nd ser., X, 1957, 46-48. Reprinted with additions in Hobsbawm (4287), listed above, 64-104.

4613 —— and Hartwell, R. M., 'The standard of living during the Industrial Revolution: a discussion', *Ec.H.R.*, 2nd ser., XVI, 1963, 120-46.

4614 **Inglis**, B., *Poverty and the Industrial Revolution*, 1971. Largely an attack on the Classical Economists.

4615 **Neale**, R. S., 'The standard of living, 1780-1844: a regional and class study', *Ec.H.R.*, 2nd ser., XIX, 1966, 590-606.

4616 **Pollard**, S., 'Investment, consumption and the Industrial Revolution', *Ec.H.R.*, 2nd ser., XI, 1958, 215-36.

4617 **Taylor**, A. J., ed., *The Standard of Living in Britain in the Industrial Revolution*, 1975. Reprints key contributions to the debate from Gilboy, Tucker, Ashton, Hartwell, Hobsbawm, Thompson and Neale.

4618 **Tucker**, R. S., 'Real wages of artisans in London, 1729-1935', *J.American Statistical Assn.*, XXXI, 1936, 73-84.

4619 **Williams**, J. E., 'The British standard of living, 1750-1850', *Ec.H.R.*, 2nd ser., XIX, 1966, 581-9.

4620 **Wilsher**, P., *The Pound in Your Pocket, 1870-1970*, 1970.

4621 **Woodruff**, W., 'Capitalism and the Victorians: a contribution to the discussion on the Industrial Revolution', *J.Ec.H.*, XVI, 1956, 1-17.

ECONOMIC THOUGHT AND POLICY

4622 **Bahmueller**, C. F., *The National Charity Company. Jeremy Bentham's Silent Revolution*, 1982.

4623 **Berg**, Maxine, *The Machinery Question and the Making of Political Economy, 1815-48*, 1980. A major study of the politico-economic debate on the machinery question.

4624 **Bowley**, Marian, *Nassau Senior and Classical Economics*, 1937.

4625 **Brebner**, J. B., 'Laissez-faire and state intervention in nineteenth-century Britain' in Carus-Wilson ed. (245), listed above, III, 252-62.

4626 **Cheyney**, E. P., *Modern English Reform, from Individualism to Socialism*, Philadelphia, 1931.

4627 **Clark**, G. K., 'Statesmen in disguise', *H. J.*, II, 1959, 19-39.

4628 **Coats**, A. W., ed., *The Classical Economists and Economic Policy*, 1971.

4629 **Cromwell**, Valerie, 'Interpretations of nineteenth-century administration: an analysis', *Vic.Studs.*, IX, 1965-6, 245-58.

4630 —— *Revolution or Evolution. British Government in the Nineteenth Century*, 1977.

4631 **Cullen**, M. J., *The Statistical Movement in Early Victorian Britain. The Foundations of Empirical Social Research*, 1975.

4632 **Deane**, Phyllis, *The Evolution of Economic Ideas*, 1978.

4633 **Dicey**, A. V., *Lectures on the Relation between Law and Public Opinion in England During the Nineteenth Century*, 1905, 2nd ed., 1914. Reprinted 1952.

4634 **Fetter**, F. W., *The Economist in Parliament, 1780-1868*, 1980.

4635 **French**, D., *British Economic and Strategic Planning, 1905-15*, 1982.

4636 **Gordon**, B., *Economic Doctrine and Tory Liberalism, 1824-30*, 1980.

4637 —— *Political Economy in Parliament*, 1976.

4638 **Gore**, C., ed., *Property: Its Rights and Duties*, 1914, 2nd ed., 1915 with an additional essay.

4639 **Halévy**, E., *The Growth of Philosophic Radicalism*, Eng.trans., 1928, rev. ed., 1952.

4640 **Harrod**, R. F., *The Life of John Maynard Keynes*, 1951.

4641 **Hart**, Jenifer M., 'Nineteenth-century social reform: a Tory interpretation of history', *P.P.*, 31, 1965, 39-61.

4642 **Hilton**, B., *Corn, Cash, Commerce: The Economic Policies of Tory Governments, 1815-30*, 1977.

4643 **Hollander**, S., 'Ricardo and the Corn Laws: A Revision', *Hist.Pol.Econ*, IX, 1977, 1-47.

4644 **Holmes**, C. J., 'Laissez faire in theory and practice: Britain, 1800-75', *J.Europ.Ec.H.*, V, 1976, 671-88.

4645 **Horne**, T. A., *The Social Thought of Bernard Mandeville. Virtue and Commerce in Early Eighteenth-Century England*, 1978.

4646 **Howson**, Susan, and Winch, D., *The Economic Advisory Council, 1930-39*, 1977.

4647 **Hume**, L. J., *Bentham and Bureaucracy*, 1981.

4648 **Hutchinson**, T. W., *A Review of Economic Doctrines, 1870-1929*, 1953.

4649 **James**, Patricia, *Population Malthus: His Life and Times*, 1979. See also Peterson (4665), below.

4650 **Jha**, N., *The Age of Marshall: Aspects of British Economic Thought, 1890-1915*, 2nd ed., 1973.

4651 **Lekachman**, R., *The Age of Keynes: A Biographical Study*, 1967.

4652 **Levy**, S. L., *Nassau W. Senior, 1790-1864*, 1970.

4653 **Lubenow**, W. C., *The Politics of Government Growth: Early Victorian Attitudes Towards State Intervention, 1853-1848*, 1971.

4654 **MacDonagh**, O., *A Pattern of Government Growth 1800-60: The Passenger Acts and their Enforcement*, 1961.

4655 —— 'The nineteenth-century revolution in government: a reappraisal', *H. J.*, I, 1958, 52-67.

4656 —— *Early Victorian Government, 1830-70*, 1977.

4657 **McGregor**, O. R., 'Social research and social policy in the nineteenth century', *Brit.J.Soc.*, VIII, 1957, 146-57.

4658 **McKibbin**, R., 'The economic policy of the second Labour government, 1929-31', *P.P.*, 68, 1975, 95-123.

4659 **Mack**, Mary P., 'The Fabians and Utilitarianism', *J.H.Ideas*, XVI, 1955, 76-88.

4660 **O'Brien**, D. P., *The Classical Economists*, 1975.

4661 **Parris**, H., *Constitutional Bureaucracy: The Development of Central Administration since the Eighteenth Century*, 1969.

4662 —— 'The nineteenth-century revolution in government: a reappraisal reappraised', *H. J.*, III, 1960, 17-37.

4663 **Peden**, G. C., *British Re-armament and the Treasury, 1932-9*, 1979.

4664 **Pellew**, Jill, *The Home Office, 1848-1914: From Clerks to Bureaucrats*, 1982.

4665 **Peterson**, W., *Malthus*, 1979. See also James (4649), above.

4666 **Pollard**, S., *The Wasting of the British Economy. British Economic Policy, 1945 to the Present*, 1982.

4667 **Robbins**, L., *The Theory of Economic Policy in English Classical Political Economy*, 1952.

4668 —— *Political Economy: Past and Present. A Review of Leading Theories of Economic Policy*, 1976.

4669 **Shelton**, G., *Dean Tucker and Eighteenth-Century Economic and Political Thought*, 1981.

4670 **Skinner**, A. S., and Wilson, T., eds., *Essays on Adam Smith*, 1976.

4671 **Stark**, W., ed., *Economic Writings of Jeremy Bentham*, 1952, I, (introduction).

4672 **Sturges**, R. P., *Economists' Papers, 1750-1950. A Guide to Archive and other Sources for the History of British and Irish Economic Thought*, 1975.

4673 **Sykes**, A., *Tariff Reform in British Politics, 1903-13*, 1979.

4674 **Taylor**, A. J., *Laissez-faire and State Intervention in Nineteenth Century Britain*, 1972.

4675 **Tomlinson**, J., *Problems of British Economic Policy, 1870-1945*, 1981.

4676 **Wilson**, T. and Skinner, A. S., eds., *The Market and the State. Essays in Honour of Adam Smith*, 1976. See also Skinner and Wilson (4670), above.

4677 **Winch**, D., *Economics and Policy: An Historical Study*, 1970. Covers Britain 1900-60. See also Tucker (2009), listed above.

4678 **Wright**, J. F., *Britain in the Age of Economic Management*, 1979.

POOR LAW, CHARITY AND SOCIAL PROTECTION, THE WELFARE STATE

(a) POOR LAW

4679 **Checkland**, S. G. and E. Olive A., eds., *The Poor Law Report of 1834*, 1974.

4680 **Gray**, I., ed., *Cheltenham Settlement Examinations, 1815-1826*, Bristol and Gloucs. Arch.Soc.,

1969.

681 **Rose**, M. E., *The English Poor Law 1780-1930*, 1971. Select documents with commentary.

682 **Watkin**, B., ed., *Documents on Health and Social Services, 1834 to the Present Day*, 1975.

683 **Ashby**, A. W., *One Hundred Years of Poor Law Administration in a Warwickshire Village*, 1912.

684 **Beales**, H. L., 'The New Poor Law', *Hist.*, XV, 1930-31, 308-19.

685 **Blaug**, M., 'The myth of the Old Poor Law and the making of the New', *J.Ec.H.*, XXIII, 1963, 151-84.

686 —— 'The Poor Law Report re-examined', *J.Ec.H.*, XXIV, 1964, 229-45.

687 **Boyson**, R., 'The New Poor Law in North East Lancashire, 1834-71', *T.L.C.A.S.*, LXX, 1960, 45-56.

688 **Branson**, Noreen, *Poplarism, 1919-25. George Lansbury and the Councillors' Revolt*, 1979. See also Keith-Lucas (4708) and Postgate (4716), below.

689 **Brundage**, A., *The Making of the New Poor Law. The Politics of Inquiry, Enactment and Implementation, 1832-79*, 1978.

690 **Coats**, A. W., 'Economic thought and poor law policy in the eighteenth century', *Ec.H.R.*, 2nd ser., XIII, 1960, 39-51.

691 **Cormack**, Una, 'The Royal Commission on the Poor Laws and the Welfare State'. In A.V.S., Lockhead, *A Reader in Social Administration*, 1968.

692 **Cowherd**, R. G., 'The humanitarian reform of the English Poor laws from 1782-1815', *Proc.American Phil.Soc.*, CIV, 1960, 328-42.

693 —— *Political Economists and the English Poor Laws*, Athens, Ohio, 1977. Appraises the influence of economists on social policy from Adam Smith to J. S. Mill.

694 **Crowther**, M. A., *The Workhouse System, 1834-1929*, 1981.

695 **Cuttle**, G., *The Legacy of the Rural Guardians: A Study of Conditions in Mid-Essex*, 1934.

696 **Digby**, Anne, *Pauper Palaces*, 1978. A study of workhouses.

697 —— *The Poor Law in Nineteenth-Century England and Wales*, 1982.

698 **Edsall**, N. C., *The Anti-Poor Law Movement, 1934-44*, 1971.

699 **Fearn**, H., 'The apprenticing of pauper children in the incorporated Hundreds of Suffolk', *Proc.Suffolk Institute of Arch.*, XXVI, 1953,

85-96.

4700 —— 'The financing of the poor law incorporations for the Hundreds of Colneis and Carlford in Suffolk, 1758-1820', *Proc.Suffolk Institute of Arch.*, XXVII, 1956, 96-111.

4701 **Finnegan**, Frances and Sigsworth, E. M., *Poverty and Social Policy. An Historical Study of Batley*, 1978.

4702 **Flinn**, M. W., 'The Poor Employment Act of 1817', *Ec.H.R.*, 2nd ser., XIV, 1961, 82-92.

4703 **Fraser**, D., ed., *The New Poor Law in the Nineteenth Century*, 1976. Has chapters on the working of the Poor Law in urban and rural areas, pauper education, medical provision under the Poor Law, and on the relationship between the Poor Law and philanthropy.

4704 **Hastings**, R. P., *Poverty and the Poor Law in the North Riding of Yorkshire, c.1780-1837*, Borthwick Papers, 61, 1982.

4705 **Henriques**, Ursula R. Q., 'How cruel was the Victorian poor law?', *H. J.*, XI, 1968, 365-71. See also Roberts (4719), below.

4706 —— *Before the Welfare State. Social Administration in Early Industrial Britain*, 1979.

4707 **Hindle**, G. B., *Provision for the Relief of the Poor in Manchester, 1754-1826*, Chet.Soc., 3rd ser., 22, 1975.

4708 **Keith-Lucas**, B., 'Poplarism', *Public Law*, Spring 1962, 52-80.

4709 **Marshall**, Dorothy, *The English Poor in the Eighteenth Century: A Study in Social and Administrative History*, 1926.

4710 —— 'The Old Poor Law, 1662-1795'. In Carus-Wilson, ed. (245), listed above, I, 295-305. Ineffectiveness of law of settlement and removal as a brake on mobility of labour.

4711 **Marshall**, J. D., *The Old Poor Law, 1795-1834*, 1968; Select bibliography, 47-8.

4712 —— 'The Nottinghamshire reformers and their contribution to the Old Poor Law', *Ec.H.R.*, 2nd ser., XIII, 1961, 382-96.

4713 **Mitchelson**, N., *The Old Poor Law in East Yorkshire*, 1953.

4714 **Oxley**, G. W., 'The relief of the permanent poor in S. W. Lancashire under the Old Poor Law'. In Harris, ed. (3839), listed above, 16-49.

4715 —— *Parish Relief in England and Wales, 1601-1834*, 1974.

4716 **Postgate**, R., *Life of George Lansbury*, 1951 Poplarism.

4717 **Poynter**, J. R., *Society and Pauperism: English Ideas on Poor Relief, 1795-1834*, 1969.

4718 **Proctor**, Winifred, 'Poor law administration in

Preston Union, 1838-1848', *T.H.S.L.C.*, 117, 1965, 145-66.

4719 **Roberts**, D., 'How cruel was the Victorian Poor Law?' *H. J.*, VI, 1963, 97-107.

4720 **Rose**, M. E., *The Relief of Poverty, 1834-1914*, 1972.

4721 —— 'The allowance system under the New Poor Law', *Ec.H.R.*, 2nd ser., XIX, 1966, 607-20.

4722 —— 'The Anti-Poor Law agitation'. In Ward (4195), listed above, 78-94, with bibliographical note.

4723 —— 'The Anti-Poor Law Movement in the North of England', *Northern H.*, I, 1966, 70-91.

4724 **Searby**, P., 'The Relief of the Poor in Coventry, 1830-63', *Hist. Jnl.*, XX, 1977, 345-61.

4725 **Taylor**, G., *The Problem of Poverty, 1660-1834*, 1969. Useful short textbook.

4726 **Treble**, J. H., *Urban Poverty in Britain, 1830-1914*, 1979.

4727 **Vorspan**, R., 'Vagrancy and the New Poor Law in late Victorian and Edwardian England', *E.H.R.*, XCII, 1977, 59-81.

4728 **Webb**, Beatrice, *My Apprenticeship*, 1926.

4729 **Webb**, S. and Beatrice, *English Poor Law History: Part I: The Old Poor Law* (to 1832), 1927, 2nd ed., with new introduction, 1963.

4730 —— *English Poor Law History: Part II: The Last Hundred Years*, 2 vols., 1929, 2nd ed., 1963.

4731 —— *English Poor Law Policy*, 1909. Reissued 1963.

4732 **Wells**, R. A. E., *Dearth and Distress in Yorkshire, 1793-1802*, Borthwick Papers, 52, 1977.

4733 **Williams**, K., *From Pauperism to Poverty*, 1981. An uneasy mixture of polemics and empiricism. See also Cutlack (2139), Eden (2157), Gray (2160), Hampson (2161), Jones (2167), Melling (2143) and Nicholls (2178), listed above.

(b) CHARITY AND SOCIAL PROTECTION

4734 **Binfield**, C., *George Williams and the Y.M.C.A.*, 1973.

4735 **Briggs**, A., *Social Thought and Social Action: A Study of the Work of Seebohm Rowntree, 1871-1954*, 1961.

4736 **Cohen**, P., *The British System of Social Insurance: A History and Description*, 1932.

4737 **Fried**, A., and Elman, R. M., *Charles Booth's London: Portrait of the Poor at the Turn of the Century, Drawn from his 'Life and Labour of the People of London'*, 1969.

4738 **Gilbert**, B. B., *The Evolution of National Insurance in Great Britain: The Origins of the Welfare State*, 1966.

4739 —— *British Social Policy, 1914-1939*, 197. Better on the period 1914-31 than on the 1930. critical bibliography, 325-36.

4740 **Hanes**, D. G., *The First British Workmen Compensation Act, 1897*, Yale, 1968.

4741 **Harris**, R. W., *National Health Insurance Great Britain, 1911-1946*, 1946.

4742 **Harrison**, B., 'Philanthropy and the Victorians *Vict.Studs.*, IX, 1965-6, 353-74.

4743 **Lewis**, J., *The Politics of Motherhood. Chi and Maternal Welfare in England, 1900-39*, 198

4744 **MacNicol**, J., *The Movement for Fami Allowances, 1918-45. A Study in Social Polic Development*, 1980.

4745 **Moore**, M. J., 'Social work and social welfar the organisation of philanthropic resources in Br tain, 1900-14', *J.Brit.Studs.*, XVI, 1977, 85-104

4746 **Mowat**, C. L., *The Charity Organisation So iety, 1869-1913: Its Ideas and Work*, 1961.

4747 **Owen**, D., *English Philanthropy, 1660-196* Cambridge, Mass., 1965. Useful, although t time-span clearly hampered the author. See als Harrison (4742), listed above.

4748 **Roberts**, D., *The Victorian Origins of the We fare State*, New Haven, Conn., 1960.

4749 —— *Paternalism in Early Victorian En land*, 1979.

4750 **Rooff**, M., *A Hundred Years of Family We fare. A Study of the Family Welfare Associatio 1869-1969*, 1972.

4751 **Schweinitz**, K. de, *England's Road to Socia Security*, 1943.

4752 **Seldon**, A., ed., *The Long Debate on Poverty* 1972. Essays on the history of social welfare.

4753 **Simey**, Margaret B., *Charitable Effort i Liverpool in the Nineteenth Century*, 1951.

4754 **Simey**, T. S., and Margaret B., *Charles Boot Social Scientist*, 1960.

4755 **Thane**, Pat, ed., *The Origins of British Socia Policy*, 1978.

4756 **Tompson**, R., *The Charity Commission an the Age of Reform*, 1979. A detailed examinatio of the first major Royal Commission of Enquiry int social reform.

4757 **Whiteside**, Noelle, 'Welfare insurance an casual labour: a study of administrative inte vention in industrial employment, 1906-26 *Ec.H.R.*, 2nd ser., XXXII, 1979, 507-22.

4758 **Woodroofe**, Kathleen, *From Charity to Socia Work: A History of Social Work in England an* the United States, 1962.

4759 **Young**, A. F., and Ashton, E. T., *British Social Work in the Nineteenth Century*, 1956.

(c) THE WELFARE STATE

4760 **Bruce**, M., *The Coming of the Welfare State*, 1961, 4th rev. ed., 1968. Extensive bibliographical references from Tudor to modern times.

4761 **Fraser**, D., *The Evolution of the British Wel-* fare State: A History of Social Policy since the Industrial Revolution, 1973.

4762 **Gregg**, Pauline, *The Welfare State: An Economic and Social History of Britain, from 1945 to the Present Day*, 1967. Useful select bibliography, 368-76.

4763 **Harris**, José, *William Beveridge. A Biography*, 1977.

4764 **Hay**, J. R., *The Development of the British Welfare State, 1880-1975*, 1978.

LAW AND ORDER

4765 **Bailey**, V., ed., *Policing and Punishment in Nineteenth-Century Britain*, 1981.

4766 **Beloff**, M., *Public Order and Popular Disturbances, 1660-1714*, 1938, new imp., 1963.

4767 **Booth**, A., 'Food riots in the north west of England, 1790-1801', *P.P.*, 86, 1977, 84-107.

4768 **Browne**, D. G., *The Rise of Scotland Yard: A History of the Metropolitan Police*, 1956.

4769 **Cornish**, W. R., ed., *Crime and Law in Nineteenth-Century Britain*, 1979.

4770 **Darvall**, F. O., *Popular Disturbances and Public Order in Regency England*, 1934, 2nd ed., 1970, with new introduction.

4771 **Hart**, Jenifer M., *The British Police*, 1951. Useful for administrative history.

4772 —— 'The reform of the borough police, 1835-1856', *E.H.R.*, LXX, 1955, 411-27.

4773 **Hay**, D. et al., *Albion's Fatal Tree. Crime and Society in Eighteenth-Century England*, 1975.

4774 —— 'War, dearth and theft in the eighteenth century: the record of the English courts', *P.P.*, 95, 1982, 117-60.

4775 **Howard**, P. A., Smith, B. S., and Wrattan, N. A., *Crime and Punishment in Gloucestershire, 1700-1800*, 1978.

4776 **James**, D. W., ed., *Crime and Punishment in Nineteenth-Century England*, 1975.

4777 **Jones**, D., *Crime, Protest, Community and Police in Nineteenth-Century Britain*, 1982.

4778 —— 'The poacher. A study in Victorian crime and protest', *H.J.*, XXII, 1979, 825-60.

4779 **Mannheim**, H., *Social Aspects of Crime in England between the Wars*, 1940.

4780 **Melossi**, D. and Pavarini, M., *The Prison and the Factory. The Origins of the Penitentiary System*, 1981.

4781 **Midwinter**, E. C., *Law and Order in Early Victorian Lancashire*, 1968.

4782 **Munsche**, P. B., *Gentlemen and Poachers. The English Game Laws, 1671-1831*, 1982. The first full-length study of this subject. The author rejects the view that the Game Laws imposed unjustifiably high penalties, but agrees that they represented notorious examples of class legislation.

4783 **Phillips**, D., *Crime and Authority in Victorian England. The Black Country, 1835-60*, 1977.

4784 **Rogers**, N., 'Popular protest in early Hanoverian London', *P.P.*, 79, 1978, 70-100.

4785 **Rule**, J. G., 'Social crime in the rural South in the eighteenth and early nineteenth centuries', *Southern H.*, I, 1979, 135-54.

4786 **Stevenson**, J., *Popular Disturbances in England, 1700-1870*, 1979.

4787 **Thomas**, J. E., *The English Prison Officer since 1850: A Study in Conflict*, 1972.

4788 **Thomis**, M. I. and Holt, P., *Threats of Revolution in Britain, 1789-1848*, 1977.

4789 **Thompson**, E. P., *Whigs and Hunters. The Origin of the Black Act*, 1975. 'History from below' challenging accepted orthodoxies about eighteenth-century stability.

4790 **Tobias**, J. J., *Crime and Industrial Society in the Nineteenth Century*, 1967.

4791 —— *Crime and Police in England 1700-1900*, 1979.

4792 **Vamplew**, W., 'Ungentlemanly conduct. The control of soccer crowd behaviour in England, 1888-1914', in Smout (2578), 139-54.

4793 **Western**, J. R., *The English Militia in the Eighteenth Century. The Story of a Political Issue, 1660-1802*, 1965. See also Cockburn (2066), Hobsbawm and Rudé (2988), and Mather (4225).

PUBLIC HEALTH AND MORALITY

(a) PUBLIC HEALTH

4794 **Brockington**, C. F., ed., *Papers relating to the Sanitary State of the People of England*, 1973. Reprints the study made by E. H. Greenhow for the General Board of Health.

4795 **Chadwick**, E., *Report on the Sanitary Conditions of the Labouring Population of Great Britain*, 1842, ed. M. W. Flinn, 1965.

4796 **Kay-Shuttleworth**, J. P., *The Moral and Physical Condition of the Working Classes employed in the Cotton Manufacture in Manchester*, 1832. Reprinted with a preface by W. H. Chaloner, 1970.

4797 **Abel-Smith**, B. and Pinker, R., *The Hospitals, 1800-1948: A Study in Social Administration in England and Wales*, 1964.

4798 **Ayers**, Gwendoline M., *England's First State Hospitals and the Metropolitan Asylums Board, 1867-1930*, 1971.

4799 **Briggs**, A., 'Cholera and society in the nineteenth century', *P.P.*, 19, 1961, 76-96.

4800 **Brockington**, C. F., *Medical Officers of Health, 1848-1855*, 1957.

4801 —— *A Short History of Public Health*, 1956.

4802 **Brotherston**, J. H. F., *Observations on the Early Public Health Movement in Scotland*, 1952.

4803 **Bullough**, V. L. and B., *The Care of the Sick: The Emergence of Modern Nursing*, 1979.

4804 **Cartwright**, F. F., *A Social History of Medicine*, 1977.

4805 **Doerner**, K., *Madmen and the Bourgeoisie: A Social History of Insanity and Psychiatry*, 1981.

4806 **Durey**, M., *The Return of the Plague. British Society and the Cholera, 1831-2*, 1979. Comprehensive bibliography.

4807 **Eversley**, D. E. C., 'The cholera in England in 1831-2'. In L. Chevalier, ed., *Le Choléra: la Première Epidémie du XIXe siècle*, La Roche-Sur-Yon, 1958, 157-88.

4808 **Finer**, S. E., *The Life and Times of Sir Edwin Chadwick*, 1952, 2nd ed., 1970.

4809 **Flinn**, M. W., *Public Health Reform in Britain*, 1968. Excellent bibliography, 69-70.

4810 **Frazer**, W. M., *A History of English Public Health, 1834-1939*, 1950.

4811 **Hodgkinson**, Ruth G., *The Origins of the National Health Service: The Medical Services of the New Poor Law 1834-1871*, 1967.

4812 **Jones**, Kathleen, *A History of the Mental Health Services*, 1972.

4813 **Lambert**, R. J., *Sir John Simon, 1816-190 and English Social Administration*, 1963.

4814 —— 'A Victorian National Health Service: sta vaccination, 1855-77', *H. J.*, V, 1962, 1-18.

4815 **Lewis**, R. A., *Edwin Chadwick and the Publ Health Movement, 1832-1854*, 1952.

4816 **Longmate**, N., *King Cholera: The Biograph of a Disease*, 1966.

4817 **McLeod**, R. M., 'The Alkali Acts Admin stration, 1863-84: the emergence of the civil scie tist', *Vict.Studs.*, IX, 1965-66, 85-112.

4818 **Midwinter**, E. C., *Social Administration Lancashire: 1830-1860: Poor Law, Publ Health and Police*, 1969.

4819 —— *Victorian Social Reform*, 1968.

4820 **Morris**, R. J., *Cholera, 1832*, 1976.

4821 **Navarro**, V., *Class Struggle, the State a Medicine: An Historical and Contempora Analysis of the Medical Sector in Great Britai 1978.

4822 **Newsholme**, A., *Fifty Years in Public Healt A Personal Narrative with Comments: T Years Preceding 1909*, 1935.

4823 **Poynter**, F. N. L., ed., *The Evolution of H pitals in Britain*, 1964.

4824 **Scull**, A. T., *Museums of Madness. The Soc Organisation of Insanity in Nineteenth-Centu England*, 1979.

4825 **Simon**, J., *English Sanitary Institution 1890.

4826 **Smith**, F. B., *The People's Health, 1830-19 1979.

4827 **Spink**, W. W., *Infectious Diseases, Preventi and Treatment in the Nineteenth and Twentie Centuries*, 1979.

4828 **Timms**, N., *Psychiatric Social Work in Gre Britain, 1939-62*, 1964.

4829 **Willcocks**, A. J., *The Creation of the Natior Health Service. A Study of Pressure Groups a a Major Policy Decision*, 1967.

4830 **Woodward**, J., *To Do The Sick No Harm: Study of the British Voluntary Hospital Syst to 1875*, 1974.

4831 **Woodward**, J., and Richards, D., eds., *Hea and Popular Medicine in Nineteenth-Centu England. Essays in the Social History Medicine*, 1977.

4832 **Youngson**, A. J., *The Scientific Revolution Victorian Medicine*, 1979.

(b) MORALITY

4833 **Acton**, W., *Prostitution*, 2nd ed., 1870, 3rd abridged ed., 1968, with introduction by P. Fryer, 4th unabridged ed., 1972, with introduction by Anne Humpherys.

4834 **Neild**, K., ed., *Prostitution in the Victorian Age*, 1973. Reprints articles from contemporary periodicals.

4835 **Berridge**, Virginia and Edwards, G., *Opium and the People. Opiate Use in Nineteenth-Century England*, 1982.

4836 **Chaloner**, W. H., 'How immoral were the Victorians? A bibliographical reconsideration', *B. John Rylands Lib.*, LX, 1978, 362-75.

4837 **Chesney**, K., *The Victorian Underworld*, 1970. Chiefly about London.

4838 **Dingle**, A. E., *The Campaign for Prohibition in Victorian England: The United Kingdom Alliance, 1872-95*, 1980.

4839 **Finnegan**, Frances, *Poverty and Prostitution: A Study of Victorian Prostitutes in York*, 1979.

4840 **McHugh**, P., *Prostitution and Victorian Social Reform*, 1980.

4841 **Marcus**, S., *The Other Victorians*, 1966.

4842 **Marsh**, P., *The Conscience of the Victorian State*, 1979.

4843 **Pearsall**, R., *The Worm in the Bud: The World of Victorian Sexuality*, 1969. Excellent references, 529-44.

4844 —— *Public Purity, Private Shame: Victorian Sexual Hypocrisy Exposed*, 1976.

4845 **Pearson**, M., *The Age of Consent. Victorian Prostitution and its Enemies*, 1972.

4846 **Trudgill**, E., *Madonnas and Magdalens. The Origins and Development of Victorian Sexual Attitudes*, 1976.

4847 **Walkowitz**, Judith R., *Prostitution and Victorian Society. Women, Class and the State*, 1980.

4848 **Weeks**, J., *Sex, Politics and Society. The Regulation of Sexuality since 1800*, 1981.

(c) THE TEMPERANCE MOVEMENT

4849 **Harrison**, B., *Drink and the Victorians: The Temperance Question in England 1815-1872*, 1971.

4850 —— *Dictionary of British Temperance Biography*, 1973.

4851 —— 'The British prohibitionists, 1853-1872: a biographical analysis', *Internat. R.Soc.H.*, XV, 1970, 375-467.

4852 **Longmate**, N., *The Waterdrinkers: A History of Temperance*, 1968.

4853 **Reid**, Caroline, 'Temperance, Teetotalism, and Local Culture', *Northern H.*, XIII, 1977, 248-64.

4854 **Wilson**, G. B., *Alcohol and the Nation, 1800-1935*, 1940.

LEISURE AND RECREATION

(a) GENERAL WORKS

4855 **Bailey**, P., *Leisure and Class in Victorian England. Rational Recreation and the Contest for Control, 1830-85*, 1978.

4856 **Chalklin**, C. W., 'Capital expenditure on building for cultural purposes in provincial England, 1730-1830', *Bus. H.*, XXII, 1980, 51-70.

4857 **Clark**, J. and Johnson, R., eds., *Working-Class Culture*, 1979.

4858 **Cunningham**, H., *Leisure in the Industrial Revolution, c.1780-c.1880*, 1980. Analyses the processes of privatisation, institutionalisation and commercialisation of leisure.

4859 **Davidoff**, Leonore, *The Best Circles: Society, Etiquette and the Season*, 1973.

4860 **Dawes**, F., *A Cry from the Streets. The Boys'* Club Movement in Britain from the 1850s to the Present Day, 1975.

4861 **Malcolmson**, R. W., *Popular Recreations in English Society, 1700-1850*, 1973.

4862 **Meller**, Helen E., *Leisure and the Changing City, 1870-1914*, 1976. A case study of Bristol.

4863 **Minihan**, J., *The Nationalisation of Culture. The Development of State Subsidies to the Arts in Great Britain*, 1977.

4864 **Phillips**, J. and P., *Victorians Home and Away*, 1978.

4865 **Plumb**, J. H., *The Commercialisation of Leisure in Eighteenth-Century England*, 1973.

4866 **Rowntree**, B. S. and Lavers, G. R., *English Life and Leisure. A Social Study*, 1951.

4867 **Smith**, M. A., Parker, S., and Smith, C. S., eds., *Leisure and Society in Britain*, 1973.

4868 **Storch**, R. D., 'The problem of working-class leisure: some roots of middle-class moral reform in the industrial north, 1825-50', in Donajgrodzki (4058), above, 138-62.

4869 **Thompson**, E. P., 'Patrician society, plebeian culture', *J.Soc.H.*, VII, 1974, 382-405.

4870 **Waites**, B., Bennett, T., and Martin, G., eds., *Popular Culture: Past and Present*, 1982.

4871 **Walvin**, J., *Leisure and Society, 1830-1950*, 1978.

4872 **Yeo**, Eileen and S., *Popular Culture and Class Conflict, 1590-1914. Explorations in the History of Labour and Leisure*, 1981. A collection of essays dealing predominantly with the nineteenth century.

(b) HOLIDAYS

4873 **Granville**, A. B., *The Spas of England: Principal Sea-Bathing Places*, 3 vols., 1841. Reprinted with an introduction by G. H. Martin, 1971.

4874 **Gilbert**, E. W., 'The holiday industry and seaside towns in England and Wales'. In *Festschrift Leopold G. Scheidl zum 60. Geburtstag*, Vienna, 1965, I, 235-47.

4875 **Hern**, A., *The Seaside Holiday: The History of the English Seaside Resort*, 1967.

4876 **Lickorish**, J. and Kershaw, A. G., *The Travel Trade*, 1958.

4877 **Marsden**, C., *The English at the Seaside*, 1947.

4878 **Pimlott**, J. A. R., *The Englishman's Holiday*, 1947.

4879 —— *The Englishman's Christmas. A Social History*, 1978.

4880 **Pudney**, J., *The Thomas Cook Story*, 1953.

4881 **Walton**, J. K., *The Blackpool Landlady. A Social History*, 1978.

4882 —— 'The demand for working-class seaside holidays in Victorian England', *Ec.H.R.*, 2nd ser., XXXIV, 1981, 249-65.

4883 —— 'Residential amenity, respectable morality and the rise of the entertainment industry: the case of Blackpool', *Lit.&Hist.*, I, 1975, 62-78.

4884 **Walvin**, J., *Beside the Seaside. A Social History of the Popular Seaside Holiday*, 1978.

(c) ENTERTAINMENT

4885 **Bratton**, J. S., *The Victorian Popular Ballad*, 1975.

4886 **Chanan**, M., *The Dream that Kicks. The Pre-*

history and Early Years of Cinema in Britai 1979.

4887 **Colls**, R., *The Collier's Rant. Song and Cu ture in the Industrial Village*, 1977.

4888 **Cunningham**, H., 'The metropolitan fairs: case study in the social control of leisure', in Dona grodzki (4058), above, 163-84.

4889 **Darcy**, C. P., *The Encouragement of the Fi Arts in Lancashire, 1760-1860*, Chet.Soc., 3 ser., 24, 1976.

4890 **Ehrlich**, C., *The Piano: A History*, 1976. Tl history of a Victorian social symbol.

4891 **Elbourne**, R., *Music and Tradition in Ear Industrial Lancashire, 1780-1840*, 1980.

4892 **Gaskell**, S. M., 'Gardens for the working clas Victorian practical pleasure', *Vict.Studs.*, XXII 1980, 479-501.

4893 **Hollingsworth**, B., ed., *Songs of the Peopl Lancashire Dialect Poetry of the Industri Revolution*, 1977.

4894 **Hudson**, K., *A Social History of Museum* 1975.

4895 **Low**, Rachel and Manvell, R., *History of tl British Film*, 3 vols., 1948-50. These cov 1896-1906; 1906-14; and 1914-18.

4896 **McKibbin**, R., 'Working class gambling in Br tain, 1890-1939', *P.P.*, 82, 1979, 147-78.

4897 **Rubinstein**, D., 'Cycling in the 1890s', *Vi Studs.*, XXI, 1977, 47-71.

4898 **Scott**, H., *The Early Doors*, 1946. A soci history of Music Hall.

4899 **Vamplew**, W., *The Turf. A Social an Economic History*, 1976.

4900 **Weber**, W., *Music and the Middle Classes. Tl Social Structure of Concert Life in London, Par and Vienna between 1830 and 1848*, 1975.

4901 **Young**, P., *The Concert Tradition*, 1961.

(d) SPORT

4902 **Baker**, W. J., 'The making of a working-cla football culture in Victorian England', *J.Soc.H* XIII, 1979, 241-52.

4903 **Bale**, J. R., 'Geographical diffusion and tl adoption of professionalism in football in Englar and Wales', *Geog.*, LXIII, 1978, 188-97.

4904 **Carr**, R., *English Fox Hunting: A Histor* 1976.

4905 **Dunning**, E. and Sheard, K., *Barbarians, Ger lemen and Players: A Sociological Study of tl Development of Rugby Football*, 1979.

4906 **Mason**, A., *Association Football and Engli Society, 1863-1915*, 1980. Examines the tran formation of football to a mass working-class sport.

4907 **Walvin**, J., *The People's Game: A Social History of Football*, 1975.

(c) READING HABITS (INCLUDING THE DEVELOPMENT OF PUBLIC LIBRARIES)

4908 **Altick**, R. D., *The English Common Reader: A Social History of the Mass Reading Public 1800-1900*, Chicago, Ill., 1957.

4909 **Hoggart**, R., *The Uses of Literacy*, 1958. A classic study of working-class reading habits.

4910 **James**, L., *Fiction for the Working Man, 1830-1850*, 1963.

4911 —— *Print and People, 1819-51*, 1975.

4912 **Kelly**, T., *Books for the People. An Illustrated History of the British Public Library*, 1977.

4913 —— *Early Public Libraries: A History of Public Libraries in Great Britain before 1850*, 1966.

4914 **Munford**, W. A., *William Ewart, M.P., 1798-1869: Portrait of a Radical*, 1960. Prominent in the free public library movement.

4915 **Neuburg**, V. E., *Popular Literature: A History and Guide*, 1977.

4916 **Rivers**, Isabel, ed., *Books and their Readers in Eighteenth-Century England*, 1982.

4917 **Shattock**, Joanne and Wolff, M., eds., *The Victorian Periodical Press: Samplings and Soundings*, 1982.

4918 **Suvin**, D., 'The social addressees of Victorian Fiction: a preliminary enquiry', *Lit.&H.*, VIII: 1, 1982, 11-40.

4919 **Webb**, R. K., *The British Working-Class Reader, 1790-1848: Literary and Social Tension*, 1955.

THE PRESS AND BROADCASTING

(a) THE PRESS

4920 **Adburgham**, Alison, *Women in Print*, 1972. Covers women authors and women's magazines from 1660 to 1837.

4921 **Anon.**, *History of the Times*, 4 vols., 1935-52.

4922 **Aspinall**, A., *Politics and the Press, 1780-1850*, 1949.

4923 **Ayerst**, D., *Guardian: Biography of a Newspaper*, 1971.

4924 **Camrose**, Lord, *London Newspapers: Their Owners and Controllers*, 1939.

4925 **Collet**, C. D., *History of the Taxes on Knowledge: Their Origin and Repeal*, 2 vols., 1899, 2nd abridged ed., 1933.

4926 **Cranfield**, G. A., *The Development of the Provincial Newspaper, 1700-1760*, 1962. Bibliography, 274-8.

4927 **Ewald**, W. B., *The Newsmen of Queen Anne*, 1956.

4928 **Ffrench**, Yvonne, ed., *News from the Past, 1805-1887: The Autobiography of the Nineteenth Century*, 1934. Extracts from the newspaper press.

4929 **Hanson**, L., *Government and the Press, 1695-1763*, 1936.

4930 **Hollis**, Patricia M., *The Pauper Press: A Study in Working-class Radicalism of the 1830s*, 1970.

4931 **Knight**, C., *Passages of a Working Life during half a century*, 1864-5. Reprinted 1971.

4932 **Lee**, A. J., *The Origins of the Popular Press*, 1976.

4933 **Mills**, W. H., *The Manchester Guardian: A Century of History*, 1921.

4934 **Milne**, M., *Newspapers of Northumberland and Durham in the Nineteenth Century*, 1971.

4935 **Political and Economic Planning**, *Report on the British Press*, 1938.

4936 **Price**, R. G. G., *A History of Punch*, 1957.

4937 **Read**, D., *Press and People, 1790-1850: Opinion in Three English Cities*. (Manchester, Leeds and Sheffield), 1961.

4938 **Siebert**, F. S., *Freedom of the Press in England, 1476-1776: The Rise and Decline of Government Control*, Urbana, Ill., 1965.

4939 **Smith**, A. C. H., *Paper Voices. The Popular Press and Social Change 1935-65*, 1975.

4940 **Weed**, K. K., and Bond, R. P., 'Studies of British newspapers and periodicals from their beginning to 1800: a bibliography'. In *Studies in Philology*, Durham, N. C., 1946.

4941 **White**, Cynthia L., *Women's Magazines, 1693-1968*, 1970.

4942 **Wickwar**, W. H., *The Struggle for the Freedom of the Press, 1819-1832*, 1928.

4943 **Wiener**, J. H., *A Descriptive Finding List of*

Unstamped British Periodicals, 1830-1836, 1970.

4944 —— *The War of the Unstamped: A History of the Movement to Repeal the British Newspaper Tax, 1830-1836*, 1970.

4945 **Wiles**, R. M., *Freshest Advices: Early Provincial Newspapers in England*, Columbus, Ohio, 1965.

(b) BROADCASTING

4946 **Baker**, W. J., *A History of the Marconi Company*, 1970.

4947 **Briggs**, A., *A History of Broadcasting in the United Kingdom*, I: *The Birth of Broadcasting*, 1961; II: *The Golden Age of Wireless*, 1965; III: *The War of Words*, 1970; IV: *Sound and Vision*, 1979.

4948 **Coase**, R. H., *British Broadcasting: A Study in Monopoly*, 1950.

RELIGION, SOCIETY AND ECONOMIC LIFE

(a) GENERAL WORKS

4949 **Briggs**, J. and Sellars, I., eds., *Victorian Nonconformity*, 1973. A documentary collection.

4950 **Thompson**, D. M., *Nonconformity in the Nineteenth Century*, 1972. A very useful collection of documents with an introduction and bibliography.

4951 **Bebbington**, D. W., *The Nonconformist Conscience. Chapel and Politics, 1870-1914*, 1982.

4952 **Binfield**, C., *So Down to Prayers. Studies in English Nonconformity, 1780-1920*, 1977.

4953 **Bradley**, I., *The Call to Seriousness. The Evangelical Impact on the Victorians*, 1976.

4954 **Coleman**, B. I., *The Church of England in the mid Nineteenth Century. A Social Geography*, 1980.

4955 **Everitt**, A. M., *The Pattern of Rural Dissent: The Nineteenth Century*, 1972.

4956 **Field**, C. D., 'The 1851 Religious Census: A select bibliography of materials relating to England and Wales', *Proc.Wesley H.Soc.*, XLI, 1978, 175-82.

4957 **Gay**, J. D., *The Geography of Religion in England*, 1971. Deals mainly with the period after 1750. Useful on the Religious Census of 1851.

4958 **McLeod**, H., *Class and Religion in the Late Victorian City*, 1974. Compares and analyses the social organisation of religion in the East and West Ends and suburbs of London in a critical period of church history.

4959 **Norman**, E. R., *Church and Society in England, 1770-1970: A Historical Study*, 1976.

4960 **Studdert-Kennedy**, K., *Dog Collar Democracy. The Industrial Christian Fellowship, 1919-29*, 1982.

4961 **Wigley**, J., *The Rise and Fall of the Victorian Sunday*, 1980. Relates Sabbatarianism to the position and preferences of the middle classes.

(b) NONCONFORMITY AND ECONOMIC DEVELOPMENT

4962 **Emden**, P. H., *Quakers in Commerce*, 1939.

4963 **Field**, C. D., 'The social structure of English Methodism: eighteenth to twentieth centuries', *Brit. J.Soc.*, XXVIII, 1977, 199-225.

4964 **Gilbert**, A. D., *Religion and Society in Industrial England. Church, Chapel and Social Change, 1740-1914*, 1976.

4965 **Grubb**, Isobel, *Quakerism and Industry before 1800*, 1930.

4966 **Holt**, R. V., *The Unitarian Contribution to Social Progress in England*, 1938, 2nd rev. ed. 1952.

4967 **Isichei**, Elizabeth, *Victorian Quakers*, 1970.

4968 **Raistrick**, A., *Quakers in Science and Industry in the Seventeenth and Eighteenth Centuries*, 1950.

(c) RELIGION AND THE WORKING CLASS

4969 **Armstrong**, A., *The Church of England, the Methodists and Society 1700-1850*, 1973.

4970 **Bebbington**, D. W., 'The city, the countryside and the social gospel in late Victorian Nonconformity', *Studs.Church H.*, XVI, 1979, 415-26.

4971 **Billington**, L., 'Popular religion and social reform: a study of Revivalism and Teetotalism 1830-50', *J.Rel.H.*, X, 1979, 266-93.

4972 **Clark**, G. K., *Churchmen and the Condition*

England, 1832-1885, 1973. See also Soloway (4983), listed below.

73 **Hart**, Jenifer M., 'Religion and social control in the mid nineteenth century' in Donajgrodzki (4058), 108-37.

74 **Himmelfarb**, Gertrude, 'Postscript on the Halévy thesis', *Victorian Minds*, 1968, 292-9.

75 **Hobsbawm**, E. J., 'Methodism and the threat of revolution in Britain'. In (4287), listed above, 23-33.

76 **Inglis**, K. S., *Churches and the Working Classes in Victorian England*, 1963.

77 **McEntee**, G. P., *The Social Catholic Movement in Great Britain*, N. Y., 1927.

78 **Mayor**, S. H., *The Churches and the Labour Movement*, 1967. Deals mainly with the period 1848-1914.

79 **Moore**, R. S., *Pitmen, Preachers and Politics. The Effects of Methodism in a Durham Mining Community*, 1974. Focuses particularly on four mining villages in period 1870 to 1926.

80 **Obelkevich**, J., *Religion and Rural Society. South Lindsey, 1825-75*, 1976.

81 **Semmel**, B., *The Methodist Revolution*, 1974. Reassesses the Methodist synthesis of liberty, order, and national mission.

82 **Smith**, A., *The Established Church and Popular Religion, 1750-1850*, 1971. A collection of documents with commentary.

83 **Soloway**, R. A., *Prelates and People: Ecclesiastical Social Thought in England 1783-1852*, 1969. See also Clark (4972) listed above.

84 **Taylor**, E. R., *Methodism and Politics 1791-1831*, 1935.

85 **Wagner**, D. O., *The Church of England and Social Reform since 1854*, N. Y., 1930.

86 **Ward**, W. R., *Religion and Society in England 1790-1850*, 1972. Based largely on unpublished sources.

87 **Wearmouth**, R. F., *Methodism and the Common People of the Eighteenth Century*, 1945.

88 —— *Methodism and the Working-class Movements of England, 1800-1850*, 1937.

4989 —— *Methodism and the Struggle of the Working Classes 1850-1900*, 1954.

4990 —— *Some Working Class Movements of the Nineteenth Century*, 1948.

4991 —— *The Social and Political Influence of Methodism in the Twentieth Century*, 1957.

4992 **Wickham**, E. R., *Church and People in an Industrial City*, 1957. A pioneer work on the social history of religion. The city is Sheffield.

4993 **Yeo**, S., *Religion and Voluntary Organisations in Crisis*, 1976. A case study (based on Reading) of the impact of capitalism and poverty on the churches between 1890 and 1914.

(d) CHRISTIAN SOCIALISM

4994 **Backstrom**, P. N., *Christian Socialism and Co-operation in Victorian England: Edward Vansittart Neale and the Co-operative Movements*, 1974.

4995 **Jones**, P. d'A., *The Christian Socialist Revival, 1877-1914: Religion, Class and Social Conscience in Late Victorian England*, Princeton, N. J., 1968.

4996 **Masterman**, N. C., *John Malcolm Ludlow: The Builder of Christian Socialism*, 1963.

4997 **Raven**, C. E., *Christian Socialism, 1848-1854*, 1920.

4998 **Saville**, J., 'The Christian Socialists of 1848'. In Saville (4165), listed above, 135-59.

(e) FREETHOUGHT

4999 **Budd**, Susan, *Varieties of Unbelief: Atheists and Agnostics in English Society, 1850-1960*, 1977.

5000 **Gilbert**, A. D., *The Making of Post-Christian Britain. A History of the Secularisation of Modern Society*, 1980.

5001 **Royle**, E., *Radicals, Secularists and Republicans*, 1980.

5002 —— *Victorian Infidels. The Origins of the British Secularist Movement, 1791-1866*, 1975.

EDUCATION

(a) SCHOOLING

03 **Digby**, Anne, and Searby, P., eds., *Children, School and Society in Nineteenth-Century Eng-*

land, 1981. A sourcebook with sections on religion, social class and the economy, teachers, and girls' education. Bibliography.

5004 **Maclure**, J. S., *Educational Documents: Eng-*

land and Wales, 1816-1967, 1968.

5005 **Archer**, R. L., *Secondary Education in the Nineteenth Century*, 1966.

5006 **Armytage**, W. H. G., *Four Hundred Years of English Education*, 1964.

5007 **Banks**, Olive, *Parity and Prestige in English Secondary Education*, 1955.

5008 **Bardshaw**, D. C. A., ed., *Studies in the Government and Control of Education since 1860*, 1970.

5009 **Cruikshank**, Marjorie, *Church and State in English Education, 1870 to the Present Day*, 1964.

5010 **Curtis**, S. J., *The History of Education in Great Britain*, 6th ed., 1965. Bibliography, 711-28.

5011 **Dent**, H. C., *The Training of Teachers in England and Wales, 1800-1975*, 1977.

5012 **Evans**, K., *The Development and Structure of the English Educational System*, 1975.

5013 **Goldstrom**, J. M., *The Social Content of Education, 1808-70. A Study of the Urban Working-Class Reader in England and Ireland*, 1972.

5014 **Gordon**, P., *The Victorian School Manager*, 1974.

5015 **Gosden**, P. H. J. H., *The Development of Educational Administration in England and Wales*, 1966.

5016 —— *Education in the Second World War. A Study in Policy and Administration*, 1976.

5017 **Horn**, Pamela L., *Education in Rural England, 1800-1914*, 1978.

5018 **Hurt**, J., *Education in Evolution: Church, State, Society and Popular Education, 1800-1870*, 1971.

5019 —— *Elementary Schooling and the Working Classes, 1860-1918*, 1979.

5020 **Johnson**, R., 'Educational policy and social control in early Victorian England', *P.P.*, 49, 1970, 96-119.

5021 **Jones**, M. G., *The Charity School Movement: A Study of Eighteenth-century Puritanism in Action*, 1938.

5022 **Kazamias**, A. M., *Politics, Society and Secondary Education in England*, 1966.

5023 **Laqueur**, T. W., *Religion and Respectability. Sunday Schools and English Working-Class Culture, 1780-1850*, New Haven, 1976.

5024 **Lawson**, J. and Silver, H., *A Social History of Education in England*, 1973. A general survey extending from the Middle Ages to the present day. The main emphasis is on the post-1760 period.

5025 **Lowndes**, G. A., *The Silent Social Revolu-tion: An Account of the Expansion of Pub.. Education in England and Wales 1895-193 1950.

5026 **McCann**, P., ed., *Popular Education a: Socialisation in the Nineteenth Century*, 1977

5027 **McLachlan**, H., *English Education under t Test Acts*, 1931. Covers Dissenting academi 1663-1820.

5028 **Maclure**, J. S., *One Hundred Years of Lond Education, 1870-1970*, 1970.

5029 **Murphy**, J., *Church, State and Schools in B tain, 1800-1870*, 1971.

5030 **Musgrave, P. W.**, *Society and Education England since 1800*, 1968, 5th ed., 1972.

5031 **Neuburg**, V. E., *Popular Education Eighteenth-Century England. A Study in Origins of the Mass Reading Public*, 1971.

5032 **Parker**, I., *Dissenting Academies in Englan 1914. See also McLachlan (5027), above.

5033 **Pinchbeck**, Ivy and Hewitt, Margaret, *Childr in English Society, Vol. 2: From the Eighteer Century to the Children Act, 1948*, 1973. See a Vol. I (2180), listed above.

5034 **Rich**, E. E., *The Education Act, 1870, 19*

5035 **Roach**, J., *Public Examinations in Engla 1850-1900*, 1971.

5036 **Robson**, D., *Some Aspects of Education Cheshire in the Eighteenth Century*, 1966.

5037 **Seaborne**, M. and Lowe, R., *The Engl School, its Architecture and Organization. 1870-1970*, 1977. Vol. I of this work is listed ab (2471).

5038 **Selleck**, R. J. W., *English Primary Educat and the Progressives, 1914-1939*, 1972.

5039 **Sherington**, G. E., *English Education, Soc Change and War, 1911-20*, 1981. Places the 1 Education Act firmly in context.

5040 **Simon**, B., *Studies in the History of E cation: The Two Nations and the Educatio Structure 1780-1870*, 1960.

5041 —— *Studies in the History of Educat Education and the Labour Movement, 1870-19 1965.

5042 —— *Studies in the History of Education: Politics of Educational Reform 1920-1940*, 19

5043 **Smith**, J. W. A., *The Birth of Modern E cation: The Contribution of the Dissen Academies, 1660-1800*, 1954.

5044 **Sturt**, Mary, *The Education of the Peop 1967. The growth of English elementary educa in the nineteenth century.

5045 **Sutherland**, Gillian, *Policy-making Elementary Education, 1870-1895*, 1974.

5046 **Tompson**, R. S., *Classics or Charity?: The Dilemma of the Eighteenth-century Grammar School*, 1971. A re-assessment of the condition and functions of the grammar schools. Useful bibliography, 144-64.

5047 **Wardle**, D., *English Popular Education, 1780-1970*, 1970.

5048 —— *Education and Society in Nineteenth-Century Nottingham*, 1971.

5049 **West**, E. G., *Education and the Industrial Revolution*, 1975. Its interpretation differs markedly from Hurt (5018), above.

(b) THE PUBLIC SCHOOLS

5050 **Bamford**, T. W., *The Rise of the Public Schools*, 1967.

5051 **Mack**, E. C., *Public Schools and British Opinion, 1780-1860*, 1938.

5052 —— *Public Schools and British Opinion since 1860*, N. Y., 1941. Covers the period up to 1914.

5053 **Simon**, B. and Bradley, I., eds., *The Victorian Public School*, 1975.

(c) ADULT EDUCATION

5054 **Harrison**, J. F. C., *Learning and Living, 1790-1860*, 1961.

5055 **Kelly**, T., *George Birkbeck, Pioneer of Adult Education*, 1957.

5056 **Porter**, J., ed., *Education and Labour in the South-West*, 1975.

5057 **Stephens**, W. B., *Adult Education and Society in an Industrial Town: Warrington, 1800-1900*, 1980.

5058 **Stocks**, Mary D., *The Workers' Educational Association: The First Fifty Years*, 1953.

5059 **Tylecote**, Mabel, *The Mechanics Institutes of Lancashire and Yorkshire before 1851*, 1956.

(d) TECHNICAL EDUCATION

5060 **Ahlström**, G., *Engineers and Industrial Growth*, 1982. Contrasts the education of engineers on the Continent and in England.

5061 **Argles**, M., *South Kensington to Robbins*, 1964. A survey of the development of technical education in the nineteenth and twentieth centuries.

5062 **Cotgrove**, S. F., *Technical Education and Social Change*, 1958.

5063 **Roderick**, G. W. and Stephens, M. D., *Education and Industry in the Nineteenth Century: the English Disease?*, 1978.

(e) THE UNIVERSITIES

5064 **Berdhal**, R. O., *British Universities and the State*, 1959.

5065 **Sanderson**, M., *The Universities and British Industry, 1850-1970*, 1972. Excellent select bibliography, 398-419.

5066 —— *The Universities in the Nineteenth Century*, 1975.

5067 **Ward**, W. R., *Georgian Oxford*, 1958. Excellent bibliography.

5068 —— *Victorian Oxford*, 1965.

WALES
BEFORE 1700

GENERAL WORKS

(a) BIBLIOGRAPHIES

5069 **Jenkins**, R. T. and Rees, W., comps., *Bibliography of the History of Wales*, 2nd ed., 1962.

(b) SOURCES

5070 **Jack**, I. R., ed., *Medieval Wales*, 1972. (Sources of History Series.)

5071 **Rees**, W., ed., *Survey of the Duchy of Lancaster Lordships in Wales, 1609-13*, 1953.

(c) SURVEYS

(i) MEDIEVAL

5072 **Davies**, R. R., *Lordship and Society in the Marches of Wales, 1282-1400*, 1978.

5073 **Davies**, Wendy, 'Land and power in early medieval Wales', *P.P.*, 81, 1978, 3-23.

5074 **Denholm-Young**, N., *Collected Papers*, 1969. Covers a variety of medieval topics.

5075 **Dodd**, A. H., *Life in Wales*, 1971. Extends from ancient to modern times.

5076 **Jones**, G. R. J., 'Early territorial organisation in Gwynedd and Elmet', *Northern H.*, X, 1975, 3-27.

5077 **Lewis**, E. A., 'The development of industry and commerce in Wales during the Middle Ages', *T.R.H.S.*, new ser., XVII, 1903, 121-73.

5078 **Lloyd**, J. E., *History of Wales from the Earliest Times to the Edwardian Conquest*, 1911, 3rd ed., 2 vols., 1939.

5079 **Owen**, D. H., 'The Englishry of Denbigh: an English colony in medieval Wales', *T.Hon.Soc.Cymmrod.*, 1975, 57-76.

5080 **Pierce**, T. J., *Medieval Welsh Society: Selected Essays*, 1973.

5081 **Pugh**, T. B., ed., *Glamorgan County History Series. III: The Middle Ages*, 1971. Traces the history of the Marcher lordships of Glamorgan and Gower from the Norman Conquest to the Act of Union.

5082 **Rees**, W., *South Wales and the March, 1234-1415*, 1924.

5083 **Strayer**, J. R., and Rudishill, G., 'Taxation and community in Wales and Ireland, 1272-1327', *Speculum*, XXIX, 1954, 410-16.

5084 **Walker**, D., 'The Norman Settlement in Wales' in Brown, R. A., ed., *Proc.Battle Conference on Anglo-Norman Studs.*, I, 1979, 131-43.

(ii) EARLY MODERN

5085 **Davies**, D. J., *The Economic History of Wales prior to 1800*, 1933.

5086 **Dodd**, A. H., *Studies in Stuart Wales*, 1952.

5087 —— *A History of Caernarvonshire 1284-1900*, 1968.

5088 **Johnson**, A. M., 'Wales during the Commonwealth and Protectorate' in Pennington and Thomas (1214), above, 233-56.

5089 **Lynch**, A. L., *Pembrokeshire in the Civil War* 1937.

5090 **Phillips**, J. R. S., ed., *The Justices of the*

Peace in Wales and Monmouthshire, 1541-1689, 1975.

5091 **Williams**, G., ed., *Glamorgan County History Series*. IV: *Early Modern Glamorgan*, 1974. Covers the period from 1536 to c.1770.

5092 **Williams**, P., *The Council in the Marches of Wales under Elizabeth I*, 1958.

5093 **Williams**, W. O., 'The social order in Tudor Wales', *T.Hon.Soc.Cymmrod.*, 1967, 167-78.

POPULATION

(a) MEDIEVAL

5094 **Williams-Jones**, K., ed., *The Merioneth Lay Subsidy Roll, 1292-3*, 1976.

5095 **Davies**, R., 'Race relations in post-Conquest Wales: confrontation and compromise', *T.Hon.Soc.Cymmrod.*, 1975, 32-56.

(b) EARLY MODERN

5096 **Griffiths**, M., 'The Vale of Glamorgan in the 1543 Lay Subsidy Returns', *B.Bd.Celtic Studs.*, XXIX, 1982, 709-48.

5097 **Owen**, L., 'The population of Wales in the sixteenth and seventeenth centuries', *T.Hon.Soc.Cymmrod.*, 1959, 99-113.

5098 **Parry**, O., 'The Hearth Tax of 1662 in Merioneth', *J.Merion.H.Rec.Soc.*, II, 1953-4, 16-38.

5099 **Richards**, T., *The Religious Census of 1676. An Enquiry into its Historical Value mainly in reference to Wales*, 1927.

AGRICULTURE AND RURAL SOCIETY

(a) MEDIEVAL

5100 **Howells**, B., 'The distribution of customary acres in South Wales', *Nat.Lib.Wales J.*, XV, 1967, 226-35.

5101 **Pierce**, T. J., 'Some tendencies in the agricultural history of Caernarvonshire during the later Middle Ages', *T.Caerns.H.Soc.*, I, 1939, 18-36.

5102 —— 'The growth of commutation in Gwynedd during the thirteenth century', *B.Bd.Celtic Studs.*, X, 1941, 309-32.

5103 **Smith**, L. B., 'The gage and the land market in late medieval Wales', *Ec.H.R.*, 2nd ser., XXIX, 1976, 537-50.

(b) EARLY MODERN

5104 **James**, D. W., *St David's and Dewisland*, 1981. A comprehensive social history.

5105 **Jones**, T. I. J., 'A study of rents and fines in South Wales in the sixteenth and early seventeenth centuries' in B. B. Thomas, ed., *Harlech Studies: Essays presented to Thomas Jones*, 1938, 215-44.

5106 **Lloyd**, H. A., *The Gentry of South-West Wales, 1540-1640*, 1968.

5107 **Pierce**, T. J., 'Landlords in Wales. Nobility and Gentry' in Thirsk (1414), above, 357-80.

5108 **Smith**, P., 'Rural housing in Wales' in Thirsk (1414) above, 767-813.

5109 **Williams**, G., 'Landlords in Wales. The Church' in Thirsk (1414), above, 381-95.

5110 —— 'The Dissolution of the Monasteries in Glamorgan', *Welsh H.R.*, III, 1966, 23-43.

5111 **Williams**, W. O., 'The Anglesey gentry as businessmen in Tudor and Stuart times', *Anglesey Antiq.Soc. & Field Club*, 1948, 100-14.

INDUSTRY

(a) MEDIEVAL

5112 **Edwards**, J. G., 'Edward I's castle-building in Wales', *Proc.Brit.Acad.*, XXXII, 1946, 15-81.

5113 **Jack**, I. R., 'The cloth industry in medieval Wales', *Welsh H.R.*, X, 1981, 443-60.

5114 **Taylor**, A. J., 'Castle building in Wales in the late thirteenth century: the prelude to construction', in E. M. Jope, ed., *Studies in Building History*, 1961, 104-33.

(b) EARLY MODERN

5115 **Jenkins**, J. G., *The Welsh Woollen Industry*, 1969.

5116 **Lewis**, W. J., 'A Welsh salt-mining venture the sixteenth century', *Nat.Lib.Wales J.*, VII 1953-4, 419-25.

5117 —— *Lead Mining in Wales*, 1967. The fir four chapters deal with the pre-1700 period.

5118 **Skeel**, Caroline A. J., 'The Welsh woolle industry in the sixteenth and seventeenth ce turies', *Arch.Camb.*, seventh ser., II, 192: 220-57.

5119 **Williams**, L. J., 'A Welsh iron works at the clo of the seventeenth century', *Nat.Lib.Wales J* XI, 1959-60, 266-84.

TOWNS

5120 **Griffiths**, R. A., ed., *Boroughs of Medieval Wales*, 1978. Has chapters on Aberystwyth, Brecon, Caernarvon, Cardiff, Carmarthen, Denbigh, Newport, Oswestry, Ruthin, Swansea, and Tenby.

5121 **Morgan**, R., 'The foundation of the borough of Welshpool', *Montgom.Collns.*, LXV, 1977, 7-24.

5122 **Owen**, H., 'The two foundation charters of the borough of Denbigh', *B.Bd.Celtic Studs.*, XXVIII, 1979, 253-66.

5123 **Pierce**, T. J., 'A Caernarvonshire manori borough. Studies in the medieval history Pwllheli', *T.Caerns.H.Soc.* (for 1941), 1942, 9-3: (for 1942-3), 1943, 35-50, (for 1944), 1945, 12-4(

5124 **Sanders**, I. J., 'The boroughs of Aberystwyt and Cardigan in the early fourteenth century *B.Bd.Celtic Studs.*, XV, 1952-4, 282-92.

5125 **Usher**, G., 'Holyhead as a fourteenth-centur port', *B.Bd.Celtic Studs.*, XV, 1952-4, 209-12.

TRADE

(a) MEDIEVAL

5126 **Lewis**, E. A., 'A contribution to the commercial history of medieval Wales with tabulated accounts from 1301 to 1547', *T.Hon.Soc.Cymmrod.*, 1913, 86-188.

(b) EARLY MODERN

5127 **Lewis**, E. A., 'The toll books of some nort Pembrokeshire fairs, 1599-1603', *B.Bd.Celt Studs.*, VII, 1934, 283-318.

5128 —— ed., *The Welsh Port Books, 1550-160:* Cymmrod.Rec.series., XII, 1927.

RELIGION

(a) MEDIEVAL

5129 **Cowley**, F. G., *The Monastic Order in South Wales, 1066-1349*, 1977.

5130 **Williams**, D. H., *The Welsh Cistercians. Aspects of their Economic History*, 1969.

5131 **Williams**, G., *The Welsh Church from the Conquest to the Reformation*, 1952, 2nd ed., 1976.

(a) EARLY MODERN

5132 **Richards**, T., *The Puritan Movement in Wales, 1639-53*, 1920.

5133 —— *Religious Developments in Wales, 1654-62*, 1923.

5134 —— *Wales under the Penal Code, 1662-87*, 1925.

5135 —— *Wales under the Indulgence, 1672-75*, 1928.

5136 **Williams**, G., *Religion, Language and Nationality in Wales*, 1979. Collected essays extending from late medieval to modern times.

WALES
AFTER 1700

GENERAL WORKS

5137 **Morgan**, J., *A Select List of Parliamentary Papers relating to Wales, 1801-51*, 1974.

5138 —— *A Breviate of Parliamentary Papers relating to Wales, 1868-1964*, 1975.

5139 **Davies**, A. E., 'Some aspects of the operation of the Old Poor Law in Cardiganshire, 1750-1834', *J.Cardigan.Antiq.Soc.*, VI, 1968, 1-44.

5140 **Davies**, D., *The Influence of the French Revolution on Welsh Life and Literature*, 1926.

5141 **Evans**, E. D., *A History of Wales, 1660-1815*, 1976.

5142 **Gray-Jones**, A., *A History of Ebbw Vale*, 1970.

5143 **John**, A. H. and Williams, G., eds., *Glamorgan County History Series. V: Industrial, Glamorgan*, 1980. One of the major industrial regions of the British Isles examined in its expansion, depression and recovery.

5144 **Jones**, E. D., ed., *Victorian and Edwardian Wales from Old Photographs*, 1972.

5145 **Jones**, I. G., *Explorations and Explanations: Essays in the Social History of Victorian Wales*, 1981. Includes essays on the 1851 Religious Census and on the emergence of an independent middle class in the country towns.

5146 —— *Health, Wealth and Politics in Victorian Wales*, 1979.

5147 **Moore**, D., ed., *Wales in the Eighteenth Century*, 1976.

5148 **Morgan**, K. O., *Re-birth of a Nation: Wales 1880-1980*, 1981. Devotes three full chapters to economic issues.

5149 **Peate**, I. C., *The Welsh House: A Study in Folk Culture*, 1940, 2nd ed., 1944.

5150 **Price**, C., *English Theatre in Wales in the Eighteenth and Early Nineteenth Centuries*, 1948.

5151 **Pryce**, W. T. R., 'Industrialism, urbanisation and the maintenance of culture areas in North East Wales in the mid nineteenth century', *Welsh H.R.*, VII, 1975, 307-40

5152 **Smith**, D. and Williams, G., *Fields of Praise*, 1980. A social history of Welsh Rugby Union from 1881 placing the game firmly in the context of the Welsh economy and of working-class experience.

5153 **Thomas**, B., ed., *The Welsh Economy: Studies in Expansion*, 1962.

5154 **Williams**, D., *A History of Modern Wales*, 1950.

POPULATION

5155 **Alderman**, G., 'The Jew as scapegoat? The settlement and reception of Jews in South Wales before 1914', *T. Jewish H.Soc.*, XXVI, 1979, 62-70.

5156 **Beddoe**, D., *Welsh Convict Women: A Study of Women Transported from Wales to Australia, 1787-1852*, 1979.

5157 **Conway**, A., *The Welsh in America*, 1961.

5158 **Dodd**, A. H., *The Character of Early Welsh Emigration to the United States*, 1953.

5159 **Jenkins**, J. P., 'The demographic decline of the landed gentry in the eighteenth century: A South Wales study', *Welsh H.R.*, XI, 1982, 31-49.

5160 **Jones**, D. J. V., 'The criminal vagrant in nineteenth-century Wales', *Welsh H.R.*, VIII, 1977, 312-43.

5161 **Jones**, E., 'The Welsh in London in the seventeenth and eighteenth centuries', *Welsh H.R.*, X, 1981, 461-79.

5162 **Williams**, D., *Wales and America*, 1975.

AGRICULTURE AND RURAL SOCIETY

5163 **Bowen**, I., *The Great Enclosures of Common Lands in Wales*, 1914.

5164 **Colyer**, R. J., 'The gentry and the county in nineteenth-century Cardiganshire', *Welsh H.R.*, X, 1981, 497-535.

5165 —— 'The Land Agent in nineteenth-century Wales', *Welsh H.R.*, VIII, 1977, 401-25.

5166 —— *The Welsh Cattle Drovers*, 1976. See also Godwin (5168) and Hughes (5172), below.

5167 **Davies**, J., 'The end of the great estates and the rise of freehold farming in Wales', *Welsh H.R.*, VII, 1974, 186-212.

5168 **Godwin**, Fay and Toulson, Shirley, *The Drovers' Roads of Wales*, 1971. Well illustrated.

5169 **Howell**, D. W., 'The economy of the landed estates of Pembrokeshire, c. 1680-1830', *Welsh H.R.*, III, 1967, 265-86.

5170 ——'The impact of railways on agricultural development in nineteenth-century Wales', *Welsh H.R.*, VII, 1974, 40-62.

5171 —— *Land and People in Nineteenth-Century Wales*, 1978.

5172 **Hughes**, P. G., *Wales and the Drovers*, 1947.

5173 **Jenkins**, D., *The Agricultural Community in South West Wales at the turn of the Twentieth Century*, 1971.

5174 **Jenkins**, D. G., *Agricultural Transport in Wales*, 1962.

5175 **Martin**, Joanna, 'Estate stewards and their work in Glamorgan, 1660-1760', *Morgannwg*, XXIII, 1979, 9-28.

5176 —— 'Private enterprise *versus* manorial rights: mineral property disputes in mid eighteenth-century Glamorgan', *Welsh H.R.*, IX, 1978, 155-75.

5177 **Roberts**, R. O., ed., *Farming in Caernarvonshire around 1800*, 1973. Documents on the Vaenol estate.

5178 **Thomas**, D., *Agriculture in Wales During the Napoleonic Wars*, 1963.

INDUSTRY

5179 **Bevan-Evans**, M., 'Gadlys and Flintshire lead-mining in the eighteenth century', Parts I, II, III, *Flints.H.Soc.*, XVIII, 1960, 75-130; XIX, 1961, 32-60; XX, 1962, 58-89.

5180 **Chappell**, E. L., *Historic Melingriffith: An Account of the Pentyrch Iron Works*, 1940.

5181 **Daunton**, M. J., 'Miners' houses: South Wales and the Great Northern Coalfield, 1880-1914',

Internat.R.Soc.H., XXV, 1980, 143-75.

5182 **Davies**, J. I., 'The history of printing in Montgomeryshire, 1789-1960', *Montgom.Collns.*, LXVIII, 1980, 7-28.

5183 **Dodd**, A. H., *The Industrial Revolution in North Wales*, 1933, 3rd ed., with corrections and additions, 1971.

5184 **Evans**, J. D., 'The uncrowned Iron King (the

first William Crawshay)', *Nat.Lib.Wales J.*, VII, 1951, 12-32. See also Fell (1601), listed above.

5185 **Harris**, J. R., *The Copper King: A Biography of Thomas Williams of Llanidan*, 1964.

5186 **John**, A. H., *The Industrial Development of South Wales, 1750-1850*, 1950. See also Davies (5085), listed above.

5187 **Jones**, J. R., *The Welsh Builder on Merseyside: Annals and Lives*, 1946.

5188 **Jones**, R. M., *The North Wales Quarrymen, 1874-1922*, 1981.

5189 **Lambert**, W. R., 'Drink and work discipline in industrial South Wales, c.1800-1870', *Welsh H.R.*, VII, 1975, 289-306.

5190 **Lerry**, G. G., *The Collieries of Denbighshire*, 1946.

5191 **Lewis**, E. D., *The Rhondda Valleys: A Study in Industrial Development, 1800 to the Present Day*, 1959.

5192 **Lindsay**, Jean, *A History of the North Wales Slate Industry*, 1974.

5193 **Minchinton**, W. E., ed., *Industrial South Wales, 1750-1914: Essays in Welsh Economic History*, 1969.

5194 **Morris**, J. H. and Williams, L. J., *The South Wales Coal Industry, 1841-75*, 1958.

5195 **North**, F. J., *The Slates of Wales*, 3rd rev. ed., 1946.

5196 **Roberts**, R. O., 'Enterprise and capital for nonferrous metal smelting in Glamorgan, 1694-1924', *Morgannwg*, XXIII, 1979, 48-82.

5197 **Tucker**, D. G., 'The leadmines of Glamorgan and Gwent', *Morgannwg*, XX, 1976, 37-52.

5198 **Tucker**, Mary, 'The slate industry of Pembrokeshire and its borders', *Ind.Arch.R.*, III, 1979, 203-27.

5199 **Walters**, R., 'Capital formation in the South Wales coal industry, 1840-1914', *Welsh H.R.*, X, 1980, 69-92.

5200 **Williams**, L. J., 'The coal owners of South Wales, 1873-80: problems of unity', *Welsh H.R.*, VIII, 1976, 75-93.

5201 —— 'A Carmarthenshire ironmaster and the Seven Years War', *Bus.H.*, II, 1959-60, 32-43.

TRADE, TRANSPORT AND COMMUNICATIONS

5202 **Archer**, M. S., *The Welsh Post Towns before 1840*, 1970.

5203 **George**, Barbara J., 'Pembrokeshire seatrading before 1900', *Field Studs.*, II, 1964, 1-39.

5204 **Hadfield**, C., *The Canals of South Wales and the Border*, 1960.

5205 **Jones**, P. N., 'Workmen's trains in the South Wales Coalfield, 1870-1926', *Trans.H.*, 1970, 21-35.

See also the section on towns below.

TOWNS

5206 **Carter**, H. and Wheatley, Sandra, 'Some aspects of the spatial structure of two Glamorgan towns in the nineteenth century', *Welsh H.R.*, IX, 1978, 32-56. Deals with Neath and Merthyr Tydfil.

5207 **Davies**, J. I., *Cardiff and the Marquesses of Bute*, 1980. A case study of aristocratic participation in economic development concentrating on the Butes' contribution to the rise of the port of Cardiff and to the growth of the South Wales iron and coal trade.

5208 **Daunton**, M. J., *Coal Metropolis: Cardiff, 1870-1914*, 1977.

BANKING

5209 **Davies**, A. S., *The Early Banks of Mid-Wales*, 1935.

5210 **Dodd**, A. H., 'The beginnings of banking in North Wales', *Economica*, VI, 1926, 16-30.

5211 **Green**, F., 'Early banks in West Wales', *H.Soc. West Wales*, VI, 1916, 129-64.

LABOUR

5212 **Arnot**, R. P., *The South Wales Miners. A History of the South Wales Miners Federation, 1898-1914*, 1967.

5213 **Evans**, E. W., *Mabon: William Abraham, 1842-1922. A Study in Trade Union Leadership*, 1959. The leader of the South Wales miners.

5214 **Jones**, D. J. V., *Before Rebecca: Popular Protests in Wales, 1793-1835*, 1973.

5215 **Smith**, D., ed., *A People and a Proletariat. Essays in the History of Wales, 1780-1980*, 1980.

Some of the essays are local case studies, others range widely in considering the problems of 'locating' the working class in Wales and the links between language and community.

5216 **Williams**, D., *The Rebecca Riots. A Study in Agrarian Discontent*, 1955.

5217 **Williams**, G. A., ed., *Merthyr Politics. The Making of a Working-Class Tradition*, 1966.

5218 **Williams**, G. A., *The Merthyr Rising*, 1978.

RELIGION AND EDUCATION

5219 **Clement**, Mary, ed., *Correspondence and Minutes of the S.P.C.K. relating to Wales*, 1952. Covers the first half of the eighteenth century.

5220 **Jones**, I. G. and Williams, D., eds., *The Religious Census of 1851. A Calendar of the Returns relating to Wales*. I: *South Wales*, 1976; II: *North Wales*, 1980.

5221 **Williams**, A. H., *John Wesley in Wales, 1739-90*, 1971. Edited extracts from his journals and diaries.

5222 **Davies**, E. T., *Religion in the Industrial Revolution in South Wales*, 1965.

5223 **Evans**, L. W., *Studies in Welsh Education.*

Welsh Educational Structure and Administration, 1800-1925, 1975.

5224 **Harvest**, L., 'The Welsh Educational Alliance and the 1870 Elementary Education Act', *Welsh H.R.*, X, 1980, 172-206.

5225 **Lewis**, G. J., 'The geography of religion in the middle borderlands of Wales in 1851', *T.Hon. Soc.Cymmrod*, 1980, 123-42.

5226 **Randall**, P. J., 'The origins and establishment of the Welsh Department of Education', *Welsh H.R.*, VII, 1975, 450-71.

5227 **Roberts**, H. P., 'Nonconformist Academies in Wales', *T.Hon.Soc.Cymmrod.*, 1928-9, 1-98.

SCOTLAND
BEFORE 1700

GENERAL WORKS

(a) BIBLIOGRAPHIES

5228 **Hancock**, P. D., *Bibliography of Works Relating to Scotland*, 2 vols., 1959-60.

5229 **Keith**, Theodora, *Bibliography of Scottish Economic History*, 1914. Now obviously very inadequate and out of date.

5230 **Mackie**, J. D., *Scottish History*, 1956.

5231 **Marwick**, W. H., 'A bibliography of Scottish business history'. In Payne, (5473), below, 77-99.

5232 —— 'A bibliography of Scottish economic history', *Ec.H.R.*, III, 1931-2, 117-37.

5233 —— 'A bibliography of Scottish economic history, 1931-51', *Ec.H.R.*, 2nd ser., IV, 1951-2, 376-82.

5234 —— 'A bibliography of Scottish economic history, 1951-62', *Ec.H.R.*, 2nd ser., XVI, 1963-4, 147-54.

5235 —— 'A bibliography of Scottish economic history, 1963-70', *Ec.H.R.*, 2nd ser., XXIV, 1971, 469-79.

5236 **Scott**, W. R., *Scottish Economic Literature to 1800*, 1911.

(b) SOURCES

5237 **Anderson**, A. O., ed., *The Early Sources of Scottish History, A. D. 500-1286*, 2 vols., 1922.

5238 **Brown**, P. H., ed., *Scotland Before 1700 from Contemporary Documents*, 1893.

5239 **Dickinson**, W. C., *A Source Book of Scottish History to 1707*, 3 vols., 1952-4. Vol. I: *From the Earliest times to 1424:* Vol. II: *1424-1567* and Vol. III, *1567-1707*.

5240 **Donaldson**, G., ed., *Scottish Historical Documents*, 1970. A useful source book covering the medieval and early modern periods. See also Browning, ed., (1142), listed above, which contains a substantial section, 591-698, on Scotland.

(c) SURVEYS
(i) MEDIEVAL

5241 **Barbé**, L. A., *Sidelights on the History, Industries and Social Life of Scotland*, 1919.

5242 **Barrow**, G. W. S., *The Kingdom of the Scots. Government, Church and Society from the Eleventh to the Fourteenth Century*, 1973.

5243 —— *The Anglo-Norman Era in Scottish History*, 1980.

5244 **Brown**, J. M., ed., *Scottish Society in the Fifteenth Century*, 1977.

5245 **Brown**, P. H., *Early Travellers in Scotland*, 1891. The accounts range in date from 1295 to 1689.

5246 **Campbell**, J., 'England, Scotland and the Hundred Years War in the fourteenth century'. In J. R. Hale, ed., *Europe in the Late Middle Ages*, 1965, 184-216.

5247 **Dickinson**, W. C., *Scotland from the Earliest Times to 1603*, 1961. A useful textbook: bibliography.

5248 **Grant**, I. F., *Social and Economic Develop-*

ment of Scotland before 1603, 1930, 2nd ed., Westport, Conn., 1971.

5249 **Lythe**, S. G. E. and Butt, J., *An Economic History of Scotland, 1100-1939*, 1975. Primarily a thematic approach though with sections dividing at 1707 and 1870.

5250 **Mackenzie**, W. C., *The Highlands and Isles of Scotland: An Historical Survey*, 1937, 2nd ed., 1949.

5251 **Mackie**, J. D., *History of Scotland*, 1964.

5252 **Nicholson**, R., *The Edinburgh History of Scotland. II. The Later Middle Ages*, 1974.

5253 **Rait**, R. S., *An Outline of the Relations between England and Scotland, 500-1707*, 1901.

5254 **Ritchie**, R. L. G., *The Normans in Scotland*, 1954.

See also Barrow (265), listed above, a general survey which devotes more space than usual to Scottish history, and Mitchison (5266), listed below.

(ii) EARLY MODERN

5255 **Barrow**, G. W. S., ed., *The Scottish Tradition. Essays in Honour of R. G. Cant*, 1974. Includes essays on the Scottish advocates, aristocratic education, the management of forfeited estates and on the burghs.

5256 **Butt**, J. and Ward, J. T., eds., *Scottish Themes. Essays in Honour of Professor S. G. E. Lythe*, 1976.

5257 **Carstairs**, A. M., 'Some economic aspects of the union of the Parliaments', *Scot. J.Pol.Econ.*, II, 1955, 64-72.

5258 **Donaldson**, G., *Scotland, James V to James VII*, 1965. Mainly of value on political and ecclesiastical aspects.

5259 ——*Shetland Life under Earl Patrick*, 1958.

5260 **Insh**, G. P., *Scotland and the Modern World*, 1932.

5261 **Keith**, Theodora, 'The influence of the Convention of the Royal Boroughs of Scotland on the economic development of Scotland before 1707', *Scot.H.R.*, X, 1914, 250-71.

5262 **Lythe**, S. G. E., *The Economy of Scotland in its European Setting, 1550-1625*, 1960.

5263 —— 'The Union of the Crowns in 1603 and the debate on economic integration', *Scot. J. Pol.Econ.*, V, 1958, 219-28.

5264 **Mathew**, D., *Scotland under Charles I*, 1955.

5265 **Meikle**, H. W., *Some Aspects of Seventeenth Century Scotland*, 1947.

5266 **Mitchison**, Rosalind, *A History of Scotland*, 1970. A general survey of Scottish history, particularly weighted, however, towards the seventeenth century – 'the key period for the understanding of modern Scotland' (ix). A useful critical bibliography is appended, 430-42.

5267 —— *Life in Scotland*, 1978.

5268 **Nobbs**, D., *England and Scotland, 1560-1707*, 1952.

5269 **Notestein**, W., *The Scot in History*, New Haven, Conn., 1946.

5270 **Paul**, J. B., 'Social life in Scotland in the sixteenth century', *Scot.H.R.*, XVII, 1919-20, 296-309.

5271 **Pryde**, G. S., *Scotland from 1603 to the Present Day*, 1962.

5272 **Shaw**, Frances J., *The Northern and Western Islands of Scotland: Their Economy and Society in the Seventeenth Century*, 1980.

5273 **Smout**, T. C., *A History of the Scottish People, 1560-1830*, 1969. Strong on economic and social aspects. Useful aids to further reading are appended to each chapter.

5274 **Warrack**, J., *Domestic Life in Scotland, 1488-1688*, 1920. Deals mainly with furniture and household effects.

5275 **Willson**, D. H., 'King James I and Anglo-Scottish unity'. In Aiken and Henning (2250), 41-56.

5276 **Wormald**, Jenny, *Court, Kirk and Community. Scotland 1470-1625*, 1981.

See also Dickinson (5247), Grant (5248), and Mackie (5251), listed above, and Ferguson (5515), listed below.

POPULATION

(a) MEDIEVAL

5277 **Barrow**, G. W. S., 'Rural settlement in central and eastern Scotland: the medieval evidence', *Scot.Studs.*, VI, 1962, 123-44.

5278 **Cooper**, Lord, 'The numbers and distribution of the population in medieval Scotland', *Scot.H.R.*, n.s., I, 1947, 2-9. Rather unsatisfactory.

(b) EARLY MODERN

5279 **Adamson**, D., ed., *West Lothian Hearth Tax, 1691*. Scot.Rec.Soc., new ser., IX, 1981.

5280 **Walton**, K., 'The distribution of population in Aberdeenshire, 1696', *Scot.Geog.Mag.*, LXVI, 1950, 17-25.

AGRICULTURE AND RURAL SOCIETY

(a) MEDIEVAL

5281 **Anderson**, M. L., *A History of Scottish Forestry*, Vol. I: *From the Ice Age to the French Revolution*, ed. C. J. Taylor, 1967.

5282 **Dodgshon**, R. A., *Land and Society in Early Scotland*, 1982.

5283 **Franklin**, T. B., *A History of Scottish Farming*, 1952.

5284 **Madden**, C. A., 'The Royal Demesne in Northern Scotland during the late Middle Ages', *Northern Scot.*, III, 1979, 1-24.

5285 **Marwick**, H., *Medieval Lairds*, 1936, 2nd ed., 1939.

5286 **Murray**, A., 'The crown lands in Galloway, 1455-1543', *Trans.Dumfriesshire and Galloway Nat.Hist.& Antiq.Soc.*, XXXVII, 1960, 9-25.

5287 **Symon**, J. A., *Scottish Farming Past and Present*, 1959.

(b) EARLY MODERN

5288 **Fenton**, A., ed., 'Skene of Hallyard's Ms. of Husbandrie', *Ag.H.R.*, XI, 1963, 65-81. A seventeenth-century account.

5289 **Donaldson**, G., 'Sources for Scottish agrarian history before the eighteenth century', *Ag.H.R.*, VIII, 1959, 82-90.

5290 **Fenton**, A., 'The rural economy of East Lothian in the seventeenth and eighteenth centuries', *Trans.East Lothian Antiq. and Field Naturalists' Soc.*, IX, 1963, 1-23.

5291 —— 'Farm servant life in the seventeenth to nineteenth centuries', *Scot.Agriculture*, XLIV, 1965, 281-5.

5292 —— *Scottish Country Life*, 1975.

5293 **Mackerral**, A., *Kintyre in the Seventeenth Century*, 1948.

5294 **Millman**, R. L., *The Making of the Scottish Landscape*, 1975.

5295 **Murray**, J. E. L., 'The agriculture of Crail, 1550-1600', *Scot.Studs.*, VIII, 1964, 85-95.

5296 **Smout**, T. C., 'Problems of timber supply in later seventeenth-century Scotland', *Scottish Forestry*, XIV, 1960, 3-13.

5297 —— 'Scottish landowners and economic growth 1650-1850', *Scot. J.Pol.Econ.*, XI, 1964, 218-34. See also Smout (5429), listed below.

5298 —— 'Goat keeping in the old highland economy: 4', *Scot.Studs.*, IX, 1965, 186-9. Assesses the significance of earlier contributions on this subject.

5299 —— and Fenton, A., 'Scottish agriculture before the improvers – an exploration', *Ag.H.R.*, XIII, 1965, 73-93.

5300 **Whyte**, I. D., *Agriculture and Society in Seventeenth-Century Scotland*, 1979.

INDUSTRY

(a) MEDIEVAL

5301 **Cochran-Patrick**, R. W., ed., *Early Records Relating to Mining in Scotland*, 1878.

5302 **Adams**, I. H., 'The salt industry of the Forth Basin', *Scot.Geog.Mag.*, LXXXI, 1965, 153-62. See also Arnot (5498), listed below.

(b) EARLY MODERN

5303 **Knoop**, D. and Jones, G. P., *The Scottish Mason and Mason Word*, 1939.

5304 **Lumsden**, H., ed., *The Records of the Trades House of Glasgow, 1605-1678*, 1910.

5305 —— *History of the Skinners, Furriers and Glovers of Glasgow: A Study of a Scottish Craft*

Guild in its Various Relations, 1937.

5306 —— and Aitken, P. H., *History of the Hammermen of Glasgow*, 1912.

5307 **Marwick**, J. D., *Edinbugh Gilds and Crafts*, Scottish Burgh Record Society, 1909.

5308 **Scott**, W. R., ed., *Records of a Scottish Cloth Manufactory at New Mills, Haddingtonshire,*

1681-1703, Scot.H.Soc., 1905.

5309 **Smout**, T. C., 'The early Scottish sugar houses, 1660-1720', *Ec.H.R.*, 2nd ser., XIV, 1961, 240-53.

5310 —— 'Lead-mining in Scotland, 1650-1850'. In Payne, (5473), below, 103-35.

See also Nef (1589), listed above, and Scott (1777), vol. III of which deals with Scottish joint stock companies.

TOWNS

(a) MEDIEVAL

5311 **Dickinson**, W. C., ed., *Early Records of Aberdeen, 1317, 1398-1407*, Scot.H.Soc., 1957.

5312 **Ballard**, A., 'The theory of the Scottish burgh', *Scot.H.R.*, XIII, 1916, 16-29.

5313 **Dunlop**, Annie I., *The Royal Burgh of Ayr*, 1953. An able account of the medieval period in particular.

5314 **Lythe**, S. G. E., 'The origin and development of Dundee', *Scot.Geog.Mag.*, LIV, 1939, 344-57.

5315 **Mackenzie**, W. M., *The Scottish Burghs*, 1949. Covers both the medieval and early modern periods.

(b) EARLY MODERN

5316 **Roberts**, F. and MacPhail, I. M. M., eds., *Dumbarton Common Goods Accounts 1614-1660*, 1972.

5317 **Shearer**, A., ed., *Extracts from the Burgh*

Records of Dunfermline in the Sixteenth and Seventeenth Centuries, 1951.

5318 **Taylor**, Louise B., ed., *Aberdeen Council Letters 1552-1681*, 6 vols., 1942-61.

5319 —— ed., *Aberdeen Shore Works Accounts 1596-1670*, 1972. Lists ships and their cargoes entering and leaving the harbour.

5320 **Lythe**, S. G. E., *Life and Labour in Dundee from the Reformation to the Civil War*, Abertay H.Soc., 5, 1958.

5321 **Murray**, D., *Early Burgh Organisation in Scotland, as Illustrated in the History of Glasgow and of Some Neighbouring Burghs*, 2 vols., 1924.

5322 **Pagan**, Theodora (née Keith), *The Convention of the Royal Burghs of Scotland*, 1926. Deals with the burghs' relations with the state and with each other.

5323 **Smout**, T. C., 'Development and enterprise of Glasgow, 1556-1707', *Scot. J.Pol.Econ.*, VII, 1960, 194-212.

TRADE

(a) MEDIEVAL

5324 **Dilley**, J. W., 'German merchants in Scotland, 1297-1327', *Scot.H.R.*, XXVII, 1948, 142-55.

5325 **Reid**, W. S., 'Trade, traders and Scottish independence', *Speculum*, XXIX, 1954, 210-22.

5326 **Rooseboom**, M. P., *The Scottish Staple in the Netherlands, 1292-1676*, The Hague, 1916.

(b) EARLY MODERN

5327 **Davidson**, A. and Gray, A., *The Scottish*

Staple at Veere, 1909.

5328 **Dow**, J., 'Scottish trade with Sweden, 1512-80', *Scot.H.R.*, XLVIII, 1969, 64-79.

5329 —— 'Scottish trade with Sweden, 1580-1622', *Scot.H.R.*, XLVIII, 1969, 124-50.

5330 —— 'A comparative note on the Sound Toll registers, Stockholm customs accounts, and Dundee shipping lists 1589, 1613-1622', *Scand.Ec.H.R.*, XII, 1964, 79-85.

5331 **Elder**, J. R., *Royal Fishery Companies of the Seventeenth Century*, 1912.

5332 **Ferguson**, W., *Scotland's Relations with Eng-*

land. *A Study to 1707*, 1977.

5333 **Hart**, F. R., *The Disaster of Darien: The Story of the Scots Settlement, 1699-1701*, 1930.

5334 **Insh**, G. P., *Scottish Colonial Schemes, 1620-86*, 1922.

5335 —— *The Company of Scotland trading to Africa and the Indies*, 1932.

5336 —— *The Darien Scheme*, Hist.Ass. pamphlet, 1947.

5337 —— ed., *Darien Shipping Papers: Papers Relating to the Ships and Voyages of the Company of Scotland Trading to Africa and the Indies, 1696-1707*, Scot.H.Soc., 3rd ser., VI, 1934.

5338 **Keith**, Theodora, *Commercial Relations of England and Scotland 1603-1707*, 1910.

5339 **Lythe**, S. G. E., 'Scottish trade with the Baltic 1550-1650'. In J. K. Eastham, ed., *Economic Essays in Commemoration of the Dundee School of Economics*, 1955, 63-84.

5340 **Prebble**, J., *The Darien Disaster*, 1968.

5341 **Scott**, W. W., 'The use of money in Scotland, 1124-1230', *Scot.H.R.*, LVII, 1979, 105-31.

5342 **Smout**, T. C., *Scottish Trade on the Eve of the Union, 1660-1707*, 1963.

5343 —— 'The overseas trade of Ayrshire 1660-1707', *Ayrshire Arch.Collns.*, 2nd ser., VI, 1961, 56-80.

5344 —— 'Scottish commercial factors in the Baltic at the end of the seventeenth century', *Scot.H.R.* XXXIX, 1960, 122-8.

5345 —— 'The foreign trade of Dumfries and Kirkcudbright, 1672-1696', *T.Dumfriesshire and Galloway Nat. H. & Antiq. Soc.*, XXXVII for 1958-9, 1960, 36-47.

5346 —— 'The Glasgow merchant community in the seventeenth century', *Scot.H.R.*, XLVII, 1968, 53-71.

5347 **Woodward**, D. M., 'Anglo-Scottish trade and English commercial policy during the 1660s', *Scot.H.R.*, LVI, 1977, 153-74.

5348 **Zupco**, R. E., 'The weights and measures of Scotland before the Union', *Scot.H.R.*, LVI, 1977, 119-45.

PRICES, PUBLIC FINANCE AND BANKING

(a) MEDIEVAL

5349 **Cochran-Patrick**, R. W., *Records of Coinage, 1357 to the Union*, 2 vols., 1876.

5350 **Stewart**, I. H., *The Scottish Coinage*, 1955.

(b) EARLY MODERN

5351 **Mitchison**, Rosalind, 'The movement of Scottish corn prices in the seventeenth and eighteenth centuries', *Ec.H.R.*, 2nd ser., XVIII, 1965, 278-91.

5352 **Murray**, A., 'The procedure of the Scottish Exchequer in the early sixteenth century' *Scot.H.R.*, XL, 1961, 89-117.

5353 —— 'The pre-Union records of the Scottish Exchequer', *J.Soc.Archivists*, II, 1961, 89-100.

5354 —— 'The Scottish treasury, 1667-1708' *Scot.H.R.*, XLV, 1966, 89-104.

See also Yamey, Edey and Thomson (2011), listed above.

COMMUNICATIONS

5355 **Hardie**, R. P., *The Roads of Medieval Lauderdale*, 1942.

5356 **Taylor**, W., 'The King's mails, 1603-25', *Scot.H.R.*, XLII, 1963, 143-7.

See also Haldane (5482), listed below, for an introductory chapter on 'The early drovers' (i.e., before 1700).

POOR RELIEF

357 **Cormack**, A., *Poor Relief in Scotland: An Outline of the Growth and Administration of the Poor Laws in Scotland from the Middle Ages to the Present Day*, 1923.

358 **McPherson**, J. M., *The Kirk's Care of the Poor*, 1941.

5359 **Nicholls**, G., *A History of the Scotch Poor Law*, 1856. Reprinted 1968. See also Ferguson (5515), below.

EDUCATION

360 **Boyd**, W., *Education in Ayrshire through Seven Centuries*, 1961.

361 **Cant**, R. G., 'The Scottish universities in the seventeenth century', *Aberdeen University R.*, XLIII, 1970, 323-33.

362 —— *The College of St Salvator*, 1950.

363 **Durkan**, J., 'Education in the century of the Reformation'. In McRoberts (5382), listed below, 145-68.

364 **Henderson**, G. D., *The Founding of Marischal College, Aberdeen*, 1947.

5365 **Mackie**, J. D., *The University of Glasgow 1451-1951. A Short History*, 1954.

5366 **Scotland**, J., *The History of Scottish Education*, 1973.

5367 **Simpson**, I. J., *Education in Aberdeenshire before 1872*, 1947.

5368 **Withrington**, D. J., ed., 'List of schoolmasters teaching Latin, 1690', *Miscellany of the Scot.H.Soc.*, X, 1965, 121-42.

RELIGION AND LAW

(a) MEDIEVAL

369 **Coulton**, G. G., *Scottish Abbeys and Social Life*, 1933.

370 **Cowan**, I. B., *The Parishes of Medieval Scotland*, Scot.Rec.Soc., XCIII, 1967.

371 **Easson**, D. E., *Medieval Religious Houses: Scotland*, 1957.

372 **Levy**, A., 'The origins of Scottish Jewry', *T. Jewish H.Soc.*, XIX, 1960, for 1955-9, 129-62.

373 **Morgan**, M., 'The organisation of the Scottish church in the twelfth century', *T.R.H.S.*, 4th ser., XXIX, 1947, 135-49.

374 **Stevenson**, Wendy B., 'The monastic presence in Scottish burghs in the twelfth and thirteenth centuries', *Scot.H.R.*, LX, 1981, 97-118.

(b) EARLY MODERN

375 **Cowan**, I. B., 'The Covenanters: a revision article', *Scot.H.R.*, XLVII, 1968, 35-52.

376 **Donaldson**, G., *The Scottish Reformation*, 1960.

5377 —— 'The legal profession in Scottish society in the sixteenth and seventeenth centuries', *Juridical R.*, VII, 1976, 1-19.

5378 **Foster**, W. R., *Bishop and Presbytery: The Church of Scotland 1661-1688*, 1958.

5379 **Henderson**, G. D., *Religious Life in Seventeenth-century Scotland*, 1937.

5380 —— *The Scottish Ruling Elder*, 1935.

5381 **Lee**, M., 'Revision article: the Scottish Reformation after 400 years', *Scot.H.R.*, XLIV, 1965, 135-47.

5382 **McRoberts**, D., ed., *Essays on the Scottish Reformation, 1513-1625*, 1962.

5383 **Makey**, W., *The Church of the Covenant, 1637-51: Revolution and Social Change in Scotland*, 1979.

5384 **Marshall**, G., *Presbyteries and Profits. Calvinism and the Development of Capitalism in Scotland, 1560-1707*, 1980.

5385 **Trevor-Roper**, H. R., 'Scotland and the Puritan Revolution'. In H. E. Bell and R. L. Ollard, eds., *Historical Essays, 1600-1750, Presented to David Ogg*, 1963, 78-130.

SCOTLAND
AFTER 1700

GENERAL WORKS

5386 **Campbell**, R. H. and Dow, J. B. A., *Source Book of Scottish Economic and Social History*, 1968.

5387 **Campbell**, R. H., *Scotland from 1707: The Rise of an Industrial Society*, 1964.

5388 **Dickson**, T., ed., *Scottish Capitalism: Class, State and Nation from before the Union to the Present*, 1980.

5389 **Grant**, I. F., *The Economic History of Scotland*, 1934. List of books for further reading, 283-5.

5390 **Hamilton**, H., *An Economic History of Scotland in the Eighteenth Century*, 1963.

5391 **Harvie**, C., *No Gods and Precious Few Heroes. Scotland, 1914-80*, 1981.

5392 **Hill**, C. W., *Edwardian Scotland*, 1976.

5393 **Hook**, A., *Scotland and America: A Study of Cultural Relations, 1750-1835*, 1975.

5394 **Lenman**, B., *An Economic History of Modern Scotland, 1660-1976*, 1977.

5395 —— *Integration, Enlightenment and Industrialisation. Scotland, 1746-1832*, 1981.

5396 **Mackinnon**, J., *The Social and Industri[al] History of Scotland*, 2 vols., 1920-1. See Marwic[k] (5399) and Smout (5273).

5397 **MacLaren**, A. A., ed., *Social Class in Sco[t]land: Past and Present*, 1976.

5398 **Marwick**, W. H., *Economic Developments i[n] Victorian Scotland*, 1936.

5399 —— *Scotland in Modern Times: An Outline [of] Economic and Social Development since th[e] Union of 1707*, 1964.

5400 **Niven**, D., *The Development of Housing i[n] Scotland*, 1979.

5401 **Phillipson**, N. T. and Mitchison, Rosalind[,] eds., *Scotland in the Age of Improvement[.] Essays in Scottish History in the Eighteent[h] Century*, 1970.

5402 **Prattis**, J. I., *Economic Structures in the High[lands] lands of Scotland*, 1977.

5403 **Slaven**, A., *The Development of the West [of] Scotland, 1750-1960*, 1975.

POPULATION

5404 **Donaldson**, G., *The Scots Overseas*, 1966. Excellent bibliography.

5405 **Flinn**, M. W., ed., *Scottish Population History from the Seventeenth Century to the 1930s*, 1977.

5406 **Hollingsworth**, T. H., *Migration: A Stud[y] based on Scottish Experience between 1939 an[d] 1944*, 1970.

5407 **Kyd**, K. D., *Scottish Population Statistics*, Scot.H.Soc., 1952.
5408 **Macdonald**, D. F., *Scotland's Shifting Population, 1770-1850*, 1937.
5409 **Macmillan**, D., *Scotland and Australia 1788-1850. Emigration, Commerce and Investment*, 1967.
5410 **Osborne**, R. H., 'The movement of people in Scotland, 1851-1951', *Scot.Studs.*, II, 1958, 1-46.

AGRICULTURE AND RURAL SOCIETY

5411 **Adams**, I. H., ed., *Peter May, Land Surveyor, 1749-93*. Scot.H.Soc., XV, 1979.
5412 **Cregeen**, E., 'Recollections of an Argyllshire drover, with historical notes on the West Highland cattle trade', *Scot.Studs.*, III, 1959, 143-62.

5413 **Adam**, Margaret I., 'Eighteenth-century highland landlords and the poverty problem', *Scot.H.R.*, XIX, 1921-2, 1-20, 161-79.
5414 **Carter**, I., *Farm Life in North East Scotland, 1840-1914: The Poor Man's Country*, 1979.
5415 **Collier**, A., *The Crofting Problem*, 1953.
5416 **Devine**, T. M., 'Social stability and agrarian change in the eastern lowlands of Scotland, 1810-40', *Soc.H.*, III, 1978, 331-46.
5417 **Donaldson**, J. E., *Caithness in the Eighteenth Century*, 1938.
5418 **Fenton**, A. and Walker, B., *The Rural Architecture of Scotland*, 1981.
5419 **Gaskell**, P., *Morvern Transformed. A Highland Parish in the Nineteenth Century*, 1968. A comprehensive analysis of the problems of the west coast.
5420 **Gray**, M., *The Highland Economy, 1750-1850*, 1957.
5421 **Handley**, J. E., *Scottish Farming in the Eighteenth Century*, 1953.
5422 **Hunter**, J., *The Making of the Crofting Community*, 1976.
5423 **Jones**, D. T., Duncan, J. F., Conacher, H. M., and Scott, W. R., *Rural Scotland During the War*, 1926.
5424 **Mitchison**, Rosalind, *Agricultural Sir John*, 1962. Definitive biography of Sir John Sinclair.
5425 —— 'Scottish landowners and communal responsibility in the eighteenth century', *Brit. J.Eighteenth Century Studs.*, I, 1978, 41-5.
5426 **Richards**, E., *A History of the Highland Clearances: Agrarian Transformation and the Evictions, 1746-1886*, 1982.
5427 —— *The Leviathan of Wealth: The Sutherland Fortune in the Industrial Revolution*, 1973.
5428 **Rosie**, J. and Kelly, L., *Agriculture in Lanarkshire, 1760-1840*, 1978.
5429 **Smout**, T. C., 'The landowner and the planned villages in Scotland, 1730-1830'. In G. Phillipson and Rosalind Mitchison, eds., *Scotland in the Age of Improvement*, 1970. See also Smout (5297), listed above.
5430 **Timperley**, L. R., ed., *A Directory of Landownership in Scotland c.1770*, Scot.Rec.Soc., new ser., V, 1976.
5431 **Ward**, W. R., 'The land tax in Scotland, 1707-98', *B. John Rylands Lib*, XXXVII, 1954, 288-308.
5432 **Wheeler**, P. T., 'Landownership and the crofting system in Sutherland since 1800', *Ag.H.R.*, XIX, 1971, 45-56.
5433 **Youngson**, A. J., *After the Forty-Five: The Economic Impact on the Scottish Highlands*, 1973. Covers period up to 1840s.

INDUSTRY

5434 **Gulvin**, C., ed., *Journal of Henry Brown, Woollen Manufacturer, Galashiels, 1828-9*, Scot.H.Soc., XIV, 1978, 53-136.
5435 **Smout**, T. C., ed., *Journal of Henry Kalmeter's Travels in Scotland, 1719-20*, Scot.H.Soc., XIV, 1978, 1-52. A Swedish industrial spy.
5436 **Bremner**, D., *The Industries of Scotland: Their Rise, Progress and Present Condition*, 1869, 2nd ed., with new introduction, 1969.
5437 **Butt**, J., *The Industrial Archaeology of Scotland*, 1968.
5438 **Buxton**, N. K., 'Economic growth in Scotland

between the Wars: the role of production structure and rationalization', *Ec.H.R.*, 2nd ser., XXXIII, 1980, 538-55.

5439 —— 'The Scottish shipbuilding industry between the Wars', *Bus.H.*, X, 1968, 101-20.

5440 **Cairncross**, A. K., ed., *The Scottish Economy*, 1954.

5441 **Campbell**, R. H., *The Rise and Fall of Scottish Industry, 1707-1939*, 1980. Focuses on the key industries – textiles, coal, iron, engineering, and shipbuilding – in the principal phases of their expansion and stagnation.

5442 **Cotterill**, M. S., 'The development of Scottish gas technology, 1817-1914: inspiration and motivation. *Ind.Arch.R.*, V, 1981, 19-40.

5443 **Devine**, T. M., 'The Rise and fall of illicit whiskey making in northern Scotland, c.1780-1840', *Scot.H.R.*, LIV, 1975, 155-77.

5444 **Donnachie**, I. L., *A History of the Brewing Industry in Scotland*, 1979.

5445 **Donnelly**, T., 'Shipbuilding in Aberdeen, 1750-1914', *Northern Scot.*, IV, 1981, 23-42.

5446 **Duckham**, B. F., *A History of the Scottish Coal Industry I: 1700-1815*, 1970.

5447 **Duncan**, W. R. H., 'Aberdeen and the early development of the whaling industry, 1750-1800', *Northern Scot.*, III, 1979, 47-59.

5448 **Durie**, A. J., *The Scottish Linen Industry in the Eighteenth Century*, 1979.

5449 **Gulvin**, C., *The Tweedmakers: A History of the Scottish Fancy Woollen Industry, 1600-1914*, 1973.

5450 **Hamilton**, H., *The Industrial Revolution in Scotland*, 1932, 2nd ed., 1966.

5451 **Hume**, J. R., *The Industrial Archaeology of Scotland. I: The Lowlands and Borders*, 1976; II: *The Highlands and Islands*, 1977.

5452 —— and Moss, M. S., *Beardmore. The History of a Scottish Industrial Giant*, 1979.

5453 **McClain**, N. E., 'Scottish lintmills, 1729-70',

Textile H., I, 1970, 293-308.

5454 **McVeigh**, P., *Scottish East Coast Potteries, 1750-1840*, 1979.

5455 **Michie**, R. C., 'North East Scotland and northern whale fishing, 1752-1893', *Northern Scot.*, III, 1979, 60-85.

5456 **Moss**, M. S. and Hume, J. R., *A History of the Scotch Whisky Distilling Industry*, 1981.

5457 —— *Workshop of the British Empire. Engineering and Shipbuilding in the West of Scotland*, 1977. A mixture of general surveys of the two industries together with case studies of individual firms.

5458 **Payne**, P. L., *Colvilles and the Scottish Steel Industry*, 1979. Explores the heyday of this major Scottish company and its failure to adapt sufficiently to changing economic circumstances.

5459 —— *The Early Scottish Limited Companies*, 1982.

5460 —— 'Rationality and Personality: A study of mergers in the Scottish iron and steel industry 1916-36', *Bus.H.*, XIX, 1977, 162-91.

5461 **Perren**, R., 'Oligopoly and competition: price fixing and market sharing among timber firms in northern Scotland, 1890-1939', *Bus.H.*, XXI, 1979, 213-25.

5462 **Robertson**, A. J., 'The decline of the Scottish cotton industry, 1800-1914', *Bus.H.*, XII, 1970, 116-28.

5463 **Thompson**, F. G., *Harris Tweed: The Story of a Hebridean Industry*, 1969.

5464 **Thomson**, A. G., *The Paper Industry in Scotland, 1590-1861*, 1974. See also Coleman (1632) and Shorter (1633), listed above.

5465 **Tucker**, G. D., 'The slate islands of Scotland: the history of the Scottish slate industry', *Bus.H.*, XIX, 1977, 18-36.

5466 **Ward**, J. T., 'The Factory Reform Movement in Scotland', *Scot.H.R.*, XLI, 1962, 100-23.

TRADE AND BUSINESS HISTORY

5467 **Campbell**, R. H., 'The Anglo-Scottish Union of 1707: the economic consequences', *Ec.H.R.*, 2nd ser., XVI, 1964, 468-77.

5468 **Devine**, T. M., 'An eighteenth-century business elite: Glasgow West India merchants c.1750-1815', *Scot.H.R.*, LVII, 1978, 40-67.

5469 —— *The Tobacco Lords*, 1975. Deals with the

merchant princes of Glasgow.

5470 **Kinloch**, J. and Butt, J., *History of the Scottish Co-operative Wholesale Society Ltd.*, 1981.

5471 **Lenman**, B., *From Esk to Tweed: Harbours, Ships and Men of the East Coast of Scotland*, 1975.

5472 **Morris**, A. S., 'The nineteenth-century Scottish

carrier trade: patterns of decline', *Scot.Geog.Mag.*, XCVI, 1980, 74-82.

5473 **Payne**, P. L., ed., *Studies in Scottish Business History*, 1967. Contains a copious bibliography of the subject, 79-99.

5474 **Riley**, P. W. J., *The Union of England and Scotland*, 1978. Chapter six deals with trade and propaganda. See also Campbell (5467), above.

5475 **Scott**, J. and Hughes, M., *The Anatomy of Scottish Capital: Scottish Companies and Scottish Capital, 1900-79*, 1980.

5476 **Vamplew**, W., *Salvesen of Leith*, 1975. A case study of the nineteenth and twentieth-century trading operations of this major Norwegian-owned Scottish company.

See also Smout (5273), above.

BANKING AND INVESTMENT

5477 **Checkland**, S. G., *Scottish Banking: A History, 1695-1973*, 1975.

5478 **Jackson**, W. T., *The Enterprising Scot: Investors in the American West after 1873*, 1968.

5479 **Munn**, C. W., *The Scottish Provincial Banking Companies, 1747-1864*, 1981.

TRANSPORT AND COMMUNICATIONS

5480 **Fyfe**, J., ed., *Autobiography of John McAdam (1806-83)*. Scot.H.Soc., 4th ser., XVI, 1980.

5481 **Acworth**, W., *The Railways of Scotland*, 1890.

5482 **Haldane**, A. R. B., *The Drove Roads of Scotland*, 1952.

5483 —— *New Ways through the Glens*, 1962. Telford's roadmaking in the Highlands.

5484 —— *Three Centuries of Scottish Posts*, 1971.

5485 **Lindsay**, Jean, *The Canals of Scotland*, 1968.

5486 **Riddell**, J. F., *Clyde Navigation: A History of the Development and Deepening of the River Clyde*, 1979.

5487 **Vamplew**, W., 'Railways and the transformation of the Scottish economy', *Ec.H.R.*, 2nd ser., XXIV, 1971, 37-54.

5488 —— 'Scottish railways and the development of Scottish locomotive building in the nineteenth century', *Bus.H.R.*, XLVI, 1972, 320-38.

URBAN HISTORY

5489 **Glasgow, City of**, *Municipal Committee on the Housing of the Poor*, 2 vols., 1902-3. A major social enquiry.

5490 **Allan**, C. M., 'The genesis of British urban redevelopment with special reference to Glasgow', *Ec.H.R.*, 2nd ser., XXIII, 1965, 598-613. Deals with the urban renewal programme of the 1860s and '70s.

5491 **Allison**, E. and Beaton, M., *Dumbarton, 1815-51*, 1979.

5492 **Checkland**, S. G., 'The British industrial city as history: the Glasgow case', *Urban Studs.*, I, 1964,

34-54.

5493 **Marwick**, W. H., *The River Clyde and the Clyde Burghs*, 1909. Useful for the burghs other than Glasgow.

5494 **Walker**, W. M., *Juteopolis: Dundee and its Textile Workers, 1885-1923*, 1980.

5495 **Worsdall**, F., *The Tenement: A Way of Life. A Social, Historical and Architectural Study of Housing in Glasgow*, 1979.

5496 **Youngson**, A. J., *The Making of Classical Edinburgh*, 1966. The major study of the building of the new town.

LABOUR

5497 **McDougall**, I., ed., *A Catalogue of Some Labour Records in Scotland and Some Scottish Records outside Scotland*, 1978.

5498 **Arnot**, R. P., *A History of the Scottish Miners from the Earliest Times*, 1955.

5499 **Buckley**, K. D., *Trade Unionism in Aberdeen, 1878-1900*, 1955.

5500 **Gillespie**, Sarah C., *A Hundred Years of Progress: The Record of the Scottish Typographical Association, 1853-1952*, 1953.

5501 **Gourvish**, T. R., 'The cost of living in Glasgow in the early nineteenth century', *Ec.H.R.*, 2nd ser., XXV, 1972, 65-80.

5502 **Gray**, R. Q., *The Labour Aristocracy in Victorian Edinburgh*, 1976.

5503 **Handley**, J. E., *The Irish in Scotland, 1798-1845*, 2nd rev. ed., 1945.

5504 —— *The Irish in Modern Scotland*, 1947.

5505 —— *The Navvy in Scotland*, 1970.

5506 **Levitt**, I. and Smout, T. C., eds., *The State of the Scottish Working Class in 1843*, 1980. A statistical and geographical investigation based on data collected for the Poor Law Commission Report of 1843.

5507 **Logue**, K. J., *Popular Disturbances in Scotland, 1780-1815*, 1979.

5508 **McDougall**, I., ed., *Essays in Scottish Labour History: A Tribute to W. H. Marwick*, 1978.

5509 **Marwick**, W. H., *A Short History of Labour in Scotland*, 1967.

5510 **Murray**, N., *The Scottish Handloom Weavers 1790-1850. A Social History*, 1978.

5511 **Trickett**, Ann, *The Scottish Carter: The History of the Scottish Horse and Motormen' Association, 1898-1960*, 1967.

5512 **Young**, G. D., *The Rousing of the Scottish Working Class*, 1979.

POOR RELIEF

5513 **Cage**, R. A., *The Scottish Poor Law, 1745-1845*, 1981.

5514 **Checkland**, E. Olive A., *Philanthropy in Victorian Scotland. Social Welfare and the Voluntary Principle*, 1980.

5515 **Ferguson**, T., *Dawn of Scottish Social Welfare: A Survey from Medieval Times to 1863*, 1948.

5516 —— *Scottish Social Welfare, 1864-1914*, 1958.

5517 **Lindsay**, J., *The Scottish Poor Law. Its Operation in the North East from 1745 to 1845*, 1976.

5518 **Mitchison**, Rosalind, 'The Making of the Old Scottish Poor Law', *P.P.*, 63, 1974, 58-93.

5519 **Paterson**, Audrey, 'The Poor Law in nineteenth-century Scotland' in Fraser (4703), above, 171-93. See also Cormack (5357) and Nicholls (5359), above.

SOCIAL LIFE AND INTELLECTUAL DEVELOPMENT

5520 **Chitnis**, A., *The Scottish Enlightenment. A Social History*, 1976.

5521 **Cowan**, R. M. W., *The Newspaper in Scotland, 1815-60*, 1946.

5522 **Davie**, G. E., *The Democratic Intellect: Scotland and her Universities in the Nineteenth Century*, 1961.

5523 —— *The Scottish Enlightenment*, 1981. Hist.Ass.pamphlet.

5524 **Graham**, H. G., *The Social Life of Scotland in the Eighteenth Century*, 1899, 2nd rev. ed., 1900, 4th ed., 1937. Reprinted 1950, 1964.

5525 **McKinnon**, K. M., 'Education and social control: the case of Gaelic Scotland', *Scot. Educational*

Studs., IV, 1972, 2, 125-37.

5526 **Meikle**, H. W., *Scotland and the French Revolution*, 1912. Reprinted 1969.

5527 **Minto**, C. S., *Victorian and Edwardian Scotland from Old Photographs*, 1970.

5528 **Montgomery**, F. A., 'The unstamped press: the contribution of Glasgow, 1831-6', *Scot.H.R.*, LIX, 1980, 154-70.

5529 **Plant**, Marjorie, *The Domestic Life of Scotland in the Eighteenth Century*, 1952.

5530 **Rendall**, Jane, *The Origins of the Scottish Enlightenment*, 1978. Chapters five and six cover social institutions and commerce and civilisation.

5531 **Saunders**, L. J., *Scottish Democracy, 1815-40: The Social and Intellectual Background*, 1950.

RELIGION

5532 **Chambers**, D., 'The Church of Scotland's Highlands and Islands Education Scheme, 1824-43', *J.Educ.Admin.& H.*, VII, 1975, 8-17.

5533 **Enright**, W. G., 'Urbanisation and the evangelical pulpit in nineteenth-century Scotland', *Church H.*, XLVII, 1978, 400-7.

5534 **MacLaren**, A. A., *Religion and Social Class. The Disruption Years in Aberdeen*, 1974.

5535 **Mechie**, S., *The Church and Scottish Social Development, 1780-1870*, 1960.

IRELAND
BEFORE 1700

GENERAL WORKS

(a) BIBLIOGRAPHIES

5536 **Asplin**, P. W. A., *Medieval Ireland, c. 1170-1495. A Bibliography of Secondary Works*, 1970.

5537 **Eager**, A. R., ed., *A Guide to Irish Bibliographical Material*, 1964.

5538 **Edwards**, R. D., and Quinn, D. B., 'Thirty years' work in Irish history: sixteenth-century Ireland', *Irish H.Studs.*, XVI, 1969, 15-32. One of a series of very useful bibliographical articles.

5539 **Johnston**, Edith M., ed., *Irish History: Select Bibliography*, Hist.Ass., 1969.

5540 **Kavanagh**, M., ed., *A Bibliography of the County Galway*, 1965.

5541 **Maclysaght**, E., ed., *Bibliography of Irish Family History*, 1981.

5542 **Mulvey**, H. F., 'Modern Irish history since 1940: a bibliographical survey, 1600-1922', *Historian*, XXVIII, 1965, 516-59.

5543 **Otway-Ruthven**, J., 'Thirty years' work in Irish history: medieval Ireland, 1169-1485', *Irish H.Studs.*, XV, 1967, 359-65.

5544 **Povey**, K., 'The sources for a bibliography of Irish history, 1500-1700', *Irish H.Studs.*, I, 1939, 393-403.

5545 **Prendeville**, P. L., 'Bibliography of Irish history', *Ec.H.R.*, III, 1931-2, 274-92, and *ibid.*, IV, 1932, 81-90.

5546 **Simms**, J. G., 'Thirty years' work in Irish history: seventeenth-century Ireland, 1603-1702', *Irish H.Studs.*, XV, 1967, 366-75.

(b) SOURCES

5547 **Curtis**, E. and McDowell, R. B., eds., *Irish Historical Documents, 1172-1922*, 1943. Overwhelmingly constitutional.

5548 **Edwards**, Ruth D., *An Atlas of Irish History*, 1973.

5549 **Maxwell**, Constantia, *Irish History from Contemporary Sources, 1509-1610*, 1932. A useful collection, with sections on social and economic conditions and on Tudor efforts at colonisation. See also Browning (1142), listed above. Part VIII, 701-83 deals with Ireland.

(c) SURVEYS
(i) MEDIEVAL

5550 **Beckett**, J. C., *A Short History of Ireland* 1952, 3rd ed., 1966.

5551 **Chart**, D. A., *An Economic History of Ireland*, 1920. An elementary textbook.

5552 **Curtis**, E., *A History of Ireland*, 1936, 6th ed. 1950.

5553 —— *A History of Medieval Ireland from 1086 to 1513*, 1923, enlarged ed., 1938. Bibliography.

5554 **Frame**, R., 'Power and society in the lordship of Ireland, 1272-1377', *P.P.*, 76, 1977, 3-33.

5555 **Lydon**, J. F., *The Lordship of Ireland in the Middle Ages*, 1972.

5556 —— *Ireland in the Later Middle Ages*, 1973.

5557 **McNeill**, T. E., *Anglo-Norman Ulster. The History and Archaeology of an Irish Barony*,

1177-1400, 1980.

5558 Nicholls, K., *Gaelic and Gaelicised Ireland in the Middle Ages*, 1972.

5559 O'Brien, Maire and C. C., *A Concise History of Ireland*, 1972.

5560 O'Domhnall, S., 'Magna Carta Hiberniae', *Irish H.Studs.*, III, 1942, 31-8.

5561 O'Sullivan, M. J. D., *Old Galway: The History of a Norman Colony in Ireland*, 1942.

5562 Orpen, G. H., *Ireland under the Normans, 1169-1333*, 4 vols., 1911-20.

5563 Otway-Ruthven, J., *A History of Medieval Ireland*, 1968. 2nd ed. 1980. Mainly political. Good bibliography.

5564 Richardson, H. G. and Sayles, G. O., *The Administration of Ireland, 1172-1377*, 1963.

(ii) EARLY MODERN

5565 Bagwell, R., *Ireland under the Tudors*, 3 vols., 1885-90. Reprinted 1963.

5566 —— *Ireland under the Stuarts and During the Interregnum*, 3 vols., 1909-16. Reprinted 1963.

5567 Beckett, J. C., *The Making of Modern Ireland, 1603-1923*, 1969. Mainly political but some coverage of economic and social aspects is attempted. Bibliography.

5568 Butler, W. F. T., *Gleanings from Irish History*, 1925. Has chapters on the Irish lordships, on the Tudor policy of surrender and re-grant and on the Cromwellian confiscations in Ireland.

5569 Cullen, L. M., *Life in Ireland*, 1968. A useful social history, although the weight is on post-1700 developments.

5570 Dunlop, R., 'Ireland, to the settlement of Ulster: from the beginning of the sixteenth century to 1611', *Cambridge Modern History*, III, 1904, 579-616.

5571 —— 'Ireland from the Plantation of Ulster to the Cromwellian Settlement, 1611-59', *Cambridge Modern History*, IV, 1906, 513-38.

5572 —— 'Ireland from the Restoration to the Act of Resumption, 1660-1700', *Cambridge Modern History*, V, 1908, 301-23.

5572a —— *Ireland under the Commonwealth*, 1913.

5573 Edwards, R. D., *Ireland in the Age of the Tudors. The Destruction of Hiberno-Norman Civilisation*, 1977.

5574 Hinton, E. M., *Ireland through Tudor Eyes*, Philadelphia, 1935.

5575 MacCurtain, Margaret, *Tudor and Stuart Ireland*, 1972.

5576 Maclysaght, E., *Irish Life in the Seventeenth Century*, 1939, 2nd ed. enlarged and revised 1950. Has chapters on rural and urban life, communications, recreations. Documentary appendices and bibliography.

5577 Moody, T. W., Martin, F. X. and Byrne, F. J., eds., *A New History of Ireland. III: Early Modern Ireland, 1534-1691*, 1976. Economic and social developments are well covered. There is a separate chapter on the Irish coinage.

5578 O'Brien, G., *The Economic History of Ireland in the Seventeenth Century*, 1919. Vintage polemics, urgently in need of replacement.

5579 Quinn, D. B., *The Elizabethans and the Irish*, Ithaca, N. Y., 1966.

5580 —— 'Ireland and sixteenth-century European expansion'. In T. D. Williams, ed., *H.Studs.*, 1958, 20-32.

5581 Rowse, A. L., *The Expansion of Elizabethan England*, 1955. Has two chapters on Ireland.

5582 Simms, J. G., *Jacobite Ireland, 1685-91*, 1969.

5583 White, D. G., 'The reign of Edward VI in Ireland: some political, social and economic aspects', *Irish H.Studs.*, XIV, 1964-5, 197-211.

See also Black (1168) and Salaman (4600), listed above.

POPULATION

(a) MEDIEVAL

5584 Graham, B. J., 'Anglo-Norman settlement in County Meath', *Proc.Roy.Irish.Acad.*, LXXV, Sect. C, 1975, 223-48.

5585 Gwynn, A., 'The Black Death in Ireland', *Studies*, XXIV, 1935, 25-42.

5586 Russell, J. C., 'Late thirteenth-century Ireland as a region', *Demography*, III, 1966, 500-12.

(b) EARLY MODERN

5587 Pender, S., ed., *A Census of Ireland, c. 1659*, 1939.

5588 Butlin, R. A., 'The population of Dublin in the late seventeenth century', *Irish Geog.*, V, 1965, 51-66.

5589 Lee, Grace L., *The Huguenot Settlements in*

Ireland, 1936.

5590 **Maclysaght**, E., 'Seventeenth-century hearth money rolls with full transcript relating to County Sligo', *Analecta Hibernica*, XXIV, 1967, 1-89.

5591 **Paterson**, T. G. F., 'County Armagh householders, 1664-5', *Seanchas Ardmhacha*, III, 1958,

92-142.

5592 **Percival-Maxwell**, M., *The Scottish Migration to Ulster in the Reign of James I*, 1973.

5593 **Robinson**, P., 'British settlement in County Tyrone, 1610-66', *Irish Ec. & Soc.H.*, V, 1978, 5-26.

AGRICULTURE AND RURAL SOCIETY

5594 **Aalen**, F. H. A., 'Enclosures in eastern Ireland: report of a symposium', *Irish Geog.*, V, 1965, 29-39.

5595 **Canny**, N. P., *The Formation of the Old English Elite in Ireland*, 1975.

5596 **Crawford**, W. H., 'Landlord-tenant relations in Ulster, 1609-1820', *Irish Ec.& Soc.H.*, II, 1975, 5-21.

5597 **Fitzpatrick**, H. M., ed., *The Forest of Ireland: An Account of the Forests of Ireland from Early*

Times until the Present Day, 1966.

5598 **Nicholls**, K., *Land, Law and Society in Sixteenth-Century Ireland*, 1976.

5599 **O'Donovan**, J., *The Economic History of Livestock in Ireland*, 1940.

5600 **Otway-Ruthven**, J., 'The organisation of Anglo-Irish agriculture in the Middle Ages', *J.Roy.Soc. Antiquaries of Ireland*, LXXXI, 1951, 1-13.

See also McCracken (5714), below.

INDUSTRY

5601 **Boyle**, E., 'Irish embroidery and lace-making, 1600-1800', *Ulster Folk Life*, XXI, 1966, 52-65.

5602 **Breathnach**, B., 'The Huguenots and the silk weaving industry in Ireland, *Eire-Ireland*, II, 1967, 11-18.

5603 **Longfield**, Ada K., 'History of tapestry making in Ireland and in the seventeenth and eighteenth centuries', *J.Roy.Soc. Antiquaries of Ireland*, LXVIII, 1938, 91-105.

5604 **McCracken**, Eileen, 'Charcoal-burning ironworks in seventeenth- and eighteenth-century Ireland', *Ulster J.Arch.*, XX, 1957, 123-38.

5605 **O'Sullivan**, D., 'The exploitation of the mines of Ireland in the sixteenth century', *Studies*, XXIV, 1935, 442-52.

See also Gill (5731), listed below, 1-30, on the linen industry in Stuart Ireland.

ANGLO-IRISH RELATIONS IN THE SIXTEENTH AND SEVENTEENTH CENTURIES

5606 **Hogan**, J., ed., *Letters and Papers relating to the Irish Rebellion Between 1642-6*, Irish Manuscripts Commission, 1936.

5607 **Moody**, T. W., ed., 'Ulster Plantation Papers, 1608-13', *Analecta Hibernica*, VIII, 179-297.

5608 **Barnard**, T. C., *Cromwellian Ireland: English Government and Reform in Ireland, 1649-60*,

1975.

5609 **Bottigheimer**, K. S., *English Money and Irish Land: The 'Adventurers' in the Cromwellian Settlement of Ireland*, 1971.

5610 **Butler**, W. F. T., *Confiscation in Irish History*, 1917.

5611 **Clarke**, A., *The Old English in Ireland, 1625-42*, 1966.

12 **Dunlop**, R., 'Sixteenth-century schemes for the plantation of Ulster', *Scot. H. R.*, XXII, 1924-1925, 51-60, 115-26, 199-212.

13 **Kearney**, H. F., *Strafford in Ireland, 1633-41: A Study in Absolutism*, 1959.

14 —— 'The Court of Wards and Liveries in Ireland, 1622-24', *Proc.Roy. Irish Acad.*, C, 1956, 29-68.

15 **Mayes**, C. R., 'The early Stuarts and the Irish peerage', *E.H.R.*, LXXIII, 1958, 227-51.

16 **Moody**, T. W., *The Londonderry Plantation*, 1939. The main work on the subject.

17 —— 'The treatment of the native population under the scheme for the plantation in Ulster', *Irish H.Studs.*, I, 1938, 59-63.

18 **Morton**, R. G., 'The enterprise of Ulster', *H.Today*, 17, 1967, 114-21. Deals with

Elizabethan efforts at plantation.

5619 **Prendergast**, J. P., *The Cromwellian Settlement of Ireland*, 1865, 3rd ed., 1922.

5620 **Quinn**, D. B., *The Elizabethans and the Irish*, Ithaca, N. Y., 1966.

5621 —— 'The Munster Plantation: problems and opportunities', *J.Cork H. and Arch.Soc.*, LXXI, 1966, 19-40.

5622 **Ranger**, T. O., 'Strafford in Ireland: a revaluation', *P.P.*, 19, 1961, 26-45. Reprinted in Aston (1164), listed above, 271-94.

5623 **Simms**, J. G., *The Williamite Confiscation in Ireland, 1609-1703*, 1956.

5624 —— 'The Civil Survey, 1654-56', *Irish H.Studs.*, IX, 1954-5, 253-63.

5625 **Treadwell**, V., 'The Irish Court of Wards under James I', *Irish H.Studs.*, XII, 1960, 1-27.

PRICES AND PUBLIC FINANCE

(a) MEDIEVAL

26 **Dolley**, R. H. M., *Medieval Anglo-Irish Coins*, 1972.

27 **Lydon**, J. F., 'Edward II and the revenues of Ireland in 1311-12', *Irish H.Studs.*, XIV, 1964, 39-57.

28 —— 'Survey of the memoranda rolls of the Irish Exchequer, 1294-1509', *Analecta Hibernica*, XXII, 1966, 49-134.

29 **Nolan**, D., *A Monetary History of Ireland*, 2 vols., 1926. Vol. 2 covers the period from the Anglo-Norman invasion to the death of Elizabeth.

30 **O'Sullivan**, M. D., *Italian Merchant Bankers in Ireland in the Thirteenth Century: A Study in* the Social and Economic History of Medieval Ireland, 1962.

5631 **O'Sullivan**, W., *The Earliest Anglo-Irish Coinage*, 1950. Reprinted 1964.

5632 **Richardson**, H. G. and Sayles, G. O., 'Irish revenue, 1278-1384', *Proc.Roy.Irish Acad.*, LXII, 1961-3, 87-100.

(b) EARLY MODERN

5633 **Quinn**, D. B., 'Guide to English financial records for Irish history, 1461-1558, with illustrative extracts, 1461-1509', *Analecta Hibernica*, X, 1941, 1-69.

TRADE

34 **Kearney**, H. F., ed., 'The Irish wine trade, 1614-15' (document), *Irish H.Studs.*, IX, 1955, 400-42.

35 **O'Brien**, G., 'The Irish staple organisation in the reign of James I', *Ec. J.Ec.H.Supp.*, I, 1920, 42-56.

36 **Treadwell**, V., 'The establishment of the farm of the Irish customs, 1603-13', *E.H.R.*, XCIII, 1978, 580-602.

5637 —— 'The Irish customs administration in the sixteenth century', *Irish H.Studs.*, XX, 1978, 384-417.

5638 **Woodward**, D. M., 'The Anglo-Irish livestock trade in the seventeenth century', *Irish H. Studs.*, XVIII, 1973, 489-523.

See also Cullen (1852), and Longfield (1866), listed above.

TOWNS

5639 **Pender**, S., ed., *Council Books of the Corporation of Waterford*, Irish Manuscripts Commission, 1964.

5640 **Butlin**, R. A., ed., *The Development of the Irish Town*, 1977.

5641 **Camblin**, G., *The Town in Ulster: An Account of the Origin and Building of the Towns of the Province and the Development of their Rural Setting*, 1951. Illustrated.

5642 **Harkness**, D. and O'Dowd, M. eds., *The Town in Ireland*, H.Studs., XIII, 1979. Includes essay on medieval plantation boroughs, the social structure of fifteenth-century Dublin and early seventeenth-century urban development.

5643 **O'Sullivan**, W., *The Economic History of Cork City from the Earliest Times to the Act of Union*, 1937. One of the best of Irish urban studies. Documentary and statistical appendices. Good bibliography.

5644 **Simms**, J. G., 'Dublin in 1685', *Irish H.Studs.* XIV, 1965, 212-26.

RELIGION AND EDUCATION

5645 **White**, N. B., ed., *Extents of Irish Monastic Possessions, 1540-41*, Irish Manuscripts Commission, 1943.

5646 **Beckett**, J. C., *Protestant Dissent in Ireland, 1687-1780*, 1948.

5647 **Coonan**, T. L., *The Irish Catholic Confederacy and the Puritan Revolution*, 1954. Bibliography. Needs to be used with great care.

5648 **Douglas**, J. M., 'Early Quakerism in Ireland' *J.Friends' H.Soc.*, XLVIII, 1956, 3-32.

5649 **Edwards**, R. D., *Church and State in Tudor Ireland: A History of the Penal Laws against Irish Catholics, 1534-1603*, 1935. Bibliography.

5650 **McGrath**, F., *Education in Ancient and Medieval Ireland*, 1979.

5651 **Miller**, D. W., 'Presbyterianism and 'modernisation' in Ulster', *P.P.*, 80, 1978, 66-90.

MISCELLANEOUS

(a) MEDIEVAL

5652 **Hand**, G. J., 'The status of the native Irish in the Lordship of Ireland, 1272-1331', *The Irish Jurist*, n.s., I, 1966, 93-115.

5653 **Lydon**, J. F., 'The problem of the frontier in medieval Ireland', *Topic*, XIII, 1967, 5-22.

5654 **Otway-Ruthven**, J., 'Knight service in Ireland', *J.Roy.Soc. Antiquaries of Ireland*, LXXXIX, 1959, 1-15.

5655 —— 'The medieval county of Kildare', *Irish H.Studs.*, XI, 1959, 181-99.

5656 **Richardson**, H. G. and Sayles, G. O., *The Irish Parliament in the later Middle Ages*, Philadelphia, 1952. Reprinted 1964.

(b) EARLY MODERN

5657 **Gleeson**, D. F., *The Last Lords of Ormond: A History of the 'Countrie of the three O'Kennedys' During the Seventeenth Century*, 1938.

5658 **Goodbody**, O. C., 'Anthony Sharp, wool merchant, 1643-1707, and the Quaker community in Dublin', *J.Friends' H.Soc.*, XLVIII, 1956, 38-50.

5659 **Knox**, S. J., *Ireland's Debt to the Huguenots*, 1959.

5660 **Nicholls**, G., *A History of the Irish Poor Law in Connection with the State of the Country and Condition of the People*, 1856. Reprinted 1968.

5661 **Ranger**, T. O., 'Richard Boyle and the making of an Irish fortune, 1588-1614', *Irish H.Studs.*, X 1956-57, 257-97.

IRELAND
AFTER 1700

GENERAL WORKS

5662 **Hutton**, A. W., ed., *Young's Tour in Ireland, 1776-79*, 2 vols., 1892.

5663 **Public Record Office of Northern Ireland** (H. M. Stationery Office, Belfast), *Irish Economic Documents*, 1967.

5664 **Coyne**, W. P., ed., *Ireland, Industrial and Agricultural*, 1902.

5665 **Cullen**, L. M., *Economic History of Ireland since 1660*, 1972.

5666 —— *The Emergence of Modern Ireland, 1600-1900*, 1981. Weighted heavily towards the eighteenth century, the book examines the juxtaposition of 'modern' and 'archaic' elements in Irish society.

5667 —— (ed.), *The Formation of the Irish Economy*, 1969.

5668 —— 'Problems in the interpretation and revision of eighteenth-century Irish economic history', *T.R.H.S.*, 5th ser., XVII, 1967, 1-22.

5669 —— 'The value of contemporary printed sources for Irish economic history in the eighteenth century', *Irish H.Studs.*, XIV, 1964, 142-55.

5670 —— and Smout, T. C., eds., *Comparative Aspects of Scottish and Irish Economic and Social History, 1600-1900*, 1978.

5671 **Freeman**, T. W., *Pre-Famine Ireland*, 1957.

5672 **Johnson**, D. S., 'The economic history of Ireland between the Wars', *Irish Ec.& Soc.H.*, I, 1974, 49-61.

5673 **Johnston**, Edith M., *Ireland in the Eighteenth Century*, 1974.

5674 **Lee**, J. P., *The Modernisation of Irish Society, 1848-1918*, 1973.

5675 **Lyons**, F. S. L., *Ireland since the Famine*, 1971.

5676 —— *Culture and Anarchy in Ireland, 1890-1939*, 1979.

5677 **McDowell**, R. B., ed., *Social Life in Ireland, 1800-45*, 1952.

5678 —— *Ireland in the Age of Imperialism and Revolution, 1760-1801*, 1979.

5679 **Maxwell**, Constantia, *Country and Town in Ireland under the Georges*, 1940.

5680 —— *The Stranger in Ireland from the Reign of Elizabeth to the Great Famine*, 1954.

5681 **Meenan**, J., *The Irish Economy since 1922*, 1970.

5682 **Moody**, T. W. and Beckett, J. C., eds., *Ulster since 1800: A Political and Economic Survey*, 1954.

5683 —— *Ulster since 1800, Second Series: A Social Survey*, 1957. Bibliography, 236-40.

5684 —— and Martin, F. X. (eds.), *The Course of Irish History*, 1967.

5685 **O'Brien**, G., *Economic History of Ireland in the Eighteenth Century*, 1918.

5686 —— *Economic History of Ireland from the Union to the Famine*, 1921. Vintage polemic.

5687 **Opel**, H., ed., *Irish History and Culture. Aspects of a People's Heritage*, Lawrence, Kansas, 1976.

5688 **O'Tuathaigh**, G., *Ireland before the Famine, 1798-1848*, 1972.

5689 **Roebuck**, P., ed., *Plantation to Partition. Essays in Ulster History in Honour of J. L. McCracken*, 1981. A valuable *festschrift* which includes essays on Ulster's population, 1660-1760, economic diversification, agricultural develop-ment, the industrial structure of Belfast in 190 and on cross-border trade in the 1920s.

5690 **Wilson**, T., ed., *Ulster under Home Rule: . Study of the Political and Economic Problems Northern Ireland*, 1955.

POPULATION

5691 **Adams**, W. F., *Ireland and Irish Emigration to the New World from 1815 to the Famine*, New Haven, Conn., 1932.

5692 **Black**, R. D. C., *Economic Thought and the Irish Question, 1817-1870*, 1960.

5693 **Collins**, Brenda, 'Proto-industrialisation and pre-famine emigration', *Soc.H.*, VII, 1982, 127-46.

5694 **Connell**, K. H., *The Population of Ireland, 1750-1845*, 1950.

5695 —— *Irish Peasant Society*, 1968.

5696 **Connolly**, S. J., 'Illegitimacy and pre-nuptial pregnancy in Ireland before 1864: the evidence of some Catholic parish registers', *Irish Ec. & Soc.H.*, VI, 1979, 5-23.

5697 **Drake**, M., 'The Irish demographic crisis of 1740-41', *H.Studs.*, VI, ed. T. W. Moody, 1968, 101-24.

5698 —— 'Marriage and population growth in Ire-land, 1750-1845', *Ec.H.R.*, 2nd ser., XVI, 196 301-13.

5699 **Edwards**, R. D. and Williams, T. D., eds., *Th Great Famine: Studies in Irish Histor 1845-1852*, 1956.

5700 **Ellis**, P. B., *A History of the Irish Workin Class*, 1972.

5701 **Goldstrom**, J. M. and Clarkson, L. A., eds *Irish Population, Economy and Society: Essay in Honour of the late K. H. Connell*, 1982.

5702 **Kennedy**, R. E., *The Irish. Emigration, Mai riage, and Fertility*, Berkeley, Cal., 1973.

5703 **Wall**, Maureen, 'The rise of a Catholic middl class in eighteenth-century Ireland', *Iris H.Studs.*, XI, 1958, 91-115.

5704 **Woodham-Smith**, Cecil, *The Great Hunger Ireland, 1845-9*, 1962.

AGRICULTURE AND RURAL SOCIETY

5705 **Crawford**, W. H., ed., *Letters from an Ulster Land Agent, 1774-85. The Letterbooks of John Moore of Clough, Co. Down*, 1976.

5706 **Beames**, M. R., 'Rural conflict in pre-Famine Ireland', *P.P.*, 81, 1978, 75-91.

5707 **Bew**, P., *Land and the National Question in Ireland, 1858-82*, 1978.

5708 **Casey**, D. J. and Rhodes, R. E., eds., *Views of the Irish Peasantry, 1800-1916*, Hamden, Conn., 1977.

5709 **Clark**, S., 'The importance of agrarian classes. Agrarian class structure and collective action in nineteenth-century Ireland', *Brit. J.Soc.*, XXIX, 1978, 22-40.

5710 **Crotty**, R. D., *Irish Agriculture. Its Volume and Structure*, 1976.

5711 **Curtis**, L. P., 'Incumbered wealth. Landed indebtedness in post-Famine Ireland', *A.H.R LXXXV*, 1980, 332-67.

5712 **Donnelly**, J. S., 'The Irish agricultural depre sion of 1859-64', *Irish Ec.& Soc.H.*, III, 197€ 33-54.

5713 —— *The Land and People of Nineteenth Century Cork*, 1975.

5714 **McCracken**, Eileen, *The Irish Woods sinc Tudor Times: Their Distribution and Exploita tion*, 1971.

5715 **Maguire**, W. A., *The Downshire Estates i Ireland, 1801-45. The Management of Iris Landed Estates in the Early Nineteenth Century* 1972.

5716 **Malcolmson**, A. P. W., 'Absenteeism in eight eenth-century Ireland', *Irish Ec.& Soc.H.*, 1974, 15-35.

5717 **Nolan**, W., *Fassadinin: Land Settlement an*

Society in South-East Ireland, 1600-1850, 1979.

18 **O'Gráda**, C., 'The beginnings of the Irish creamery system, 1880-1914', *Ec.H.R.*, 2nd ser., XXX, 1977, 284-305.

19 —— 'Primogeniture and ultimogeniture in rural

Ireland', *J.Interdis.H.*, X, 1980, 491-7.

5720 **Solow**, Barbara L., *The Land Question and the Irish Economy, 1870-1903*, 1971.

5721 **Steele**, E. D., *Irish Land and British Politics. Tenant Right and Nationality, 1865-70*, 1974.

TRANSPORT AND INDUSTRY

22 **Barker**, T. C., 'The beginnings of the canal age in the British Isles' (the Newry Canal). In Pressnell, ed. (2575), 1-22.

23 **Bianconi**, M. A. and Watson, S. J., *Bianconi, King of the Irish Roads*, 1962.

24 **Boyd**, A., *The Rise of the Irish Trade Unions, 1729-1970*, 1972. Should be used with caution.

25 **Casserley**, H. C., *Outline of Irish Railway History*, 1974.

26 **Coe**, W. E., *The Engineering Industry of the North of Ireland*, 1969.

27 **Conroy**, J. C., *A History of Railways in Ireland*, 1928. Needs revision.

28 **Cullen**, L. M., 'Eighteenth-century flour milling in Ireland', *Irish Ec.& Soc.H.*, IV, 1977, 5-25.

29 **Delany**, R., *The Grand Canal of Ireland*, 1973.

30 **Delany**, V. T. H. and D. R., *The Canals of the South of Ireland*, 1966.

31 **Gill**, C., *The Rise of the Irish Linen Industry*, 1925. Reprinted 1964.

32 **Green**, E. R. R., *The Industrial Archaeology of County Down*, 1963.

33 —— *The Lagan Valley, 1800-50: A Local History of the Industrial Revolution*, 1949.

34 **Gribbon**, H. D., *The History of Water Power in Ulster*, 1969.

35 **Irvine**, H. S., 'Some aspects of passenger traffic

between Britain and Ireland, 1820-1850', *J.Trans.H.*, IV, 1960, 224-41.

5736 **Kane**, R., *Industrial Resources of Ireland*, 2nd ed., 1845.

5737 **Lee**, J. P., 'The constructional costs of early Irish railways, 1830-52', *Bus.H.*, IX, 1967, 95-109.

5738 —— 'The provision of capital for early Irish railways', *Irish H.Studs.*, XVI, 1968, 33-63.

5739 **Lynch**, P. and Vaizey, J., *Guinness's Brewery in the Irish Economy, 1759-1876*, 1960.

5740 **McCutcheon**, W. A., *The Canals of the North of Ireland*, 1968.

5741 —— *The Industrial Archaeology of Northern Ireland*, 1981.

5742 **McGuire**, E. B., *Irish Whisky. A History of Distilling, the Spirit Trade and Excise Controls in England*, 1974.

5743 **McNeil**, D. B., *Irish Passenger Steamship Services. I: North of Ireland*, 1969.

5744 **Murray**, K. A., *The Great Northern Railway (Ireland)*, 1944.

5745 **Nowlan**, K. B., *Travel and Transport in Ireland*, 1973.

5746 **Petree**, J. F., 'Charles Wye Williams (1780-1866) a pioneer in steam navigation and fuel efficiency', *Trans.Newcomen Soc.*, XXXIX, 1966-7, 35-46. Steam navigation in Irish waters.

5747 **Swift**, J., *History of the Dublin Bakers*, 1949.

TRADE

48 **Bourke**, P. M. A., 'The Irish grain trade, 1839-48', *Irish H. Studs.*, XX, 1976, 156-69.

49 **Kennedy**, L., 'Traders in the Irish rural economy, 1880-1914', *Ec.H.R.*, 2nd ser., XXXII, 1979, 201-10.

50 —— 'Retail markets in rural Ireland at the end of the nineteenth century', *Irish Ec.& Soc.H.*, V, 1978, 46-63.

51 **Murray**, Alice E., *A History of the Commer-*

cial and Financial Relations Between England and Ireland from the Period of the Restoration, 1907.

5752 **Wall**, Maureen, 'The Catholic merchants, manufacturers and traders of Dublin, 1778-1782'. *Reportorium Novum: Dublin Diocesan Historical Record*, II, 1959-60, 298-323.

See also Cullen and Smout (5670), above.

TOWNS

5753 **Beckett**, J. C., and Glasscock, R. E., *Belfast, the Origin and Growth of an Industrial City*, 1967.

5754 **Chart**, D. A., *A History of Dublin*, 1932.

5755 **Clarkson**, L. A., 'An anatomy of an Irish town: the economy of Armagh, 1770', *Irish Ec.& Soc.H.*, V, 1978, 27-45.

5756 **Craig**, M., *Dublin, 1660-1860*, 1952.

5757 **Daly**, S., *Cork, A City in Crisis. A History Social Conflict and Misery, 1870-2*, 1978.

5758 **Harvey**, J., *Dublin: A Study in Environme* 1949.

5759 **Maxwell**, Constantia, *Dublin under Georges, 1714-1830*, 1936, 2nd rev. ed., 1956.
See also Harkness and O'Dowd (5642), above.

FINANCE AND BANKING

5760 **Barrow**, G. L., *The Emergence of the Irish Banking System, 1820-45*, 1974.

5761 **Dillon**, M., *The History and Development of Banking in Ireland*, 1889.

5762 **Fetter**, F. W., ed., *The Irish Pound, 1797-1826: A Reprint of the Committee of 1804 of the British House of Commons on the Condition of the Irish Currency*, 1955.

5763 **Hall**, F. G., *History of the Bank of Ireland, 1783-1946*, 1949.

5764 **Moynihan**, M., *Currency and Central Bank in Ireland, 1922-60*, 1975.

5765 **O'Kelly**, E., *The Old Private Banks and B kers of Munster*, 1959.

5766 **Robinson**, H. W., *A History of Accountant. Ireland*, 1964.

5767 **Simpson**, N., *The Belfast Bank, 1827-19* 1975.

5768 **Tanning**, R., *The Irish Department Finance, 1922-58*, 1978.

RELIGION AND EDUCATION

5769 **Akenson**, D. H., *The Irish Education Experiment. The National System of Education in the Nineteenth Century*, 1970.

5770 **Atkinson**, N., *Irish Education. A History of Educational Institutions*, 1969.

5771 **Burns**, R. E., 'The Catholic Relief Act in Ireland, 1778', *Church H.*, XXXII, 1963, 181-206.

5772 **Connolly**, S. J., *Priests and People in Pre-Famine Ireland, 1780-1845*, 1982.

5773 **MacElligott**, T. J., *Secondary Education in* *Ireland, 1870-1921*, 1981.

5774 **Macourt**, M. P. A., 'The religious enquiry in Irish census of 1861', *Irish H.Studs.*, XXI, 19 167-87.

5775 **Parkes**, S. M., *Irish Education in Brit Parliamentary Papers in the Nineteenth Cent and After, 1801-1920*, 1978.

5776 **Quane**, M., 'The Diocesan Schools, 1570-18 *J.Cork H. and Arch.Soc.*, LXVI, 1961, 26-5

MISCELLANEOUS

5777 **Broeker**, G., *Rural Disorder and Police Reform in Ireland, 1812-36*, 1970.

5778 **Curtis**, L. P., *Apes and Angels. Irishmen in Victorian Caricature*, 1971.

5779 **Finnane**, M., *Insanity and the Insane Post-Famine Ireland*, 1981.

5780 **Inglis**, B., *The Freedom of the Press in land, 1784-1841*, 1954.

5781 **Munter**, R., *The History of the Irish News-paper, 1685-1760*, 1967.

5782 **Sheehy**, Jeanne, *The Rediscovery of Ireland's Past. The Celtic Revival, 1830-1930*, 1980.

INDEX
OF AUTHORS
AND EDITORS

Numbers refer to items in the bibliography